Advanced Topics in Electronic Commerce

Volume 1

Mehdi Khosrow-Pour
Information Resources Management Association, USA

IDEA GROUP PUBLISHING
Hershey • London • Melbourne • Singapore

Acquisitions Editor:	Renée Davies
Development Editor:	Kristin Roth
Senior Managing Editor:	Amanda Appicello
Managing Editor:	Jennifer Neidig
Copy Editor:	Shanelle Ramello
Typesetter:	Amanda Kirlin
Cover Design:	Lisa Tosheff
Printed at:	Integrated Book Technology

Published in the United States of America by
Idea Group Publishing (an imprint of Idea Group Inc.)
701 E. Chocolate Avenue, Suite 200
Hershey PA 17033
Tel: 717-533-8845
Fax: 717-533-8661
E-mail: cust@idea-group.com
Web site: http://www.idea-group.com

and in the United Kingdom by
Idea Group Publishing (an imprint of Idea Group Inc.)
3 Henrietta Street
Covent Garden
London WC2E 8LU
Tel: 44 20 7240 0856
Fax: 44 20 7379 3313
Web site: http://www.eurospan.co.uk

Library of Congress Cataloging-in-Publication Data

Advanced topics in electronic commerce / Mehdi Khosrow-Pour, editor.
p. cm.
Summary: "This book provides comprehensive coverage and understanding of the social, cultural, organizational, and cognitive impacts of e-commerce technologies and advances on organizations around the world"--Provided by publisher.
Includes bibliographical references and index.
ISBN 1-59140-819-9 (hardcover) -- ISBN 1-59140-820-2 (softcover) -- ISBN 1-59140-821-0 (ebook)
1. Electronic commerce. I. Khosrowpour, Mehdi, 1951-
HF5548.32.A324 2005
658.8'72--dc22

2005004530

British Cataloguing in Publication Data
A Cataloguing in Publication record for this book is available from the British Library.

Advanced Topics in Electronic Commerce
Volume 1

Table of Contents

Preface

We are pleased to bring you this inaugural volume of *Advanced Topics in Electronic Commerce*. In our present era, electronic commerce has taken the stage as a necessary ingredient in education, manufacturing, and even research. Individuals involved in researching, improving, and using e-commerce need a strong resource to provide ideas and information on the utilization of these new technologies and what possibilities e-commerce offers. *Advanced Topics in Electronic Commerce, Volume 1* presents a wide range of the most current research in the adoption of e-commerce, e-business, and e-government. This inaugural volume will assist researchers, educators, and professionals in understanding the necessary components for e-technologies and how to best adopt these elements into their own classrooms, workplaces, and organizations throughout the world.

Chapter I, "Role of Small-Business Strategic Alliances in the Perception of Benefits and Disadvantages of E-Commerce Adoption in SME" by Robert MacGregor and Lejla Vrazalic, University of Wollongong (Australia), addresses the lack of research into comparing e-commerce use in small businesses that are members of a strategic alliance to those that have opted to remain outside such arrangements. This chapter presents the findings of a study of 176 regional small businesses in Sweden that investigated the impact of strategic-alliance membership on benefits and disadvantages associated with e-commerce adoption. The study also shows that correlations between e-commerce benefits exist and that the benefits can be grouped according to three distinct factors: costs, efficiency, and sales or inventory.

Chapter II, "The Effects of Animated Banner and Pop-Up Ads on Commercial Web Sites" by Yuan Gao, Ramapo College of New Jersey (USA), and Marios Koufaris and Robert H. Ducoffe, Baruch College (CUNY) (USA), explores the effects of two specific message-delivery techniques frequently adopted by online stores: continuously animated site banners and unexpected pop-up ads.

Results from 128 surveys collected in a 2x2 factorial design showed that each of the two techniques had a significant effect on perceived irritation in the hypothesized direction. This chapter also confirms that perceived irritation has a significant negative relationship with a visitor's attitude toward the Web site. This study fills a vacuum in academic research with respect to the negative effects of Web advertising and advises caution in the deployment of certain techniques. This chapter encourages future research exploring the effects of cross-site ads on consumer attitude and advocates additional studies linking format attributes and presentation techniques with attitudinal consequences in the design of commercial Web sites.

Chapter III, "Managing Security Vulnerabilities in a Business-to-Business Electronic Commerce Organization" by Shirley Ann Becker, Northern Arizona University (USA), and Anthony Berkemeyer, Texas Instruments, Inc. (USA), profiles the security risks associated with a business-to-business (B2B) e-commerce firm that recently experienced a denial-of-service attack. Its security vulnerabilities are described from both an internal and external perspective. Risk-management processes are recommended to improve overall security in the organization. The chapter concludes with a discussion of security challenges facing the B2B firm taking into account increasingly sophisticated security threats.

Chapter IV, "Government-to-Government Enterprises: A Road Map for Success" by Luiz Antonio Joia, Brazilian School of Public and Business Administration - Getulio Vargas Foundation and the Rio de Janiero State University (Brazil), aims to present a heuristic frame to implement government-to-government endeavors effectively. The frame presented in this article was largely drawn from an actual government-to-government case study successfully implemented in Brazil. From the analysis of this explanatory case study involving the Brazilian Central Bank and the Brazilian Justice Department, some key success factors were singled out as well as the major hurdles to be overcome and causes thereof. These findings led the researcher to propose a heuristic frame not only to explain the conclusions drawn from the case study presented, but also to help researchers, practitioners, and policy makers to deploy government-to-government projects adequately.

Chapter V, "Effective Web Site Design: Insight from Information Processing" by Deborah E. Rosen and Scott J. Lloyd, University of Rhode Island (USA), and Elizabeth F. Purinton, Marist College (USA), focuses on Web design from an information-processing perspective. Studies are described using cognitive maps and preferences as a possible framework for understanding why some designs are more effective than others in terms of viewers' likelihood of revisit and overall impression.

Chapter VI, "Personalization of E-Commerce Applications in SMEs: Conclusions from an Empirical Study in Switzerland" by Petra Schubert and Uwe

Leimstoll, University of Applied Sciences, Basel (FHBB) (Switzerland), investigates the potential for personalization from the particular angle of SMEs. In addition to some theoretical fundamentals of personalization, this chapter presents the results of an empirical study. With the help of a survey, the application potential for personalization tools in Swiss companies is investigated. The conclusions show that SMEs are skeptical toward e-commerce applications that use personalization. It furthermore becomes clear that the heterogeneity of organizational and technical conditions impedes the development of standardized tools.

Chapter VII, "An Interventionist Approach to E-Commerce Implementation in SMEs" by David Tucker and Anthony Lafferty, Manchester Metropolitan University Business School (U.K.), sets out the main factors that are inhibiting SMEs from adopting e-commerce. It reports on a two-year teaching company scheme (TCS) between the Manchester Metropolitan University Business School (MMUBS) and Partwell Ltd., a U.K.-based manufacturing SME. The chapter highlights the philosophy and objectives of the TCS programme, and describes the process of technology transfer between Partwell and MMUBS. The action learning method by which e-commerce was introduced into the company is described and the results are evaluated against contemporary technology-diffusion literature. It is shown that gaining the trust of key employees at Partwell, coupled with the adoption of a soft approach to e-commerce implementation, was a critical success factor. Finally, the chapter reports on the benefits that Partwell has gained through the TCS experience.

Chapter VIII, "E-Government Evolution in Ireland: A Framework for Successful Implementation" by William Golden, Martin Hughes, and Murray Scott, National University of Ireland, Galway analyzes the Irish government's evolutionary path to the provision of successful e-government. The success factors and stages of the evolution of e-government are identified and a detailed examination of how the Irish government successfully implemented its e-government strategy is presented. The lessons learned from this case provide a valuable road map for the successful attainment of citizen-centred e-government in other jurisdictions.

Chapter IX, "E-Taxation: An Introduction to the Use of TaxXML for Corporate Tax Reporting" by Vikramaditya Pant, M. Susan Stiner, and William Wagner, Villanova University (USA), provides some background for the study of TaxXML and will suggest why TaxXML is a very significant development in the realm of online tax systems. Online tax systems are rapidly replacing paper-based tax-reporting systems. Promising many advantages over the traditional method of hard-copy tax filing, these systems promise faster processing, lower costs, and increased efficiency. Using a specific language from the extensible markup language (XML) family called TaxXML, TIGERS, a government subcommittee for the establishment of electronic taxation standards, is looking to revolutionize the way government administers taxation. TaxXML draws upon the concepts and constructs of basic XML and utilizes tax-related vocabularies to create a standardized and systematized framework of electronic tax preparation and reporting. While it is still in its early stages of development, it is unclear how hard the government will impose this technology onto the industry and also how the industry will react to this new technology.

Chapter X, "Online Consumer Trust: A Multi-Dimensional Model" by Felix B. Tan, Auckland University of Technology (New Zealand), and Paul Sutherland, The University of Auckland (New Zealand), aims to synthesize the viewpoints on consumer trust from across the disciplines and bring them together in a multidimensional trust model. It is hoped that in doing so, this broad assortment of views will highlight the true underlying nature of trust in the online environment. From these multiple disciplines, three dimensions of trust emerged — dispositional trust, institutional trust, and interpersonal trust — each bringing its own influencing factors into the overall intention to trust. From this model emerged the notion that the consumer as an individual is central to the understanding of trust, and in turn, that the individual's personality and culture form the foundation for the development of trust.

Chapter XI, "A Customer Relationship Management System to Target Customers at Cisco" by Rahul Bhaskar, California State University - Fullerton (USA), describes the implementation of Internet-empowered customer-relationship management (CRM) at Cisco Systems Inc. After describing the organizational background of Cisco, the case takes the student into the issues that the executives faced after the market crash in 2001. John Chambers, Cisco CEO (chief executive officer), and his team decided to strengthen Cisco's relationship with the customers so that the company could emerge stronger when the markets recovered. Questions are raised as to the implementation of technology and supporting processes in a company that traditionally had not considered CRM as its core marketing strategy.

Chapter XII, "E-Government and Social Exclusion: An Empirical Study" by Liz Lee-Kelley and Thomas James, University of Surrey (U.K.), examines the possibility of social exclusion from e-government implementation as a widening gap surfaces between those who are e-literate and those who are not. This gap is a result of the U.K. central government's vision to deploy all local government services electronically by 2005. Anchored on two questions — (a) What are the factors influencing the adoption of e-government initiatives and (b) is the implementation of e-government likely to result in the social exclusion of certain groups in the community? — the study sampled members of the public from two local authorities in the U.K. to investigate their dispositions toward the new offering of online government services. This study contributes to a better understanding of the factors required for effective online public-services delivery and the ways to direct resources into increasing Internet literacy and use.

Chapter XIII, "From Seeking Information to Transacting: The Impact of Web-Site Quality on E-Taxation" by Stuart J. Barnes, Victoria University of Wellington (New Zealand), and Richard Vidgen, University of Bath (U.K.), examines the results of a survey of the quality of a Web site provided by the U.K. government (Inland Revenue). The survey was administered directly after the launch of a new system to enable the online submission of self-assessed tax returns. The instrument, E-Qual, draws on previous work in Web-site usability, information quality, and service-interaction quality to provide a rounded framework for assessing e-government offerings. The metrics and qualitative comments provide some detailed insights into the perceptions of users who attempted to interact with the online taxation system. The results point to specific areas in need of development on the Web site, which are found to be consistent with initiatives launched recently by the Inland Revenue.

Chapter XIV, "The Strategic Importance of E-Commerce in Modern Supply Chains" by Peter R. Gibson, University of Wollongong (Australia), and Janet Edwards, Loughborough University (U.K.), outlines strategic opportunities for e-commerce-enabled supply chains, considering some aspects of the motor industry, and greatly improved responses to customers. The authors demonstrate that there will be resulting strategic advantage for firms that become enabled to take the further step of making changes to their much wider manufacturing process philosophies. The developed knowledge associated with these changes will not be easily copied by competitors, and as such, provides the basis for a sustainable competitive advantage for those firms that are able to lead the way with the enabling technology of e-commerce in supply chains. However, leadership and change management are identified as key issues requiring further investigation.

Chapter XV, "On E-Markets in Emerging Economy: An Indian Experience" by Ashis K. Pani and Amit Agrahari, XLRI, Jamshedpur (India), presents MetalJunction.com, a joint venture of TISCO and SAIL, the steel makers contributing more than 60% to India's total steel production. This chapter illustrates how organizations can use information technology to spin off key processes such as procurement and selling. In its first year of operations, MetalJunction.com generated substantial savings for TISCO and SAIL. The case also supports the argument that the business context in emerging economies is significantly different from the context in developed economies; hence, setting up a successful B2B marketplace may require the creation of basic services that are taken for granted in developed economies.

Chapter XVI, "An E-Government Model" by Sushil K. Sharma, Ball State University (USA), and Jatinder N.D. Gupta, The University of Alabama in Huntsville (USA), discusses how the movement toward electronic government is rapidly advancing as nations exploit new electronic means of communication such as the Internet. The e-government transformation process can be and often is seriously hindered when initiatives are disjointed and not coordinated by an overall strategy. Although many countries are creating e-government services, there is no documentation of an e-government framework to guide the process. Guidelines for the implementation of e-government are also missing from the literature. This chapter conceptualizes a framework that could guide the transformation process toward an e-government model, and also suggests various actions needed for e-government implementation.

Chapter XVII, "Beauty is More than Skin Deep: Organisational Strategies for Online Consumer Risk Mitigation in Apparel Retailing" by Mary Tate, Beverley Hope, and Brent Coker, Victoria University of Wellington (New Zealand), investigates the reasons for the increase in online sales of apparel through an examination of the literature and research of best practice in a successful Australasian multichannel e-tailer. The chapter describes the apparel industry and examines online shopping risks and their consequences, paying particular attention to consumer risks and consequences in the apparel industry. Finally, a set of organizational strategies that can mitigate customer perceived risk and six key strategies for success in online apparel retailing are presented.

The field of e-commerce has become extremely prevalent within the past few years, and this new form of technology continues to grow and expand at a rapid pace. Professionals and educators alike will find that the *Advanced Topics in Electronic Commerce* series is a constantly up-to-date tool necessary for understanding and implementing e-technologies into the daily lives of professors, researchers, scholars, professionals, and all individuals in general. An outstanding collection of the latest research associated with the effective utilization of e-commerce, e-business, and e-government, *Advanced Topics in Electronic Commerce, Volume 1* provides the latest research on e-technologies and their integral role in our ever-changing technological world.

Mehdi Khosrow-Pour, DBA

Editor-in-Chief

Advanced Topics in Electronic Commerce, Volume 1

Chapter I

Role of Small-Business Strategic Alliances in the Perception of Benefits and Disadvantages of E-Commerce Adoption in SMEs

Robert MacGregor, University of Wollongong, Australia

Lejla Vrazalic, University of Wollongong, Australia

Abstract

Despite the proclaimed advantages of small-business strategic alliances, little research has been carried out to determine whether these structures promote the benefits and/or "cushion" the disadvantages arising from e-commerce adoption for member businesses. There has also been a lack of research into comparing e-commerce use in those small businesses that are members of a strategic alliance to those that have opted to remain outside such arrangements. This chapter aims to correct the situation by presenting the findings of a study of 176 regional small businesses in Sweden that investigated the impact of strategic-alliance membership on the benefits and disadvantages associated with e-commerce adoption. The results of the study indicate that there are no significant differences between strategic-alliance members and nonmembers where benefits of e-commerce are concerned. In contrast, e-commerce disadvantages are often dissipated through a strategic-alliance structure more easily than through a single self-directed unit. The study also shows that correlations between e-commerce benefits exist and that the benefits can be grouped according to three distinct factors: costs, efficiency, and sales or inventory.

Introduction

The diffusion and assimilation of e-commerce in small to medium enterprises (SMEs) represents a critical area of investigation. As SMEs confront an environment that is increasingly complex, technologically uncertain, and globally focused, there is a growing need to be flexible and proactive in business dealings. Miles, Preece, and Baetz (1999) have suggested that this has prompted many businesses (both large and small) to turn toward some form of strategic alliance, where the locus of the impact of change is interorganisational rather than organisational. There are many studies that advocate the importance of strategic alliances or networks in the early adoption of e-commerce, particularly by SMEs (see Donckels & Lambrecht, 1997; Jarratt, 1998; Overby & Min, 2001). These studies not only suggest that formal networking provides a ready source of technical information, market expertise, and business know-how, but that the network structure provides a more flexible arrangement than the hierarchy in dealing with environmental turbulence.

Despite the proposed advantages of a strategic alliance in adopting e-commerce in the SME environment, little research has been carried out concerning the ongoing success with e-commerce under such arrangements. Even less work has been done comparing those SMEs that do work within a formal network and those who have opted to remain outside such arrangements.

This chapter compares the perception of benefits and disadvantages derived from the adoption of e-commerce by regional SMEs that are part of a small-business strategic alliance with those that are not. The chapter begins by examining the nature of SMEs. This is followed by a brief overview of the adoption of e-commerce by SMEs, particularly focusing on the benefits and disadvantages of that adoption. Next, the chapter presents a study of 176 Swedish small businesses that have adopted e-commerce technology in their day-to-day activity. The study compares the rating and grouping of benefits and disadvantages arising from e-commerce use between those SMEs that are part of a small-business strategic alliance and those that are not. Finally, the limitations of the study are presented along with the conclusions and future research directions.

The Nature of SMEs

There are a number of definitions of what constitutes an SME. Some of these definitions are based on quantitative measures such as staffing levels, turnover, or assets, while others employ a qualitative approach. Meredith (1994) suggests that any description or definition must include a quantitative component that takes into account staff levels, turnover, and assets together with financial and nonfinancial measurements, but that the description must also include a qualitative component that reflects how the business is organised and how it operates.

More recently there has been a tendency for researchers to simply utilise a mailing list of SMEs supplied by a government agency, thus implying that making decisions about the definitions of SMEs is the responsibility of government agencies rather than researchers. Examples of this approach can be seen in studies by DeLone (1988) and Pendergraft, Morris, and Savage (1987). For the purposes of the study presented in this chapter, the Swedish definition of an SME, namely, less than 50 employees, will be used.

There have been many studies in the literature that have attempted to define the characteristics of SMEs. SMEs are not simply scaled-down versions of large businesses (Wynarczyk, Watson, Storey, Short, & Keasey, 1993). Although size is a major distinguishing factor, SMEs have a number of other unique features that set them apart from large businesses. There have been various studies carried out in order to isolate these features (Bunker & MacGregor, 2000; Dennis, 2000; Hill & Stewart, 2000; Miller & Besser, 2000; Reynolds, Savage, & Williams, 1994; Tetteh & Burn, 2001). An extensive review of the available literature was undertaken to identify the features and create a context for the study. Following this process, an analysis of the features identified revealed that they could be classified as being internal or external to the business. Internal features include management, decision-making and planning processes within the organisation, and the availability of resources, while external features are related to the market (products or services and customers) and the external environment (risk taking and uncertainty). These are presented in Table 1.

It is now appropriate that we examine the nature of e-commerce, in particular, e-commerce and SMEs.

Table 1. Internal and external features unique to small businesses

Features Unique to Small Businesses	Related Literature	
Features Related to Management, Decision Making and Planning Processes		INTERNAL FEATURES
Small businesses have a centralised management strategy with a short range planning perspective	Bunker & MacGregor (2000) Welsh & White (1981)	
Small businesses have poor management and business skills	Blili & Raymond (1993)	
Small businesses exhibit a strong desire for independence and avoid business ventures which impinge on their independence	Dennis (2000) Reynolds et al. (1994)	
Small business owners often withhold information from colleagues	Dennis (2000)	
Decision making processes in small businesses are intuitive, rather than based on detailed planning and exhaustive study	Bunker & MacGregor (2000) Reynolds et al. (1994)	
Small business owners have a strong influence in the decision making process	Bunker & MacGregor (2000) Reynolds et al. (1994)	
Family values and concerns may intrude with the decision making processes of small businesses	Bunker & MacGregor (2000) Dennis (2000)	
Small businesses have informal and inadequate planning and record keeping processes	Tetteh & Burn (2001) Miller & Besser (2000) Rotch (1981)	
Features Related to Resource Availability		
Small businesses face difficulties obtaining finance and other resources, and as a result have fewer resources	Blili & Raymond (1993) Cragg & King (1993) Welsh & White (1981)	
Small businesses are more reluctant to spend on information technology and therefore have limited use of technology	Walczuch et al. (2000) Dennis (2000) Poon & Swatman (1997) MacGregor & Bunker (1996)	
Small businesses have a lack of technical knowledge and specialist staff and provide little information technology training for staff	Martin & Matlay (2001) Bunker & MacGregor (2000) Blili & Raymond (1993) Cragg & King (1993) Welsh & White (1981)	
Features Related to Products/Services and Markets		EXTERNAL FEATURES
Small businesses have a narrow product/service range	Bunker & MacGregor (2000) Reynolds et al. (1994)	
Small businesses have a limited share of the market (often confined towards a niche market) and therefore heavily rely on few customers	Quayle (2002) Hadjimonolis (1999) Lawrence (1997) Reynolds et al. (1994)	
Small businesses s are product oriented, while large businesses are more customer oriented	Bunker & MacGregor (2000) MacGregor et al. (1998) Reynolds et al. (1994)	
Small businesses are not interested in large shares of the market	MacGregor et al. (1998) Reynolds et al. (1994)	
Small businesses are unable to compete with their larger counterparts	Lawrence (1997)	
Features Related to Risk Taking and Dealing with Uncertainty		
Small businesses have lower control over their external environment than larger businesses, and therefore face more uncertainty	Hill & Stewart (2000) Westhead & Storey (1996)	
Small businesses face more risks than large businesses because their failure rates are higher	DeLone (1988) Cochran (1981) Brigham & Smith (1967)	
Small businesses are more reluctant to take risks	Walczuch et al. (2000) Dennis (2000)	

E-Commerce

There are nearly as many definitions of e-commerce as there are contributions to the literature. Turban et al. (2002, p. 4) define e-commerce as "an emerging concept that describes the process of buying, selling or exchanging services and information via computer networks." Choi et al. (as cited in Turban et al.) draw a distinction between what they term pure e-commerce and partial e-commerce. According to Choi et al., pure e-commerce has a digital product, a digital process, and a digital agent. All other interactions (including those that might have one or two of the three nominated by Choi et al.) are termed partial e-commerce. Raymond (2001, p. 411) defines e-commerce as "functions of information exchange and commercial transaction support that operate on telecommunications networks linking business partners (typically customers and suppliers)." Damanpour (2001, p. 18), in comparison, defines e-commerce as "any 'net' business activity that transforms internal and external relationships to create value and exploit market opportunities driven by new rules of the connected economy." For the purposes of this study, which examines changes to the organisation brought about by involvement in e-commerce, the definition provided by Damanpour is used. While it may be argued that other definitions do not preclude organisational transformation, only the definition of Damanpour demands those transformations and is consistent with the concept in the literature, generally.

As already stated, e-commerce is not just another mechanism to sustain or enhance existing business practices. It is a paradigm shift that is radically changing traditional ways of doing business. Dignum (2002) believes that although IT is an important component, the biggest mistake made by many organisations is that they believe that by simply introducing e-commerce technology, they will succeed without having to worry about their organisational structure. If, as suggested by Treacy and Wiersema (1997), e-commerce transforms a company from one geared toward "production excellence" to one geared toward "customer intimacy," e-commerce is not about technology but about a new way of treating customers and suppliers. Achrol and Kotler (1999), in a discussion of marketing within a network economy, describe this transformation as a shift from being an "agent of the seller" to being an "agent of the buyer." Thus, according to Lee (2001), the biggest challenge for most organisations is not how to imitate or benchmark the best e-commerce model, but how to fundamentally change the mind-set of management away from operating as a traditional business.

Fundamental to any changes to traditional business procedures is the realisation that e-commerce, unlike any previous technological innovation, has a locus of impact not within the organisation but at an interorganisational level. Thus, a traditional management focus, which included total quality management, lean manufacturing, and business-process reengineering (collectively termed "economics of scarcity" by Lee, 2001), is replaced by the gathering, synthesis, and distribution of information (collectively termed "economics of abundance" by Lee). Output for organisations can no longer simply be finished products, but must include information and information services bundled for customer use.

Not only has e-commerce changed the rules pertaining to processes within the organisation, it has had a profound effect on the structure of organisations. The advent of e-commerce has seen a radical change away from the hierarchical-based philosophy. Organisations that were once housed within strict product-based boundaries are now having to operate and compete at a global level, and strict hierarchies appear less adept in the turbulent global market. Functions such as marketing that were once organisational and product based (i.e., a select set of products was marketed by an individual organisation) are now becoming interorganisational and knowledge based (multiple organisations continually adjusting their operations to meet changing customer needs, and passing on information rather than products to their customers). Indeed, Achrol and Kotler (1999, p. 146) suggest that "[d]riven by a dynamic and knowledge-rich environment, the hierarchical organisations of the 20th century are disaggregating into a variety of strategic alliance forms."

Not only has e-commerce altered perceptions of organisational structure and function (see Giaglis, Klein, & O'Keefe, 1999; Kuljis, Macredie, & Paul, 1998), it has altered the use of technology within the organisation (Fuller, 2000; Kendall & Kendall, 2001). Where once technology supported the hierarchical structure, it is technology that is driving the evolution away from it.

For larger businesses there has been a variety of approaches. Some businesses are moving entirely to a Web-based presence (Lee, 2001), some are establishing subsidiaries that ultimately become stand-alone, online businesses (see Gulati & Garino, 2000), and others are merging with online businesses. In all cases, there has been a realisation that multilevel hierarchies, with their inability to react to external change, need to be replaced by flatter structures that are adaptable to an ever-changing external environment.

In light of the above discussion, the adoption and use of e-commerce in SMEs will now be considered.

E-Commerce and SMEs

Studies carried out at the onset of e-commerce (Acs, Morck, Shaver, & Yeung, 1997; Auger & Gallaugher, 1997; Gessin, 1996; McRea, 1996; Murphy, 1996; Nooteboom, 1994) predicted that, since SMEs had always operated in an externally uncertain environment, they were more likely to benefit from e-commerce. Other authors, while agreeing in principle with this viewpoint, did so with a degree of caution. Hutt and Speh (1998) felt that most areas of the SME sector, with the exception of those SMEs involved in the industrial market, would benefit from e-commerce. They suggest that the industrial SMEs already concentrated on an established base of customers and product offerings. Swartz and Iacobucci (2000) felt that the service industries would benefit far more than other areas of the SME community. Other studies (Donckels & Lambrecht, 1997; Reuber & Fischer, 1999) felt that the business age was a strong predictor of the relative benefit of e-commerce adoption, suggesting that older businesses would not adopt as easily as newer ones. Among the predicted benefits available to SMEs were the following.

- A global presence presenting customers with a global choice (Barry & Milner, 2002)
- Improved competitiveness (Auger & Gallaugher, 1997)
- Mass customisation and "customerisation," presenting customers with personalised products and services (Fuller, 2000)
- A shortening of supply chains providing rapid response to customer needs (Barry & Milner)

Recent studies have found that these predictions have not eventuated and that it has been the larger businesses that have been more active with respect to e-commerce (see Barry & Milner, 2002; Riquelme, 2002; Roberts & Wood, 2002). A number of reasons have been put forward, including poor security, high costs, and lack of requisite skills. However, some researchers have begun to examine how decisions concerning IT adoption and use are made in the SME sector.

There have been many governmental as well as privately funded projects attempting to further the cause of adoption of e-commerce by SMEs. Unfortunately many of these projects relied on pre-e-commerce criteria and focused on internal systems within the SME rather than interorganisational interaction (Fallon & Moran, 2000; Martin & Matlay, 2001; Poon & Swatman, 1997). The resulting models were stepwise or linear, beginning with e-mail and progressing through Web site, to e-commerce adoption, and finally to organisational transformation. Not only are these models based on inappropriate or oversimplified criteria (Kai-Uwe Brock, 2000), but they recommend the adoption of e-commerce prior to any form of organisational change.

E-commerce brings with it changes in communication (Chellappa, Barua, & Whinston, 1996), business method (Henning, 1998), market structure, and the approach to marketing (Giaglis et al., 1999), as well as changes in day-to-day activities (Doukidis, Smithson, & Naoum, 1998). These changes are exacerbated in the SME sector as many SMEs have no overall plan and, for the most part, fail to understand the need for competitive strategies (Jeffcoate, Chappell, & Feindt, 2002).

Unlike previous technological innovations, e-commerce brings with it changes to both procedures within the organisation as well as changes to the structure of the organisation itself. These changes include the way businesses interact; their approaches to marketing, products, and customers; and the way decisions are made and disseminated, particularly decisions concerning technology adoption and use. For SMEs, these changes can have both positive and negative effects. Those SME owners and managers who have developed an organisation-wide strategy for e-commerce adoption report increases in efficiency. Those who have not often find that the changes reduce flexibility within their businesses. The following section will examine the benefits and disadvantages derived by SMEs through e-commerce adoption and use.

Benefits and Disadvantages of E-Commerce in SMEs

For SMEs, the changes associated with e-commerce have produced both positive and negative effects. Studies by Raymond (2001) and Ritchie and Brindley (2000) found that, while e-commerce adoption has eroded trading barriers for SMEs, this has often come at the price of altering or eliminating commercial relationships and exposing the business to external risks. Lawrence (1997), Lee (2001), and Tetteh and Burn (2001) contend that e-commerce adoption fundamentally alters the internal procedures within SMEs. Indeed, Lee adds that the biggest challenge to SMEs is not to find the best e-commerce model, but to change the mind-set of the owners and managers themselves. For those who have developed an organisation-wide strategy (in anticipation of e-commerce), these changes can lead to an increase in efficiency in the business; for those who have not, the changes can reduce the flexibility of the business (Tetteh & Burn) and often lead to a duplication of the work effort (MacGregor et al., 1998).

A number of studies have examined both the tangible and intangible benefits achieved by SMEs from the adoption of e-commerce. Studies by Abell and Limm (1996), Poon and Swatman (1997), and Quayle (2002) found that the tangible benefits (such as reduced administration costs, reduced production costs, reduced lead time, increased sales) derived from electronic commerce were marginal in terms of direct earnings. These same studies found that the intangible benefits (such as improvement in the quality of information, improved internal control of the business, improved relations with business partners) were of far greater value to SMEs.

A number of studies has provided conflicting results. Raymond (2001), in a study of the effect of e-commerce on travel agents, found that very often electronic commerce replaced previously held business partners. He suggested that e-commerce removed the need for intermediaries in many small-business dealings. Stauber (2000) also noted the negative effect of e-commerce on small businesses. Specifically, he found that many firms felt that there was a decline in contact with customers; in some cases, managers felt that this had led to a loss of revenue. In comparison, a study by Poon and Swatman (1997) found that electronic commerce had led to an improved relationship with customers but not with suppliers. In their study they found that small-business operators complained that e-commerce failed to meet expectations concerning marketing or sales, and they had not experienced any savings in terms of communications costs.

A number of studies (MacGregor et al., 1998; Sparkes & Thomas, 2001) has also suggested that indirect drawbacks of e-commerce use in SMEs include dependence on the technology and the high cost of maintenance of the technology itself.

It is interesting to note that various authors (Abell & Limm, 1996; Martin & Matlay, 2001; Poon & Swatman, 1997) all suggest that tangible benefits are marginal in the short term, contrary to the expectations of small-business operators, and that at best these may be more fruitful in the longer term. This is supported in a recent article by Vrazalic, Bunker, MacGregor, Carlsson, and Magnusson (2002). For summary purposes, the benefits and disadvantages of e-commerce adoption are listed in Tables 2 and 3 respectively.

The role of strategic alliances in SMEs will now be discussed.

Table 2. Summary of e-commerce adoption benefits reported by previous studies

E-Commerce Benefits	Related Literature
E-commerce had led to increased sales.	Abell & Limm (1996)
E-commerce has given us access to new customers and markets.	Quayle (2002) ; Raymond (2001); Ritchie & Brindley (2001); Sparkes & Thomas (2001)
E-commerce has improved our competitiveness.	Vescovi (2000)
E-commerce has lowered our administration costs.	Abell & Limm (1996); Poon & Swatman (1997); Quayle (2002)
E-commerce has lowered our production costs.	Abell & Limm (1996); Poon & Swatman (1997); Quayle (2002)
E-commerce has reduced the lead time from order to delivery.	Abell & Limm (1996); Poon & Swatman (1997); Quayle (2002)
E-commerce has reduced the stock levels.	Quayle (2002)
E-commerce has increased internal efficiency.	MacGregor et al. (1998); Tetteh & Burn (2001)
E-commerce has improved our relations with business partners.	Poon & Swatman (1997)
E-commerce has improved the quality of information in our organisation.	Abell & Limm (1996); Poon & Swatman (1997); Quayle (2002)

Table 3. Summary of e-commerce adoption disadvantages reported by previous studies

E-Commerce Disadvantages	Related Literature
E-commerce has resulted in a deterioration of our organisation's relations with business partners.	Raymond (2001); Stauber (2000)
E-commerce has increased our costs.	Stauber (2000)
E-commerce has increased the computer maintenance in our organisation.	MacGregor et al. (1998)
E-commerce has doubled the work in our organisation.	MacGregor et al. (1998)
E-commerce has reduced the flexibility of the work.	Lawrence (1997); Lee (2001); MacGregor et al. (1998)
E-commerce has increased security concerns and issues.	Ritchie & Brindley (2001)
Our organisation has become too dependent on e-commerce.	Sparkes & Thomas (2001)

Role of Strategic Alliances in SMEs

It could be argued that by the very nature of business, all organisations relate to others and are thus part of some form of strategic alliance or network arrangement. On the surface these relationships may appear to be nothing more than exchanges of goods and payments, but relationships with customers, suppliers, and competitors can never be simply described in terms of financial transactions. Dennis (2000) suggests that any dealings with other organisations must impinge on the decision-making process even if these decisions only involve the strengthening or relaxing of the relationships themselves. Brandenburg and Nalebuff (1996) state that for a relationship to be truly an alliance, it must be conscious, interdependent, and cooperating toward a predetermined set of goals.

Viewed then as "self-designing" partnerships, Eccles and Crane (as cited in Dennis, 2000) suggest that alliances or networks are a dynamic arrangement evolving and adjusting to accommodate changes in the business environment. Achrol and Kotler (1999, p. 147) take this a step further by stating, "Networks are more adaptable and flexible because of loose coupling and openness to information. Environmental disturbances transfer imperfectly through loose coupled networks and tend to dissipate in intensity as they spread through the system." Thus, member organisations have interconnected linkages that allow more efficient movement toward predetermined objectives than would be the case if they operated as a single separate entity. By developing and organising functional components, alliances or networks provide a better mechanism to learn and adapt to changes in their environment.

In addition to providing much needed information, alliances often provide legitimacy to their members. For businesses that provide a service and whose products are intangible, company image and reputation become crucial since customers can rarely test or inspect the service before purchase. Cropper (1996) suggests that alliance membership very often supplies this image to potential customers.

The advent of e-commerce technology has given rise to a new wave of research examining the role of strategic alliances, particularly in SMEs. Much of this research has been prompted by the realisation that old hierarchical forms of company organisation produce relationships that are too tightly coupled (Marchewka & Towell, 2000) and do not fit in an often turbulent marketplace (Overby & Min, 2000; Tikkanen, 1998).

While recent studies (Keeble et al., 1999; O'Donnell et al., 2001; Overby & Min, 2001) stress the importance of informal interorganisational links, the definition of these links in small business varies widely. As this study has as its focus SME networks with some form of governance (be they organisationally linked small businesses or firms that have made use of small-business associations), the definition provided by Achrol and Kotler (1999, p. 148) will be adopted:

an independent coalition of task- or skill-specialised economic entities (independent firms or autonomous organisational units) that operates without hierarchical control but is embedded by dense lateral connections, mutuality, and reciprocity, in a shared value system that defines "membership" roles and responsibilities.

Properly utilised, strategic alliances can provide a number of advantages over stand-alone organisations. These include the sharing of financial risk (Jorde & Teece, 1989), technical knowledge (Marchewka & Towell, 2000), market penetration (Achrol & Kotler, 1999), and internal efficiency (Datta, 1988). Early studies of SME networks (Gibb, 1993; Ozcan, 1995) concentrated on formal alliances. Indeed, Golden and Dollinger (1993), in a study of small manufacturing firms, concluded that few small firms were able to function without some form of interorganisational relationship having been established. They added that these interorganisational relationships were associated with successful strategic adaptation by small businesses. Dean et al. (1997, p. 78) suggested that formal networks were used by SMEs to "pool resources and talents together to reap results which would not be possible (due to cost constraints and economies of scale) if the enterprise operated in isolation."

In the 1990s many SME alliances took a more semiformal approach. Local or government agencies such as small-business associations and chambers of commerce provided a formal umbrella in the form of advisory services that assisted in legal, financial, training, or technical advice. Individual members operated formally with the umbrella organisation but could interact informally with fellow members.

While researchers, government agencies, and practitioners have continued to examine and refine both formal and semiformal networks, recent literature

(Premaratne, 2001; Rosenfeld, 1996) suggests that informal or social linkages may provide a higher and more stable flow of information and resources in the SME environment. If, as suggested in the literature, many SMEs are moving toward some type of strategic-alliance arrangement through which e-commerce adoption and use is possible, it is appropriate to examine whether the perceptions of benefits and disadvantages differs between those SMEs that are part of a strategic alliance and those that are not. This was done in a study described in the following section.

Methodology

A series of six in-depth interviews was undertaken to determine whether the e-commerce benefits and disadvantages listed in Tables 2 and 3 respectively were applicable and complete. All of the benefits and disadvantages were found to be applicable and no additional ones were forthcoming. Based on the six in-depth interviews, a survey instrument was developed to collect data about e-commerce-adoption benefits and disadvantages (amongst other things). Respondents were asked whether their firms were part of strategic alliances of small businesses or organisations for small businesses. They were also asked whether they had adopted electronic commerce. Those respondents who indicated that they had adopted e-commerce were asked to rate each of the benefits and disadvantages across a five-point Likert scale. The Likert scale responses were assumed to possess the characteristics of an interval measurement scale for data-analysis purposes. An example of a Likert-scale question in the survey is shown in Figure 1.

This question relates to the disadvantages experienced by your organisation following e-commerce adoption. Below is a list of statements indicating possible disadvantages your organisation may have experienced after implementing e-commerce. Please rank each of the statements on a scale of 1 to 5 to indicate to what extent each is applicable to your organisation, as follows:

The study was primarily concerned with small businesses located in regional areas, especially since no other research has investigated e-commerce-adoption disadvantages in these areas specifically. As a result, this study was conceived primarily as exploratory in nature. To qualify as a regional area, the following criteria was developed and applied to several areas in Sweden.

- The location must be an urban regional area and not a major or capital city or rural area.

Figure 1. Question about e-commerce adoption disadvantages used in survey

This question relates to the disadvantages experienced by your organisation following e-commerce adoption. Below is a list of statements indicating possible disadvantages your organisation may have experienced after implementing e-commerce. Please rank each of the statements on a scale of 1 to 5 to indicate to what extent each is applicable to your organisation, as follows:

1 = highly inapplicable to our organisation's experience

2 = inapplicable to our organisation's experience

3 = neither applicable nor inapplicable to our organisation's experience

4 = applicable to our organisation's experience

5 = highly applicable to our organisation's experience

Following e-commerce adoption, our organisation experienced the following disadvantages.	Rating				
E-commerce adoption resulted in a deterioration of relations with our business partners.	1	2	3	4	5
E-commerce adoption increased costs in our organisation.	1	2	3	4	5
E-commerce adoption increased the computer maintenance required in our organisation.	1	2	3	4	5
E-commerce adoption doubled the work in our organisation.	1	2	3	4	5
E-commerce adoption reduced the flexibility of the business processes in our organisation.	1	2	3	4	5
E-commerce adoption raised security concerns in our organisation.	1	2	3	4	5
Since adopting e-commerce, our organisation has become increasingly dependent on this technology.	1	2	3	4	5

- A viable government-initiated chamber of commerce must exist and be well-patronised by the small-business community.
- The location should have a full range of educational facilities (including a university).
- The business community must represent a cross section of business ages, sizes, sectors, and market foci.

As a result, 1,170 surveys were distributed by post to randomly selected SMEs in Karlstad, Filipstad, Saffle, and Arvika. The mode of the data collection was selected based on previous research by de Heer (1999), which indicated that Scandinavian countries (including Sweden) had historically high survey response rates (although he notes that this is declining).

Analysis of Responses

Responses were obtained from 339 SME organisations, giving a response rate of almost 29%. Of the 339 responses, 148 indicated that they belonged to a small-business strategic alliance. These have been termed member respondents. Meanwhile, 191 respondents indicated that they were not part of such an arrangement. These have been termed nonmember respondents. Table 4 provides a summary profile of the respondents. Of the 339 that responded, 176 SMEs indicated that they had adopted e-commerce.

A comparison of the means of the ratings of benefits and disadvantages (in members and nonmembers) was carried out using a two-tailed t-test. Table 5 provides the means and the t values.

A correlation analysis of the ratings of benefits and of disadvantages was carried out for the complete set of data. The results of this analysis are shown in the following tables.

The correlation matrix shows an interesting pattern of results. The first two benefits, A and B, correlate (this benefit group has been termed costs), and benefits C, D, and E also show strong correlation (this benefit group has been termed sales or inventory). Similarly, it appears that correlations exist between the last six benefits in the correlation matrix (this benefit group has been termed efficiency). Therefore, three distinct groupings of results can be identified in the correlation matrix: costs, inventory, and efficiency.

These findings suggested the use of factor analysis to investigate any separate underlying factors and to reduce the redundancy of certain benefits indicated in

Table 4. Profile of survey respondents

Number of Years in Business	**Total**	**%**
Less than 1 year	5	1%
1 to 2 years	14	4%
3 to 5 years	45	13%
6 to 10 years	61	18%
11 to 20 years	83	24%
More than 20 years	131	39%
Market Focus		
Local	174	51%
Regional	30	9%
National	96	28%
International	39	12%
Business Sector		
Industrial	84	25%
Service	118	35%
Retail	63	19%
Finance	9	3%
Other	54	16%
Missing	*11*	*3%*

Table 5. A comparison of the means of benefits and disadvantages of e-commerce adoption in member and nonmember SMEs

	Members of Strategic Alliance	Nonmembers of Strategic Alliance	t Value
BENEFITS			
E-commerce has led to increased sales.	2.51	2.43	-0.321
E-commerce has given us access to new customers and markets.	2.67	2.95	1.085
E-commerce has improved our competitiveness.	2.00	1.97	-0.128
E-commerce has lowered our administration costs.	2.85	2.76	-0.349
E-commerce has lowered our production costs.	2.64	2.80	0.372
E-commerce has reduced the lead time from order to delivery.	2.82	2.75	-0.265
E-commerce has reduced the stock levels.	1.85	2.06	0.897
E-commerce has increased internal efficiency.	2.57	2.87	1.204
E-commerce has improved our relations with business partners.	2.56	2.50	-0.231
E-commerce has improved the quality of information in our organisation.	2.66	2.85	0.733
DISADVANTAGES			
E-commerce has resulted in a deterioration of our organisation's relations with business partners.	1.16	1.29	0.912
E-commerce has increased our costs.	1.59	1.98	1.923*
E-commerce has increased the computer maintenance in our organisation.	1.89	2.24	1.728*
E-commerce has doubled the work in our organisation.	1.44	1.83	2.146*
E-commerce has reduced the flexibility of the work.	1.05	1.25	1.650*
E-commerce has increased security concerns and issues.	1.13	1.50	2.642**
Our organisation has become too dependent on e-commerce.	1.44	1.64	1.110

* *significant at 0.05 level* ** *significant at 0.01 level*

the correlation matrix. The results of Kaiser-Meyer-Olkin MSA (0.798) and Bartlett's Test of Sphericity ($c^2 = 576$, $p = 0.000$) indicated that the data set satisfied the assumptions for factorability. Principle components analysis was chosen as the method of extraction in order to account for maximum variance in the data using a minimum number of factors. A three-factor solution was extracted with eigenvalues of 4.083, 1.657, and 1.007, and was supported by an inspection of the screen plot. These three factors accounted for 67.476% of the total variance as shown in Table 7.

The three resulting components were rotated using the Varimax procedure, and a simple structure was achieved as shown in the rotated component matrix in Table 8. Five benefits loaded highly on the first component. These benefits are related to internal efficiency and marketing. This component has been termed the efficiency factor. Three benefits highly loaded on the second component are termed the costs factor, and two benefits loaded onto the final factor are termed the sales or inventory factor. These three factors are independent and uncorrelated as an orthogonal rotation procedure was used.

Table 6. Correlations of benefits for the entire sample group (i.e., members and nonmembers)

		A	B	C	D	E	F	G	H	I	J
Lower administration costs	**A**	**1**									
Lower production costs	**B**	**.259**	**1**								
Reduced lead time	**C**	**.343**	.099	**1**							
Reduced stock	**D**	**.274**	.239**	**.506**	**1**						
Increased sales	**E**	**.307**	**.270**	**.364**	**.283**	**1**					
Increased internal efficiency	**F**	**.644**	.214**	**.372**	.241**	**.397**	**1**				
Improved relations with business partners	**G**	**.298**	.166*	**.364**	**.355**	**.457**	**.365**	**1**			
New customers and markets	**H**	.103	.161*	.151	.098	**.709**	**.315**	**.393**	**1**		
Improved competitiveness	**I**	**.316**	.192*	**.291**	.160	**.558**	**.395**	**.602**	**.620**	**1**	
Improved quality of information	**J**	.031	.127	.127	.059	**.535**	.180*	**.291**	**.674**	**.519**	**1**

*** Correlation is significant at the 0.01 level (two-tailed); * Correlation is significant at the 0.05 level (two-tailed); **Bold**: Correlation significant at the 0.001 level (two-tailed)*

Table 7. Total variance explained

	Rotation Sums of Squared Loadings		
Component	***Eigenvalue***	***% of Variance***	***Cumulative %***
1. Efficiency	4.083	29.911	29.911
2. Costs	1.657	19.985	49.897
3. Sales/Inventory	1.007	17.580	67.476

The same analysis was carried out for e-commerce disadvantages. Table 9 presents the correlations of the disadvantages.

As can be seen in Table 9, there is only a single grouping of disadvantages, indicating that factor-analysis techniques are not applicable in this case.

The data was then subdivided into two groups: members (respondents that were members of small-business strategic alliances) and nonmembers (respondents that were not). Correlations of benefits were carried out for each group of respondents separately (see Tables 10 and 11).

The correlation matrix for nonmember respondents (Table 10), as before, shows that the first two benefits correlate (this benefit group has been termed costs), and benefits C, D, and E again show strong correlation (this benefit group has been termed sales or inventory). Similarly, correlations exist between the last six benefits in the correlation matrix (this benefit group has been termed efficiency). Therefore, for the nonmember respondents, three distinct groupings of results can be identified in the correlation matrix.

The correlation matrix for member respondents (Table 11) shows two groupings only: benefits A, B, and C forming one grouping, and benefits E through J forming

Table 8. Rotated component matrix

E-Commerce Benefits	Component 1 – Efficiency	Component 2 – Costs	Component 3 – Sales/Inventory
Lower administration costs	.022	.822	.184
Lower production costs	.133	.447	.079
Reduced lead time	.116	.255	.788
Reduced stock	.048	.081	.874
Increased sales	.759	.271	.255
Increased internal efficiency	.221	.820	.161
Improved relations with business partners	.489	.282	.462
New customers and markets	.905	.106	.018
Improved competitiveness	.742	.334	.163
Improved quality of information	.850	-.025	-.004

Table 9. Correlations of disadvantages for the entire sample group (i.e., members and nonmembers)

		A	B	C	D	E	F	G
Deterioration of relations with business partners	A	1						
Higher costs	B	**.322**	1					
Computer maintenance	C	**.358**	**.494**	1				
Doubling of work	D	**.319**	**.340**	**.416**	1			
Reduced flexibility of work	E	**.633**	**.336**	**.360**	**.443**	1		
Security	F	**.453**	**.343**	**.394**	**.401**	**.578**	1	
Dependence on e-commerce	G	**.336**	**.407**	**.527**	**.333**	**.389**	**.570**	1

***Bold**: Correlation significant at the 0.001 level (two-tailed)*

Table 10. Correlations of benefits for nonmembers

		A	B	C	D	E	F	G	H	I	J
Lower administration costs	A	1									
Lower production costs	B	.209*	1								
Reduced lead time	C	.262**	.028	1							
Reduced stock	D	**.346**	.243*	**.608**	1						
Increased sales	E	.242*	.239*	**.342**	**.400**	1					
Increased internal efficiency	F	**.701**	.175	.249*	.313**	.236*	1				
Improved relations with business partners	G	**.319**	.141	**.386**	**.516**	.308**	.282**	1			
New customers and markets	H	.007	.134	.126	.139	**.638**	.182	.253*	1		
Improved competitiveness	I	.307**	.173	.308**	.291**	**.452**	.312**	**.570**	**.533**	1	
Improved quality of information	J	-.063	.106	.141	.041	**.444**	.042	.237*	**.611**	**.473**	1

*** Correlation is significant at the 0.01 level (two-tailed); * Correlation is significant at the 0.05 level (two-tailed); **Bold**: Correlation significant at the 0.001 level (two-tailed)*

Table 11. Correlations of benefits for members

		A	B	C	D	E	F	G	H	I	J
Lower administration costs	**A**	**1**									
Lower production costs	**B**	**.676**	**1**								
Reduced lead time	**C**	**.481**	**.568**	**1**							
Reduced stock	**D**	.158	.294*	.344*	**1**						
Increased sales	**E**	.385**	**.616**	.399**	.116	**1**					
Increased internal efficiency	**F**	**.570**	**.573**	**.577**	.172	**.613**	**1**				
Improved relations with business partners	**G**	.281*	.378**	.352**	.035	**.671**	**.525**	**1**			
New customers and markets	**H**	.254	.412**	.197	.049	**.829**	**.506**	**.617**	**1**		
Improved competitiveness	**I**	.324*	.417**	.267	-.073	**.694**	**.523**	**.649**	**.760**	**1**	
Improved quality of information	**J**	.171	.317*	.097	.126	**.672**	.378**	.374**	**.765**	**.585**	**1**

*** Correlation is significant at the 0.01 level (two-tailed); * Correlation is significant at the 0.05 level (two-tailed);* ***Bold****: Correlation significant at the 0.001 level (two-tailed)*

Table 12. Total variance explained (nonmembers)

	Rotation Sums of Squared Loadings		
Component	***Eigenvalue***	***% of Variance***	***Cumulative %***
1. Efficiency	3.776	37.765	37.765
2. Costs	1.774	17.741	55.505
3. Sales/Inventory	1.131	11.311	66.817

a second group. Interestingly, benefit D (reduced stock) does not appear to correlate with either group.

Again, these findings suggested the use of factor analysis to investigate any separate underlying factors and to reduce the redundancy of certain benefits indicated in the correlation matrix. The results of Kaiser-Meyer-Olkin MSA (0.738 for nonmembers and 0.836 for members) and Bartlett's Test of Sphericity ($c^2 = 351$ and $p = 0.000$ for nonmembers, and $c^2 = 292$ and $p = 0.000$ for members) indicated that the data set satisfied the assumptions for factorability. Principle components analysis was chosen as the method of extraction in order to account for maximum variance in the data using a minimum number of factors. For the nonmember respondents, a three-factor solution was extracted with eigenvalues of 3.776, 1.774, and 1.131, and was supported by an inspection of the screen plot. These three factors accounted for 66.817% of the total variance as shown in Table 12. For the member respondents, a two-factor solution was extracted with eigenvalues of 5.083 and 1.683, accounting for 67.657% of the total variance as shown in Table 13.

Both sets of components were rotated using the Varimax procedure, and a simple structure was achieved as shown in the rotated component matrix in Table 14. In both cases, the factors are independent and uncorrelated as an orthogonal rotation procedure was used.

Table 13. Total variance explained (members)

	Rotation Sums of Squared Loadings		
Component	*Eigenvalue*	*% of Variance*	*Cumulative %*
1. Efficiency	5.083	50.830	50.830
2. Costs & Inventory	1.683	16.827	67.657

Table 14. Rotated component matrix

	NONMEMBERS			MEMBERS	
BENEFITS	**Efficiency**	**Sales/ Inventory**	**Cost**	**Efficiency**	**Costs & Inventory**
Lower administration costs	-.004	.260	.867	.216	.771
Lower production costs	.188	.001	.452	.399	.743
Reduced lead time	.006	.860	.005	.161	.822
Reduced stock	.008	.850	.181	-.114	.501
Increased sales	.701	.335	.184	.875	.301
Increased internal efficiency	.006	.187	.853	.522	.646
Improved relations with business partners	.296	.639	.232	.720	.267
New customers and markets	.898	.004	.005	.927	.122
Improved competitiveness	.637	.337	.339	.876	.124
Improved quality of information	.846	.002	-.002	.808	-.003

As there was only one factor for disadvantages, no further statistical analysis was possible.

Discussion

Before examining the data in detail, it is interesting to note that of the 339 respondents, only 148 (43.7%) indicated that they considered that their businesses were part of strategic alliances. There are two possibilities for this lower-than-expected result.

1. While many respondents may have dealt with other businesses, these interactions were informal rather than under some form of enforced governance. This is supported by the findings of Premaratne (2001).
2. As the study was conducted on regional SMEs, the ability to form and maintain any form of network was more difficult than it might have been for city-based SMEs. This is supported by the findings of Dahlstrand (1999), who suggests that geographic proximity is essential for the development and maintenance of alliances, particularly in the small-business arena.

Table 4 presents a profile of the respondents that had adopted e-commerce. In relation to the number of years in business (business age), Table 4 shows that the majority of respondents were SMEs that had been in operation for more than 10 years (i.e., established SMEs). In relation to market focus, Table 4 indicates that the respondents predominantly had a local focus, with the majority of their customers being located in their local areas. In contrast, studies by Blackburn and Athayde (2000) suggest that e-commerce adoption is positively associated with an international market focus. Finally, in relation to the business sector, the majority of the respondents were in the service and industrial sectors.

Before examining the data in Table 5 in detail, it is interesting to note that the mean for all the e-commerce benefits and disadvantages was below the median value of 3. This implies that the benefits and disadvantages found by other researchers (and listed in Tables 2 and 3) are not as apparent in the current study. Table 5 also shows that only the disadvantages showed significant difference between the member and nonmember respondents. In contrast, there were no significant differences between members and nonmembers where e-commerce benefits were concerned. This would appear to suggest that belonging to a strategic alliance does not result in achieving more benefits through e-commerce adoption, which is in contrast to the views of Achrol and Kotler (1999), and Marchewka and Towell (2000).

In relation to the e-commerce disadvantages, the two groups differed on all but two disadvantages (deterioration of relations with business partners and dependence on e-commerce). While still below the median point, the other e-commerce disadvantages were all rated higher by the nonmember group than by their strategic-alliance-member counterparts. One possible explanation for this is that sufficient technical support and business know-how existed within the SME strategic-alliance arrangement to satisfy its members. This expertise may not have been available to the individual nonmember businesses. This would tend to support the views of Foy (as cited in Dennis, 2000), Keeble et al. (1999), and Overby and Min (2000), who suggest that many SMEs seek out strategic alliances to acquire these skills that are absent in their own organisations.

The results presented in Tables 6, 7, and 8 indicate that correlations between e-commerce benefits exist and enable the grouping of these benefits according to three factors. These factors have been termed costs, efficiency, and sales or inventory. The costs factor is related to those benefits that have resulted in reduced costs following e-commerce implementation. The efficiency factor is related to the improved way of doing business brought about as a result of e-commerce adoption, including internal efficiency, improved relations with partners, the ability to reach new customers and increase competitiveness, and the improved quality of information. The final factor has been termed sales or inventory, and it concerns those benefits related to higher sales and lower levels of inventory or stock.

Table 9 indicates that there exists only a single grouping of e-commerce disadvantages, suggesting that all of the e-commerce disadvantages are correlated.

Tables 10 to 14 provide the results of dividing the respondents into two subsets (members and nonmembers of a strategic alliance) and the correlations between the e-commerce benefits in each subset. Tables 10 and 12 indicate that the benefits in the nonmember subset can be grouped according to the same three factors that apply to the entire set: costs, efficiency, and sales or inventory. In contrast, the member subset showed only two clear groupings of benefits, with the reduced-stock benefit not showing any correlations with either group. However, a comparison of Tables 12 and 13 shows that only 38% of the nonmembers achieved efficiency benefits compared to almost 51% of the members of strategic alliances. This would appear to suggest that pooling resources via a strategic alliance may result in improved internal efficiency and quality of information, as well as improved competitiveness and relations with business partners.

The results of this study are significant in several ways. The analysis has shown that e-commerce benefits can be grouped in relation to three main factors. This gives researchers a powerful explanatory tool because it reduces the noise in the data. Instead of accounting for 10 different benefits, the advantages of e-commerce use can be explained in relation to one of three factors. The rotated component matrix shown in Table 8 also enables the prediction of the scores of each individual benefit based on the score of the three factors, and vice versa, for an SME. This has implications for research into e-commerce benefits. Whereas before, researchers had identified various benefits (such as the ones listed in Table 2), this is the first time a study has shown that certain benefits are correlated and can be logically grouped according to three factors. This makes it simpler not only to explain but also to predict benefits of e-commerce adoption in SMEs.

Limitations

It should be noted that the study presented here has several limitations. First, the membership or nonmembership in some type of small-business strategic alliance may be biased by the lack of geographic proximity to other small businesses needed to form and maintain some type of viable alliance. It may also be biased by the perception of the respondent as to what constitutes a small-business strategic alliance. Second, the choice of variables selected for the study is somewhat problematic because of the complex nature of e-commerce benefits and disadvantages, which change over time. Furthermore, according to Sohal and Ng (1998), the views expressed in the surveys are of a single individual from the responding organisation, and only those interested in the study are likely to complete and return the survey. However, previous empirical studies (Raymond, 2001) have demonstrated this methodology to be valid. Finally, this is a quantitative study, and further qualitative research is required to gain a better understanding of the key issues.

Conclusion

Unlike previous studies that have focused on small businesses that are part of a strategic alliance, the data presented in this chapter have attempted to compare and contrast those small businesses that are part of a strategic alliance with those that are not. The results of the study presented in this chapter suggest that there are no significant differences between those SMEs that are members of a strategic alliance and those that are not in relation to benefits of e-commerce use. In contrast, the disadvantages experienced by SMEs following e-commerce adoption do show significant differences, implying that these disadvantages are often dissipated through a strategic-alliance structure more easily than through a single self-directed unit. However, the results also show that not all of the e-commerce disadvantages are reduced by a strategic alliance.

The study presented in this chapter also demonstrates that e-commerce benefits can be grouped according to three distinct factors, namely, costs, efficiency, and sales or inventory. This is significant because it consolidates our understanding of e-commerce-adoption benefits and provides an explanatory tool to researchers. The results of this study are significant in other ways as well. This has been the first attempt at understanding the relationship between strategic-alliance membership and e-commerce benefits and disadvantages. The research presented here indicates that this relationship is worthy of further examination because by formally explicating it, researchers and government organisations engaged in promoting e-commerce adoption will have more comprehensive knowledge about the issues and factors that have an effect on the relationship and will be able to provide better advice to SMEs on e-commerce adoption.

References

Abell, W., & Limm, L. (1996). Business use of the Internet in New Zealand: An exploratory study. In *Proceedings of AUSWeb 96*.

Achrol, R. S., & Kotler, P. (1999). Marketing in the network economy. *Journal of Marketing, 63*, 146-163.

Acs, Z. J., Morck, R., Shaver, J. M., & Yeung, B. (1997). The internationalisation of small and medium sized enterprises: A policy perspective. *Small Business Economics, 9*(1), 7-20.

Auger, P., & Gallaugher, J. M. (1997). Factors affecting adoption of an Internet-based sales presence for small businesses. *The Information Society, 13*(1), 55-74.

Barry, H., & Milner, B. (2002). SME's and electronic commerce: A departure from the traditional prioritisation of training? *Journal of European Industrial Training, 25*(7), 316-326.

Blili, S., & Raymond, L. (1993). Threats and opportunities for small and medium-sized enterprises. *International Journal of Information Management, 13*, 439-448.

Brandenburg, A., & Nalebuff, B. (1996). *Co-opetition.* Doubleday Broadway Books.

Brigham, E. F., & Smith, K. V. (1967). The cost of capital to the small firm. *The Engineering Economist, 13*(1), 1-26.

Bunker, D. J., & MacGregor, R. C. (2000). Successful generation of information technology (IT) requirements for small/medium enterprises (SME's): Cases from regional Australia. In *Proceedings of SMEs in a Global Economy* (pp. 72-84).

Chellappa, R., Barua, A., & Whinston, A. (1996). Looking beyond internal corporate Web servers. In R. Kalakota & A. Whinston (Eds.), *Readings in electronic commerce* (pp. 311-321). Reading, MA: Addison Wesley.

Cochran, A. B. (1981). Small business mortality rates: A review of the literature. *Journal of Small Business Management, 19*(4), 50-59.

Cragg, P. B., & King, M. (1993). Small-firm computing: Motivators and inhibitors. *MIS Quarterly, 17*(1), 47-60.

Cropper, S. (1996). Collaborative working and the issue of sustainability. In C. Huxham (Ed.), *Creating collaborative advantage* (pp. 80-100). London: Sage.

Damanpour, F. (2001). E-Business e-commerce evolution: Perspective and strategy. *Managerial Finance, 27*(7), 16-33.

DeLone, W. H. (1988). Determinants for success for computer usage in small business. *MIS Quarterly*, 51-61.

Dennis, C. (2000). Networking for marketing advantage. *Management Decision, 38*(4), 287-292.

Dignum, F. (2002). E-commerce in production: Some experiences. *Integrated Manufacturing Systems, 13*(5), 283-294.

Donckels, R., & Lambrecht, J. (1997). The network position of small businesses: An explanatory model. *Journal of Small Business Management, 35*(2), 13-28.

Doukidis, G. I., Smithson, S., & Naoum, G. (1992). Information systems management in Greece: Issues and perceptions. *Journal of Strategic Information Systems, 1*, 139-148.

Fallon, M., & Moran, P. (2000). Information communications technology (ICT) and manufacturing SMEs. In *Proceedings of the 2000 Small Business and Enterprise Development Conference* (pp. 100-109).

Fuller, T. (2000). The small business guide to the Internet: A practical approach to going online. *International Small Business Journal, 19*(1), 105-107.

Gessin, J. (1996). Impact of electronic commerce on small and medium sized enterprises. *Management*, 11-12.

Giaglas, G., Klein, S., & O'Keefe, R. (1999). Disintermediation, reintermediation, or cybermediation? The future of intermediaries in electronic marketplaces. In *Proceedings of the 12th Bled Electronic Commerce Conference*.

Gulati, R., & Garino, J. (2000). Getting the right mix of bricks and clicks for your company. *Harvard Business Review*, 107-114.

Hadjimonolis, A. (1999). Barriers to innovation for SMEs in a small less developed country (Cyprus). *Technovation, 19*(9), 561-570.

Henning, K. (1998). *The digital enterprise: How digitisation is redefining business*. New York: Random House Business Books.

Hill, R., & Stewart, J. (2000). Human resource development in small organisations. *Journal of European Industrial Training, 24*(2/3/4), 105-117.

Hutt, M. D., & Speh, T. W. (1998). *Business marketing management: A strategic view of industrial and organisational markets*. Fort Worth, TX: Dryden Press.

Jarratt, D. G. (1998). A strategic classification of business alliances: A qualitative perspective built from a study of small and medium-sized enterprises. *Qualitative Market Research: An International Journal, 1*(1), 39-49.

Jeffcoate, J., Chappell, C., & Feindt, S. (2002). Best practice in SME adoption of e-commerce. *Benchmarking: An International Journal, 9*(2), 122-132.

Kai-Uwe Brock, J. (2000). Information and technology in the small firm. In S. Carter & Jones-Evans (Eds.), *Enterprise and the small business* (pp. 384-408). Prentice Hall, Pearson Education.

Kendall, J. E., & Kendall, K. E. (2001). A paradoxically peaceful coexistence between commerce and Ecommerce. *Journal of Information Technology, Theory and Application, 3*(4), 1-6.

Kuljis, J., Macredie, R., & Paul, R. J. (1998). Information gathering problems in multinational banking. *Journal of Strategic Information Systems, 7*, 233-245.

Lawrence, K. L. (1997). Factors inhibiting the utilisation of electronic commerce facilities in Tasmanian small- to medium-sized enterprises. In *Proceedings of the Eighth Australasian Conference on Information Systems* (pp. 587-597).

Lee, C. S. (2001). An analytical framework for evaluating e-commerce business models and strategies. *Internet Research: Electronic Network Applications and Policy, 11*(4), 349-359.

MacGregor, R. C., & Bunker, D. J. (1996). The effect of priorities introduced during computer acquisition on continuing success with IT in small business environments. In *Proceedings of the Information Resource Management Association International Conference* (pp. 271-277).

MacGregor, R. C., Bunker, D. J., & Waugh, P. (1998). Electronic commerce and small/medium enterprises (SME's) in Australia: An electronic data interchange (EDI) pilot study. In *Proceedings of the 11th International Bled Electronic Commerce Conference*.

Martin, L. M., & Matlay, H. (2001). "Blanket" approaches to promoting ICT in small firms: Some lessons from the DTI ladder adoption model in the UK. *Internet Research: Electronic Networking Applications and Policy, 11*(5), 399-410.

McRea, P. (1996). Reshaping industry with the Internet. *Management*, 7-10.

Meredith, G. G. (1994). *Small business management in Australia* (4th ed.). Sydney, Australia: McGraw Hill.

Miles, G., Preece, S., & Baetz, M. C. (1999). Dangers of dependence: The impact of strategic alliance use by small technology based firms. *Journal of Small Business Management*, 20-29.

Miller, N. L., & Besser, T. L. (2000). The importance of community values in small business strategy formation: Evidence from rural Iowa. *Journal of Small Business Management, 38*(1), 68-85.

Murphy, J. (1996). *Small business management.* London: Pitman.

Nooteboom, B. (1994). Innovation and diffusion in small firms: Theory and evidence. *Small Business Economics, 6*(5), 327-347.

Overby, J. W., & Min, S. (2001). International supply chain management in an Internet environment: A network-oriented approach to internationalisation. *International Marketing Review, 18*(4), 392-420.

Pendergraft, N., Morris, L., & Savage, K. (1987). Small business computer security. *Journal of Small Business Management, 25*(4).

Poon, S., & Swatman, P. (1997). The Internet for small businesses: An enabling infrastructure. In *Proceedings of the Fifth Internet Society Conference,* (pp. 221-231).

Quayle, M. (2002). E-commerce: The challenge for UK SMEs in the 21st century. *International Journal of Operations and Production Management, 22*(10), 1148-1161.

Raymond, L. (2001). Determinants of Web site implementation in small business. *Internet Research: Electronic Network Applications and Policy, 11*(5), 411-422.

Reuber, A. R., & Fischer, E. (1999). Understanding the consequences of founders' experience. *Journal of Small Business Management, 3*(2), 30-45.

Reynolds, W., Savage, W., & Williams, A. (1994). *Your own business: A practical guide to success.* ITP.

Riquelme, H. (2002). Commercial Internet adoption in China: Comparing the experience of small, medium and large businesses. *Internet Research: Electronic Networking Applications and Policy, 12*(3), 276-286.

Ritchie, R., & Brindley, C. (2001). Disintermediation, disintegration and risk in the SME. *Global Supply Chain Management Decision, 38*(8), 575-583.

Roberts, M., & Wood, M. (2002). The strategic use of computerised information systems by a micro enterprise. *Logistics Information Management, 15*(2), 115-125.

Rotch, W. (1987). *Management of small enterprises: Cases and readings.* Charlottesville, VA: University of Virginia Press.

Sparkes, A., & Thomas, B. (2001). The use of the Internet as a critical success factor for the marketing of Welsh agri-food SMEs in the 21st century. *British Food Journal, 103*(4), 331-347.

Stauber, A. (2000). *A survey of the incorporation of electronic commerce in Tasmanian small and medium sized enterprises.* Tasmania: Tasmanian Electronic Commerce Centre.

Swartz, T. A., & Iacobucci, D. (2000). *Handbook of services marketing and management*. CA: Sage.

Tetteh, E., & Burn, J. (2001). Global strategies for SME-business: Applying the SMALL framework. *Logistics Information Management, 14*(1/2), 171-180.

Treacy, M., & Wiersema, F. (1997). *The discipline of market leaders*. Cambridge, MA: Perseus Press.

Turban, E., Lee, J., King, D., & Chung, H. (2000). *Electronic commerce: A managerial perspective*. NJ: Prentice Hall.

Vescovi, T. (2000). Internet communication: The Italian SME case. *Corporate Communications: An International Journal, 5*(2), 107-112.

Vrazalic, L., Bunker, D., MacGregor, R. C., Carlsson, S., & Magnusson, M. (2002). Electronic commerce and market focus: Some findings from a study of Swedish small to medium enterprises. *Australian Journal of Information Systems, 10*(1), 110-119.

Walczuch, R., Van Braven, G., & Lundgren, H. (2000). Internet adoption barriers for small firms in the Netherlands. *European Management Journal, 18*(5), 561-572.

Welsh, J. A., & White, J. F. (1981). A small business is not a little big business. *Harvard Business Review, 59*(4), 46-58.

Westhead, P., & Storey, D. J. (1996). Management training and small firm performance: Why is the link so weak? *International Small Business Journal, 14*(4), 13-24.

Wynarczyk, P., Watson, R., Storey, D. J., Short, H., & Keasey, K. (1993). *The managerial labour market in small and medium sized enterprises*. London: Routledge.

Chapter II

The Effects of Animated Banner and Pop-Up Ads on Commercial Web Sites

Yuan Gao, Ramapo College of New Jersey, USA

Marios Koufaris, Baruch College (CUNY), USA

Robert H. Ducoffe, Baruch College (CUNY), USA

Abstract

This chapter explores the effects of two specific message-delivery techniques frequently adopted by online stores: continuously animated site banners and unexpected pop-up ads. Results from 128 surveys collected in a two-by-two factorial design showed that each of the two techniques had a significant effect on perceived irritation in the hypothesized direction. This chapter also confirmed that perceived irritation has a significant negative relationship with a visitor's attitude toward the Web site. This study fills a vacuum in academic research with respect to the negative effects of Web advertising and advises caution in the deployment of certain techniques. This chapter encourages future research exploring the effects of cross-site ads on consumer attitude and advocates additional studies linking format attributes and presentation techniques with attitudinal consequences in the design of commercial Web sites.

Introduction

The Web offers many tools a firm can explore to reap the benefits of this rich medium. Companies find themselves dwelling at the intersection of the real and the virtual, and are faced with a task that is more complex than delivering an attractive Web site (Mitra, 2003). Both practitioners and scholars are beginning to investigate ways to take full advantage of the techniques used in site promotion (Berthon, Pitt, & Watson, 1996; Coyle & Thorson, 2001; Ducoffe, 1996). These techniques may include the overall structure of the online retailing interface (Westland & Au, 1998) and such individual features as banners, animation, sound, video, interstitials, and pop-up ads (Rodgers & Thorson, 2000). Features like banner size, image maps, audio, and Web-site interactivity have been found to enhance site appeal (Coyle & Thorson; Li & Bukovac, 1999). In a recent study, banner-ad effectiveness was found to be affected by incentive offerings contained in the ads as well as the emotional appeal imbedded in the ad (Xie, Donthu, Lohtia, & Osmonbekow, 2004). Nonetheless, the use of such promotional techniques also comes with its negative effects. Such effects have been largely overlooked in the academic literature. The question of how certain advertising techniques have influenced consumers' perceptions of and attitude toward a site calls for more research in this field.

Traditional advertising research has established a hierarchical model of advertising effects, spanning the spectrum from ad content to cognition, attitude, and behavior (Holbrook, 1986; Olney, Holbrook, & Batra, 1991). Olney et al. saw TV advertising content and techniques influence consumers' emotional dimensions, attitude, and subsequent viewing behavior, for example, zipping and zapping in watching TV and video programs. This chain of links has been well documented in advertising and marketing research where both content and form variables were examined as predictors of attention, memory, recall, click-through, informativeness, attractiveness, and attitude (Rodgers & Thorson, 2000).

Nevertheless, the study of the effects of executional factors extended to the Web involves new factors to be considered and requires a higher level of comprehensiveness due to the volume and scope of a Web site in comparison to print or TV ads. While maintaining that many of the ad features found in traditional media (such as color, size, and typeface in print media, and audio, sound level, animation, and movement in broadcast) are relevant to the Web, Rodgers and Thorson (2000) consider such techniques as banners, sponsorships, interstitials, pop-up windows, and hyperlinks additions to ad formats in interactive marketing. A brief description of each type, based on Rodgers and Thorson, is presented in Table 1.

In addition to information content, format and presentation attributes that contribute to the delivery of Web-site appeal have also been examined (Huizingh,

Table 1. Ad formats in interactive marketing

Ad Format	Description
Banners	Rectangular-shaped graphics, mostly horizontal but some vertical
Interstitials	Full-screen ads between two content pages
Pop-ups	A separate window on top of the user's content window
Sponsorships	Indirect persuasion, such as brand name, associated with key content
Hyperlink	A highlighted word, phrase, or graphic that allows the user to click to go to another page or site

2000; Palmer & Griffith, 1998). Consumer behavior related to online shopping experience is gradually explored in the information systems literature (Bhatnagar, Misra, & Raw, 2000; Jarvenpaa & Todd, 1997; Koufaris, 2002; Koufaris, Kambil, & Labarbera, 2001). In a recent study, Vijayasarathy (2003) performed a psychographic profiling of online shoppers and studied the relationship between consumers' shopping orientations (home, community, and apathetic) and their intention of use and actual use of the online shopping medium. Researchers have also examined Web-site design from the perspective of building a cognitive framework, emphasizing enhanced usability through the coherent choice of design elements and composition of the layout (Rosen, Purinton, & Lloyd, 2004). We recognize the interdisciplinary nature of research in this field, and would like to supplement existing research in this collection of theories and studies that relate content and forms of commercial Web sites to visitor perceptions of and attitude toward a site.

Irritation

Several studies have explored factors addressing consumer behavior, attitude, and perceptions in the online environment (Chen & Wells, 1999; Ducoffe, 1996; Eighmey, 1997; Koufaris, 2002; Koufaris et al., 2001). Eighmey finds that users are helped by information in an enjoyable context, whereas Ducoffe argues that the value of advertising comes from informative claims in an entertaining form. Several studies have shown that product representation and the quality of the shopping experience online have a significant effect on attitude toward online shopping and intention to buy (Burke et al., 1992; Jarvenpaa & Todd, 1997; Novak, Hoffman, & Yung, 2000). Perceived usefulness and ease of use of the Web site have both been shown to have a strong impact on online customer attitudes and behavior (Koufaris, 2002; Gefen, Karahanna, & Straub, 2003).

Such research has provided valuable measuring tools of consumer perceptions and attitude, both in traditional media and the online environment, that might result from a visitor's experience at a Web site.

Online consumers place great value on the Web as a source of information. In a Jupiter Research survey, 48% of respondents indicated they use the Web extensively for product research and information gathering on health or medical information, local events, and/or job postings (Johnson, Slack, & Keane, 1999). With regard to online ads, 40% of respondents said a banner that is informative would grab their attention, and an even larger number (49%) would pay attention to ads that contain some discount or coupon information.

However, the experience and perceptions of a visitor are individual specific. While one individual might find the Flash entrance screen of the Coca-Cola Web site entertaining, another person could find it annoying. The frequent pop-up ads that appear on the New York Times Web site may be irritating to many of its readers, but there may be some that find the information in the ads informative and helpful. The same could be said for the continuously animated skyscrapers that frequently appear in the news articles in Yahoo! News. Some users may find them distracting while others may enjoy their content.

An unintended outcome from visiting a Web site is a user's feeling of irritation. Irritation is a factor that has been studied in traditional advertising (Greyser, 1973). It could be caused by tactics perceived to be annoying, offensive, or insulting. Ad features that are overly manipulative could also cause irritation (Ducoffe, 1996). Even though research in traditional advertising identified irritation as a significant factor that influences consumer attitude, it has not been widely explored in the online context. Specifically, scarce research has been done to address the specific features or content elements of a Web site that relate to higher levels of irritation by the visitors and its influence on attitude toward the site.

In the traditional media, an irritating commercial is one that provokes and causes displeasure and momentary impatience (Aaker & Bruzzone, 1985). In the Web context, irritation can indicate a user's confusion and distraction or the messiness of the site, all due to the way a Web site is presented and the site's features that are present (Chen & Wells, 1999). The source of irritation may be the negative feelings about the organization of the site, a feature of the site, or the visitor's frustration with a particular design element.

Certain Web-based features may have negative effects on visitor perceptions and attitude. These negative elements include scrolling text across the screen or the status bar, continuously running animation, nonstandard link colors, outdated information, complex URLs (uniform resource locators), broken links or anchors, error messages, and pop-ups (Nielsen, 1996). For example, it has become standard in most Web browsers that links change from blue to purple or red after being accessed. Any deviation from this convention seems to cause visitor confusion and irritation.

Animation as a design tool facilitates the communication of product information between the Web site and its visitors. For example, Ford Motor Company's Web site at http://www.fordvehicles.com includes a virtual showroom that allows the visitor, under his or her control, to view a three-dimensional presentation of the exterior and interior of each model. Such use of animation helps the visitor visualize a three-dimensional structure and better understand the features offered in a product. Another example of wise use of animation is at http://www.weather.com. When the visitor chooses to view the Doppler radar in motion, the site provides an animated view of a satellite weather map showing the cloud cover, among other things, changing over time. At other sites featuring computer games and outdoor activities, animation may also increase the perceived realism of information presented. For example, in a study of the effects of interactivity and vividness on consumer attitude, Coyle and Thorson (2001) find that a more vivid site, operationalized through the use of audio and moderate animation, was related to a more positive attitude toward the site.

Animation can also be used to draw a visitor's attention. We recognize that the use of continuous animation on many Web sites is for the purpose of alerting the visitor of a particular product or event, or an attempt to entertain the visitor while he or she is at the site. In that case, Nielsen (1999) suggests that animation should be done on a one-time-only basis, and then the animated object should become a still image. Nielsen (1995) argues that "a web page should not emulate Times Square in New York City in its constant attack on the human senses: give your user some peace and quiet to actually read the text!"

Due to the overpowering effect of moving images on the human peripheral vision, the presence of continuous animation on a page makes it very hard to read the text in the middle of a page (Nielsen, 1995). We argue that the continuousness poses a problem that is similar to TV advertising in terms of intrusiveness. Greyser (1973) found that people felt more irritated by TV commercials than by other media due to the intrusiveness of TV commercials. Continuous animation is much like scrolling text at the bottom of a television screen that cries for attention. It is a form of intrusive presentation of information to Web-site visitors. Such intrusiveness demands attention like TV commercials, and will similarly cause irritation like any other intrusive means of advertising. Thus, we so hypothesize.

H1: Perceived irritation of the Web site is positively related to the use of continuous animation.

Another frequently adopted Web-based promotional technique is the pop-up ad. We observe that pop-up ads, like animated banners, can be used for both cross-site and in-house advertising. Whether a site deploys cross-site ads or in-house ads depends on the main type of business the site is conducting. For a portal site such as Yahoo! or Microsoft Network (MSN), whose revenue comes at least partially from third-party advertising, cross-site ads are a necessary source of its income. Nielsen (2003) maintains that users at search sites are more receptive to targeted ads than in other contexts because these ads often relate to what the users are after, and subsequently the users are more likely to follow the ads. While some people often find them annoying, many others find them informative and related to their search goal, and thus consider them less irritating than in other circumstances.

On the other hand, firms selling their own products or services online are less inclined to deploy cross-site ads, either in the form of a banner or pop-up, because it is not in their interest to have visitors click away from their own Web site. However, we observe that many such e-commerce sites do use pop-up ads, along with animated banners, to inform visitors of certain promotions and events. While the business model of portal sites relies on selling advertising space to generate income from third-party ads, an e-commerce site selling its own products or services online has a choice between whether to adopt or not to adopt any such ads. Our research question here is whether the use of such techniques for in-house advertising cause a higher level of irritation than the absence of them. Both animated site-banner and pop-up ads are ways to reach the consumer within the site, but are they good delivery mechanisms for the store?

We have argued that such techniques will cause more irritation in the case of a continuously animated site banner. We also argue that unexpected pop-up ads could have similar negative effects. In traditional advertising, Greyser (1973) found that interruption was a predominant reason why the British public considered TV advertisements more irritating than print media. The Internet is a hybrid of print and broadcast media. The use of unexpected pop-up ads closely mirrors the TV commercials' interruptible nature. In addition, the visitor has to find a way to get rid of the popped-up window, the process of which increases the level of irritation.

In a study linking the use of interruption implemented via pop-up windows, Xia and Sudharshan (2000) manipulated the frequency of interruptions and found that interruptions had a negative impact on consumer decision-making processes. Intrusive formats of advertising like interstitials are found to have "backlash risks" online according to Johnson et al. (1999), whose survey found that 69% of users consider pop-up ads mildly to very annoying, and 23% of them said they would never come back to the site again. In light of the above discussion, we hypothesize the following.

H2: Perceived irritation of the Web site is positively related to the use of pop-up ads.

Attitude Toward the Site

Attitude toward the site (Ast) is a measure parallel to attitude toward the Ad (Aad) and was developed in response to a need to evaluate site effectiveness, like using Aad to evaluate advertising in traditional media (Chen & Wells, 1999). Aad mediates advertising responses to influence brand attitudes and purchase intentions (Brown & Stayman, 1992). It is an important factor for marketing and advertising strategies. Ast is an equally useful indicator of a Web user's predisposition to respond either favorably or unfavorably to the content of a Web site in a natural exposure situation (Chen & Wells). In this chapter, we define attitude to be a positive affective variable.

The similarity between Aad and Ast arises from the fact that a commercial Web site contains information similar to that contained in traditional advertising. Chen and Wells (1999) developed and tested a scale assessing a surfer's general attitude toward Web sites through a six-item scale, incorporating various perspectives that reflect a visitor's positive or negative impressions of a sponsoring company. A Web site high in organization and low in irritation is likely to be appreciated by the site visitors and hence is likely to receive a favorable attitude toward the site, a finding that has been validated by Chen and Wells and Ducoffe (1996). Ast is a direct result of a visitor's perceptual dimensions such as perceived entertainment and perceived irritation (Ducoffe, 1995, 1996). A visitor's affective response to a Web site may result from his or her experience at the Web site.

In traditional media, annoyance and irritation are the main reasons why people criticize advertising (Bauer & Greyser, 1968). Irritation leads to reduction in advertising effectiveness (Aaker & Bruzzone, 1985). Irritation is also a cause for visitors to leave a site (Johnson et al., 1999; Nielsen, 1999). Ducoffe (1995) finds a negative and significant correlation of -0.52 between irritation and the perceived value of advertising. Chen and Wells (1999) find a positive 0.44 correlation between organization and Ast, where organization is measured through descriptions such as *not messy*, *not cumbersome*, *not confusing*, and *not irritating*.

To validate whether such a negative correlation holds in the context of a Web site, especially in the presence of Web advertising techniques like pop-up ads and continuously animated banners, we hypothesize the following.

Figure 1. Research framework

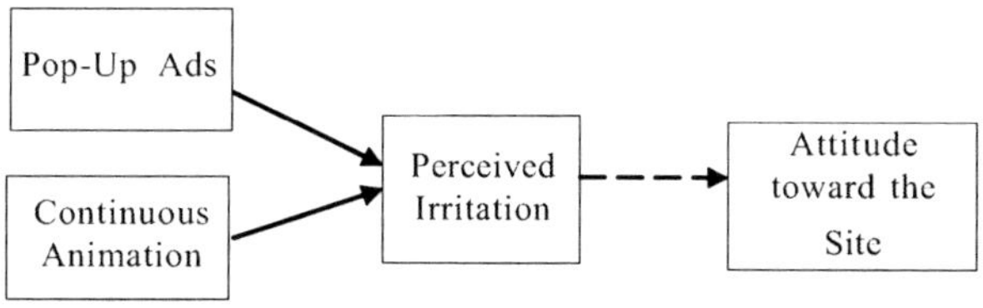

Note: Solid lines represent positive associations; a dashed line represents a negative association.

H3: Attitude toward the site is negatively related to perceived irritation.

Figure 1 summarizes the research questions proposed in this study.

We note that perceived irritation is just one of the perceptual antecedents to a visitor's attitude toward the site. In Web-related research, Chen and Wells (1999), Ducoffe (1996), and Eighmey (1997) find perceived entertainment and perceived informativeness predictors of Ast, while Coyle and Thorson (2001) find that perceived telepresence is an important factor in predicting Ast. We believe that testing the negative relationship between irritation and Ast in this study will help us understand the direct relationship between the use of Web-site techniques and Ast, and may shed light on the direction of future research in this area.

Research Methodology

Based on Simmon's Market Research Database (Choices II, 2000), consumer electronics are researched and purchased by customers between the ages of 18 and 24 at a rate that is proportional to their percentage of the population overall. Therefore, adults of this age group represent an important segment of the real target demographic. They represent about 15% of electronics customers who purchase electronics such as cameras. A commercial Web site selling a variety of cameras was chosen as the site for the experiment involved in this study. The Web site, by its own design, makes use of a framed page that contains a navigational header — the site banner — and a main frame underneath it. Hyperlinks in the header change the main frame. Hyperlinks in the main frame change the main frame only. Thus, the header is present all the time. Both the header and the main frame were borderless so that they integrated into each other seamlessly.

This Web site was peripherally modified to operationalize the constructs in the study through a two-by-two factorial design. Four versions were created based on the site through the presence or absence of continuously running animation in the site banner, and the presence or absence of pop-up ads during a user's visit. There was light animation in the original banner. We modified the banner to create an animated version that included an animated logo, an animated neon sign saying, "open 24 hours," animated images of a phone and e-mail icons linking to customer-service and contact pages, and an animated text banner linking to a prize contest. Still pictures were used in the nonanimated version. Thus, both versions of the header were custom made and resided on the local server. The main frame pointed to the main frame of the real commercial Web site. Content in the main frame was not manipulated. The functionalities of the hyperlinks (in both the custom header and the real site main frame) were maintained and tested to be robust when the custom headers were integrated into the real site main frame.

The pop-up ads included a message of quantity discount (save 5% on $200 or more) offered by the site and a picture linking to a sweepstakes entry form then running at the site. The first pop-up contained an expiration date of the offer and a close button. The second pop-up contained, in addition to an image of a camera, a line of instruction that said, "Click the image above to enter the sweepstakes." Both were created with the theme of the Web site and used existing images of the site. The two windows popped up at 30 seconds and three minutes into the visit, respectively. Hence, the four treatment conditions were (1) animation without pop-up, (2) pop-up without animation, (3) animation and pop-up, and (4) neither animation nor pop-up. In all four conditions, hyperlinks in the custom header changed the main frame, and hyperlinks in the main frame changed the main frame only. Thus, to each visitor, the custom header was present all the time. As in the original site, both the header and the main frame were borderless. This experimental design maintained internal validity through the factor manipulations and external validity through the use of a slightly modified real commercial Web site.

Voluntary participation was sought from students on the campus of a northeast college. One hundred and thirty-six undergraduate students participated in this study through a gift incentive (a disposable camera valued at about $7) and entry into a lottery of four cash prizes (one $100 and three $50 prizes). Each participant was randomly assigned to one of the four treatment conditions, that is, the four versions of the same Web site. They were instructed to explore the site for product information and help in finding a model of digital camera for one of his or her close friends.

The task-assignment approach has been used in involvement research to manipulate levels of involvement (Buchholz & Smith, 1991; Laczniak & Carlson,

1989). Our study adopted this approach to bring all participants to a similar level of involvement in the task they were assigned. We chose not to instruct them to go into an "I-am-ready-to-buy" mode because we believe that the scenario we presented them with better represents an initial exchange between a visitor and a Web site. Opinions about or attitudes toward the site formed from this initial exchange would be a key indicator of the effectiveness of the site in retaining site visitors and thus attracting return customers. Additionally, we believe that the I-am-ready-to-buy type of engagement would be more difficult to attain across all participants than the informational search type we assigned them. Finally, a homogenous level of engagement in the assigned task across the entire sample was desirable in our experimental study.

Each participant completed a survey after visiting the site. On average, participants spent slightly under 20 minutes to complete the visit and the survey. The measures taken are explained in the following section. The data collection was done over four weeks. Among surveys returned, 128 were substantially complete and used in data analysis of this study.

Measures

This study was part of a larger research project and it adapted existing scales from the current literature. With respect to the variables involved in this experiment, perceived irritation was measured through three items indicating whether the site was annoying, irritating, and frustrating. These scale items have been developed, tested, and used in measuring perceived irritation of TV advertising and Web advertising, and have yielded fairly high Cronbach's alpha values (> 0.8; Ducoffe, 1995, 1996). In Ducoffe's (1996) Web advertising survey, 57% of respondents considered an entire Web site a form of advertising. Firms initially displayed brochures and promotional pieces onto the Web site to deliver a message that was much like an ad in the online environment (Singh & Dalal, 1999). Rodgers and Thorson (2000) consider an entire Web site a format of interactive marketing. We maintain that the use of these items developed for measuring perceived irritation of Web advertising was appropriate for measuring perceived irritation of a Web site as a whole.

Ast was measured through the following three pairs of descriptions: like or dislike, favorable or unfavorable, and good or bad (Coyle & Thorson, 2001). Since product involvement has been found to be a significant predictor of consumer attitude and behavior in e-commerce (Coyle & Thorson, 2001; Koufaris et al., 2001), product involvement using the Revised Personal Involvement Inventory (RPII) (Zaichkowsky, 1985) was taken as a potential covariate.

Additionally, to check the effectiveness of our manipulations, after participants completed the attitudinal part of the questionnaire, they were asked to check off whether they saw continuously running animation and whether they experienced pop-up ads during their visit. The appendix shows details of the scale items used in this study.

Results

Demographic information taken with the survey shows that about 60% of the respondents were under 24, and all were roughly evenly split between male and female participants. About 20% spent between four to six hours per week online, another 20% spent between seven to 10 hours online, and more than 32% spent more than 10 hours per week online. With respect to the site, the participants seem to have a generally favorable attitude toward the site, with a mean Ast score of 5.47 on a seven-point scale.

Cronbach's alphas on multi-item scales adopted in this study indicate strong scale reliability. Table 2 summarizes the means and standard deviations (S.D.) of each scale item.

Table 2. Summary statistics and Cronbach's alpha values

Scale	Mean	S.D.	Cronbach's Alpha
IRRITATION			0.9473
This Web site is frustrating.	2.52	1.49	
This Web site is annoying.	2.48	1.67	
This Web site is irritating.	2.57	1.69	
ATTITUDE TOWARD SITE (Ast)			0.9525
Bad...Good	5.54	1.27	
Unfavorable...Favorable	5.40	1.31	
Dislike...Like	5.38	1.37	
PRODUCT INVOLVEMENT			0.9352
Important...Unimportant	4.89	1.68	
Irrelevant...Relevant	5.09	1.51	
Means a lot to me...Means nothing to me	4.89	1.68	
Unexciting...Exciting	4.91	1.51	
Dull...Neat	5.18	1.51	
Matters to me...Does not matter to me	4.66	1.54	
Boring...Interesting	5.17	1.47	
Fun...Not fun	4.84	1.73	
Appealing...Unappealing	4.89	1.59	
Of no concern to me...Of concern to me	4.91	1.35	

To examine construct validity of the measures adopted in this study, evidence of the dimensionality of each scale and its discriminant validity was obtained through factor analyses. Construct validity addresses whether a measure measures the construct or variable that is supposed to be measured. A principle component analysis with direct oblimin rotation was performed on each group of scales. The results indicate that items within each scale load on the same factor, and thus are all unidimensional. Items belonging to different scales load on their own separate factors, showing evidence of discriminant validity. Table 3 shows that perceived irritation (the first three items) loads on the second factor, Ast (the next three items) loads on the third factor, while product involvement (the last 10 items) loads on the first factor. We thus conclude that evidence supports construct validity for all scales adopted.

Manipulation checks were performed via one-way ANOVAs (analyses of variance), with each fixed factor (animation or pop-up) as independent variables and a participant's acknowledgment of perceiving (or noticing) the features as the dependent variables. Those who were exposed to the animated sites were significantly more likely to agree that the site had continuous animation ($M = 0.8281$) than those who were exposed to the nonanimated versions ($M = 0.1406$; $F[1, 126] = 113.14$, $p < 0.001$). Those who were exposed to the sites with pop-

Table 3. Structure matrix

	Component		
	1	2	3
Annoying	-.174	**.930**	-.490
Frustrating	-.231	**.915**	-.463
Irritating	-.229	**.938**	-.503
Good	.355	-.559	**.913**
Favorable	.365	-.569	**.931**
Like	.322	-.592	**.912**
Relevant	**.819**	-.088	.229
Exciting	**.844**	-.145	.346
Neat	**.830**	-.179	.381
Interesting	**.807**	-.216	.369
Of concern to me	**.881**	-.185	.236
Important	**.859**	-.085	.264
Means something to me	**.859**	-.085	.264
Matters to me	**.774**	-.237	.095
Fun	**.819**	-.277	.064
Appealing	**.787**	-.329	.091

Extaction method: Principal component; Rotation method: Oblimin with Kaiser

up ads were significantly more likely to agree that they saw pop-up ads (M = 0.8438) than those that were not exposed to versions with pop-up ads (M = 0.2500; $F[1, 126] = 69.55$, $p < 0.001$). Thus, the manipulations were successful. Age, gender, and weekly Web usage were not significantly correlated with either irritation or attitude and thus were dropped from further analyses.

Sample probability plots showed patterns of a normal distribution. An equal number of observations (32 per cell) was collected from each treatment group, and thus we had a balanced design that protected against any potential violations of assumptions in an ANOVA analysis (Hildebrand, 1986). Product involvement, age, gender, and hours spent weekly on the Internet were considered as potential control variables. An ANOVA analysis would be necessary with these control variables as covariates if they have a strong linear correlation with the dependent variable of irritation. Such a correlation coefficient would have to be at least 0.30 according to Cohen's standard of a medium effect (Cohen, 1988). We examined the correlation between irritation and product involvement, hours spent on the Internet, age, and gender. Among them, only the correlation between product involvement and irritation was significant ($p = 0.008$), with a correlation coefficient of -0.232. Since the strength of this correlation is under 0.30, it not included as a covariate and neither were age, gender, and hours spent on the Internet, whose correlations were not significant.

A two-way ANOVA was performed treating perceived irritation as the dependent variable and manipulation of the presence of continuous animation and unexpected pop-up ads as fixed factors in a two-by-two design. Both continuous animation ($F[1, 124] = 9.78$, $p = 0.002$) and pop-up ads ($F[1, 124] = 7.87$, $p = 0.006$) had a significant effect on perceived irritation at $p < 0.01$. No interaction effect emerged ($F[1, 124] = 0.026$, $p = 0.872$). Table 4 shows the ANOVA results.

Table 4. ANOVA for effects of continuous animation and pop-up ads on irritation

Source	Type III Sum of Squares	df	Mean Square	F	Sig.	Partial η^2
Corrected Model	[a]	3	12.561	5.892	.001	.125
Intercept	833.681	1	833.681	391.045	.000	.759
MANIM	20.855	1	20.855	9.782	.002	.073
MPOP	16.772	1	16.772	7.867	.006	.060
MANIM * MPOP	5.556E-02	1	5.556E-02	.026	.872	.000
Error	264.359	124	2.132			
Total	1135.722	128				
Corrected Total	302.042	127				

[a] *R Squared = 0.125 (Adjusted R Squared = 0.104)*

To confirm the direction of the effects of these two factors, we observed from descriptive statistics that those who were exposed to versions with continuous animation perceived the site as significantly more irritating ($M = 2.9557$) than did those who were not ($M = 2.1484$). We also observe that those who were exposed to pop-up ads perceived the site as significantly more irritating ($M = 2.9141$) than did those who were not ($M = 2.1901$). Separate t-tests comparing means further verified our conclusion from the above ANOVA analysis. Related statistics are shown in Table 5. We thus conclude that both hypotheses H1 and H2 were supported in this study.

To test hypothesis H3, a Pearson correlation analysis was performed between perceived irritation and Ast. Irritation was significantly ($p < 0.001$) and negatively correlated with Ast with a Pearson correlation coefficient of -0.613. To validate that such a strong correlation was not the artifact of a large sample, we constructed a confidence interval to see whether zero falls within that interval. If zero does fall within the confidence interval, we cannot reject the null hypothesis of the correlation being zero (Hildebrand, 1986).

The confidence interval of [r - t * standard error, r + t * standard error] was created. With 99% confidence interval (Hildebrand, 1986, p. 141, Formula 3.1.37) and the table value of the t distribution with 120 degrees of freedom (p. 757, Table 4), the t statistic is 2.62. The standard error is 0.061. Thus, the 99% confidence interval is [-0.773, -0.453], which does not include zero. Thus, we conclude that the negative correlation between irritation and Ast is statistically significant. Hypothesis H3 was supported in this study.

Though not formally hypothesized, the direct impact of continuous animation and pop-up ads on Ast was also examined via an ANOVA model where Ast was treated as the dependent variable. Table 6 shows the results. Once again, no interaction effect emerged ($p = 0.322$). Both factors had a negative effect on Ast. Those who were exposed to animation had a less favorable attitude toward

Table 5. Mean comparison of perceived irritation conditioned upon manipulated factor

Manipulated Factor	Condition	Mean	S.D.	t	df	Sig. (two-tailed)
Animation	Present	2.9557	1.7684	3.057	126	0.003
	Absent	2.1484	1.1559			
Pop-Up Ads	Present	2.9141	1.7069	2.722	126	0.007
	Absent	2.1901	1.2706			

Table 6. ANOVA for effects of continuous animation and pop-up ads on attitude

Tests of Between-Subjects Effects

Dependent Variable: Attitude

Source	Type III Sum of Squares	df	Mean Square	F	Sig.	Partial η^2
Corrected Model	20.628[a]	3	6.876	4.817	.003	.109
Intercept	3663.626	1	3663.626	2566.419	.000	.956
MANIM	10.214	1	10.214	7.155	.009	.057
MPOP	9.563	1	9.563	6.699	.011	.054
MANIM * MPOP	1.410	1	1.410	.988	.322	.008
Error	168.448	118	1.428			
Total	3843.000	122				
Corrected Total	189.076	121				

[a] *R Squared = 0.109 (Adjusted R Squared = 0.086)*

Table 7. Effect size on irritation

Treatment Factor	Sig.	η^2	Qualitative Description	Cohen's Standard (1969, p. 276, Table 8.2.2; pp. 277-281)	
Continuous Animation	.002	.073	Medium	*Large*	$\eta^2 = .1379$
Pop-Up Ads	.006	.060	Medium	*Medium*	$\eta^2 = .0588$
				Small	$\eta^2 = .0099$

the site (M = 5.1913) than those who were not (M = 5.7541). Those who were exposed to pop-up ads also had a less favorable attitude toward the site (M = 5.2063) than those who were not (M = 5.7571). Both relationships were statistically significant at p = 0.009 and p = 0.011 respectively for animation and pop-up ads.

To put these statistically significant findings in a proper perspective, we include a discussion on effect size, which is "an index of degree of departure from the null hypothesis" (Cohen, 1969, p. 10). In a fixed-factor experiment, it can be measured through the "variance-accounted-for" indicator η^2, which was produced by the ANOVA analysis. Cohen (p. 77) observed that the "difficulty arising from the use of PV (percentage of variance) measures lies in the fact that in many, perhaps all, of the areas of behavioral science, they turn out to be so small!" Based on his subjective averaging of PVs in behavioral-science literature, Cohen offered a convention of various effect-size measures as a general guideline in behavioral-science research. These conventions were used by many researches that reported effect sizes in their studies, and they were restated in the second edition of his book (Cohen, 1988). With these considerations in mind, Table 7 presents a summary report of the effect sizes of each promotional technique examined in this chapter and their relative strength in Cohen's convention.

We note that the two techniques examined in this study had a medium to strong-medium effect on perceived irritation. Given Cohen's (1969) standard, these effect sizes were in line with other behavioral-science research results. Though the decision whether to accept or reject a null hypothesis is solely based on statistical significance, reporting effect sizes enables readers to evaluate study and sample replicability, and facilitates meta-analyses as needed in future research (Wilkinson, 1999).

Discussion and Future Research

This experimental study examined the effects of continuous animation and pop-up ads on perceived irritation by online customers, and the correlation between perceived irritation and attitude toward the Web site. Specifically, we focused on the use of pop-up ads and continuous animation for in-house presentation of information on discounts, special offers, and announcements. This study examined the effect of using such techniques as delivery mechanisms to reach out to visitors already at the site. Both factors were found to significantly influence perceived irritation. In turn, irritation is a significant predictor of attitude toward the site. Even though irritation is not the only factor in determining attitude toward the Web site, our results showed that it had a significant negative correlation with attitude. To Web marketers and site designers, it means that they should never overlook factors contributing to perceived irritation while exploring factors that may contribute to consumer perceptions in the positive direction. A recent study found that consumers have a generally negative attitude toward advertising through intrusive means of short messages delivered to their mobile phones without their prior consent (Tsang, Ho, & Liang, 2004).

The results of our current study also validated observations in industry surveys (Johnson et al., 1999) and practitioners' advice (Nielson, 2000). The implication of the findings from this study is that practitioners need to exercise caution in deploying certain Web advertising techniques. Companies selling products or services online may want to reconsider using pop-up ads and continuous animation as delivery mechanisms to communicate information to customers visiting their Web sites. Nielsen (2004) advises that users have learned to stop paying attention to anything that looks like an advertisement through what he calls banner blindness, animation avoidance, and pop-up purges. This presents a new challenge to Web marketers and site designers.

We presented our participants with the scenario of an initial exchange with a Web site. We believe that such an initial exchange plays a significant role in an e-store's ability to attract users and convert them to buyers. We believe that for ready-to-buy visitors, the effect of online advertising may vary. They may be hardly annoyed by the ads if they go directly to what they want. They may be excited about an offer in the ads and buy something right away. They may also be frustrated by the annoying ads and quit using the site altogether. Among an e-commerce site's functions of presales product introduction, sales transaction, and postsales service and support, we focused on the first-stage exposure of a potential customer to the Web site. We examined techniques that may impact a visitor's attitude toward the site, which may subsequently influence a visitor's intention to revisit the site and become a buyer. Whether similar results will be seen in the population of ready-to-buy shoppers remains to be studied in future research.

As we have discussed earlier, we studied the effect of pop-up ads and animated site banners as delivery mechanisms of same-company announcements, promotions, and discounts, but not for third-party advertisements. Such content may be more relevant to customers searching for general product information than ready-to-buy shoppers. However, our results cast doubts on whether these mechanisms are truly effective. Nevertheless, we recognize the use of cross-site ads, which are most likely used by portals and online publishing sites to generate revenue (as part of their business model). A recent study by Yoo, Kim, and Stout (2004) focused on just this type of cross-site animated banner ads and found that animated banners prompted better attention-grabbing capabilities and higher recalls, as well as a more favorable attitude toward the ad than static banner ads. In the meantime, Yoo et al. recognize that too much animation, though eye catching, may reduce advertising effectiveness due to the potential negative affective responses such as irritation or annoyance. We also suspect that results could be very different from our current study in search-engine sites due to the fact that users visiting those sites have an explicit intention to leave them once they find a link of interest, be it a text link or picture ad. What effects such cross-site ads may have remains to be examined in further studies.

A possible limitation of the study was the use of student samples. Students are deemed appropriate participants in that they make a significant portion of the Internet population ("GVU's 10th WWW Survey," 1998). One of the arguments for using a homogenous sample such as undergraduate college students is that it makes it easier to achieve internal validity (Greenberg, 1987). While the use of students may threaten external validity, that threat is mitigated by the fact that our student population was from a university in a densely populated suburban area. Such students may be more representative of the general population and may be more appropriate for consumer behavioral studies than more traditional college students that attend universities in remote rural areas (James & Sonner, 2001).

The use of an experimental approach with a custom-tailored version of a Web site in this study is another limitation. If a real-life Web site was used, visitors might have a different reaction to the promotional techniques. Our research design called for manipulation of the two factors while holding everything else constant. To implement such a design with multiple versions of a real-life Web site would have been prohibitively costly. On the other hand, we argue that an experimental study has its advantage in its ability to validate causal relationships between the treatment effects and the dependent variables. Experimental research, though limited in scope, goes beyond the predictive power of observational research. In completely randomized design fixed-factor experiments, the differences in dependent variables can be reasonably attributed to the participants' membership in different treatment groups, and thus a causal effect between the treatment factor and the dependent variable can be validated (Huck, Cormier, & Bounds, 1974).

Despite the limitations addressed above, we were encouraged by the findings of this study. To answer the question whether the causal relationship between executional factors and attitudinal outcome exists online, experiments that can be used in cross-group comparisons are required. Such research is now common in the literature (Coyle & Thorson, 2001; Li & Bukovac, 1999; Yoo et al., 2004), and our study represents an addition to this line of research that explores the effects of different combinations of elements online.

Future research should explore the effects of the use of such promotional techniques in combination with influences of situational factors, such as portal sites vs. e-store sites, surfers vs. buyers, on visitor perceptions and attitude. Future research should also examine the impact of other media presentation factors in e-business. In summary, this study extended and validated existing theories in advertising research in the Web context and considered new content and format factors that may influence visitor perceptions and attitude. It is necessary to take a rigorous and scientific look at the various components that go into doing business online in order to help electronic business develop in a structured, efficient, and effective way (Koufaris et al., 2001). Our study joins the pursuit that is beginning to explore the effects of presentation formats and system attributes on consumer perceptions and attitude, which in turn may impact the bottom line of firms who conduct business online.

References

Aaker, D. A., & Bruzzone, D. E. (1985). Causes of irritation in advertising. *Journal of Marketing, 49*, 47-57.

Bauer, R. A., & Greyser, S. A. (1968). *Advertising in America consumer view*. Boston: Harvard University Press.

Berthon, P., Pitt, L. F., & Watson, R. T. (1996). The World Wide Web as an advertising medium: Toward an understanding of conversion efficiency. *Journal of Advertising Research, 36*(1), 43-54.

Bhatnagar, A., Misra, S., & Raw, H. R. (2000). On risk, convenience, and Internet shopping behavior. *Communications of the ACM, 43*(11), 98-105.

Brown, S. P., & Stayman, D. M. (1992). Antecedents and consequences of attitude toward the ad: A meta-analysis. *Journal of Consumer Research, 19*(1), 34-51.

Buchholz, L. M., & Smith, R. E. (1991). The role of consumer involvement in determining cognitive response to broadcast advertising. *Journal of Advertising, 20*(1), 4-17.

Burke, R. R. (1997). Do you see what I see? The future of virtual shopping. *Journal of the Academy of Marketing Science, 25*(4), 352-360.

Chen, Q., & Wells, W. D. (1999). Attitude toward the site. *Journal of Advertising Research, 39*(5), 27-38.

Choices II. (2000). Retrieved from Simmon's Market Research Database.

Cohen, J. (1988). *Statistical power analysis for the behavioral sciences* (2nd ed.). Hillsdale, NJ: Erlbaum.

Coyle, J. R., & Thorson, E. (2001). The effects of progressive levels of interactivity and vividness in Web marketing sites. *Journal of Advertising, 30*(3), 65-77.

Ducoffe, R. H. (1995). How consumers assess the value of advertising. *Journal of Current Issues and Research in Advertising, 17*(1), 1-18.

Ducoffe, R. H. (1996). Advertising value and advertising on the Web. *Journal of Advertising Research, 36*(5), 21-34.

Eighmey, J. (1997). Profiling user responses to commercial Web site. *Journal of Advertising Research, 37*(3), 59-66.

Gefen, D., Karahanna, E., & Straub, D. W. (2003). Trust and TAM in online shopping: An integrated model. *MIS Quarterly, 27*(1), 51-90.

Greenberg, J. (1987). The college sophomore as guinea pig: Setting the record straight/Student guinea pigs: Porcine predictors and particularistic phenomena. *The Academy of Management Review, 12*(1), 157-159.

Greyser, S. A. (1973). Irritation in advertising. *Journal of Advertising Research, 13*(1), 3-10.

GVU's 10th WWW user survey. (1998). Retrieved from *http://www.cc.gatech.edu/user_surveys/survey-1998-10/*

Hildebrand, D. K. (1986). *Statistical thinking for behavioral scientists.* Boston: Duxbury Press.

Holbrook, M. B. (1986). Emotion in the consumption experience: Toward a new model of the human consumer. In R. A. Perterson et al. (Eds.), *The role of affect in consumer behavior: Emerging theories and applications* (pp. 17-52). Lexington, MA: Heath Publishing.

Huck, S. W., Cormier, W. H., & Bounds, W. G. (1974). *Reading statistics and research.* New York: Harper & Row.

Huizingh, E. K. R. E. (2000). The content and design of Web sites: An empirical study. *Information & Management, 37*, 123-134.

James, W. L., & Sonner, B. S. (2001). Just say no to traditional student samples. *Journal of Advertising Research, 41*(5), 63-71.

Jarvenpaa, S. L., & Todd, P. T. (1997). Consumer reactions to electronic shopping on the World Wide Web. *International Journal of Electronic Commerce, 1*(2), 59-88.

Johnson, M., Slack, M., & Keane, P. (1999). *Inside the mind of the online consumer: Increasing advertising effectiveness* (Vol. 18). Jupiter Research. Retrieved from *http://www.jupiter.com*

Koufaris, M. (2002). Applying the technology acceptance model and flow theory to online consumer behavior. *Information Systems Research, 13*(2), 205-223.

Koufaris, M., Kambil, M. A., & Labarbera, P. A. (2001). Consumer behavior in Web-based commerce: An empirical study. *International Journal of Electronic Commerce, 6*(2), 131-154.

Laczniak, R. N., & Carlson, L. (1989). Examining the influence of attitude-toward-the-ad on brand attitudes. *Journal of Business Research, 19*(4), 303-311.

Li, H., & Bukovac, J. L. (1999). Cognitive impact of banner ad characteristics: An experimental study. *Journalism and Mass Communication Quarterly, 76*(2), 341-353.

Lohse, G. L., & Spiller, P. (1998). Electronic shopping. *Communications of the ACM, 41*(7), 81-86.

Mitra, A. (2003). Cybernetic space: Bringing the virtual and the real together. *Journal of Interactive Advertising, 3*(2). Retrieved from *http://www.jiad.org*

Nielsen, J. (1995). Multimedia guidelines. *Jakob Nielsen's Alertbox*. Retrieved from *http://www.useit.com/alertbox*

Nielsen, J. (1996). Top ten mistakes in Web design. *Jakob Nielsen's Alertbox.* Retrieved from *http://www.useit.com/alertbox*

Nielsen, J. (1999). User interface directions for the Web. *Communications of the ACM, 42*(1), 65-72.

Nielsen, J. (2000). Is navigation useful? *Jakob Nielsen's Alertbox*. Retrieved from *http://www.useit.com/alertbox*

Nielsen, J. (2003). Making Web advertisements work. *Jakob Nielsen's Alertbox*. Retrieved from *http://www.useit.com/alertbox*

Nielsen, J. (2004). Top ten mistakes in Web design (Rev. ed.). *Jakob Nielsen's Alertbox*. Retrieved from *http://www.useit.com/alertbox/9605.html*

Novak, T. P., Hoffman, D. L., & Yung, Y. (2000). Measuring the customer experience in online environments: A structural modeling approach. *Marketing Science, 19*(1), 22-42.

Olney, T. J., Holbrook, M. B., & Batra, R. (1991). Consumer responses to advertising: The effects of ad content, emotions, and attitude toward the ad on viewing time. *Journal of Consumer Research, 17*, 440-453.

Palmer, J. W., & Griffith, D. A. (1998). An emerging model of Web site design for marketing. *Communications of the ACM, 41*(3), 45-51.

Rodgers, S., & Thorson, E. (2000). The interactive advertising model: How users perceive and process online ads. *Journal of Interactive Advertising, 1*(1). Retrieved from *http://jiad.org/vol1/no1/rodgers*

Rosen, D. E., Purinton, E., & Lloyd, S. J. (2004). Web site design: Building a cognitive framework. *Journal of Electronic Commerce in Organizations, 2*(1), 15-28.

Singh, S. N., & Dalal, N. P. (1999). Web homepages as advertisements. *Communications of the ACM, 42*(8), 91-98.

Tsang, M. M., Ho, S., & Liang, T. (2004). Consumer attitude toward mobile advertising: An empirical study. *International Journal of Electronic Commerce, 8*(3), 65-78.

Vijayasarathy, L. R. (2003). Psychographic profiling of the online shopper. *Journal of Electronic Commerce in Organizations, 1*(3), 48-72.

Westland, J. C., & Au, G. (1998). A comparison of shopping experience across three competing digital retailing interfaces. *International Journal of Electronic Commerce, 2*(2), 57-69.

Xia, L., & Sudharshan, D. (2000). An examination of the effects of cognitive interruptions on consumer on-line decision processes. Paper presented at the *Second Marketing Science and the Internet Conference*, Los Angeles.

Xie, F. T., Donthu, N., Lohtia, R., & Osmonbekow, T. (2004). Emotional appeal and incentive offering in banner advertisements. *Journal of Interactive Advertising, 4*(2). Retrieved from *http://www.jiad.org*

Yoo, C. Y., Kim, K., & Stout, P.A. (2004). Assessing the effects of animation in online banner advertising: Hierarchy of effects model. *Journal of Interactive Advertising, 4*(2). Retrieved from *http://www.jiad.org*

Zaichkowsky, J. L. (1985). Measuring the involvement construct. *Journal of Consumer Research, 12*(3), 341-352.

Appendix: Scale Items for Measures Taken in this Study

[Perceived Irritation] Circle the number that best indicates your agreement or disagreement with each statement (anchored by 1, definitely disagree, *and 7,* definitely agree*).*

This Web site is frustrating.	1	2	3	4	5	6	7
This Web site is irritating.	1	2	3	4	5	6	7
This Web site is annoying.	1	2	3	4	5	6	7

[Attitude toward the Site] Please use the descriptive words listed below to indicate your overall impression of this site (1, negative, *and 7,* positive*).*

Bad	1	2	3	4	5	6	7	Good
Unfavorable	1	2	3	4	5	6	7	Favorable
Dislike	1	2	3	4	5	6	7	Like

[Product Involvement] We would like to know how interested you are in cameras, camcorders, or photography in general. Please use the series of descriptive words listed below to indicate your level of interest in such products.

Important	1	2	3	4	5	6	7	Unimportant
Irrelevant	1	2	3	4	5	6	7	Relevant
Means a lot to me	1	2	3	4	5	6	7	Means nothing to me
Unexciting	1	2	3	4	5	6	7	Exciting
Dull	1	2	3	4	5	6	7	Neat
Matters to me	1	2	3	4	5	6	7	Does not matter to me
Boring	1	2	3	4	5	6	7	Interesting
Fun	1	2	3	4	5	6	7	Not fun
Appealing	1	2	3	4	5	6	7	Unappealing
Of no concern to me	1	2	3	4	5	6	7	Of concern to me

[Manipulation Checks] Please check what you saw at this site. Check all that apply.

❑ Continuously Running Animation	Check this box if the site displays any animation that is continuously running on the screen. In case you need a definition, animation means an active or moving image.

❑ Pop-Up Advertising (Pop-Up Windows)	Check this box if the site uses any unexpected pop-up windows for promotional messages or advertising.

Appendix: (cont.)

[Demographics] Answers on this survey are anonymous. We appreciate your responses to the following questions.

1. How many hours a week, on average, do you spend on the Internet?

☐0 ☐1-3 ☐4-6 ☐7-10 ☐More than 10 hours

2. Your age: ☐16-24 ☐25-30 ☐31-40 ☐Over 40

3. Your gender: ☐F ☐M

Chapter III

Managing Security Vulnerabilities in a Business-to-Business Electronic Commerce Organization

Shirley Ann Becker, Florida Institute of Technology, USA

Anthony Berkemeyer, Texas Instruments, Inc., USA

Abstract

GlobalUBid.com is a B2B (business-to-business) e-commerce company offering excess and obsolete inventory to online customers. GlobalUBid is rapidly expanding into the global online marketplace, but recently, its Web site crashed due to a denial-of-service (DOS) attack. A lack of security awareness at an organizational level has left GlobalUBid's online system vulnerable to internal and external attacks. Though informal security policies are in place, many employees are not aware of them and they are not enforced on a regular basis. Unsecured aspects of the physical workplace make the organization vulnerable to disgruntled employees, hackers, and unscrupulous competition. GlobalUBid has hired URSecure consultants to conduct a security assessment in uncovering internal and external vulnerabilities. URSecure has made recommendations for improved security, though the organization must develop most of the implementation details. GlobalUBid management recognizes the need for improved security, though there is a concern about the financial implications of implementing a security plan.

Organization Background

GlobalUBid.com[1] became a start-up company in March of 1998 in order to provide online auction capabilities to U.S. companies getting rid of excess inventory. GlobalUBid is one of the first online auction sites in the B2B e-commerce industry. Inspired by the skyrocketing stock values of 1997 IPOs (initial public offerings), local venture capitalists backed the company with an initial investment of $1.5 million for building the online B2B auction site. The strategic plan was to build the system as quickly as possible with an expenditure of $1 million during the first year.

In May 1998, 10 Web developers, two database administrators (DBAs), and a system administrator (SA) were hired to apply both Oracle and Microsoft software technologies in building the system. The technology staff worked an average of 98 hours per week (14-hour days, seven days a week) with the promise of stock options significantly increasing in value when the company went public. The company had announced plans for an IPO offering in the spring of 1999. Approximately half of the Web developers left within the first three months because of the burnout associated with the mandatory overtime to complete the online system. These employees were replaced immediately but at a higher cost for salaries and increased stock options.

Management and the technical staff knew that when the venture capital ran out, the company would have to declare bankruptcy without an opportunity of going public. They were aware of the dot.com IPO offerings that made employees with stock options instant millionaires. They were also aware of the increasing number of failed dot.coms littering the Internet, many of which had insufficient venture capital to sustain development efforts.

By April 1999, the company had developed the Web technology to support online auction capabilities. The online site became available for public use in July with limited domestic support. Though the online auction site was deemed successful by GlobalUBid's management team, more customers were needed to increase inventory sales. Inventory turnover was less than 10% per month with customer growth rate increasing 2% each month. Many of the sellers were expressing their dissatisfaction with the inventory turnover rate. It was decided that the IPO would be moved back by at least one year in order to increase the customer base and the inventory turnover rate.

GlobalUBid expanded its customer base by entering the global B2B marketplace primarily through acquisitions. GlobalUBid acquired GCB.com (Global Customer Base) in December 1999 in order to double its site traffic and add over 5,000 new sellers in the European market. In February 2000, GlobalUBid acquired an online transaction system called StaticPrice from a company in Frankfurt, Germany. This B2B software component provided a powerful search engine and expanded GlobalUBid's business model to include fixed quote pricing in addition to the auctioning component. Customers could now purchase inventory that was offered at a fixed price in order to expedite the purchasing process. This acquisition provided an opportunity to expand GlobalUBid's global presence in the Asia Pacific area and Northern Africa. By the end of the 2000 fiscal year, the number of global customers exceeded 1,600 and the rate of inventory turnover doubled.

By the spring of 2000, a marketing manager was hired to manage a newly created marketing department composed of 100 employees. The objective was to have an online support system in place by early September in order to grow international sales and handle customer-service enquiries. The marketing manager would take advantage of customer and seller data in order to predict inventory sales and identify potential customer growth areas. The confidential information stored in the system's databases would be used to personalize the company's relationships with both sellers and buyers to increase sales and inventory offerings. This confidential data, though password protected, was readily accessible by management, technology personnel, and the sales staff.

A recent crisis occurred when a DOS attack crashed GlobalUBid's online server. For over 14 hours, none of its customers could access the system while the SA tried to bring the server back online. Though lost sales are projected to be over $18,000, management's primary concern is the reaction of customers and sellers over the breach of system security. The long-term impact of the DOS attack could be devastating if customers or sellers think confidential data is at risk of being stolen. The online auction component, in particular, requires anonymity in order to secure bids. Management agreed that a consultant team should be brought in to assess the potential for more security breaches within or external to the company.

Setting the Stage

GlobalUBid is hierarchically structured, as shown in Figure 1. Four vice presidents (VPs) report to Ms. Susan Dawson who is the president and chief executive officer (CEO). The CEO reports directly to the venture capitalist team who visits the company site on a quarterly basis. During each visit, the chief financial officer (CFO) presents a summary of the financial standing of the company in terms of venture capital spent, international and domestic sales by auction and fixed price quotes, and operational expenses. The venture capitalist team has final approval over any acquisitions or major expenditures until after the IPO.

Management Team

Ms. Susan Dawson, the CEO, has over 22 years of sales experience primarily in mail-order consumer products. She has an MBA and a bachelor-of-science degree in electrical engineering. Before joining GlobalUBid, she was president and CEO of a $20 million annual-sales mail-order catalog company targeting middle-class consumers. During her tenure, she increased mail-order sales by 25% while reducing shipping and handling costs by 5%. So far, Ms. Dawson's leadership in formulating GlobalUBid's corporate strategy has proven to be successful. She was primarily the one responsible for the strategic acquisitions that allowed GlobalUBid to become a major player in the international B2B marketplace.

Mr. Jacob McFurley, vice president of e-commerce, has extensive experience in managing government contracts for software systems. He has worked as a project manager for 15 years on satellite systems focusing on telecommunications software components. He also worked as a project manager for a Fortune 500 company, managing an inventory-control system using COBOL[2] business software. Mr. McFurley is new to the e-commerce area of software development, though he is knowledgeable in software processes, the C++ programming language, and large database systems. He received a master-of-science degree in computer science and a bachelor of science in physics.

Mr. John Schmitz, vice president and chief financial officer, worked in the banking industry for over 20 years. Most recently, he was the bank president of a small-town bank in Illinois. Mr. Schmitz has an MBA and a bachelor-of-science degree in mathematics. He has a close working relationship with the venture capitalists, as one of them was his college roommate at Illinois State University.

Mr. Mike Nowell, vice president of human resources, is fairly new to GlobalUBid. He was hired after the first year of operations in order to formalize the benefits

Figure 1. The organizational structure of GlobalUBid

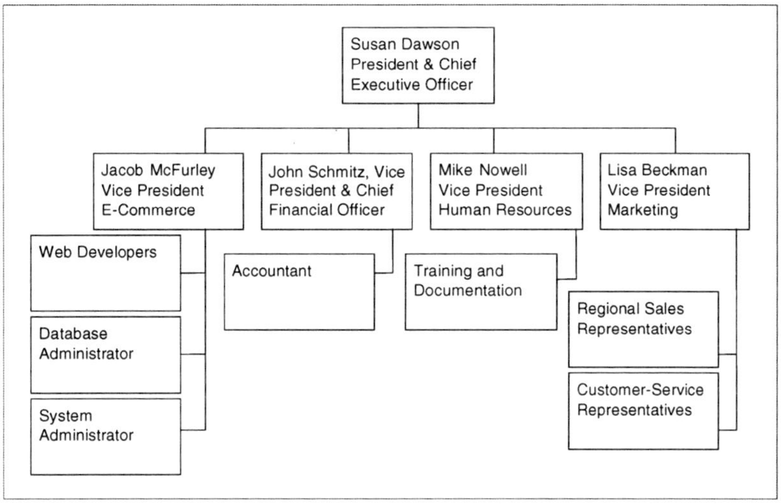

package including stock options. He was also hired to staff up in the marketing and customer-services areas. Mr. McFurley highly recommended Mr. Nowell, as they had worked together for a government contractor during the early 1980s. Mr. Nowell has an MBA and a bachelor-of-science degree in management.

Ms. Lisa Beckman is the newest addition to the management team, as she was hired in March 2000 to manage the sales and customer-support staff. She has five years of experience in managing telemarketers for the Democratic National Committee. She is a sister of the same venture capitalist who is a colleague of Mr. Schmitz.

None of the executive staff has experience in managing security risks in an organization. Though Mr. McFurley has extensive knowledge in computing and information technology, he lacks expertise in the security of online systems.

Overview of GlobalUBid

The overall objective of GlobalUBid is to provide customers ready access to inventory that may be difficult to find, obsolete, military, or special-order components. Sellers have an opportunity to liquidate inventory that otherwise might be difficult to dispose. Currently, there are over 5 million inventory items that are available for sale either through the auction or the fixed price quoting system. The customer is able to conduct sophisticated searches of hard-to-find inventory given the powerful search-engine capability that was provided by the acquisition of StaticPrice.com.

Customer and seller confidentiality is guaranteed by GlobalUBid, as stated in the privacy-policy statement on its Web site. The auction component requires anonymity between each buyer and seller, which is maintained even after the purchase has been made. Inventory is initially offered to a customer at an opening bid with a specified time period for placing bids. Each customer places a bid on an inventory item until the bidding time period lapses. The customer can place an unlimited number of bids during the bidding time period. The seller is able to monitor the bidding process throughout the bidding time period, though at no time is any type of communication allowed in terms of bidding activity. The customer may ask the seller questions via an anonymous e-mail system that is maintained by GlobalUBid.

The fixed-price-quoting system allows a seller to offer inventory at a fixed price. There is no bidding component, though the customer may ask the seller questions about the inventory via the GlobalUBid e-mail system. This system component also offers the customer an opportunity to list inventory items and request price quotes from potential sellers. This is also an anonymous selling and buying system such that fixed price quotes are made through GlobalUBid's e-mail system.

GlobalUBid handles all transactions in terms of payment processing. The customer is required to submit payment to GlobalUBid within 24 hours of winning a bid or accepting a fixed-price offer from a seller. The customer is also rated internally by GlobalUBid in order to track the payment history of a customer. The customer is flagged "yellow" when failing to make a valid payment within the specified time period. A second occurrence changes the flag to "red," and the customer is suspended from using GlobalUBid's online system unless a cash account is established for future payments.

Recently, Mr. Schmitz made a recommendation to include an electronic payment system to the GlobalUBid site in order to expedite the payment process. However, it would require a secure environment that would guarantee credit-card data could not be stolen. Mr. McFurley is responsible for identifying the system requirements for adding an electronic payment system, which would protect all transaction data in the customer database system.

Security and the Organization

The management team discusses risk primarily from a financial perspective during the executive meeting held on Friday afternoons. The primary concern is that venture capital will run out before the online auction and fixed-price-quoting systems make a profit. Management has not addressed any specific security issues including external attacks by hackers or security breaches due to disgruntled employees. However, they have identified natural disasters including tornadoes, snowstorms, and floods, which pose risks to the daily operations of GlobalUBid. To protect from natural disasters, system backups are to be made quarterly with all operational data downloaded from the server. The backup copy is stored in a local bank vault approximately 20 miles from GlobalUBid.

Both researchers and practitioners in the information-systems field recognize the importance of information-security awareness (McLean, 1992; Spurling, 1995; Straub & Welke, 1998; Thomson & von Solms, 1998). As such, research has begun to focus on an organizational perspective in minimizing vulnerabilities associated with information security (Rees, Bandyopadhyay, & Spafford, 2003; Siponen, 2001). In practice, studies are assessing current organizational practices, assigned responsibilities, and security issues facing organizations. A global information-security survey, conducted by Ernst and Young (2003), found that there are still major obstacles in terms of outdated infrastructures, fragmented approaches to deploying security tools, and a lack of top-management accountability for information security.

Though much emphasis has been placed on technological aspects of developing defenses against security breaches (Gordon & Loeb, 2002), organizations remain extremely vulnerable. Many companies lack a security vision that goes beyond a defensive mentality, such as downloading Microsoft patches when a virus attack is imminent. This was the case with the recent MSBlast worm attack that organizations could have prevented simply by installing a patch that was made available to them. A security plan with supporting processes would protect organizations from many security hazards, but too few have them.

Because of this neglect, information and software systems are far more vulnerable than need be in terms of damages that are caused by security attacks (Straub & Welke, 1998). Many organizations are left vulnerable to attacks, especially given the rise in cybercrime activities. As long as hacking know-how is easily transferable, its costs are low, technology is readily available, and industry remains reactive to security attacks, cybercrime will continue to flourish (Siponen, 2001).

Whitman (2003) points out that a security policy is perhaps the most important layer of security available to an organization. Yet, many organizations do not understand their vulnerabilities and, as such, they have neither a policy nor a plan for the prevention, detection, and correction of threats (Wood, 2000).

An important aspect of managing vulnerabilities is an organized classification of threats and an understanding of security services that target them. The ISO 7498-2 (1989) can be used as a reference model in that it identifies five types of security services (authentication, access control, data confidentiality, data integrity, nonrepudiation) and eight security mechanisms (encryption, digital signature, access control, data integrity, data switch, traffic-flow padding, route control, and validation) supporting these services. From this model, a risk-management policy may evolve taking into account each vulnerability and assessing its cost to the organization (Farahmand, Navathe, Sharp, & Enslow, 2003). It is important that organizations initiate this type of assessment as critical system failures due to security issues continue to cause major business disruptions.

Security and Personnel

The executive team promotes few security measures within and external to the operational environment of GlobalUBid. Mr. Nowell was overheard telling Ms. Beckman that he disabled virus-protection software on his laptop in order to download e-mail attachments. Managers often forget to log off computer workstations not only in their offices but also in the conference rooms. All managers rely heavily on remote e-mail access using their laptop computers to connect to GlobalUBid's server. The SA has been trying to keep up with Microsoft patches and virus-protection updates, with laptops taking precedence over all other personal computers and workstations.

The technical staff in general agrees that security policies must be defined and adhered to. However, the database administrators have conflicting opinions regarding database-backup and security policies. The system administrator has established security policies in terms of user IDs and passwords, but he lacks the authority to ensure that they are followed.

GlobalUBid personnel are only moderately concerned about following the security policies that are in place. It is not uncommon to see yellow notes on workstations with user ID, password, and customer information. All personnel are trained in security measures regarding password protection, maintaining confidentiality of customer data, and securing workstations. However, accountability is sporadic in ensuring these policies are followed.

The news about the "I love you" virus disabling computer systems around the world spread like wildfire across news sources. Mr. McFurley held an emergency meeting with his technical staff regarding virus software protection. It came as a surprise that 45% of the personal computer workstations and 90% of the laptops did not have the latest version of virus software. The cost of the virus, from an industry perspective, was devastating (refer to Appendix A). Fortunately, the love bug did not infiltrate GlobalUBid's e-mail system, and the technical staff gave each other "high fives" for updating the virus-protection software just in time.

Security and Existing Processes

The SA, Mr. Bill Jones, primarily follows the book in ensuring user profiles are set up correctly, firewall software is current, and virus software is updated. This is the extent of securing the server to eliminate vulnerabilities associated with DOS and virus attacks.

Ms. Wei Choi and Mr. Raj Tripathy, the Oracle DBAs, have system-administration access to the database systems. They provide full access rights to both Mr. Jones and Mr. McFurley in order to resolve database problems when the DBAs are not available. Mr. Tripathy sets up user profiles for each of the Web developers such that they have access to operational database components including customer, seller, inventory, and sales data. The sales and customer-service staff have restricted access to customer and seller data, though they can insert new data and update existing data as long as they enter a user identifier and password code.

User identification codes and passwords are distributed among all personnel both electronically and as a hard-copy report. Each user is asked to change his or her password upon receiving the list, though no formal process exists to ensure that this is done.

The organization has a formal policy on shredding documents. Letterhead is available with *confidential* boldly appearing on the top of it. The personnel policy to be followed is that any customer, financial, or employee content requires the use of this letterhead. There is one shredder by the copy machine for employee use, and the letterhead paper is to be kept in a locked storage cabinet with the key made available by Ms. Evelyn Arthur, the secretary.

Security and the Physical Environment

Each employee wears a badge with his or her picture, employee identification number, and title. An employee takes an elevator to the second floor of the Marshall building and gains access to the GlobalUBid work area via a badge reader. Ms. Arthur sits at a front desk facing the elevator door from 8 a.m. to 5 p.m. At times, there is no one at the front desk when Ms. Arthur runs internal errands, attends executive meetings, or takes her one-hour lunch break. Each visitor is expected to sign in at the front desk whereby Ms. Arthur issues a temporary badge to be returned at the end of the visit.

Before leaving the building, each employee secures his or her workstation by closing all electronic files, logging out, placing the computer on standby, and storing confidential documents. About 20% of the employees fail to secure workstations on a regular basis. It mostly is unnoticed by management because of the screen-reader software that automatically places the computers on standby. An employee is provided a handbook during a one-day new-employee orientation. The handbook discusses workstation maintenance including procedures on changing passwords, closing applications, and placing a computer on standby. Ms. Jessica Antony, the human-resource trainer, thoroughly covers these policies during orientation.

The server machines and the physical-data and log files are separated from other work areas by divider walls. All administrators have workstations in this area, and they are responsible for securing all operational data. Unauthorized employees are not to enter this area without being accompanied by the SA or DBAs.

Security and the System Architecture

The system architecture for GlobalUBid is shown in Figure 2. The system is comprised of both internally and externally accessible components. All components have access to the outside world through a proxy server and a firewall. The internally accessible components of the architecture include the domain, file, and mail servers and user workstations. The externally accessible components of the system architecture include the Web server and Web database.

A key part of the system architecture is that the externally accessible components can only be accessed by the internal components from the outside. That is, user workstations access the outside Internet in order to connect to and update the Web site and Web data set. Only the SA has direct access to the Web server and Web database (externally accessible components) by physically using the systems. The belief is that this increases security of company-sensitive information.

Case Description

Denial-of-Service Attack

A DOS attack took place on Monday, May 22, at 6 a.m. When Mr. Jones arrived for work at 8 a.m., panicked sales personnel were trying to locate him. None of the staff could access software applications necessary to answer customer questions or to monitor inventory bids. International phone calls were inundating the staff regarding the unavailable Web site. Mr. Jones was able to recover from the attack around 8 p.m. such that all system applications were operational.

Figure 2. System architecture

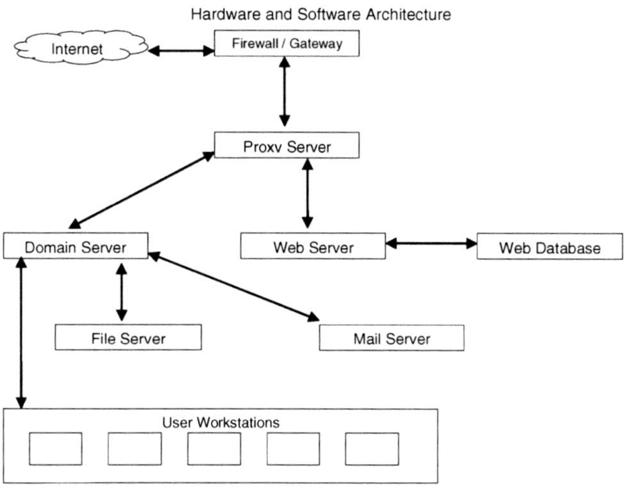

The management staff, led by Mr. McFurley, called an emergency meeting about the security breach. Mr. McFurley expressed concern about a subsequent breach with little or no recourse for ensuring system availability. Mr. Nowell expressed another concern about security and a disgruntled salesperson who recently quit. The employee had unsecured access to both customer and seller files. Mr. Nowell read an article about disgruntled employees accounting for much of the online theft and security breaches that occur in organizations (refer to Appendix B). Mr. Schmitz pointed out that the financial impact of the DOS attack was currently unknown. He stated that there might be financial consequences as the result of customer mistrust in the security of GlobalUBid's online system.

Management agreed that the consultant company, URSecure, Inc., should be contracted to conduct a full security assessment. The overall objective would be to identify potential security risks both internally and externally. Dr. Timothy Berger, the lead assessor of URSecure, Inc., proposed to GlobalUBid that a security assessment be conducted followed by a formal presentation of findings.

The Security Assessment

Dr. Berger met with GlobalUBid management to explain the security-assessment process followed by his team. He recommended that they visit Carnegie

Mellon Software Engineering Institute's CERT Coordination Center (http://www.cert.org) to learn about cybercrime, which was anticipated to reach 80,000 reported incidents by 2002. Dr. Berger explained that security threats are internal due to disgruntled or dishonest employees gaining easy access to online systems, and external due to malicious hackers or persons no longer employed. He provided them with a handout on cybercrime terminology (Appendix C). Management was told that these attacks could be devastating when the organization has few security processes.

Dr. Berger explained that the security assessment was based on recommendations made by online security resources provided by the CERT Coordination Center, the Computer Security Institute (CSI; http://www.gocsi.com), and the National Institute on Standards and Technology (http://www.nist.gov; Stonebumer, Goguen, & Feringa, 2001).

Mr. McFurley met with the technical staff in order to get support for conducting a security assessment by URSecure, Inc. Mr. McFurley explained that the assessment process would uncover high-risk factors including incomplete or missing security processes, a lack of training and documentation in existing security processes, a failure to enforce security processes, the lack of a reward and recognition system for employees, and a missing feedback mechanism for security improvements[3].

Mr. Jones scowled at Mr. McFurley while expressing his view that the security assessment was a waste of time. Mr. Jones pointed out that he was constantly updating the virus-protection and firewall software, and as such, he felt there was no need for consultants poking around in his server files. Ms. Choi also expressed her concern regarding data integrity if the consultants inadvertently made changes to the database. Mr. McFurley assured everyone that the consultant's work was strictly confidential and that at no time would they have unsupervised access to GlobalUBid data.

Security Areas

Dr. Berger outlined several areas to be included in the security assessment conducted by the URSecure team. Dr. Berger pointed out other security areas that might need to be included in a comprehensive security-assessment plan.

- *Physical security*: Physical security is assessed in terms of the building perimeter, cubicles, halls, offices, conference rooms, doors, and other public areas. The physical work area is evaluated for unsecured copiers, faxes, and printers; confidential documents; passwords; and user IDs.

- *Database security*: Database security is evaluated in terms of user profiles and access rights. Database scripts are assessed in terms of unauthorized data access by software applications. Database log files are audited for unauthorized user access to data.
- *Desktop and group policies*: Individual and group policies are audited in terms of desktop access rights, remote administration, hardware configuration, software backups, user privileges, virus protection, and software downloads.
- *Intrusion detection*: System-administration log files are audited to uncover security areas vulnerable to DOS attacks. Firewall protection is assessed in terms of security holes allowing external intruders to access sensitive data.
- *Web logs*: Web logs are audited to assess the use of cookies, content filtering, secure socket-layer encryption, plug-ins, and customer and seller data encryption.

Security Audit Form

Table 1 illustrates part of a security audit form used by the URSecure team. Each question is based on security information obtained from the CERT Web site, as extracted by the URSecure team. The form is completed by a URSecure team member while conducting an interview with employees, observing informal policies and employee behavior, auditing logs, or reviewing documents. The root cause is noted for each potential security violation. Root-cause values are *no*, *informal*, or *formal* for the three areas of training, formal processes, and baseline data. Root-cause values are as follow.

NT = No Training
NP = No Process
NB = No Baseline
IT = Informal Training
IP = Informal Process
IB = Informal Baseline
FT = Formal Training
FP = Formal Process
FB = Formal Baseline

Table 1. Part of the physical-security questionnaire

Security Item	Root Cause	Risk Rating	Security Actions
Badge is worn at all times	NT IP NB	High	There is an informal process of wearing a badge while in the work area, but it is not consistently enforced. The badge does not distinguish an employee from a visitor.
Temporary badges for visitors	NT IP NB	High	There is an informal process for visitor sign-in, but it is not consistently enforced. A badge is issued to a visitor when a secretary is at the front desk. Visitors roam the building without being escorted by an employee.
Badge request to replace lost or stolen one	NT NP NB	Severe	There is no process for replacing stolen or lost badges. A new badge can be requested without an explanation.
Controlled access to physical areas on second floor	NT NP NB	Severe	There are no employee restrictions on the conference room, server area, offices, or other work spaces. Employees often share multiple workstations and desktops without logging in.

For each item on the questionnaire, a risk-rating factor is assigned to it. The risk ratings are *severe*, *high*, *moderate*, *low*, or *none*. A *severe* rating means that due to a lack of security processes, the company is highly vulnerable to an attack. A *high* rating means that the probability of a breach is significant because security processes are informal. A *moderate* rating means that the breach is less likely to occur because security processes have been formalized. A *low* risk means that security processes have been formalized and supported with training and documentation.

Security audit forms are to be developed for each of the security-assessment areas that comprise the security-assessment plan. These forms need to specify questions that are objective and can be readily evaluated for compliance. In addition, baseline data need to be defined in quantitative terms whenever possible. Baseline data are important for comparing improvements made by the organization in each of the security-assessment areas.

Assessment Results

Physical Security

There are numerous security risks associated with the physical layout of GlobalUBid (refer to Figure 3). The peripheral of the building has windows for which the blinds are not drawn. Confidential material, including an entity-relationship diagram of the customer database, could be seen externally. Several vice presidents have unlocked doors leading from their offices to a patio where sensitive data is visible.

Figure 3. GlobalUBid's physical layout

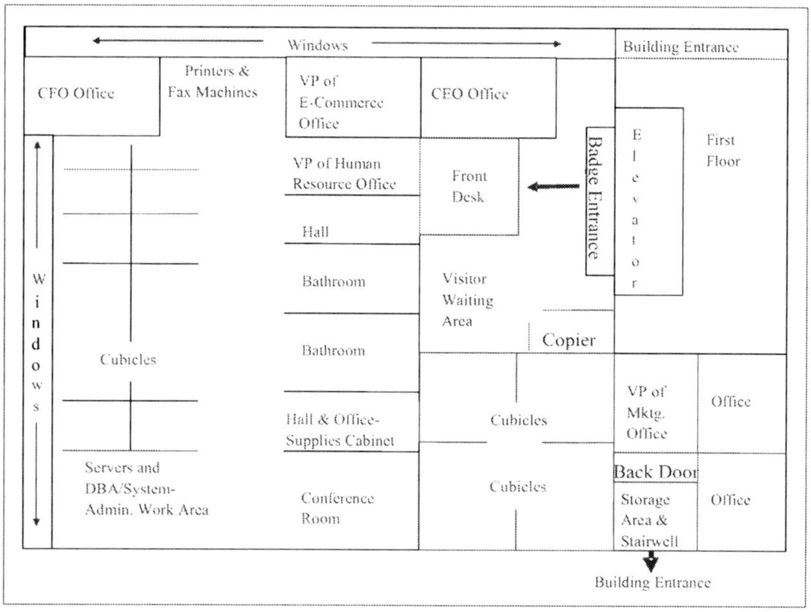

The front desk is sporadically vacated and, as such, visitors can access the GlobalUBid premises without signing in. On the first visit to GlobalUBid, two URSecure team members accessed the second floor without badges and none of the employees questioned their access. The copier, readily accessible by visitors, had confidential documents lying near it unattended.

The server machine is somewhat vulnerable to a security breach because it is accessible to anyone on the second floor. It is located in a secured cubicle next to the SA's work area; it is secured in the sense that no one is allowed in the area unaccompanied by the technical staff. Desktop computers in cubicles are also vulnerable given that many are not logged off. Several desktops are left unattended with open e-mail messages displayed. Approximately 20% of the sales staff have customer data stored as icons on the desktop. The conference-room computer was not logged off after an executive meeting. A history of Web pages with sensitive buyer and seller data is accessible using the history button in Internet Explorer.

Both the front and back entrances appear to be secure, though further assessment is needed to determine whether there are undetected security risks. The consultants acknowledged that further investigation is needed to uncover security issues associated with the physical environment.

Database Security

Mr. Tripathy, one of the database administrators, identified a security risk associated with GlobalUBid's databases in that the system administrator has unsecured access to both the operating system and databases. The SA can perform database-administration functions without notifying the DBAs. As such, there is no accountability for unauthorized database access. This security breach also exists for the production database system, as Mr. McFurley, Web developers, DBAs, and the SA have unsecured access to production data. Though this data is for development use only, if stolen, it would compromise GlobalUBid's competitive advantage.

Another security risk appears to be a lack of formal procedures for backup and recovery of operational data, though further investigation is needed. Mr. Tripathy explained that backup is typically done by Ms. Choi at the end of the workweek. However, one week's backup was not performed because the developers were fixing a software bug associated with the online bidding system. Ms. Choi explained that the week's backup was only delayed. She is confident that an in-house backup occurs each week, as documented in the database log files.

In terms of database recovery, both DBAs rely on Oracle defaults to store data in recovery logs. Neither of the DBAs knows the contents of these logs, and they rely on Oracle software to back up the logs periodically. Mr. Tripathy is somewhat concerned about the loss of operational data because he has never performed a database recovery. However, Ms. Choi is confident in fully recovering from a database failure if it were to occur. She has implemented recovery procedures many times in her previous DBA position and has relied extensively on Oracle software for 100% recovery of operational data.

Desktop Security

The URSecure team members interviewed staff from international sales, customer service, human resources, and management regarding desktop security. The questionnaire in Table 2 illustrates some of the findings uncovered during the interview activities.

The consultants found that about 25% of the surveyed employees write user IDs and passwords on notes attached to monitors, desks, and walls. This unsecured data is readily obtainable by anyone near the employee workstation. Almost a third of the employees stated that they were unaware of the company policy to change the user password on a regular basis.

GlobalUBid personnel were asked about user ID and password sharing, and the results are shown in Figure 4. Only one third stated that they would not provide

Table 2. Questionnaire results from desktop-security assessment

Is the user required to change the password for his/her account?				
Yes	No	Not sure		
54%	31%	15%		
Can the same password be used more than once?				
Yes	With restrictions	Never	Not sure	
23%	8%	23%	46%	
Are there requirements on password content? Check all that apply.				
Minimum length				50%
Maximum length				17%
Requirement on letter, digit, special character combinations				17%
What are the requirements? (No response) Not sure				16%
What happens when I forget my password? Check all that apply.				
I ask the system administrator				46%
I do not know				0%
I use a word that I will not forget				23%
I ask a coworker because he/she will remember it				0%
I look it up (I have it stored)				0%
Other (Please explain)				23%

Figure 4. Employee responses to password protection

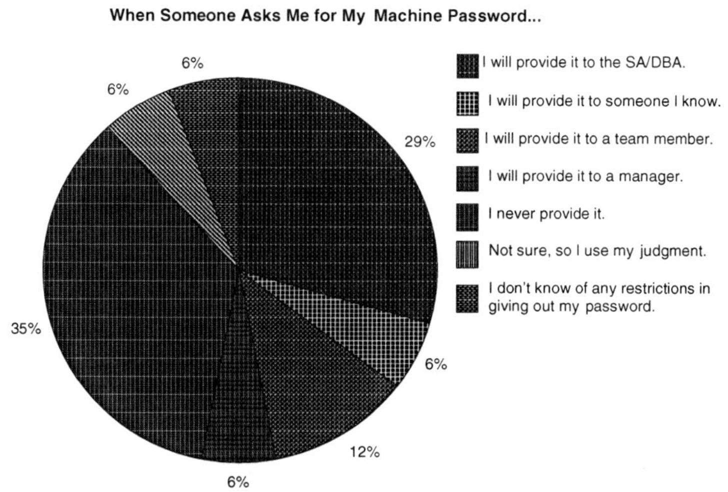

their passwords to anyone including the system administrator. Mr. McFurley told the team that all employees are informed of keeping passwords secure and changing them, as disseminated regularly in a "keeping passwords secure" e-mail note.

Recommendations

Dr. Berger was asked to present the findings, make recommendations for security improvements, and identify the current level of security maturity as a basis for setting future goals.

During the presentation, Dr. Berger showed management a chart whereby GlobalUBid was rated for security maturity. He proposed a security plan, as shown in Table 3, in order to manage security risks. Dr. Berger suggested that management implement a reward and recognition system in order to obtain buy-in from all employees. He did not provide the details, stating that management needs to address this issue.

Dr. Berger recommended the formation of a security response team (SRT) comprised of personnel from various departments. He did not specify a manager to lead the team, but did mention that human resources should play an active role. He stated that the roles and responsibilities of each SRT member should be formalized. Dr. Berger also suggested that the company establish an auditing process that would be performed by the SRT. Thus, employees would be accountable for their security actions and rewarded for security innovation and improvement.

Dr. Berger summarized the improvements for both physical and database security illustrated below. He notes that there are improvements to be made in the other security areas, with the details to be provided in a follow-up meeting with management.

Table 3. Security plan[4]

Activity	Description
Security Vulnerabilities	Each vulnerability is identified in terms of ease of exploitation, likelihood of occurrence, speed of recovery, and monetary damages.
Security Process	Security processes are formalized in terms of implementing, managing, and maintaining security in each area.
Process Improvement	Lessons learned from each incident are used to improve security processes.
Measurement System	A measurement system is established to identify costs associated with maintaining each security process, and to calculate direct and indirect costs for each incident reported.
Incident Costs	For each security incident, direct and indirect costs are calculated. Direct costs include labor, lost sales, and overhead expenses. Indirect costs include reputation and lost customers and sellers.
Security Assessment	For each security incident, data is collected on the security processes used, their effectiveness, the costs of using them, and the processes that were bypassed.
Security Monitoring	Each global security incident is monitored. Data is recorded about vulnerabilities and the recovery mechanisms used. Lessons learned from each incident are used to improve security processes.
Security Awareness	Each employee is continuously trained on security processes and the consequences of not following processes. A reward and recognition system is in place for security improvements suggested by employees.

Improved Physical Security

Many of the physical-security recommendations formalize processes for securing sensitive data both electronically and in hard-copy form. The following recommendations were made to the management team.

- Develop processes for displaying and disseminating confidential data including user IDs and passwords, customer and seller data, database schemas, and software code.
- Develop a confidentiality rating for company documents.
- Develop a process for disposing of documents based on the confidentiality rating.
- Develop a process for securing unoccupied offices, conference rooms, halls, closets, and exit doors.

Dr. Berger reminded the management team that physical security requires a commitment by all employees. However, he did not specify what measures should be taken to obtain a commitment by all employees.

Improved Database Security

The consultant team made recommendations for improving database security emphasizing backup and recovery processes to protect the company's most valuable asset: operational data. The following illustrate database-security recommendations made by the URSecure team.

- Define and document user roles and responsibilities for system administration, database administration, Web developers, and management.
- Conduct audits of database logs comparing user access rights and data manipulation in terms of inserts, deletions, and updates.
- Develop backup and recovery procedures in order to ensure 100% recovery capability for all database systems.
- Perform periodic recovery drills to determine the success rate of recovery. These drills include levels of severity inclusive of natural disasters, intrusions, nonmalicious data corruption, and system failures.

After listening to Dr. Berger's initial findings, Ms. Dawson expressed her concern regarding the lack of leadership in securing the organization. She also expressed concern that the financial cost and resources necessary to implement a full-scale security plan outweigh the benefits. She set a date for an executive meeting in order to discuss what would be financially feasible in terms of improved security.

Challenges Facing GlobalUBid

There are several challenges facing GlobalUBid as it continues to expand into the international marketplace. One of its biggest challenges is to improve organizational awareness of security issues associated with internal and external attacks. It may be difficult to change the laissez-faire attitude toward security because of the competitive nature of the dot.com industry and the software challenges facing GlobalUBid. Though management recognizes the need for increased security, their focus is on what they perceive as issues that are more critical. There are 12 online competitors who have entered the B2B international marketplace for inventory disposal. International sales continue to drop as the world economy faces a growing recession, oil prices continue to rise, and the threat of terrorist activity remains high.

In addition, the executive management team is concerned about the financial cost of implementing a security plan and the resources needed to form an SRT. Given that only one DOS attack occurred since GlobalUBid has become operational, management feels that the financial costs outweigh the security benefits.

Many desktops remain vulnerable to malicious attacks because Microsoft software patches, virus protection, and firewall updates are not done on a regular basis. Database backups appear to be scheduled around software-development deadlines, which could leave the data vulnerable to failures. Employees fail to secure their workstations, thus leaving them vulnerable to unauthorized access to sensitive data. One of the major challenges is to develop security policies that are strictly adhered to by all personnel. A reward and recognition system needs to be developed that would promote the implementation of security policies as well as identify improvements to them.

Personnel resistance to implementing security policies must be overcome in order to ensure that a high level of security is maintained. Several employees expressed a concern about the additional effort required to secure desktops and documents. The customer-service staff has complained that their workload would significantly increase if shared user IDs and passwords are banned.

Employee dissatisfaction may be an underestimated security risk, especially given the amount of overtime required by many of the employees. Over 30% of the developers have recently quit, and several more are threatening to boycott the mandatory Saturday overtime. The organization remains vulnerable to internal security breaches until this issue is addressed.

As GlobalUBid continues to expand in the international marketplace with localized Web applications for each international market, its systems become more prone to security holes. This is the case for many U.S. companies, including GlobalUBid, that have outsourced the localization of applications. The company will have to allow access to its internal systems by third parties while maintaining the integrity and safety of the information hosted on its servers.

Outsourcing will continue to be a priority in terms of securing proprietary information (e.g., source code), development servers, and sandbox servers, among others. Though the security of this information is generally addressed in nondisclosure agreements with outsourcing companies, the company's systems and business processes remain vulnerable due to open access by third parties. Additional security measures will be required in order to develop effective policies on third-party access. These policies will have to be reviewed and audited on a regular basis in order to assess effectiveness and proper enforcement.

References

Blakley, B., McDermott, E., & Geer, D. (2001). Information security is information risk management. In *Proceedings of the 2001 Workshop on New Security Paradigms* (pp. 97-104).

Cambanis, T. (2003). Worker vengeance makes its way online. *Information Security News*. Retrieved July 25, 2003, from *http://lists.insecure.org/lists/isn/2003/May/0106.html*

Cnn.com. (2000). Former student: Bug may have been spread accidentally. *Cnn.com Technology*. Retrieved July 25, 2003, from *http://www.cnn.com/2000/ASIANOW/southeast/05/11/ilove.you.02/#1*

Ernst & Young. (2003). *2003 global information security survey: A focus on CIS responses*. Retrieved August 18, 2004, from *http://www.ernstandyoung.pl/gcrdownload/TSRS_Report%202003%20eng.pdf*

Farahmand, F., Navathe, S. B., Sharp, G. P., & Enslow, P. H. (2003). Managing vulnerabilities of information systems to security incidents. In *Proceedings of the Fifth International Conference on Electronic Commerce* (pp. 348-354).

Gordon, L. A., & Loeb, M. P. (2002). The economics of information security investment. *ACM Transactions on Information and System Security, 5*(4), 438-457.

ISO 7498-2. (1989). *Information processing systems: Open systems interconnection. Basic reference model, Part 2: Security architecture.*

McLean, K. (1992). Information security awareness selling the cause. In *Proceedings of the Information Federation for Information Processing TC11* (pp. 27-20).

OnlineSecurity.com. (2001). *Recent computer forensic case studies from the Online Security files.* Retrieved July 25, 2003, from *http://www.onlinesecurity.com/Email_Files/onlinesecurity_email_v2.html*

Rees, J., Bandyopadhyay, S., & Spafford, E. H. (2003). PFIRES: A policy framework for information security. *Communications of the ACM, 46*(7), 101-106.

Siponen, M. T. (2001). Five dimensions of information security awareness. *ACM SIGCAS Computers and Society, 31*(2), 24-29.

Spurling, P. (1995). Promoting security awareness and commitment. *Information Management and Computer Security, 3*(2), 20-26.

Stonebumer, G., Goguen, A., & Feringa, A. (2001). *Risk management guide for information technology systems.* NIST Special Publications.

Straub, D. W., & Welke, R. J. (1998). Coping with systems risk: Security planning models for management decision making. *MIS Q, 22*(4), 441-469.

Thomson, M. E., & von Solms, R. (1998). Information security awareness: Educating our users effectively. *Information Management and Computer Security, 6*(4), 167-173.

Verton, D. (2001). Analysis: Insiders a major security threat. *Cnn.com Sci-Tech.* Retrieved July 25, 2003, from *http://www.cnn.com/2001/TECH/industry/07/11/insider.threat.idg/?related*

Whitman, M. (2003). Enemy at the gate: Threats to information security. *Communications of the ACM, 46*(8), 91-95.

Wood, C. C. (2000). Integrated approach includes information security. *Security, 37*(2), 43-44.

Endnotes

1 The .com associated with each online company discussed in this paper is dropped after it has been initially introduced (e.g., GlobalUBid.com is referred to as GlobalUBid).

2 COBOL (Common Business Oriented Language) was the first widely used programming language for business applications. COBOL was used in the

1960-1970's to develop many automated payroll, inventory, customer service, employee, accounting, and other business applications. There are still many COBOL programs that are operational, though they are typically viewed as "legacy" software.

3 These steps are based on Blakely, McDermott, and Geer's (2001) security risk management activities.

Appendix A: The Love Bug Virus

The Love Bug Virus

The Love Bug virus spread worldwide with surprising speed as millions of unsuspecting victims opened the e-mail, which had the subject line "ILOVEYOU" and often came from someone known to the user (Cnn.com, 2000). The virus devastated e-mail programs, and damage from the bug and variations of it were estimated at $7 to $10 billion. Once activated on a computer, the Love Bug virus destroyed files. Then, it replicated itself, accessed a program that searched for log-in names and passwords, and mailed them back to the bug's author.

Appendix B: Disgruntled Employees and Cybercrime

Disgruntled Employees and Cybercrime

According to Verton (2001), cybercrime can be devastating when knowledgeable employees become disgruntled and cause damage to online systems. One company fired two knowledgeable employees for demanding pay increases and stock options to avoid software-development problems. The next day, the company was hit with a DOS attack that allowed external access to the company's server. Two minutes after being brought online, it was attacked again.

In another case, an executive downloaded proprietary information that would help him in his new job with the company's competitor (OnlineSecurity.com, 2001). The executive zipped the files and sent them via a dial-up Internet connection to the competitor's office. E-mail retrieved from the executive's laptop discussed his cybercrime intentions to the competition.

A disgruntled employee who had been fired from a travel agency hacked into his former employer's computer system, canceling 60 customer airline tickets (Cambanis, 2003). The cost of this cybercrime was estimated to be over $90,000, not including damage to its reputation.

Appendix C

Malicious Code

Sniffing: Source code monitoring information traveling over a network. Sniffer software can be used legitimately to monitor network flow or illegitimately to steal confidential data.

Trojan Horse: Source code designed to behave unexpectedly often for the purposes of stealing user log-in and password data or destroying files. The ExploreZip Trojan horse relied on Microsoft Outlook to infect other computers. It reduced file sizes to zero, making them unrecoverable.

Virus: Source code that replicates or copies itself in order to spread to other files. Its destruction can range from a harmless message to file corruption or the reformatting of a hard drive.

Worm: Often combined with a virus, it is source code designed to spread to other computers. The ILOVEYOU virus contained a worm sending itself to addresses in the Microsoft Outlook address file.

Cyber Attacks

Black Hats: Hackers attempting to gain unauthorized access to computing systems with the intent to cause damage.

Cracker: A hacker with malicious intent in gaining access to computing systems. Malicious intent includes crashing or defacing Web sites, or accessing, stealing, or destroying unauthorized files.

Denial-of-Service (DOS) Attacks: Hackers flooding a Web site with traffic to cause a network overflow. The network is shut down resulting in a corporate Web site to be inaccessible by users.

Grey Hats: Hackers attempting to gain unauthorized access based on some justification. These hackers often look for weaknesses and then publish them. They are not White Hats because they may supply information to both software vendors and crackers.

Hacker: A user attempting to gain unauthorized access to computing systems.

Phishing: Hackers pretending to be company representatives in e-mail notes to users requesting password or credit-card data. The user is directed to a Web site that masquerades as the company site in order to steal confidential data.

Spoofing: Hackers hiding their identities by using fake e-mail addresses or pretending to use valid e-mail addresses.

White Hats: Hackers attempting to gain unauthorized access with the purpose of uncovering security breaches. They are typically employed to uncover a company's security vulnerabilities. They may also be hackers who uncover security flaws and report them to software vendors.

Security Terminology

Authenticity: The identity of a person or entity is verified to be the one claimed.

Availability: An authorized person or entity has access to information when it is needed.

Confidentiality: Information access is available only to those persons or entities with authorization.

Information Security: Confidentiality, integrity, and availability of information is preserved by the organization.

Integrity: The accuracy, correctness, and completeness of information and the use of it are maintained.

Vulnerability: Information-system weaknesses that, when exploited, lead to undesirable consequences.

Chapter IV

Government-to-Government Enterprises:
A RoadMap for Success

Luiz Antonio Joia,
Brazilian School of Public and Business Administration -
Getulio Vargas Foundation and Rio de Janeiro State University, Brazil

Abstract

Electronic government has proven a watershed in the domain of public administration despite being difficult to pin down precisely. Indeed, the government-to-government (G2G) arena is one of the least studied aspects of this newly established field of knowledge. This chapter aims to present a heuristic frame to implement government-to-government endeavors effectively. The frame presented in this article was largely drawn from an actual government-to-government case study successfully implemented in Brazil. From the analysis of this explanatory case study involving the Brazilian Central Bank (BCB) and the Brazilian Justice Department (BJD), some key success factors were singled out as well as the major hurdles to be overcome and causes thereof. These findings led the researcher to propose a heuristic frame not only to explain the conclusions drawn from the case study presented, but also to help researchers, practitioners, and policy makers to deploy government-to-government projects adequately.

Introduction

The main scope of this article is to present a heuristic frame to deploy government-to-government initiatives effectively, as well as to establish some key success factors for building G2G enterprises successfully. It also aims to show how public agencies themselves can benefit when they are electronically linked to others, thereby innovating and streamlining their working processes, in order to achieve greater agility and efficacy at reduced cost.

In order to generate a heuristic frame and pinpoint the key G2G success factors, a single explanatory and successful case-study approach was used, namely, one involving the Brazilian Central Bank and the Brazilian Justice Department. In-depth analysis of this case enables us to appreciate the barriers surrounding G2G enterprises as well as the associated causes involved and possible solutions thereto.

The BacenJud[1] system developed by the Brazilian Central Bank to be used together with the Brazilian Justice Department was analyzed in a more detailed manner. This case — considered a success — shows how this G2G project made it possible for both the Brazilian Central Bank and the Brazilian Justice Department to achieve greater agility and effectiveness regarding the processing of legal demands made by the Brazilian Justice Department, thereby handing down its sentences at reduced cost.

Therefore, this chapter intends to answer the following research questions.

- From the case study analyzed, what are the key success factors in the implementation of government-to-government processes between public agencies in Brazil?
- From the case study analyzed, what are the main barriers, causes, and potential solutions associated with electronic interorganizational cooperation between government agencies?
- From the case study analyzed, is it possible to explore a heuristic frame to be used to implement G2G endeavors successfully?

Regarding the chapter's structure, first there is a bibliographical review section for defining the theoretical background upon which this research is based. This includes the analysis of the strategic use of information and communication technologies in organizations and some discussion about e-government definition and government-to-government issues. Then, there is a research-design section where the method used by the researcher is presented. Subsequently, the case study is analyzed and presented in order to ascertain the key success factors for this kind of enterprise. The hurdles encountered, the associated causes thereof, and some possible solutions are also listed. After the case-study analysis and outcome, a heuristic framework is proposed to implement G2G projects successfully. Then, conclusions are drawn and recommendations are made by the researcher to practitioners, academics, public administrators, and policy makers so as to enable them to comprehend more clearly the dynamics and peculiarities of G2G enterprises, and to indicate options for further research.

Bibliographical Review

The Incremental Effects of Information Technology in Organizations

According to Venkatraman (1994), the contribution of IT to business was affected by skepticism in the early 1990s due to the failure to achieve the promised results. In view of this perception, the author pointed out the pressing need to create and develop new criteria to evaluate the impact of IT on business, duly reappraising automation logic, cost reduction, and internal-operation efficiency-based logic, which had prevailed until that time and might well no longer be relevant parameters.

In order to overcome this hurdle, Venkatraman (1994) developed a referential model in which five levels of IT-enabled transformations in organizations were described: localized exploration, internal integration, business-process redesign, business-network redesign, and business-scope redefinition.

According to Venkatraman (1994), the first two levels are evolutionary whereas the latter three are revolutionary. His main thesis addresses the fact that the use of IT associated with evolutionary levels only has a very slight impact on business change, despite the complexity of the technological infrastructure used. Consequently, the real benefits of IT in business only arise from the revolutionary levels, that is, the redesign of business processes and also of business networks, and the redefinition of business scope.

Internet technology enabled organizations to rethink ways of doing business. In regard to the G2G realm, the redesign of business networks among public agencies is now a reality and the bedrock for G2G enterprises, as will be seen in the case study presentation to follow.

E-Government: An Idea Lacking a Clear Definition

E-government is still an exploratory knowledge field and is consequently difficult to define accurately. Moreover, it encompasses such a broad spectrum that it is difficult to find one expression that encapsulates exactly what e-government really represents.

According to Zweers and Planqué (2001, p. 92), one can say that e-government "concerns providing or attainment of information, services or products through electronic means, by and from governmental agencies, at any given moment and place, offering an extra value for all participant parties."

Lenk and Traunmüller (2001), on the other hand, choose to see e-government as a collection of four perspectives based on citizens, processes, cooperation, and knowledge management, which is obviously merely taxonomy developed to help researchers study this field. Naturally, there is a great deal of interdependence among the facets quoted above, and they can seldom be studied individually.

Other authors define e-government in a broader sense (see, for instance, Kraemer & Dedrick, 1997; Perri, 2001). For them, e-government encompasses a broad gamut of activities, from digital data and electronic public service to online pool, e-democracy, and e-governance. Yet, the most recent definitions see e-government as the various ways government uses information and communication technologies to remain relevant in the knowledge society (ITAC, 2002).

Currently, substandard efficiency, efficacy, and effectiveness, at a high cost, in the traditional governmental processes between two or more public agencies were detected. Faced with this reality, one question arises: If enterprises have discovered the enormous benefits that the Internet can generate for them through linkages among themselves, why do not public agencies use this technology and the integration it provides in order to become more responsive at reduced cost? As public budgets are shrinking all over the world and society is increasingly calling for more accountable public administration, integrated electronic processes between public agencies via the Internet, known as government to government, can be the answer to this question (Canuto, 2001).

Internet technology has spurred governmental agencies to participate in this new paradigm. However, this step is not achieved simply by offering new services to citizens via the Web in what are now called G2C (government-to-citizen) initiatives. In Brazil, most e-government projects have addressed the provision of new digital services (G2C) for the citizen as well as the purchasing of goods and services from enterprises, mainly through Web-based reverse auctions (Joia & Zamot, 2002) in what we now call government-to-business (G2B). Unfortunately, very few projects strive to link public agencies so as to manage their knowledge and allow them to put new workflows into effect (E-GOV, 2000).

Consequently, in governmental processes involving two or more public organizations, it is detected very low efficacy and effectiveness at a very high cost. The main reason for this lies in the traditional use of paper as the linkage element between public agencies (Cavalcanti-Neto, 2002).

Government-to-Government Projects and Knowledge Management in the Public Arena

In the business sector, when all the tasks and procedures of an undertaking are centralized in a single company, it is simpler to organize and assess knowledge accrued from a project. The problem is that a handful of different players may now be involved in any major project. Consequently, the question that arises is how is it possible to manage and store the knowledge generated during a given venture in such a way as to use it in the course of a specific project and also manage to access it for use on future projects?

Some very important research has already addressed several aspects of this issue, such as Badaracco (1991), Bahrami (1992), and Baker (1994), to name but a few.

However important these articles are in their own right, the scope of this research just touches on how to create, deploy, transfer, store, and retrieve the intelligence of an undertaking encompassing a handful of different companies in different places with different — although important — duties. Therefore, the next logical step includes expanding the research to ongoing and ad hoc interorganizational groups. In order to accomplish this in the business realm, it is of paramount importance to understand how information technology can leverage and strengthen knowledge links among the players of a major project involving a host of subcontractors, suppliers, and other firms. Interestingly, this is precisely the government's environment.

Government as a collection of public agencies, each of them having their own information and knowledge, needs to ensure that these agencies are linked so as to share their explicit knowledge. It can be said that government is (or should be) similar to metabusinesses — quasi-firms or virtual firms created via digital links between several companies — in such a way that it is almost impossible to define their precise boundaries (Keen, 1991).

Information technologies have a threefold impact on metabusinesses, affecting their degree of connectivity, sharing, and structuring (Haeckel & Nolan, 1993). These three parameters are considered vital to establish the intelligence of metabusinesses and their expertise in managing the knowledge involved.

The connectivity issue addresses the degree of the penetration of the metabusiness, that is, if and how the public agencies involved are linked within the metabusiness in such a way as to transmit data and information among themselves.

The sharing issue addresses the degree of the scope of the metabusiness, that is, the type of transactions developed within the metabusiness, and the way the public agencies are working together in order to set up a work-group environment.

Finally, the structuring issue deals with the ability that the public agencies possess for extracting useful knowledge from the data and information retrieved and shared by them. It is an established fact that knowledge, either tacit or explicit, is far more than the sum of data and information compiled and, according to the theory of autopoiesis (Maturana & Varela, 1980), is generated when a "structural coupling" occurs among the workers.

This is the main reason why knowledge management within public administration cannot be adequately researched and studied other than in the government-to-government realm due to an inadequate technical infrastructure. Furthermore, no sharing exists without connectivity, no structuring can exist without sharing, and no organizational intelligence will be created without structuring.

Research Design

The researcher in this chapter used a single case-study research method. Close scrutiny was given to the case study analyzing the digital link between the Brazilian Central Bank and the Brazilian Justice Department, which was established to allow the former to assist the latter in its legal requests related to information on the investment situation of companies and citizens in the Brazilian financial system. The researcher sought out the critical success factors involved in G2G projects and also assessed the increase in efficiency over former processes conducted by these public agencies relating to this workflow.

Case studies are particularly suitable for answering *how* and *why* questions, and are ideal for generating and building theory in an area where little data or theory exists (Yin, 1994). It also enables researchers to use "controlled opportunism" to respond flexibly to new discoveries made while collecting new data (Eisenhardt, 1994). An embedded single-case research method (Type 2, according to Yin) was used in this chapter as multiple units of analysis — courts throughout the country — were taken into consideration and analyzed.

According to Yin (1994), the single case study is an appropriate design under several circumstances. One rationale for a single case is when it represents an extreme or unique case in which a specific intervention, such as that successful G2G enterprise in Brazil, may be so rare that is worth documenting and analyzing. Another rationale for a single case study is the revelatory case. This situation exists when an investigator has an opportunity to observe and analyze an intervention previously inaccessible to scientific investigation, as in this research.

Furthermore, single cases are used as a prelude to further study (Patton, 1990), such as the use of this research as an exploratory device that is supposed to be the first of possible multiple case studies to be analyzed when other G2G projects are developed and made available in Brazil, leading to a Type 4 case study, according to Yin's taxonomy.

As stated above, an explanatory approach was adopted in this case study. Explanatory case studies are useful for assessing how and why a form of intervention is working. The method verifies whether problems and modifications are needed, and attempts to explain the causal effects revealed. Different sites are necessary in order to develop a comparative analysis (Morra & Friedlander, 1999), as was the case in this study

Yin's (1994) tactics (construct validity, internal validity, external validity, and reliability) were carefully considered in this research.

In particular, construct validity was dealt with in the study through the use of multiple sources of evidence as several courts were examined and related data were collected, through the establishment of a sequence of evidence, and through having the members of the group review the draft case-study report. Internal validity in the findings was also taken into account mainly by interviewing the professionals involved in the process and asking outsiders to read the research draft. External validity was verified by using replication logic and trying to infer behavior patterns in similar environments so as not to introduce biases. Finally, the reliability of the results was ratified using a case-study protocol and developing a case-study database in order to make it possible for other researchers to reach the same outcomes and conclusions as those presented at the end of this chapter.

In conjunction with case study analysis, action research method was also used. Action research is a method that deals both with action and research (Dick, 1999): action to introduce change in any community, organization, or program, and research to leverage the researcher's understanding about what is happening. It is a method where the researcher must belong to the team involved in the proposed change (Checkland & Holwell, 1998), as in this research. In this method, both rigor and relevance are pursued. According to West and Stansfield (2001), a method that is not adequately structured in theory can lead to questionable outcomes. Furthermore, the method must be useful in practical terms in order to be relevant to the managers of the enterprise.

Therefore, theoretical background information related to this knowledge field was also analyzed in order to obtain a match between the case study, action-research practicalities, and the current theory.

Finally, so as to propose a framework to implement G2G projects, a heuristic frame method was also used. According to Winter (1998, pp. 172-173):

[a] heuristic frame corresponds to a degree of problem definition that occupies an intermediate position on the continuum between a long and indiscriminate list of things that might matter at one end and a fully formulated control-theoretic model of the problem at the other. Within a heuristic frame, there is room for a wide range of more specific formulations of the problem — but there is also enough structure provided by the frame itself to guide and focus discussion. On the other hand, a rich variety of different heuristic frames may represent plausible approaches to a given problem.

Based on this assumption, the model presented is one among many that can be used again in the near future as it represents an effort to overcome the "paralysis by analysis" effect (Ansoff, 1984), which is only too common when dealing with intangibles and leads to endless and fruitless discussion instead of producing practical results. A model is valid not by virtue of the excess of rigor it applies to itself, measured by the number of variables taken into consideration, but by the fact that it encapsulates and expresses the reality we are facing adequately. Hence, complexity is not necessarily synonymous with good results, and some flexibility is required when dealing with topics for which a considerable amount of critical perception is required (Joia, 2004).

Consequently, four methodological mainstreams were blended in this chapter: single case study (the major emphasis), action research (as one of the researcher's graduate students took part in the G2G team), bibliographical review, and heuristic frame.

Case Study[2]

The Brazilian Federal Constitution grants very few institutions the right of access to the bank accounts of both citizens and companies or, indeed, the power to freeze financial assets of either. One such institution is the justice department, which intervenes by means of judicial orders handed down by the judges of several courts nationwide.

As required, a judge can either freeze or liberate the bank accounts of both citizens and businesses, and even declare the bankruptcy of a company. Judges are further empowered to suspend a decreed bankruptcy or request financial information about organizations and citizens under scrutiny.

When it issues orders relating to information about the financial assets of either citizens or institutions, the justice department sends them directly to the Central

Bank, which then forwards the orders to the specific recipients, namely, either an institution or the Brazilian financial system. It is almost impossible for the justice department to know precisely where the request should be sent.

As there was already a computerized system in the Central Bank linking it to the Brazilian financial system, it was relatively easy to meet the justice department's requests. However, the increasing demand for this kind of information made by the justice department obliged the Central Bank to involve several employees on a full-time basis and expend considerable financial resources just to deal with this requirement. Over the years, the number of claims has increased dramatically, as can be seen in Figure 1. In the meantime, the Central Bank's legal department issued an opinion alleging that the Central Bank had no constitutional duty to assist the justice department with these specific demands. However, in order not to jeopardize its relationship with the justice department, the Central Bank decided to rethink its modus operandi in order to continue giving assistance to the justice department. Consequently, the Central Bank acknowledged the need to redesign this working process by streamlining it and achieving greater efficiency and responsiveness at reduced cost. At a time when the federal government has reduced the public spending budget and society is demanding greater efficiency, efficacy, and accountability from the public agencies, it was of paramount importance to achieve this.

An Innovative Process

By 1999, the Central Bank realized it was no longer feasible to process this operation manually, that is, receiving claims on paper and feeding them into the communication systems linked to the national financial system. In 2000, the Central Bank received 300 claims per day, totaling 71,775 claims in that year (see Figure 1). A team of 23 people working full time on this task was unable to meet the justice department's demands in time, thereby causing problems in terms of efficacy. The bank was spending approximately US$1 million per year to process these requests, including for wages, equipment, and so forth.

The bank soon realized that there was a pressing need to develop an information system where the justice department itself could formulate its requests that could then be forwarded directly by the Central Bank to the financial institutions.

The bank looked into the possibility of a revised information flow, seeking to take advantage of the deployment of the existing Internet access in most Brazilian courts. A Web-based system was developed in order to centralize the interaction of the judges with the bank so that they could file their requests directly. A Web-based system was selected such that the judges would not have to install any specific software on their desktops, thereby reducing costs involved in the process.

Figure 1. Number of requests sent by the justice department to the Central Bank

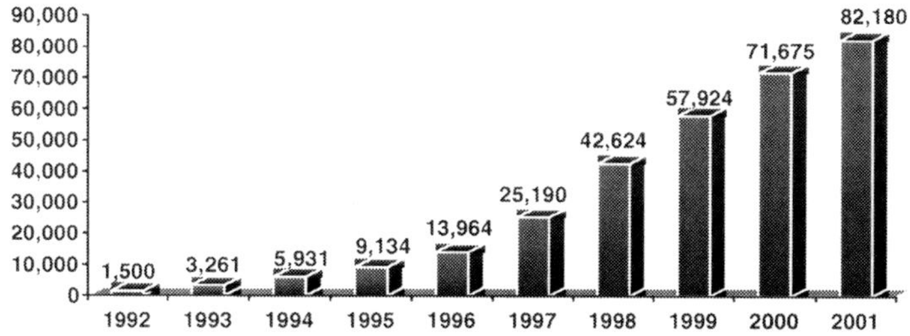

Figure 2. Process architecture

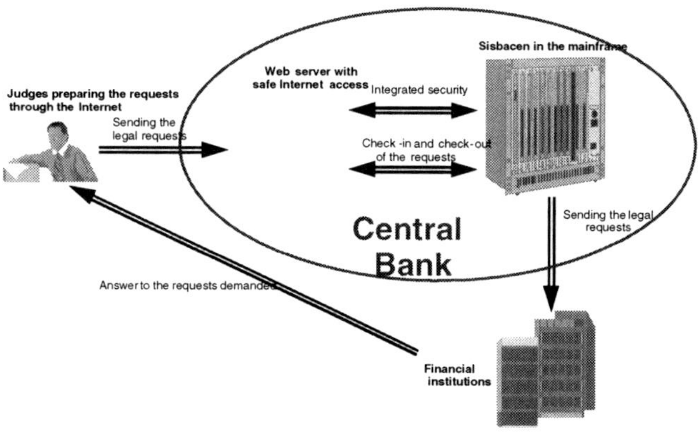

The Architecture of the New Interorganizational Process

The modus operandi between the Brazilian Central Bank and the Brazilian Justice Department is depicted in Figure 2. From the moment a court signs an agreement with the Central Bank, it designates a professional in charge of managing the system on its premises. This manager is supposed to conduct operations including adding users, altering data, changing passwords, granting permission to judges to access the system, and withdrawing this permission when necessary. These operations are done through the system itself, which has a dynamic interface according to the user profile. Users can then access a restricted site on the Internet and after their identity is verified, the system offers Web templates to allow them to fill out their requests. These are recorded directly in the Central Bank's corporate database.

At 7 p.m. every day, all requests received during the course of that day are processed and forwarded to the financial institutions as electronic files. Each institution then replies directly to the judge involved. The process allows the institutions to standardize their answers and send them directly to the judges' e-mail addresses.

Findings

Perceived Benefits

This new process has brought several benefits both to the Brazilian Central Bank and the Brazilian Justice Department, the main benefit being the marked improvement in efficiency in processing and answering requests. Under the former system, it used to take an average of five days from the moment the request was made and delivered to the financial system, though, at times it could even take as long as 20 days. Such delays can render a legal request worthless as it gives the suspects sufficient time to remove monetary assets from the banks. Using the new process, a maximum of 24 hours is needed to prepare a request, transmit it to the Central Bank, and receive the answer to it from the financial system.

The agility attained by this new process derived not only from the reduced turnaround time in handling requests, but also from the opportunity given to the institutions to make or buy their own software in order to answer the claims automatically as the e-mails of the judges are also supplied to the financial organizations (JUDNET, 2001). Another improvement in process performance arose from the tracking capabilities available in this new workflow. In the event the request is not answered in due time, the judge is aware of whom must be contacted and can follow up and demand an immediate reply.

In financial terms, the new process reduces costs both for the Central Bank and for the justice department. For the Central Bank, the main costs are related to the infrastructure needed to complete the process. For the time being, the former infrastructure still remains in place as some requests still have to be processed manually, though now that the new structure is there, there is no further pressure to improve the structure. Whereas requests used to cost the Central Bank nearly US$10 each, an automated request costs less than US$0.80. Costs to the justice department were also reduced as it is only necessary to establish Internet access in every court. The costs involved in traditional mail and personnel to handle the legal requests have also been eliminated.

Key Success Factors

From researcher observations and analysis of the interviews, it was deduced that the key success factors associated with a G2G enterprise are as follow.

Security

As the Internet has become a very important link between governmental agencies, it is of paramount importance to avoid security flaws, such as information violation by crackers, breakdowns in communication, and so forth. Losses caused by such problems are more than just financial as they can cause loss of confidence and acceptance by users and even involve the interruption of a given communication link (Endler, 2001; Huijboom & Hoogwout 2004).

In G2G processes, the issue of security is even greater as confidential information can leak and be made public. Most of this information is protected by laws of secrecy under Brazilian legislation.

According to Markus (1983), flaws in the design of an information system can be considered sources of user resistance to the adequate use of it.

Thus, as was shown generically above, it is clear that security is one of the key success factors for a G2G endeavor. An authentication failure can allow any person to issue a legal request and expose the private life of citizens and relevant organizational information to all and sundry. Several courts insisted on seeing how the process worked before actually deciding to join the network proper.

Organizational Culture

Another factor that influences the success of an electronic governance model is the culture of the public agency in which it is developed. New processes of electronic governance, at different levels within the public administration, demand changes in organizational culture (ITAC, 2002; Traunmüller, Chutimaskul, & Karning, 2004).

The influence of the culture is even more relevant when two different public agencies are working together, concurrently. The changes required in the organizational cultures in order to integrate different internal processes demand very clear prior definition of leadership and respective function. This role, itself, demands that a clear path and precise judgment be followed so as to make innovative workflows feasible (Kieley, Lane, Paquet, & Roy, 2001).

Kling (1980) and Markus (1983) have provided a very helpful approach to examining the introduction and implementation of computer-based information systems and the human resistance or acceptance that so often accompanies them.

They say that people or groups resist or accept systems because of an interaction between characteristics related to the people and characteristics related to the system. This theory, according to the author, is difficult to define but easier to describe. The operant word in the definition is *interaction*. New information systems may prescribe a division of roles and responsibilities at variance with existing ones; they may structure patterns of interaction that are at odds with the prevailing organizational culture. In this light, systems can be viewed as a vehicle for creating organizational change. Similar articulations of a variant of the interaction theory can be found in Ginzberg (1975) and Keen (1980).

It should be noted that this explanation identifies neither the system nor the organizational setting as the cause of resistance or acceptance, but rather their interaction.

A second variant of the interaction theory can be called the political version. Here, resistance or acceptance is explained as a product of the interaction of system design features with the intraorganizational distribution of power and status, defined either objectively in terms of horizontal or vertical power and status dimensions, or subjectively in terms of symbolism.

The interaction theory explains clearly what occurred in the Brazilian Justice Department regarding the BacenJud system implementation as the judges perceived their interaction with the system as valuable and as a vehicle to increase their power and status.

Besides this, it was observed that the courts that already had a culture of using computerized processes assimilated the new modus operandi very rapidly and naturally. On the other hand, courts without Internet access or that barely used information systems in their daily activities have resisted greatly in joining the G2G process.

Hence, as seen above, the success of the use of a new process depends on the culture within the organizations involved, in this case, the culture of the courts nationwide.

Training

New technologies, new processes, and new models of electronic governance require the acquisition of new knowledge not just by the persons involved directly in the process, but also by the persons in charge of administrating them. Consequently, public agencies must assess their human capital carefully as it is mandatory to train personnel before the deployment of G2G enterprises (Kieley et al., 2001).

When the process involves more than just one public agency, all players must implement training efforts in order to leverage the knowledge of the personnel in the agencies involved equally (Traunmüller et al., 2004).

Figure 3. Key success factors in G2G endeavors

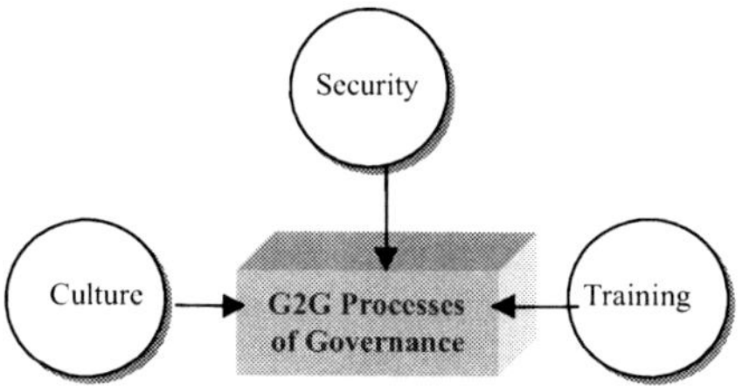

According to Markus (1983), insufficient training can impede users from using information systems, hindering the potential benefits that might be attained by this new process.

Hence, although the system was developed based on a user-friendly environment via a Web interface, the Central Bank felt it necessary to make presentations to judges across the country in order to explain how the system worked and explain the best practices associated with this new workflow.

In October 2001, the Central Bank started to make presentations to the judges in the courts in a state where only 10 judges had joined the system and a mere eight requests had been generated until that moment. In the two months following the presentations, 130 judges joined the system and nearly 100 requests were generated. Interviews made by the researcher have shown that the use of the G2G process by trained people is increasing, proving the efficacy of the training strategy.

Thus, by consolidating information from all the observations, interviews, and questionnaires, it can be seen that access and information security, organizational culture, and training were the key success factors in this G2G enterprise, as depicted in Figure 3.

Barriers: Causes and Solutions

From the case-study observations and various interviews with the major players involved, the existence of three types of barriers in a G2G project can be seen, namely, structure-based, human-based, and technology-based barriers. As shown in Table 1, the last of the three is the easiest barrier to overcome as opposed to the other two that deal with organizations as a whole and their existing personnel who are set in their ways. Table 1 consolidates the results observed by the researcher. These results are very similar to those found in the implementation of major and complex technological projects as presented by Evangelidis, Akomode, and Taylor (2002) and Joia (1998).

A Heuristic Model for Implementation of G2G

Based on the data collected and the observations made, which enabled the researcher to grasp both the critical success factors for G2G projects and the obstacles commonly encountered, as well as the causes thereof and the possible solutions thereto, the idea took the shape of consolidating these results into a heuristic frame for implementation in G2G projects of a generic nature. Einsenhardt (1989) shows how case studies may be used to validate models, and Joia (2004) and Winter (1998) establish how a heuristic frame should be structured. With these three consultation sources and methodological parameters in mind, and adapting the model proposed by Christensen (1997) to understand how innovation arises in organizations, the researcher developed the g-RPV model (resources, processes, values) applicable to G2G projects. This model explains the critical success factors listed above with respect to the Brazilian Central Bank case, and it illustrates and encapsulates the barriers, causes, and solutions presented in Table 1 of this chapter.

Resources

Resources include everything that can either be purchased and/or trained. Personnel, hardware, software, tangible assets, and monetary values, among

Table 1. Barriers, causes, and solutions for a G2G project

BARRIERS	CAUSES	SOLUTIONS
	Structural	
Focus only on direct manpower and indexes	Obsolete decision criteria	In-depth analysis of the costs and benefits involved
Failure to perceive the actual benefits	Lack of measures for intangible benefits	Intangible and tangible productive analysis
High risk for the managers	Reward system not considering innovation	Different reward systems for managers
Lack of coordination and cooperation	Organizational fragmentation	Systems to allow coordination and cooperation
High expectations and hidden costs	Selling of an unreal system	Planning strategic objectives
	Human	
Unwillingness to take risk	Fear of change and uncertainty	Communication and involvement
Resistance	Fear of loss of power and status	Board engaged in project implementation
Unplanned decisions and fear of being made redundant	Orientation and action; lack of patience with planning	Pilot project planning long-range objectives
	Technical	
Incompatibility of systems	Purchase of different hardware and software platforms	Purchase of one integrated system; write own system; neutral transfer files

others, belong to this category. They can be hired or laid off, purchased or sold, depreciated or improved.

With respect to G2G projects, the main resources needed are skilled people — usually found through training initiatives — and an adequate infrastructure, not just to develop and implement information systems, but also to link the public agencies digitally in a secure and adequate manner.

Consequently, training sessions, skilled people, Web-based information systems, network infrastructure, proxy servers, firewalls, and other computer features are necessary to deploy a G2G enterprise successfully. All of the aforementioned inputs are related to the resource dimension of the proposed g-RPV model.

Undoubtedly, training as a key success factor of the case study analyzed here is the crux of the matter. Likewise, security belongs to this area too as a key success factor as tangible assets are needed to establish it in a G2G process.

To reiterate what was already stated above regarding the specific case involving the Central Bank and the justice department, it was of paramount importance to ensure that the personnel involved was properly trained and a technological infrastructure duly implemented in order to guarantee the required security.

Processes

Organizations create value by transforming inputs (resources) — personnel, equipment, technology, information, energy, capital, and so forth — into products or services of added value to the customer or citizen. The interaction, coordination, communication, and decision choices made in order to achieve this goal are called processes (Garvin, 1998). Each public agency has its own internal processes specific to its own value chain (Porter, 1980), a concept that has been enlarged to be used in the realm of public administration (Andersen, 1999). G2G enterprises impact the workflows of these organizations, obliging them to innovate, redesign, or be more flexible (see Venkatraman, 1994). Furthermore, it is imperative nowadays for organizations to be familiar not only with their own workflows, but also with those of their partners in order to streamline their modus operandi (Hammer, 2001).

Evidently, security as a key success factor is partly centered in this dimension of the proposed model as the redesign of both the technological infrastructure (resources) and the organization's intra- and interorganizational processes are necessary, including the redefinition of the business network (Level 4 of the model proposed by Venkatraman, 1994, presented earlier), in order to be successful in a G2G project.

Values

The values of an organization are the sum of the criteria it adopts to establish and define its priorities, which is called public choice in the public administration arena. These values are the subjacent logic that explains how employees allocate their time and define their priorities, judge whether an order is attractive or not, decide whether or not a customer or citizen must be assisted or ignored, and realize if they must comply with a new modus operandi, which can either pose an opportunity or a threat for them. Therefore, within the scope of this chapter, an awareness of the values of an organization is mandatory to be in a position to assess whether or not the civil servants will assist or sabotage (even in a passive way) a new enterprise such as a G2G project.

Undoubtedly, the key success factor of culture is totally embedded in this dimension of the proposed model, almost overlapping the value dimension.

It can also be seen that most of the barriers presented in Table 1 and associated to the implementation of G2G enterprises are embedded in this dimension. Only the technical-based barriers and a few structural-based ones linked to processes cannot be associated directly to this dimension. All the human-based hurdles, for instance, are associated to this aspect of the model presented.

The Model and Its Interactions

In order to test the proposed model, called g-RPV, research was conducted to establish whether a correlation existed between the model and the key success factors found by the authors, including the barriers encountered. Hence, Figure 4 is presented showing the links of the heuristic framework with the key success factors — security, organizational culture, and training — as well as the observed barriers: the technical-, structural-, and human-based ones.

As can be seen in Figure 4, the proposed g-RPV model explains the dynamics of a G2G project adequately as all the dimensions, facets, and outcomes arising in a G2G endeavor are depicted and included within the model.

Conclusion and Further Research

From the case-study analysis and several interviews conducted with the major players involved, it is possible to conclude the following.

Figure 4. The g-RPV model and its interactions

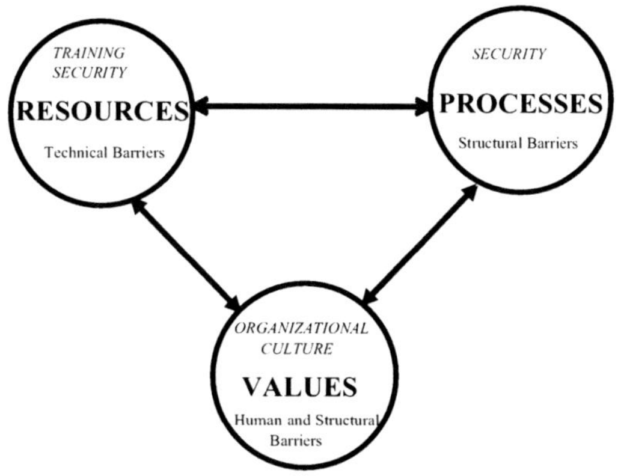

- Responsiveness to a G2G process is far greater than that obtained in traditional processes. This agility itself is of paramount importance in deploying more effective and efficient public policies.
- G2G processes are a valid alternative for Brazilian public administration, which is facing the dilemma of cutting back its operational budget to make the control of the governmental fiscal deficit feasible and to comply with citizen expectations regarding public agencies.
- The security issue in a G2G process is a critical factor as breakdowns arising from it can cause losses not only for public agencies, but for society as a whole.
- To overlook the organizational culture of a public agency by concentrating efforts on a technological facet of a G2G project may cause the undertaking to fail. Nonetheless, public administration is ruled by the same legal agenda and must comply with similar procedures and rules. However, each public agency has its own identity, values, and culture, leading it to develop different workflows, sometimes far different from workflows addressing a similar process in another public agency. To analyze the culture and values of a public agency is of paramount importance to the success of a G2G enterprise.
- The institutional setting influences the nature of innovation in government and determines its pace and selectivity. So, one has to involve qualified public employees as full partners of the change process (Traunmüller et al., 2004).
- Although technology offers people a user-friendly interface and, in some cases, the technology is already being used in the public agency, a G2G

enterprise involves a modus operandi that is new for most of the people involved. It is necessary to show the benefits this new process can bring and the best praxis as important steps for proper implementation of G2G projects.

- The structural and human barriers are far more relevant than the technological barriers. For each barrier, there are causes and possible solutions, as presented in Table 1 in this chapter.
- As several courts were analyzed by the researcher, it can be said that the overall results can be replicated within the Brazilian Justice Department as a whole. For other environments, multiple case studies and a comparison of results are needed so as to make the extrapolation of the conclusions herein presented possible.

It can also be inferred that the chapter deals with e-governance (Perri, 2001) as it taps digital support for public choices and workgroups among several public administrators of different ranks. This is important as, according to Kraemer and Dedrick (1997), it is the least researched facet of e-government. Similarly, the case study addresses the process and cooperation dimensions in the e-government taxonomy proposed by Lenk and Traunmüller (2001), as presented earlier in this chapter, as well as it allows public agencies to attain Levels 3 (business-process redesign) and 4 (business-network reconfiguration) regarding the use of information technology, according to the model proposed by Venkatraman (1994).

According to the organizational intelligence model developed by Haeckel and Nolan (1993), presented earlier in this chapter, it is clear that the degree of scope (connectivity dimension) and the degree of range (sharing dimension) of the metabusiness created between the Central Bank and the courts of the justice department were improved by this G2G endeavor. The structuring dimension of this metabusiness — the transformation of received raw data and information into knowledge — could not be evaluated.

All the research questions presented have been duly answered as the key success factors and the barriers, causes, and possible solutions associated with G2G processes have been addressed. Furthermore, a heuristic frame was also presented, explaining the outcomes derived from the case study and enabling public administrators to deploy G2G projects successfully.

Finally, more research is necessary to verify how these processes have worked in other countries in order to verify whether these conclusions can be replicated in different political, economical, social, legal, and technological environments.

This is a very recent knowledge field; therefore, far more research is needed. This chapter attempts to make a contribution in this very challenging area in the hope that the results achieved may benefit societies worldwide.

References

Andersen, K. V. (1999). Reengineering public sector organizations using information technology. In R. Heeks (Ed.), *Reinventing government in the information age* (pp. 312-330). Routledge.

Ansoff, H. I. (1984). *Implanting strategic management.* Englewood Cliffs, NJ: Prentice-Hall.

Badaracco, J. (1991). Knowledge links. In *The knowledge link: How firms compete through strategic alliances.* Harvard Business School Press.

Bahrami, H. (1992). The emerging flexible organization: Perspectives from Silicon Valley. *California Management Review, 34*(4).

Baker, W. (1994). Building intelligent networks. In *Networking smart* (chap. 3). McGraw-Hill, Inc.

Canuto, O. (2000). O comércio eletrônico e a mobilidade dos gansos. *Jornal Valor.* Retrieved May, 25, 2000, from *http://www.eco.unicamp.br/artigos/artigo131.htm*

Cavalcanti-Neto, A. A. (2002). *Fatores relevantes na construção de processos government-to-government no Banco Central do Brasil* (unpublished master's thesis), Brazilian School of Public and Business Administration, Getulio Vargas Foundation, Brazil.

Checkland, P., & Holwell, S. (1998). Action research: Its nature and validity. *Systemic Practice and Action Research, 11*(1), 13-16.

Christensen, C. M. (1997). *The innovator's dilemma.* Harvard Business School Press.

Dick, R. (1999). *What is action research?* Retrieved July 29, 2002, from *http://www.scu.edu.au/schools/gcm/ar/whatisar.html*

E-GOV. (2000). 1° Seminário Governo na Internet. Brasília: Rede Governo (Computer software).

Einsenhardt, K. M. (1989). Building theories from case study research. *Academy of Management Review, 14*(4), 532-550.

Endler, A. (2001). *Governo eletrônico: A Internet como ferramenta de gestão dos serviços públicos.* Retrieved December 26, 2001, from *http://read.adm.ufrgs.br/read14/artigo/artigo1.pdf*

Evangelidis, A., Akomode, J., & Taylor, M. (2002). Risk assessment & success factors for e-government in a UK establishment. In R. Traunmüller & K. Lenk (Eds.), In *Proceedings of the First International Conference, EGOV 2002.* Berlin, Germany: Springer.

Garvin, D. (1998). The process of organization and management. *Sloan Management Review.*

Ginzberg, M. J. (1975). *Implementation as a process of change: A framework and empirical study* (rep. no. CISR-13). Cambridge, MA: Massachusetts Institute of Technology, Center for Information System Research.

Haeckel, S., & Nolan, R. (1993). Managing by wire. *Harvard Business Review*, 122-132.

Hammer, M. (2001). The superefficient company. *Harvard Business Review*, 82-91.

Huijboom, N., & Hoogwout, M. (2004). Trust in e-government cooperation. In R. Traunmüller (Ed.), In *Proceedings of the Third International Conference, EGOV 2004* (pp. 332-335). Berlin, Germany: Springer.

ITAC. (2002). *Electronic government: The government of Canada as a model knowledge-based enterprise.* Retrieved January 6, 2002, from *http://www.itac.ca/client/ITAC/ITAC_UW_MainEngine.nsf/0/19f4c6b8e8a6bbf585256810000622b1f/$FILE/pp991015.pdf*

Joia, L. A. (1998). Large-scale reengineering on project documentation at engineering consultancy companies. *International Journal of Information Management, 18*(3), 215-224.

Joia, L. A. (2004). Geração de modelos heurísticos a partir de estudos de casos múltiplos: Da teoria à prática. In M. M. F. Vieira & D. M. Zouain (Eds.), *Pesquisa qualitativa em administração* (pp. 123-149). Rio de Janeiro, Brazil: Editora FGV.

Joia, L. A., & Zamot, F. (2002). Internet-based reverse auctions by the Brazilian government. *The Electronic Journal of Information Systems in Developing Countries, 9*, 1-12. Retrieved September 29, 2002, from *http://www.ejisdc.org*

JUDNET. (2001). *Troca de informações entre o Poder Judiciário e o Sistema Financeiro Nacional (Sistema JUDNET).* Retrieved December 18, 2001, from *http://www.ditech.com.br/judnet.htm*

Keen, P. G. W. (1980). *Information systems and organizational change* (rep. no. CISR-46). Cambridge, MA: Massachusetts Institute of Technology, Center for Information System Research.

Keen, P. G. W. (1991). *Shaping the future.* Harvard Business School Press.

Kieley, B., Lane, G., Paquet, G., & Roy, J. (2001). *E-government in Canada: Services online or public service renewal.* Retrieved December 28, 2001, from *http://www.governance.uottawa.ca/english/Publications/Downloads/Paquet/2001%20-%20EGovernment%20in%20Canada%20%20Services%20Online%20or%20Public%20Service%20Renewal.pdf*

Kling, R. (1980). Social analyses of computing: Theoretical perspectives in recent empirical research. *Comp. Surv., 12*(1), 61-110.

Kraemer, K. L., & Dedrick, J. (1997). Computing and public organizations. *Journal of Public Administration Research and Theory, 7*(1), 89-112.

Lenk, K., & Traunmüller, R. (2001). Broadening the concept of electronic government. In J. E. J. Prins (Ed.), *Designing e-government* (pp. 63-74). Kluwer Law International.

Markus, L. M. (1983). Power, politics and MIS implementation. *Communications of the ACM, 26*(3), 430-444.

Maturana, H., & Varela, F. J. (1980). *Autopoiesis and cognition: The realization of the living.* London: Reidl.

Morra, L., & Friedlander, A. C. (1999). *Case study evaluations* (working paper series no. 2). OED (Operations Evaluation Department), World Bank.

Patton, M. Q. (1990). *Qualitative evaluation and research methods* (2nd ed.). Newbury Park: Sage.

Perri. (2001). E-governance: Do digital aids make a difference in policy making? In J. E. J. Prins (Ed.), *Designing e-government* (pp. 7-27). Kluwer Law International.

Porter, M. E. (1980). *Competitive strategy: Techniques for analyzing industries and competitors.* New York: Free Press.

Traunmüller, R., Chutimaskul, W., & Karning, B. (2004). Regional developments in global connection. In R. Traunmüller (Ed.), *Proceedings of the Third International Conference, EGOV 2004* (pp. 538-542). Berlin, Germany: Springer.

Venkatraman, N. (1994). IT-enabled business transformation: From automation to business scope redefinition. *Sloan Management Review, 35*(2), 73-87.

West, D., & Stansfield, M. H. (2001). Structuring action and reflection in information systems action research studies using Checkland's FMA model. *Systemic Practice and Action Research, 14*(3), 251-281.

Winter, S. (1998). Knowledge and competence as strategic assets. In D. Klein (Ed.), *The strategic management of intellectual capital* (pp. 165-187). Butterworth-Heinemann.

Yin, R. (1994). *Case study research: Design and methods* (2nd ed.). Thousand Oaks, CA: Sage Publications.

Zweers, K., & Planqué, K. (2001). Electronic government: From an organizational based perspective towards a client oriented approach. In J. E. J. Prins (Ed.), *Designing e-government* (p. 92). Kluwer Law International.

Endnotes

1 BacenJud: Brazilian Central Bank's system to answer the justice department's legal claims

2 For further details on this case, see Cavalcanti-Neto, 2002.

Chapter V

Effective Web Site Design: Insight from Information Processing

Deborah E. Rosen, University of Rhode Island, USA

Elizabeth F. Purinton, Marist College, USA

Scott J. Lloyd, University of Rhode Island, USA

Abstract

The Web has been a destination for commerce for well over a decade, so it is time to take stock of what we know, or do not know, about Web design. A review of the literature to date provides evidence that we have really just begun to understand what makes a Web site optimal from a design standpoint. As the Web is first and foremost a source of information, this chapter focuses on Web design from an information processing perspective. Studies are described using cognitive maps and preferences as a possible framework for understanding why some designs are more effective than others in terms of viewers' likelihood of revisit and overall impression.

Introduction

The World Wide Web has been available to companies and consumers for over a decade. Whether the purpose of the site is for communication or the actual transacting of business, design should be a common concern for organizations across industries. It is reasonable, therefore, to take a step back at this time and examine what we have learned in terms of Web design.

The challenge is to sift through the research to understand what features contribute to good Web site design and exactly why this is so. If we knew what people liked in a Web site and why they liked it, we would have a better framework for developing effective Web sites than merely having a list of preferred attributes or features. There are numerous how-to guides available from the popular press. Many are based on technical knowledge (what *can* be done) and the assumption that the Web is like any other print medium (what *has* been done). But the Web, the only interactive medium, is unlike its two-dimensional print cousins. What we know about information processing in the traditional print arena, therefore, may not translate to this interactive world. Specifically, we need to know why Web visitors like what they like (what *should* be done).

Through a review of the literature, this chapter sets out to determine exactly what we know in terms of the technical, the Web as a medium, and why Web visitors actually like what they like. Insight is gained from this examination as to areas that require further investigation if we are to maximize the use of this highly unique medium.

What *Can* Be Done

A review of the literature reveals that progress on the issue of Web site design spans a wide spectrum from how to use graphics to how to optimize your site to get the best search-engine results. Discussed here are only a few of the vast array of topics of the research and handbooks.

The Technical Nature of the Web

There are many technical issues when it comes to Web design. For example, hypertext is central to what makes the Internet different from other print media. Hypertext is characterized as being nonlinear, so the viewer, rather than the writer, can determine the order in which things are read. Hypertext is what gives individual users control and makes them the masters of content (Nielsen, 2004). Albert, Goes, and Gupta (2004) examine how to make use of this Web phenomenon in designing customer-centric Web sites. The gist of this research is that by knowing something about customer behavior from their click streams, you can build a site that more readily gets them to the information they want. But the nature of that behavior is not addressed in this study.

Design Elements

This area of Web site development has probably received the most attention in the popular press. Advice on the use of graphics, banners, buttons, and so forth abound.

- *Graphics*: As a medium with a distinctive page format, the use of graphics on the Web requires specific consideration. One can find a plethora of advice on the use of graphics (mostly from the popular press): whether to use graphics, what type of graphics, how fast the graphics load, and so forth (e.g., http://www.wpdfd.com/wpdgraph.htm). This, of course, is only one element of Web-site design. Graphics appropriately chosen can make the Web site more appealing to a particular target audience, and firms seem to be getting a good handle on how to make this work. But from a research perspective, no one really knows why.
- *Banners, Pop-Ups, Interstitials*: Again, much advice can be found regarding the use of banners, pop-ups, and the like. On the Interactive Advertising Bureau site (http://www.iab.net) you can find standard guidelines for pop-ups (http://www.iab.net/standards/popup/index.asp) as well as guidelines for other Web-specific phenomena. Web guru Jakob Nielsen's Web site is currently posting advice on the use of checkboxes vs. radio buttons (http://www.useit.com/alertbox/20040927.html). Again, these are all features specific to the Web, but these are guidelines that at best allude to the underlying reasons why one option works better than others.

Interactivity and Search Engines

Due to the fact that viewers can actively search for information, search engine optimization is a major concern for all online sites. Consequently, search engine optimization is getting an excessive amount of press (e.g., Greenspan, 2004). But optimizing for search only gets people to your site; the bigger question is how to optimize your site so that surfers are able to find what they want at your site and revisit again, and again, and again.

Relying only on the technical is like focusing on the product and not the market. In spite of what we think we have learned about the value of a marketing orientation (e.g., Narver & Slater, 2000), the literature on Web site design tenaciously clings to a product orientation. In his advice, Jakob Nielsen stipulates that certain unique Web solutions do not work well even though they are technologically advanced. They do not work well because they do not take into account how people process information. The focus remains on the possibilities and idiosyncrasies of Web sites and how to exploit them (Lopuck, 2001) rather than on how Web visitors use these features and how designers can best facilitate the processing of this content.

What *Has* Been Done: The Web as a Print Medium

The Web is a print medium, albeit a very different form of print media than the newspaper or magazine. We know that Web-site designers have adopted certain design conventions (Huang, 2003), but do we know that these are the most effective or why they are effective?

It is not surprising that the initial sites on the Web, when the designers thought about Web design at all, largely borrowed design characteristics from the traditional print media (e.g., http://www.pathfinder.com). For example, the small size of the monitor screen does not allow the Web visitor to view the content in the same way as a large newspaper page, which lends itself to striking, intricate designs. In addition, Web pages cannot handle the same amount of information as a newspaper page (Nielsen, 1999). Now that we have had time to reflect on what we know about this new medium, designers have begun to recognize that the differences embodied in the Web phenomenon must be taken into account. Newspapers such as the *Wall Street Journal*, for example, have recently spent a great deal of time and money revising their Web sites as they recognize not only that these differences exist but that they should be exploited to take full advantage of this interactive medium. This effort, combined with the growing standards of design convention (Huang, 2003), means that more and more Web-design gurus are espousing new models for Web design.

The choices of Web design elements combined with graphic art seem endless. Elements of space, the use of images, the size of images, the use of animation and/or audio, the number of words per line, color, and the size of characters are among just a few of these factors. The work of content design does not stop with selecting the appropriate elements for the particular audience. Content design also involves deciding on the placement of those elements to facilitate their use. Then, of course, there is the need to decide on the type and amount of text. Add to that the fact that everything can be accessed interactively, and it is easy to see that conventional media studies may or may not play out in the same way when you move to the online environment.

What *Should* Be Done: What Makes an Effective Web Site?

Initially, measuring Web-site effectiveness was restricted to counting the number of eyeballs that hit the site. This measure soon proved to be an inaccurate reflection of activity, so organizations next turned to the click-through rate as a more robust measure. Today, sophisticated software tracks the Web surfers' click-stream data trying to understand online behavior (e.g., Sismero & Bucklin, 2004). While these methods measure traffic, none of these methods actually answer the question: What makes a Web site effective in the eyes of the Web user?

Nielsen and Norman (2000) proclaim that users first assess Web-site usability; purchase and payment are second. If a Web site does not give users a good experience, they will not come back. Because it is easier for a consumer to merely go to an alternative supplier on the Web, some organizations never get the opportunity to make a sale. They lose customers on the basis of the usability of their site before customers even explore the product offerings. Consequently, a critical factor for any organization considering an online presence must be how to assess Web-site design apart from the prices and quality of goods and services offered.

Studies have begun to emerge that attempt to address this issue. For example, Aladwani and Palvia (2002) found key that characteristics of a quality Web site include specific content, content quality, appearance, and technical adequacy. Katerattanakul (2002) examined the concept of fitness for use and found that effective Web site design should support either consumer information search, consumer transactions, or consumer enjoyment. Similarly, Chakraborty, Lala, and Warren (2002) found that informativeness and organization were among the factors that explain effective Web sites. None of these studies, however, examine how to actually build effective content or present that content in an organized fashion to facilitate information processing on the part of the Web visitor.

As the Internet is first and foremost a source of information, it seems only logical to approach designing an effective Web site from the perspective of information-processing theory. The task then becomes one of identifying the dimensions upon which to design a Web site as an effective purveyor of information.

At the heart of understanding how people make sense of their environments are the concepts of schemas and cognitive maps. Schemas are cognitive structures that guide information processing (Fiske & Linville, 1980), while cognitive maps are orienting schemas, mental representations that actively seek and integrate spatial information. The latter is, obviously, extremely important to the interactive environment of the Web. Kaplan, Kaplan, and Ryan (1998) and Kaplan and Kaplan (1982) provide insight into assessing a landscape from an information-processing perspective, in particular, the examination of cognitive maps.

Building on the work of Kaplan and Kaplan (1982), the studies described in this chapter address the issue of developing a Web-site effectiveness measure from the perspective of information-processing theory. Using the Kaplan and Kaplan framework, the authors develop the Web Site Preference Framework (WSPF). To understand the context of this framework, information processing theory, specifically the concept of cognitive maps, is first summarized. From this theory, the notion of the Web as a landscape is explored and studies are presented that identify four dimensions that appear to be relevant to assessing Web-site effectiveness.

Cognitive Landscapes

Everyone has heard about information overload. Consumers are inundated with information from a variety of sources on a daily basis. Some of this information is important; some of it is not. The concept of information overload becomes more important in the Web environment wherein a shopper is a click away from literally millions of pages. Information overload increases exponentially online, particularly when Web design is ineffective. Many Web sites appear to have been designed by just transferring a printed brochure to an HTML (hypertext markup language) document without even understanding what could be done to facilitate online usage. How, then, do marketers and Web designers choose content and a layout that does not exacerbate this confusion? Fortunately, theory from cognitive psychology can be applied to this problem. The work of Rachel Kaplan and Stephen Kaplan provides insight into how to use this theory to create environments that both encourage viewing and motivate surfers to further explore a Web site.

Kaplan and Kaplan (1982) recognized that landscape designers (e.g., architects) were not necessarily the best individuals to design a user-friendly landscape as experts see things differently than do first-time visitors. The goal of Kaplan and Kaplan's research was to develop preference patterns for environmental design that incorporate the end users' use of environmental cues in information processing. By identifying the end users' preference patterns, environments could be designed that make it easier for people to feel comfortable entering a landscape because they believe they will be able to function effectively once they actually enter the landscape.

Kaplan and Kaplan's (1982) preference framework is based on the importance of cognitive maps to information processing. Cognitive maps are mental maps that provide individuals with a means of sorting and storing information from the environment. Cognitive maps are an accumulation or summary of experiences. Humans draw on these maps to make their way through an environment. These maps influence "how the environment 'feels' to that person, what is noticed, what is ignored" (Kaplan & Kaplan, pp. 5-6).

The concept of a cognitive map allows someone to go somewhere he or she has never been before and, by recalling previous experiences, have some level of confidence in his or her ability to find his or her way. For example, having used one bank's ATM machine, a consumer would be able to draw on his or her cognitive map of an ATM and be able to quickly use another bank's ATM.

Humans must also be motivated to use and extend these maps. People appreciate and are motivated to use information that helps them expand previous knowledge contained in their cognitive maps. On the other hand, they have trouble understanding and are not motivated to use information that is not connected to the maps they already have. Furthermore, providing too much information creates a barrier to engaging the recipient's internal map. When individuals can take advantage of their cognitive maps, they become more comfortable and confident in their ability to make sense of and explore an environment, and actually prefer designs that enable them to do so (Kaplan et al., 1998).

Kaplan and Kaplan's Preference Framework

Kaplan and Kaplan's (1982) preference framework (Table 1) captures how people use information to satisfy their needs of making sense and exploring in an uncertain world. Through a series of research studies, Kaplan and Kaplan found that making sense (understanding) and exploring (involvement) represent the two basic informational needs.

Time (immediate vs. longer-term) provides a further dimension critical to understanding cognitive preferences. Specifically, individuals have preferences for environments that will enable them to meet these needs now and also in the future. For example, when we ask, "Can I comprehend this situation?" Kaplan

Table 1. Preference framework aspects

	Understanding	Exploration
Immediate	**Coherence** Comprehension Navigability Ease of interpretation	**Complexity** Richness Difference of elements Plentiful elements
Future	**Legibility** Distinctiveness Expectation of future readability Expectation of future navigability Existence of memorable components (landmarks)	**Mystery** Interest in future content Interest in the unknown Anticipation of future involvement Motivation to proceed

Source: Kaplan et al. (1998)

and Kaplan term this *coherence.* When we ask, "Is there enough going on to maintain my interest?" Kaplan and Kaplan term this *complexity*. These aspects, coherence and complexity, allow a rapid assessment of a scene or situation based upon a surface examination "of the patterns of light and dark. Elements and textures in the scene, including their grouping and location are also extracted from this more primary information" (Kaplan et al., 1998, p. 13). Neither complexity nor coherence alone, however, is sufficient to motivate activating one's cognitive map and hence make one feel confident and comfortable in an environment.

Kaplan and Kaplan (1982) found that after this immediate assessment comes an inference of what is deeper in the landscape. They have equated this with moving from an immediate assessment of the lines, patterns, and groupings (coherence and complexity) to projecting what is deeper in the scene (legibility and mystery): in other words, what happens standing at the garden gate (in the immediate environment or two-dimensional space) vs. what happens when one actually walks through the garden (in the future or three-dimensional space). Kaplan and Kaplan found that when viewing scenes, people not only infer a third dimension (a future time), but imagine themselves in the scene. The questions one would have on the latter level would be "Does this environment have a memorable component that will help me find my way in the future (legibility)?" and "Is there a chance to learn more (mystery)?" Having a memorable component (a landmark or a pattern of vegetation in the case of landscape design) assists in understanding an unfamiliar landscape, while being distinctive reduces confusion for finding the way in the future. A promise of future satisfaction will motivate someone to explore a landscape.

Assessment of both the immediate environment and the promise of the future occur rapidly and build upon each other. For example, "coherence and legibility share in common that they provide information that can help with making sense of the environment" (Kaplan et al., 1998, p. 13). An environment that is well organized and distinctive is easier to understand. Similarly, complexity and mystery capture information suggesting that there is more to be seen. Consequently, there is a preference for landscapes that score highly on all four aspects. Subsequent studies provide evidence that people favor landscapes that recognize a preference for coherence and legibility (Lynch, 1960) while at the same time desiring some complexity (Wohlwill, 1976) and mystery (R. Kaplan, 1973).

The Preference Framework and the Webscape

Though designed for physical landscapes, the applicability of the preference framework to the Internet can be easily demonstrated. Information, according to Kaplan et al. (1998), is central to human effectiveness. Thus, how information is presented, both in terms of content and organization, can facilitate or impede its utilization.

Like a physical landscape, the Internet is a highly cognitive, information-laden environment. Consequently, each of the elements of the preference framework can be associated with elements of the Webscape. For example, coherence refers to the degree to which a physical landscape is orderly, relying on the redundancy of elements and textures.

Coherence has been the outcome of many studies on Web sites, though it is not identified as such. The ease of searching out information (Eighmey, 1997; Supphellen, Magne, & Nysveen, 2001) and a nice layout (Supphellen et al.) that is not messy, not cumbersome, not confusing, and not irritating (Chen & Wells 1999, 2002) have been found to be attributes of good Web-site design. Again these studies and others ask respondents what they like in a Web site. Unfortunately, they do not follow this with the next logical step: that of linking information processing to these evaluations.

The notion of coherence also acknowledges the information overload aspect of the Web. Aside from the overabundance of Web sites and Web pages, many sites themselves include a plethora of print copy, graphics, links, banners, and ads. The perception that one needs help navigating through the excess becomes evident. Coherence provides just such help. Chen, Wang, Proctor, and Salvendy (1997) found that one should limit information to a certain range relevant to users' goals, helping users to process the information more deeply. We also know that limiting the amount of content on a Web site will also improve load time.

Complexity refers to the richness or variety of elements in an environment. This variety of elements cannot be excessive, however, as this overwhelms the individual and complicates information processing. REI, a leading purveyor of specialty outdoor equipment, provides examples of each of these elements (http://www.rei.com). REI maintains coherence through the coordinated colors of its

Web site. The dominating color of the Web site (green) gives an outdoorsy feel to the entire site. Complexity, on the other hand, refers to the variety of the elements in a setting. REI's site combines text and graphics/pictures for navigation to provide an environment that does not rely only on text or graphics to tell its story. Consequently, through the deployment of a complementary color scheme, and through a variety of design elements, the user can make sense of and become interested in the REI Webscape.

Recent research studies provide support for complexity as being relevant to Web design. Media richness (Palmer, 2002), the richness and availability of information (Supphellen et al., 2001), and resourcefulness (Chen & Wells, 1999) as attributes of good Web sites are examples of complexity.

Parallels to the Web landscape can also be illustrated for the three-dimensional space elements: legibility and mystery. Legibility is defined by distinctiveness. Memorable components become landmarks that facilitate finding one's way. On the Web, this is similar to having a site map a distinctive graphic or icon, either of which make navigation of the Web site easier and much more straightforward. Based on the premise that a curved path is far more enticing than a straight one, mystery, the final component, enhances one's desire to explore a space by conveying the feeling that much more can be found if one keeps on going. Entertainment as a recurring theme in Web site design studies (Chen & Wells, 1999; Eighmey, 1997) has hinted at the value of mystery.

Many Web sites try to establish mystery by having pages linked together not only technically through hyperlinks, but through the very content itself. On REI's Web site, the menu bar remains positioned at the top and left-hand side of the screen no matter what page one moves to, making the surfer feel that they can find their way on this Web site. REI then entices surfers into their Webscape by inviting them, for example, to "see more best-selling tents" by clicking on a link that will move them deeper into the site.

The preference matrix thus provides a useful way to begin to develop an understanding of how to effectively design a Web site that facilitates information processing. A Web developer can use coherence, complexity, legibility, and mystery to tap into the cognitive maps individuals employ to make sense of their world, thus allowing them to build sites users feel comfortable entering and returning to over and over again. In the remainder of this chapter, we present two studies that were undertaken to develop the Web Site Preference Framework. On the basis of the previous discussion, we test the following hypotheses to demonstrate the usefulness of this scale to Web site development.

H1: The stronger the score on the Web site preference framework factors, the more likely it will be that the site will be revisited.

H2: The stronger the score on the Web site preference framework factors, the more positive will be the overall impression of the site.

Methodology

Study 1

The first step in this program of research was to identify the dimensions that facilitate information processing on the Web. The first study, therefore, was designed to replicate the dimensions identified by Kaplan and Kaplan (1982): coherence, complexity, legibility, and mystery.

Questionnaire Development: The four dimensions — coherence, complexity, legibility, mystery — that comprise the WSPF were operationalized as a five-point Likert scale. Each dimension was measured using multiple items. These items were developed through a variety of techniques. First, studies used to develop the preference framework were reviewed for insight into item format. Second, to adopt these questions to the Web, the critical-incident technique was utilized. In this phase of questionnaire development, open-ended questions were administered to a student population with the same demographic characteristics as those used in the study presented below. For example, the respondents were asked to identify characteristics of Web sites they liked (e.g., what helped them to make sense of a Web site). These responses were then content analyzed using the themes from the work of Kaplan et al. (1998) and Kaplan and Kaplan (1982).

Instrument Testing: In a pretest, multiple-item measures were used in an attempt to capture the rich concepts of the WSPF. An initial draft of the scale was used to collect data, and two sets of analyses were performed to refine the scale.

In this analysis, three factors emerged that fit well with Kaplan et al.'s (1998) and Kaplan and Kaplan's (1982) dimensions of coherence, complexity, and legibility (see Table 2). Because mystery did not emerge as a factor, additional items were written in the attempt to better delineate this dimension. One item, "Is friendly to first-time visitors," was changed to "Would be friendly to first-time visitors" in the attempt to capture the future temporal aspect of mystery.

Using the three factors that emerged, item-to-total correlations and reliability analysis were performed to assess the reliability of the factors. Coefficient alphas were well above 0.70, which suggests a satisfactory level of reliability (Nunnally, 1978).

Table 2. Factor loadings: Study 1

	Coherence	Complexity	Legibility
Has logically organized information	.814		
Makes sense	.800		
Is well written	.703		
Has enough content to be interesting to repeat visitors	.675		
Is easy to navigate once you get past the home page	.652		
Caused me to want to learn more	.586		
Uses many visual images		.821	
Graphics and pictures fit with content		.804	
Uses different types of visual images		.765	
Unlike other sites I have visited			.882
Has created a distinct identity			.829
Has memorable elements			.563
Coefficient alpha	*.867*	*.838*	*.765*

Data Collection: Participants in the study were 211 undergraduate students at two Northeastern institutions of higher education. The group was comprised of an equal number of males and females with an age range of 18 to 25. Their use of the Web for research as well as purchasing indicates familiarity with the Web. Only 1% of the respondents never used the Web for research, while 47% had never purchased anything online. Over 82% use the Web for research on a weekly basis. Consequently, the participants were generally conversant with navigation on the Web and, in fact, were representative of the online population at the time of the study (Strategis Group, 1999).

The students were asked to evaluate the Web sites while thinking of the site as a whole. The sites selected represent the broad spectrum of sites that Web surfers might visit. The sites were selected from a variety of categories that this population might patronize (Table 3). As actual Web sites were chosen for this study, the participants' familiarity with the sites as well as familiarity with the brands were also assessed as a part of background data collection efforts.

Data collection took place in a controlled setting. University computer labs with one computer per participant were utilized. All students were given instructions and began the survey at the same time. The students were instructed to wander through each site as if they were searching for information using their regular surfing behavior. They were instructed not to complete the evaluation of the site until they had navigated through the home page and at least three subpages of the

Table 3. Web sites utilized in study

Study 1	Study 2
Banana Republic	The Gap
Net Grocer	Banana Republic
The Gap	J. C. Penney
Macy's	United Airlines
L. L. Bean	Southwest Airlines
Nordstrom	L. L. Bean
REI	Hershey's Chocolate
Peapod	Nordstrom's
Wall Street City	Godiva's
Market Guide	Bluefly

site. The order of site evaluation was randomly distributed to avoid an order effect. Students were supervised to minimize any discussion and to make sure Web sites, navigational software, and hardware were functioning.

Results and Discussion: Each construct was measured with multiple items and was subjected to the scale development and purification procedure (Churchill, 1979). On the basis of item-to-total correlations, three ill-fitting items were dropped. The remaining 12 WSPF items were factor analyzed. As was true in the pretest, dimensions consistent with the work of Kaplan et al. (1998) and Kaplan and Kaplan (1982) emerged; however, from this factor analysis, three, not four, factors were identified (Table 3). The three factors that emerged (coherence, complexity, and legibility) explained 69.3% percent of the total variance. These factors displayed coefficient alphas above 0.70, which suggests a satisfactory level of reliability (Nunnally, 1978). Factor scores were calculated by averaging across the items for each participant's score. A WSPF score was then calculated by summing the factors.

Coherence in this study, with one exception, is identical to Kaplan and Kaplan's (1982) construct of coherence. The items included in this factor describe an environment that is logical and friendly. In addition to Kaplan and Kaplan's development of the construct, coherence in this study captures that the site is well written and easy to navigate, two items that make making sense on the Web possible.

Complexity implies the Web-site design contains a variety of images that satisfy the desire to explore the environment. Like Kaplan and Kaplan's (1982) complexity, the construct here is defined by the use of many varied visual images. Furthermore, using images that fit the site content ties the complexity of the site to this content-enhancing comprehensibility and encourages rather than discourages exploration. This is a very important factor to online consumers. A recent study by Fram and Grady (1997) found that Web shoppers wanted more visuals and graphics as this would improve the online shopping environment.

Similarly, legibility mirrors legibility as developed by Kaplan and Kaplan (1982) and includes being memorable and distinctive. In addition, legibility in this Study 1 includes being unlike other sites. This construct provides assurances that understanding in the future can be facilitated through the creation of a distinct identity for the site. This is a must in order to stand above other sites in the eyes of Web surfers.

The factor that did not emerge as expected was that of mystery. Mystery may, in fact, not be relevant on the Web. Consumers, though purchasing online in ever-increasing numbers, actually turn to the Web more for information than purchase. According to a recent study by The Strategis Group (1999), Web use for research is four times greater than Web use for purchasing. The promise of appropriate information rather than intrigue may be far more important in explaining Web site preferences. If the information is clear, interesting, and distinctive, you will want to go on. Web surfers have a short attention span and need to know how to use a page as well as how to read it. Effort spent on intrigue would, therefore, not be an attractive characteristic to a Web surfer.

Because all of the four factors did not emerge, hypothesis testing was deferred until Study 2.

Conclusions: The fact that mystery did not emerge needs to be further examined. There are at least two possible explanations for this. One is that the construct was not effectively captured by the items. Is it really an inappropriate factor, or were the items designed to capture this factor inadequate? A second and more likely explanation is that, in fact, mystery may not be a relevant dimension to understanding information-processing behavior on the Web. As time (or the absence thereof) is one of the factors that drive people to utilize the Web, being coherent, unambiguous, and direct (as opposed to mysterious) may in fact be a distinguishing characteristic of the Web as a form of a cognitive landscape. Building on these results, Study 2 investigates an alternative construct that might be more appropriate for inclusion in the WSPF.

Study 2

The Web environment is not like any other medium. The Web's potential to surpass other media forms lies in its ability to create and sustain a two-way dialogue (Rafaeli & Sudweeks, 1997; Rogers & Allbritton, 1995). Consequently, when considering the Web as a medium, assessing its ability to only convey information is insufficient. By getting consumers to be willing to dig deeper into the Webscape, they might prefer to interact with the information presented rather than engage in mystery. Furthermore, the outcome of interactivity is engagement, in other words, a desire to pursue a relationship between the communicator and the audience. To adequately assess a Web site's effectiveness may require assessing the site's ability to provide an interactive information environment.

Definitions of interactivity have emerged as a part of the new communication technologies. Ha and James (1998) suggest that interactivity can be defined as the extent to which the communicator and the audience respond to each other's communication needs. Williams, Rice, and Rogers (1988) define interactivity as having three components: control, the exchange of roles, and mutual discourse. Control is important as it captures the element of choice in an interactive process. In an interactive communication, participants have flexibility in what they view; they have control as they can select what to access. The ability to exchange roles allows participants to be both senders and receivers of information. Mutual discourse captures the relationship-building nature of interactive communications. Communications build on previous communications in interactive communications. Focusing on the social-interaction research, Rafaeli's (1988) definition adds a hierarchical component to the definition of interactivity by describing it as a continuum having three distinctive levels: (1) two-way (noninteractive) communication, (2) reactive (or quasi-interactive) communication, and (3) fully interactive communication. To determine whether interactivity is a more relevant three-dimensional-space element that motivates the audience to explore a site further, a second study was developed.

Questionnaire Development: To capture the constructs of coherence, complexity, and legibility, items generated for this study were taken from the purified scale used in Study 1. Items designed to capture interactivity were adapted from previous studies (e.g., Fortin, 1999) so that they measured the future possibilities of interactivity afforded by a site. All items were again operationalized as a five-point Likert scale. In addition, an attempt was made in this second study to improve the validity of the instrument with a closer replication of Kaplan and Kaplan's (1982) original studies.

To be able to perform initial testing of the Web Site Preference Matrix as a measure of Web effectiveness, Web effectiveness was operationalized as two items: (1) overall impression of the site and (2) likelihood of revisit. These items were measured using a five-point Likert scale. There is precedence for the use of single-item measures (e.g., Anderson & Narus, 1990).

Data Collection: Participants in the study were 119 undergraduate students at two Northeastern institutions of higher education. The group was 48% male and 52% female, with an age range of 18 to 25. As was the case in the first study, the majority of participants were familiar with the online environment. The majority of students (84%) use the Web weekly for research, while a substantial number (39%) had never purchased anything online.

The participants were given similar instructions for their viewing assignment as described in Study 1, and the instrument was again administered in a controlled setting. Ten e-retailer sites (Table 3) selected from a variety of categories that this population might patronize were selected for this study. As actual Web sites were chosen for this study, the participants' familiarity with the sites was assessed as a part of background data collection efforts.

Results and Discussion: Each construct was measured with multiple items and was subjected to the scale development and purification procedure (Churchill, 1979; Moore & Benbasat, 1991). On the basis of item-to-total correlations, one ill-fitting item was dropped. The remaining 16 WSPF items were factor analyzed. As was true in the first study, three dimensions consistent with the work of Kaplan et al. (1998) and Kaplan and Kaplan (1982) emerged. In addition, a fourth factor emerged as well (Table 4). The four factors that emerged explain 0.73% percent of the total variance. These factors displayed coefficient alphas above 0.70, which suggests a satisfactory level of reliability (Nunnally, 1978). Factor scores were calculated by summing across the items for each participant.

As was the case in the first study, items comprising coherence, complexity, and legibility are similar to Kaplan and Kaplan's (1982) operationalization of these constructs.

The only difference in Study 2 arose from the inclusion of an item meant to capture interactivity. One item, "Really gave me some control," loaded on coherence and not on interactivity as expected. The remaining items that comprise the fourth construct capture the three levels of interactivity prescribed by Rafaeli demonstrating the hierarchical nature of the construct. On Level One, the site allows for two-way communication. On Level Two, the site will reply to a specific inquiry (reactive). On Level Three, the site made the participants feel that the company really cares about them and wants to develop a relationship (fully interactive).

On careful reading, the items that do load on this fourth construct do not appear to fully represent interactivity as defined earlier. Being allowed to have a two-way dialogue with a company that conveys the impression that someone will answer questions and, furthermore, someone cares about the customer seems much more reflective of a relational component. Consequently, the fourth dimension of the matrix is labeled connectedness rather than interactivity.

To test whether this four-factor solution was predictive of Web-site effectiveness (as measured by the overall impression and probability of revisit), nonparametric tests were conducted. General linear models were not used because

Table 4. Factor loadings: Study 2

	Coherence	Complexity	Legibility	Connectedness
Has logically organized information	.739			
Is easy to navigate once you get past the home page	.714			
Really gave me some control	.665			
Makes sense	.649			
Is well written	.539			
Uses many visual images		.892		
Uses different types of visual images		.875		
Graphics and pictures fit with content		.819		
Has created a distinct identity			.816	
Unlike other sites I have visited			.811	
Has memorable elements			.711	
Makes me feel the company cares about me				.778
Makes me feel like they are listening to me				.763
Would allow me to easily communicate with the company if I had a specific question				.740
Makes me confident that the company will respond to my requests				.705
Makes me feel the company wants to have a relationship with me				.679
Coefficient alpha	*.881*	*.903*	*.812*	*.889*

Table 5. Chi-Square Test and Kruskal-Wallis Test[1]

	Factor 1	Factor 2	Factor 3	Factor 4
Chi Square	391.5958	467.6933	579.9852	467.8144
Df	12	18	18	16
P	<.0001	<.0001	<.0001	<.0001

assumptions regarding normality could not be validated. However, under all nonparametric tests (e.g., Kruskal-Wallis, Median One-Way Analysis, Van der Waerden One-Way Analysis, and Savage One-Way Analysis), all factors were significant at the 0.0001 level (see Table 5).

Conclusion and Directions for Future Research

Developing an effective Web site design is not as easy a proposition as the numerous how-to guides would lead us to believe. Effective Web design must be built upon an understanding of how Web visitors process Web content. Through cognitive maps, the studies presented in this chapter provide evidence that Web-site design can benefit from adopting an information-processing perspective, thus providing insight for both researchers and practitioners.

The four factors (coherence, legibility, complexity, and connectedness) of the Web site preference framework (Table 6) provide four design criteria upon which to base not only the choice of design elements, but the composition of the layout as well. Furthermore, from debriefings conducted as a part of these studies, we have evidence of site design features that can be linked to the factors of this framework. For example, participants indicated that the use of categories, uncrowded presentation (simple subject headings describing broad categories rather than lengthy lists), and minimizing text contributes to coherence, while mouse-over graphics contribute to complexity. Similarly, having a mini home page on every page supports legibility while having a "contact us" section with e-mail, live chat, and/or voice mail contributes to connectedness. The links between site features and the WSPF provide Web designers with specific features that should be included in their design decisions.

From a research perspective, the Web site preference framework is important for several reasons. First, it provides a means of tying the assessment of Web site design to how individuals process information online. The Web site preference framework puts conventional wisdom (Web sites should be well written) and information-processing phenomena into a workable framework. For example, it provides evidence that being coherent is not just about being easy to navigate: It is also about being in control. Being distinctive from other sites and having memorable elements (legibility) also contributes to making sense of a Web site. Furthermore, providing individuals with the motivation to explore is accomplished by (1) selecting different visual elements that fit with the content (complexity), and (2) making the surfer feel that there is the possibility for a relationship (connectedness).

Table 6. Web site preference framework

	Understanding	Exploration
Two-dimensional	Coherence	Complexity
Three-dimensional	Legibility	Connectedness

Development of the Web site preference framework needs to be continued. Study 2 provides evidence that control is a component of coherence, and this seems to contradict previous research on interactivity. This difference could be the result of the fact that studies of interactivity have not focused on other elements of information-processing behavior that are taken into consideration in the development of the WSPF. Further work needs to be done to understand what role control plays from a broader information-processing perspective.

That connectedness was a better example of the fourth dimension rather than interactivity may lie in the very nature of the Kaplan and Kaplan (1982) theory. Their work is predicated on how an individual processes information and cues before stepping into a landscape. Similarly, the studies reported in this chapter were designed to capture that initial evaluation as this was felt to be an approach that would capture the first critical assessment made by a Web surfer. For a visitor to fully factor in the interactive capacity of a Web site, however, probably requires actually entering the Web site and testing the waters. This interpretation of the findings needs to be further explored in future studies.

While Study 2 measures the likelihood of revisit and overall impression, purchase behavior was not examined. Further research needs to be done to determine the relationship between the Web-Site Preference Framework and actual purchase behavior. In addition, the role that product choice and price plays in online purchases needs to be incorporated in future studies. Of course, as the Web continues to grow, the characteristics of the Web population will change. Further studies need to take into account the changing nature of the online population in the choice of appropriate participants for study.

A question arises as to whether information processing and Web visitor preferences would change depending on whether the Web site is used for information gathering or purchase. Chakraborty, Lala, and Warren (2003) found business-to-business Web site visitors differ in their preferences depending on whether they were purchasing or not. This research should be extended to information processing and to business-to-consumer Web visitors.

As a dynamic medium, effective Web design needs to logically take advantage of all the technology that the Web has to offer. Yet, due to its dynamic nature, what attracts Web visitors today may not be effective tomorrow because of changing tastes, changing technologies, and changing users. Through an understanding of how individuals process information online, however, we can better identify *why* Web visitors like what they like, thus providing better guidance for those designing the sites of tomorrow. The Web site preference framework is one step in this direction.

References

Aladwani, A. M., & Palvia, P. C. (2002). Developing and validating an instrument for measuring user-perceived Web quality. *Information & Management, 39*(6), 467-476.

Albert, T. C., Goes, P. B., & Gupta, A. (2004). GIST: A model for design and management of content and interactivity of customer-centric Web sites. *MIS Quarterly, 28*(2), 161-182.

Anderson, J. C., & Narus, J. A. (1990). A model of distributor firm and manufacturer firm working partnerships. *Journal of Marketing, 54*, 42-58.

Chakraborty, G., Lala, V., & Warren, D. (2002). An empirical investigation of antecedents of B2B Websites' effectiveness. *Journal of Interactive Marketing, 16*, 51-72.

Chakraborty, G., Lala, V., & Warren, D. (2003). What do customers consider important in B2B Websites? Journal of Advertising Research, *43*(1), 50-61.

Chen, B., Wang, H., Proctor, R. W., & Salvendy, G. (1997). A human-centered approach for designing World-Wide Web browsers. *Behavior Research Methods, Instruments, & Computers, 29*(2), 172-179.

Churchill, G. (1981). A paradigm for developing better measures of marketing constructs. *Journal of Marketing Research*, 64-73.

Eighmey, J. (1997). Profiling user responses to commercial Web sites. *Journal of Advertising Research, 37*(3), 59-67.

Fiske, S. T., & Linville, P. W. (1980). What does the schema concept buy us? *Personality and Social Psychology Bulletin, 6*(4).

Forrester Research, Inc. (2001, November 7). *eCommerce will prevail through the economic downturn in 2002* (press release). Retrieved from *http://www.forrester.com*

Fortin, D. R. (1997). *The impact of interactivity on advertising effectiveness in the new media.* Unpublished doctoral dissertation, University of Rhode Island, Kingston.

Fram, E. H., & Grady, D. B. (1997). Internet shoppers: Is there a surfer gender gap? *Direct Marketing*, 46-50.

Greenspan, R. (2004). *Study: Top e-tailers neglect SEO.* Retrieved from *http://www.clickz.com/stats/markets/retailing/article.php/3414941*

Heeter, C. (1989). Implications of new interactive technologies for conceptualizing communication. In J. L. Salvaggio & J. Bryant (Eds.), *Media use in the information age: Emerging patterns of adoption and consumer use* (pp. 217-236). Hillsdale, NJ: Lawrence Erlbaum Associates.

Kaplan, R. (1973). Predictors of environmental preference: Designers and clients. In W. F. E. Preiser (Ed.), *Environmental design research* (Vol. 1, pp. 265-274). Stroudsburg, PA: Dowden, Hutchinson and Ross.

Kaplan, R., Kaplan, S., & Ryan, R. L. (1982). *Cognition and environment: Functioning in an uncertain world.* New York: Praeger Publishers.

Kaplan, R., Kaplan, S., & Ryan, R. L. (1998). *With people in mind.* Washington, D.C.: Island Press.

Kaplan, S. (1973). Cognitive maps, human needs and the designed environment. In W. F. E. Preiser (Ed.), *Environmental design research* (Vol. 1, pp. 274-283). Stroudsburg, PA: Dowden, Hutchinson and Ross.

Kaplan, S., & Kaplan, R. (1982). *Cognition and environment.* New York: Praeger Publishers.

Katerattanakul, P. (2002). Framework of effective Web site design for business-to-consumer Internet commerce. *INFOR*, 57-70.

Lopuck, L. (2001). *Web design for dummies.* Hoboken: Wiley.

Lynch, K. (1960). *The image of the city.* Cambridge, MA: MIT Press.

Moore, G. C., & Benbasat, I. (1991). Development of an instrument to measure the perceptions of adopting an information technology innovation. *Information Systems Research*, 192-221.

Neisser, U. (1976). Cognitive maps. In *Cognition and reality.* San Francisco: Freemand and Company.

Nielsen, J. (1999). *Differences between print design and Web design.* Retrieved January 24, 2003, from *http://www.useit.com*

Nielsen, J. (2004). *Checkboxes vs. radio buttons.* Retrieved from *http://www.useit.com/alertbox/20040917.html*

Nielsen, J., & Norman, D. A. (2000). Usability on the Web isn't a luxury. *Informationweek*, 65-73.

Nunnally, J. C. (1978). *Psychometric theory* (2nd ed.). New York: McGraw-Hill Book Company.

Rafaeli, S., & Sudweeks, F. (1997). Networked interactivity. *Journal of Computer Mediated Communication, 2*(4).

Rogers, E. M., & Allbritton, M. M. (1995). Interactive communication technologies in business organizations. *The Journal of Business Communication, 32*(2), 177-195.

Shaw, T., Arnason, K., & Belardo, S. (1993). The effects of computer mediated interactivity on idea generation: An experimental investigation. *IEEE Transactions on Systems, Man, and Cybernetics, 23*(3), 737-745.

Sismero, C., & Bucklin, R. E. (2004). Modeling purchase behavior at an e-commerce Web site: A task-completion approach. *Journal of Marketing Research, 41*(3), 306-327.

Slater, S. F., & Narver, J. C. (2000). The positive effect of a market orientation on business profitability: A balanced replication. *Journal of Business Research, 48*(1), 69-82.

Strategis Group, The. (1999). *Internet use trends: Mid-year 1999.*

Williams, F., Rice, R. E., & Rogers, E. M. (1988). *Research methods and the new media.* New York: The Free Press.

Wohlwill, J. F. (1976). Environmental aesthetics: The environment as a source of affect. In I. Altman & J. F. Wohlwill (Eds.), *Human behavior and environment* (Vol. 2). New York: Plenum.

Endnote

1 The Median One-Way Analysis, Van der Waerden Analysis, and the Savage One-Way Analysis were also performed and yielded similar results. In the interest of space, only the Kruskal-Wallis test is shown here.

Chapter VI

Personalization of E-Commerce Applications in SMEs: Conclusions from an Empirical Study in Switzerland

Petra Schubert,
University of Applied Sciences, Basel (FHBB), Switzerland

Uwe Leimstoll,
University of Applied Sciences, Basel (FHBB), Switzerland

Abstract

Personalization of e-commerce applications is an issue that is gaining increasing importance with the advancing maturity of such systems. There is already e-commerce software on the market offering integrated e-shop and personalization functions. However, the available software is too time-consuming and expensive for SMEs. With this in mind we saw a need to investigate the potential for personalization from the particular angle of SMEs. In addition to some theoretical fundamentals of personalization, this paper presents the results of an empirical study. With the help of a survey, we investigated the application potential for personalization tools in Swiss companies. The conclusions show that SMEs are (still) skeptical towards e-commerce applications which use personalization. It furthermore becomes clear that the heterogeneity of organizational and technical conditions impedes the development of standardized tools.

Introduction

The paper presents the results of a longitudinal, publicly funded research project about "personalization of e-commerce applications run by SMEs." The quality of e-commerce applications has been constantly improved over the last few years. Especially the major suppliers run Web sites that are of noticeable usefulness and are reliable enough to assure the customer's trust (Schubert & Dettling, 2002). This is confirmed by continuously positive growth figures in online business.

Personalization is always targeted at the fulfillment of a special requirement. It can be aimed at people as well as at organizational roles in companies (e.g., a purchasing agent). Personalization — as we understand it — starts AFTER THE LOGIN. The mere speculation about a user on the basis of local cookies on the client PC which has the smack of spying on someone does not fall into the scope of our discussion. Personalization is context sensitive (regarding output for a certain user) and requires learning (by the system). The interface between the customer and the system is called "point of interaction" (POI). Personalization can be an important component for the success of an e-commerce application because it is beneficial to all interested parties (Buxel, 2001).

For the personalization of e-shops there are integrated software packages available, such as, e.g., One-to-One (Broadvision), Dynamo Relationship Commerce Suite (Art Technology Group), Personalization Manager (Net Perceptions) or ADAPTe (ResponseLogic), which already supply the full range of e-commerce applications. These products are expensive applications generally destined for use in large companies. The standardized online shops partially used in SMEs only contain rudimentary tools for the personalization of transactions.

We believe that a separate consideration of these companies is significant because SMEs differ from large corporations in many respects. In the context of the personalization of e-commerce applications the specific features of SMEs become particularly relevant. SMEs are generally characterized by the fact that they have limited resources and often lack the benefits of economies of scale. With regard to using e-commerce applications, above all limited financial resources, poor conceptual knowledge, lacking IT resources and low economies of scale can all have a negative effect. The low economies of scale result primarily from the small size of the company because the usefulness of e-commerce applications increases with the number of transactions completed and the volume of turnover generated. SMEs offer specialized, qualitative high value products in their small market segment which are tailored to customers' needs (product differentiation). It is precisely for this reason that elements of personalization should also be applied in e-commerce.

At the beginning of the project, we had to examine if the essential technical preconditions are fulfilled in SMEs and how much demand there is for personalization. The potential for personalized e-commerce applications in SMEs as well as the requirements for the development of a personalization tool, result from these aspects.

The paper starts with the description of the research design and a short literature review on personalization. The following sections present the findings of an empirical study. We summarize the findings and draw some conclusions for the currently emerging potential for the implementation of personalization software in SMEs in Switzerland.

Research Design

The research findings presented in this paper stem from a project which has been carried out since 1999 together with different SMEs in Switzerland. The reason to start this project was a perceived disadvantage regarding personalization possibilities in e-business applications suitable for SMEs, as compared to the possibilities of big companies. As mentioned earlier there are software packages for personalization available on the market but those systems are often too expensive for SMEs. The situation is comparable to the adoption of SAP in big companies and "light-weight ERP solutions" like Abacus in SMEs. SMEs need "easy" solutions — preferably standard software — which are cost-effective and can be customized according to the company's special purposes.

As shown in Figure 1, the project started with an empirical survey in the region. The result encouraged the authors to proceed with the project. On the one hand, SMEs attribute a high value to their relationship with the customer and recognize the potential of the electronic relationship which comes with an e-shop. On the other hand, the survey showed that the situation for the implementation of personalization (state of know-how, existing hard- and software, willingness to invest, etc.) is not very favorable in most SMEs. One important result was the need for setting a focus on the further development of existing ERP systems, which were already in use by SMEs (ERP II).

In order to illustrate the potentials of personalization we created a "handbook personalization" which shows the possibilities from a perspective we thought

Figure 1. Steps and results of the longitudinal research project

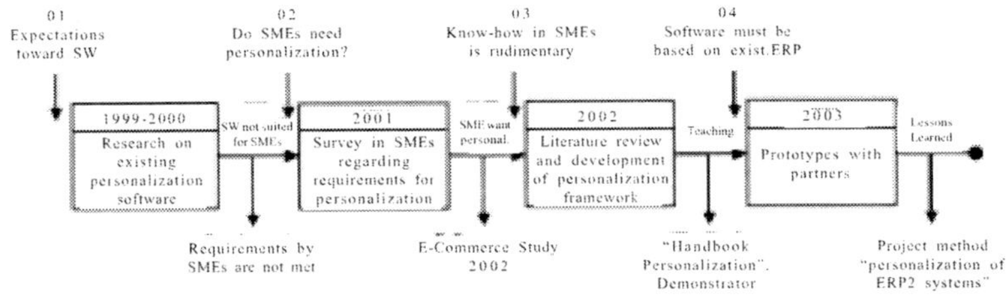

adequate for SMEs (Schubert & Leimstoll, 2002). Additionally, we built a "software demonstrator" that is publicly accessible on the Internet. It displays the possibilities in a graphical form. The following development of the personalization framework was the basis for the current development of prototypes of ERP extensions with four industry partners. The last objective was the development of a generic project method for the introduction of personalization of e-commerce applications on the basis of ERP II systems which is still going on. ERP II is a term coined by Gartner Group which they define as an application and deployment strategy to integrate all things enterprise centric. It is basically the further development of the inherently internal ERP system into a boundary-spanning system, which integrates into its peer systems run by business partners and customers. Figure 1 shows the steps of the project with its premises (01-04) and its milestones.

This article does not reflect PhD research. It is an experience report from a joint project with different small- and medium-sized companies in Switzerland. The empirical study presented in this report was not intended to be statistically sound, but was used as a guidance reference for the further orientation of the project. We intended to test some of our assumptions about the current state of development of ERP-based e-business applications at the beginning of the project. The study was meant to either confirm or refute our assumptions. Since most SMEs in Switzerland are not yet sophisticated Web users, most of the questions were phrased indirectly pointing at different aspects of personalization rather than naming the concept specifically. The outcome of the study was used for the setting of project objectives (which resulted in the development of a project method). Although the survey was based on a questionnaire and we gathered data, we did not perform a rigorous statistical testing. The project would not have benefited from a statistical analysis, but we were in need of getting some answers to our assumptions. We were especially interested in the state of technological equipment, the starting point for personalization, and a major prerequisite for our future project.

We are aware that the following analysis is focused more on the relevance of our research objectives than on academic rigor. The analysis of the survey data is simplistic. Only descriptive statistics are given and conclusions are drawn from these. This choice was made deliberately. In past projects we learned that dealing with SMEs requires a pragmatic rather than a theoretical approach. Otherwise the results cannot be made accessible because SMEs reject them as being "too academic." Given these limitations we are still convinced that academia can profit from our findings.

Literature Review on Personalization

Personalization is about selecting or filtering information objects or products for an individual by using information about the individual (his customer profile). The information displayed on the screen is specifically tailored for the user. From a technical point of view, meta information of products or information objects is matched against meta information of users (stored in the customer profile). Personalization can be tailored to a group of people or to a specific individual. In the latter case, where the information or products are only customized for one single individual, we speak of individualization as a special form of personalization. Personalization uses information about customers. The general term for stored customer information is "user profile" or in the context of electronic shopping "customer profile." There are various ways how e-shop operators can cultivate customer profiles e.g., "historically" by storing (1) interaction with the Web site (click stream) or (2) purchase transactions or "explicitly" by (3) asking for preferences or (4) ratings or by recording (5) contextual information (e.g., time, date, place). What formerly seemed to be possible only for the corner shop whose storekeeper knew all her clients personally, reaches a new potential in the online medium where every client leaves traces and thus "teaches" the system how to treat him differently from the other customers. This form of mass customization becomes feasible with the use of predefined rules, which can be built into e-commerce environments. These automatically personalized Web sites do not achieve the high quality of corner shops, but they help to establish a personal dialogue with the customer, tying him or her closer to the electronic offer. Additionally, the time spent by the client to "teach" the system leads to increased switching cost. The underlying prerequisite is that the customer really wants to be addressed personally.

What Makes Personalization Possible?

The ability to deliver personalization rests upon (1) the acquisition of a "virtual image" of the user, (2) the availability of product meta information, and (3) the

Figure 2. A multi-disciplinary view of systems and concepts in which personalization plays an important role

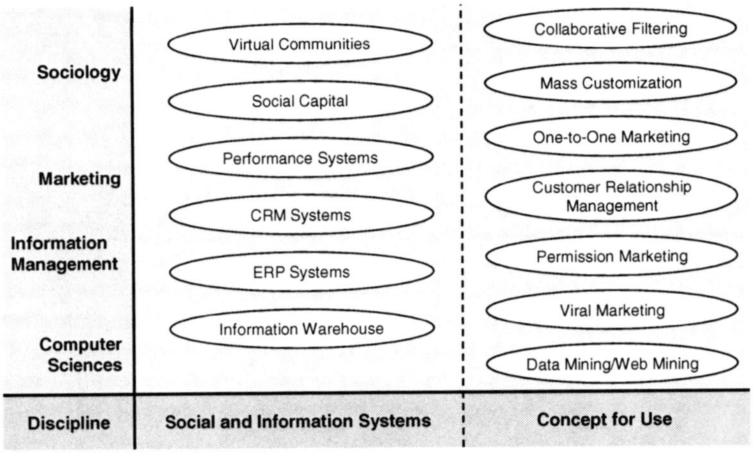

availability of methods to combine the datasets in order to derive recommendations for the customer.

In this section we will give an overview of the main concepts and systems that make (automatic) personalization possible in today's businesses. These driving forces can be categorized by disciplines, which are involved in personalization. The consideration of personalization ranges from a technical view in computer sciences, to the economic principles of information management and marketing, as far as to the global perspective of sociology. Figure 2 displays a matrix of disciplines in which personalization plays an important role.

Virtual Communities are groups of people who come together on Internet-based platforms for communication and collaboration around a common topic of interest. These community platforms gather community knowledge (stored in customer profiles), which according to Peppers and Rogers is the following:

"Community knowledge comes from the accumulation of information about a whole community of customer tastes and preferences. It is the body of knowledge that a 1:1 enterprise acquires with respect to customers who have similar tastes and needs, enabling the firm actually to anticipate what an individual customer needs, even before the customer knows he needs it." (Peppers & Rogers, 1997, p. 231)

This way, knowledge about the community can help to customize and even personalize the service for an individual member.

Social Capital was defined by Pennar (1997) as "the web of social relationships that influences individual behavior and thereby affects economic growth". The existence of social capital is the basis of many virtual communities. An example for this is the Internet Chess Club (ICC). The ICC is a virtual gaming platform on the Internet, where a large part of the leading chess masters and more than 45,000 paying members are interacting (Ginsburg & Weisband, 2002). A large number of volunteers is contributing to the smooth operation of this community. The information of all members of the community—moderators, chess masters and other active members—forms the social capital of the community. Another example is the Internet auction platform eBay (Schonfeld, 2002). Social capital enables eBay to make use of the creativity of millions of entrepreneurs (the sellers and buyers) on their Web site. By adding information themselves and by publishing their own marketing the users take on the main work on the platform. Social capital additionally leads to the subjective feeling of objectivity, which Peppers and Rogers call "agent objectivity":

"Every customer wants genuinely objective, unbiased advice in a commercial transaction, and every customer knows that sometimes this advice will run counter to the seller's own interests." (Peppers & Roger, 1997, p. 244)

If the recommendations of a seller are only based on the comparison of customer feedback, then this information is objective and without bias — it represents the subjective attitudes of other customers. Amazon.com also uses this idea in their customer reviews. The result is the development of an "objective agent," an intermediary, that just provides opinions of others on its platform.

Performance Systems were developed by product vendors in the 1990s as a solution for differentiating their own products from the competition (Belz et al., 1991). Performance systems bundle the core product or service with different additional products or services in order to propose a specific solution for individual customers or specific target groups. They thus represent a "personalization" of the standard set of products which a company offers. Peppers and Rogers (1997) call these combinations "product-service bundles." The additional services make the product unique and attractive for the customer. To design these product bundles an information basis is needed that allows the anticipation of the customers needs. An electronic offer could additionally enable bundles that include complementary products of other manufacturers, delivery, installation and training, service and an emotional customer experience. Ratings or experience reports supplied by the virtual community can e.g. be seen as such additional services.

Customer Relationship Management systems are enterprise information systems which support the relationship with the customer. They are used to communicate with the customer or to assist communication with the customer. CRM systems store all kinds of information about the customer, ranging from basic information such as name and address to the full history of company-customer interaction (e.g., inquiries, purchase transactions, claims). The databases contained in CRM systems are a valuable information source which can be harnessed for personalization. Most CRM systems are built upon existing software for Enterprise Resource Planning (ERP).

ERP systems comprise a whole class of software products that are geared at the automatization and control of business process throughout the whole company. They supply software modules which support almost all critical business processes and departments (e.g., accounting, procurement, human resources, sales, production, logistics). ERP systems can be found as core systems for Supply Chain Management, Customer Relationship Management and e-business applications. These more specialized information systems often source their data from the ERP databases which contain the critical company information, namely product catalogs, customer database, sales figures, accounting and the like. In recent years, ERP systems have been further developed to meet the requirements of the Internet. In the last three years, traditional ERP functionality has been extended into the Internet environment. Customers can directly access data in the ERP system using specially developed e-business interfaces. ERP systems which have been equipped with these new e-business interfaces (for e-shops) have been labeled "ERP II" by Gartner Group. Within the scope of our SME project we are striving to further develop SME-suitable ERP systems into ERP II systems.

An *Information Warehouse* as a result of a data mining process is an additional — extended, improved and optimized — representation of sales and customer data. Warehouses are usually used to store raw data for later use in executive information or decision support systems (EIS or DSS). In the context of our study of e-commerce applications, these databases are an important source for personalization and digital marketing.

Where is Personalization Used?

After having looked at different information systems, with their respective databases serving as "enablers of personalization" we will now look at different concepts for the "application of personalization."

In electronic business media *mass customization* can be implemented by a pre-defined rule system which combines the advantages of mass production (the same e-shop and the same product catalog for all clients) with the strength of made-to-order production (personalized web pages and customized products). *One-to-One Marketing* is the embodiment of personalization in marketing. The underlying idea is to serve and address every customer according to his or her specific needs. *Customer Relationship Management* has already been implicitly described in the section about CRM systems. It aims at supplying every employee (or even the client himself, e.g., in an e-shop) with the relevant information about a customer at the right time to be able to offer him an individualized service. *Permission Marketing* is the idea of giving the customer the chance to select the kind of marketing message he or she wants to receive (Godin, 1999). The customer grants a company "the right to supply him with marketing information" in a preferred category. Regarding electronic communication, it is a means to prevent spamming.

Viral Marketing uses the customer's network of (social and business) relationships. A marketing message is sent to one customer with an incentive to forward this message to his friends and/or business contacts. Every time the message is forwarded to more than one person it is multiplied—a process which reminds of the outbreak of a disease (thus the word "viral"). The idea is similar to what we know as "chain letters." *Data mining* is the process of storing and interpreting data recorded in business processes, e.g., POS transactions. Companies are interested in generating information warehouses which are sources for executive information systems. Whereas data mining addresses all kind of real-world business processes, *Web mining* focuses especially on data accrued from the Web. Data mining is the extraction of interesting and potentially useful information from user activity on the Internet (Kimball & Merz, 1996; Spiliopoulou, 2000; Adomavicius & Tuzhilin, 2001).

Research Instrument and Design of the Study

The survey was driven by the future objectives of the research project. In several interviews with our SME project partners, we identified possible problems which were likely to be encountered in our quest of developing personalization functions for e-business applications. Based on these assumptions, a set of questions was developed and sent to companies.

The interests of SMEs are in the forefront of the survey, which was carried out in the summer of 2001. On the one hand, the study was meant to give information about whether there is a demand on the part of SMEs for personalized e-commerce solutions and how their exploitation can be evaluated. On the other hand, the study was intended to show which technical and organizational preconditions are already met by the companies surveyed. For the recording of the primary data, a standardized questionnaire was developed and repeatedly tested in pretest interviews. The regional chamber of commerce sent the printed

Collection period	August / September 2001
Collection area	Basel-City and Basel-Country
Collection method	Written survey with standardized questionnaire
Size of companies	SMEs with from 1 to 250 employees
Target group	Mainly managers and those responsible for IT in SMEs in addition to independent IT service providers and management
Returns	271 questionnaires, 216 from SMEs and 55 from experts; rate 16%

questionnaires to 1,250 randomly chosen SMEs in the region. Excluded from the survey were several freelance professions such as doctors and other companies whose main function is construction and utilities. The questionnaire was directed to members of management and those responsible for IT in SMEs.

Besides SMEs, the survey was also meant to reach providers of IT services and management consultants with the aim of including additional expert opinions. For the group of experts, the questionnaire was slightly modified and provided online. The experts were asked to answer the questions from the point of view of a company well-known to them (one of their customers). The table above summarizes the most important details about the design of the survey.

The explanations that follow are an excerpt from the study — primarily presenting the answers given by the representatives from SMEs. The "expert" opinions will only be listed explicitly if they differ significantly from those of the SMEs.

Findings of the Study

We start by describing the characteristics of the companies surveyed. This is followed by an analysis of the significance of marketing and sales processes for SMEs. The third paragraph discusses Internet use and the exploitation of personalized e-commerce applications. Finally, the technical and financial prerequisites for the development and operation of e-shops will be discussed.

Characteristics of the Companies Surveyed

The survey reached primarily *owners or managing directors* (53%) and *people responsible for IT* (25%) in SMEs. The remaining questionnaires were

Figure 3. Number of employees (full-time equivalent)

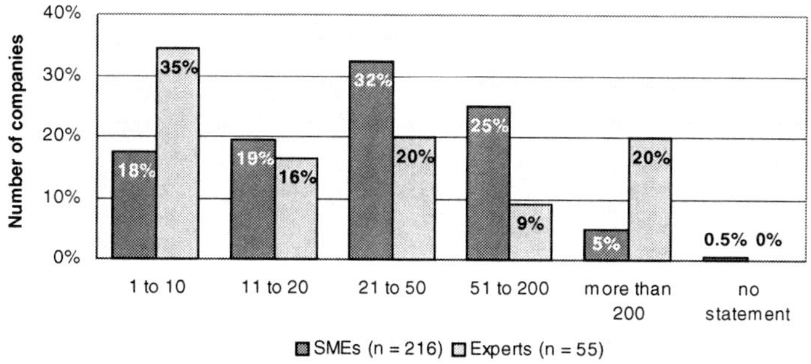

completed by people who fulfilled *both functions* (6%) and from people who had *other leadership functions*. In the group of experts, *providers of IT services* or *management consultants* (45%) were addressed. Other experts were *owners or managing directors* of the company (29%).

In the sample, almost all sectors are represented, the majority being from the industrial (22%) and services (20%) sector. Trading companies account for 12% and IT/telecommunications firms for 8% of the sample. Grouping the companies according to size categories illustrates that these SMEs are mainly represented by companies employing between 21 and 200 employees (Figure 3). They account for 57% of all SMEs surveyed. A further 37% are small firms with between one and 20 employees. Only very few larger firms with more than 200 employees are represented.

In the expert group the size distribution looks different; here there are a lot of small firms with between one and 10 employees. They account for 35% of the companies evaluated by the experts. The share of firms with more than 200 employees (20%) is noticeably high. The high proportion of small as well as large companies in the sample of experts can be explained by the fact that the IT and telecommunications field is strongly represented in this sample. Firms in this sector are often very small (e.g., IT service providers) or very large (e.g., telecommunications corporations). This relationship is also expressed in the number of customers. The SME group shows a far more balanced distribution of customer numbers.

The sample cannot be seen as representative regarding distribution of company size. We can also assume that there is a dominance of those companies which are already tackling the e-commerce issue, or at least intend to in the near future.

Significance of Marketing and Sales Processes for SMEs

The e-commerce activities of SMEs are the focus topic of the survey. In order to evaluate the future role of e-commerce in the companies, we first tried to clarify the general significance attached to sales activities. Figure 4 shows a few selected factors which were evaluated in view of their significance for the companies' future competitiveness.

The companies are in agreement that the *quality of the products* will play an important role in the future. The sales-related factors, which are of special interest here — *customer advisory service, delivery reliability*, and *close customer relations* — follow in places two to four. They are evaluated higher than the *efficiency of internal business processes*, the *application of IT* in general and *production costs*. It is somehow surprising that *marketing and advertising* rank at the bottom (Figure 4).

There are only slight differences between the appraisal of the SME representatives and the opinion of the experts. The importance of *marketing and advertising* (1.07) for example ranks higher. On the other hand, in the eyes of the experts, *efficiency of internal business processes* and *production costs* were least important (last two places).

Figure 4. Success factors of SMEs, based on the statements of SMEs

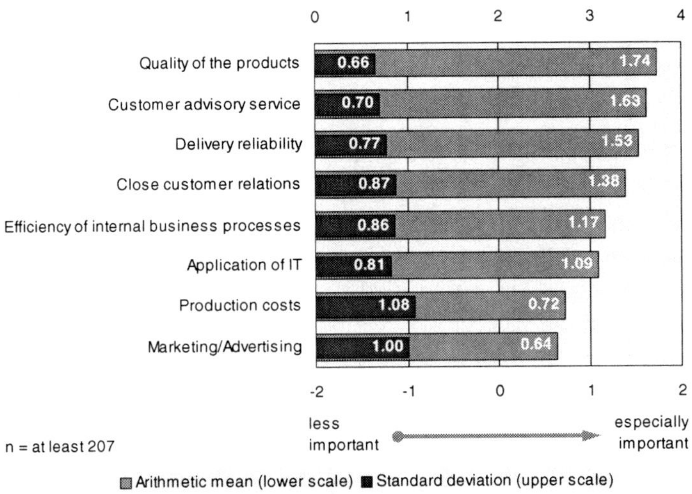

From this result it follows that sales-related activities are of high significance for the competitiveness of the companies. The support granted by information technology also plays an increasingly important role.

Current E-Commerce Activities of Swiss SMEs

Empirical studies show that the intensity of Internet use in Switzerland is steadily increasing. However, the concept of Internet use is seldom considered in a differentiated way. The following graphic shows the ways in which the Internet is used by the responding companies. The kind of use indicates to some extent the stage of maturity of the e-business applications implemented in the companies. Figure 5 shows the results of the question on Internet use. Whereas the degree of extensiveness ("yes" answers) declines from top to bottom, the degree of planning ("planned" answers) first increases, and then declines again in the area of more sophisticated applications ("no" answers).

The results regarding e-mail use show higher figures than presented by similar studies; e-mail is used by almost all of the companies surveyed, and there is no company that does not at least plan to use e-mail for communication. *Company and product presentation* is also widely realized. If we include the figures on planned use, then soon 98% of the companies will present information about the company on their Web site and 92% will present information about their products on the Internet. The evaluation of the experts hardly deviates from this.

Internet applications that go beyond the functions of e-mail and homepage are rarely encountered (Figure 5). *Ordering facilities via the Internet* (offered by 32% of companies surveyed) as well as *use of the Internet for online marketing and advertising* are also included among the functions carried out to a considerable extent. Taking into account planned use, these two forms of use will, in the future, reach a degree of 56 and 60%. They are considerably more widespread in the companies of the experts; there, *ordering via the Internet* is possible in 44% of the companies, and 53% use the Internet for *online marketing and advertising*. Together with companies planning to apply these uses, the degree of use reaches 77%.

In addition, there is a group of Internet functions which have hitherto been put into practice in very few SMEs. These are functions which take up a special position with particular relevance to the personalization of e-commerce applications (in parentheses: carried out/planned): *personal registration of the customer on the Web site* (11/14%), *customer access to previous orders* (6/11%), and *customer access to inventory* of the supplier (6/8%). Among the expert companies, 22% already offer *personal registration*. Planned use is significantly higher than reported by the SMEs; in the future, about a quarter to almost a half of the expert companies will offer these otherwise rarely implemented functions.

Figure 5. Different uses of the Internet, based on statements of SMEs

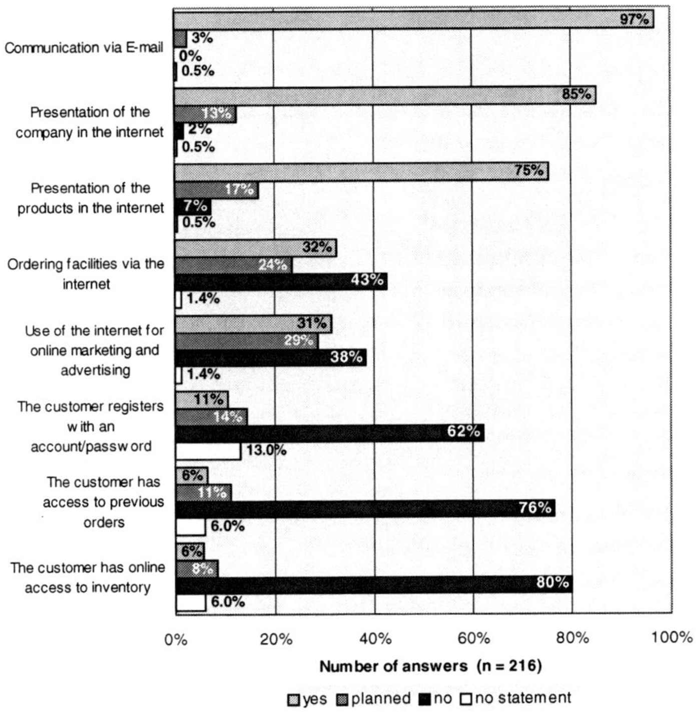

Basic Functions in Personalized E-Commerce

After the first block of more general questions about marketing and e-commerce activities, the questionnaire presented a block of questions targeted at specific functions of personalized e-commerce applications. When developing the questionnaire, we were aware that there is an abundance of functions related to personalization, but we had to limit the questionnaire to the ones that seemed most relevant to our project (Figure 6).

Out of the functions presented in Figure 6, only a few are considered truly significant. On the five-point scale (from -2 = less significant to + 2 = very significant) , only three functions score over zero, starting with *addressing the customer personally and individually*. In this case almost three-quarters of the SMEs responded to the answer with "1" or "2." The significance of *online ordering facilities* is 0.30, which means that *online ordering facilities* are in

Figure 6. Significance of the functions of a personalized e-commerce application (SMEs and experts in comparison)

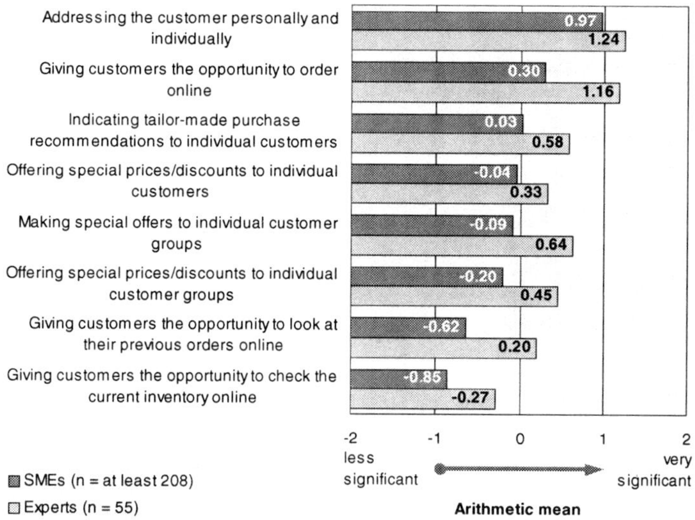

the group of functions which are considered "significant." The same is true for *purchase recommendations tailor-made to the customer* (0.03), for the *opportunity to offer special prices/discounts to individual customers* (-0.04), and for the *opportunity to make special offers to individual customer groups* (-0.09).

Ranked among the functions evaluated rather "less significant" we find *prices and discounts for individual customer groups* (-0.20), *access to previous orders* (-0.62) and *online access to inventory* (-0.85). Note that the last function, *access to inventory*, is not applicable in certain sectors (e.g., services, which comprised 14.4% of the sample).

In contrast to the SMEs, the experts attributed higher scores to the functions of personalized e-commerce applications (Figure 6). We could measure the highest difference in the evaluations for *online ordering* (D = 0.86), *previous orders* (D = 0.82) and for the *opportunity to make special offers to individual customer groups* (D = 0.73). These findings illustrate that SMEs are cautious in the assessment of personalization efforts — more cautious than the group of experts.

Figure 7. Additional functions of e-commerce applications to support marketing and sales processes (SMEs and experts in comparison)

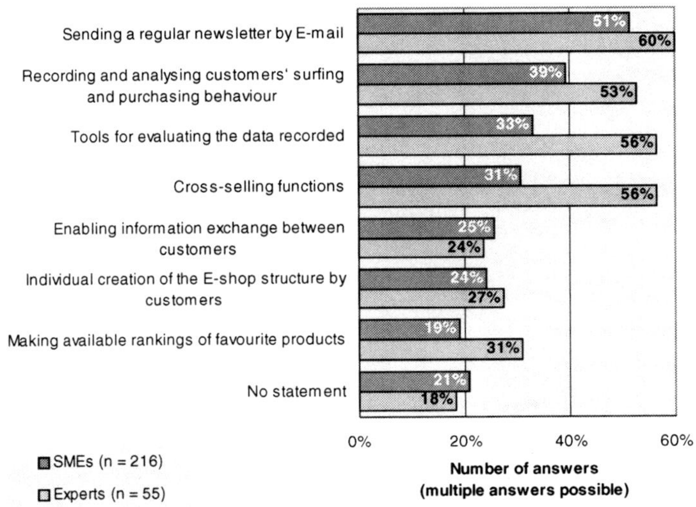

Additional Functions of Personalized E-Commerce

E-commerce solutions support and offer a number of further functions related to personalization. Figure 7 compares the opinions of SMEs and experts regarding the usefulness of the application of these additional functions. The questions were phrased abstractly (not in the language of information systems) in order to analyze which additional functions future e-commerce solutions should offer. This was evaluated indirectly with the help of questions regarding marketing and sales processes.

In the comparison both groups named the following functions most frequently: *newsletter via e-mail*, *analysis of customers' surfing and purchasing behavior*, *evaluation tools* and *cross-selling functions*. However, the frequency of these answers is far lower among the SMEs than among the experts.

The group of functions which were not mentioned frequently by neither of the two groups includes: *information exchange between customers* (a community function), *customer creation of e-shop structure* and *rankings of favorite products*. Clearly, only a few companies envision the positive effects of personalization on marketing and sales processes. However, *rankings of favorite products* was at least mentioned by 31% of the expert companies.

Figure 8. Outsourcing of Web server operation, based on statements of SMEs

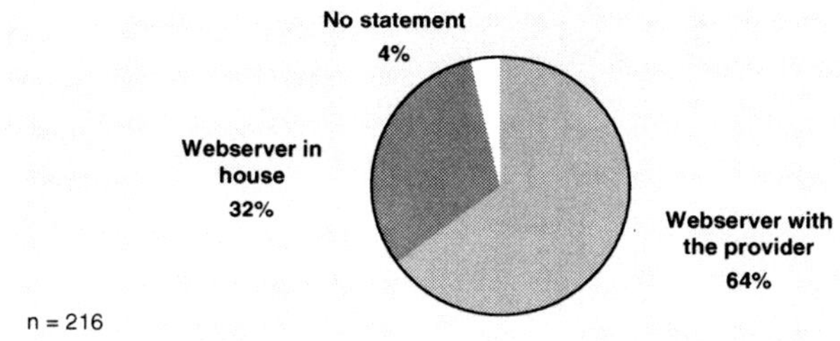

The comparison between SMEs and experts indicates that the SMEs are more skeptical towards the opportunities of personalized e-commerce solutions. Possibly they cannot yet imagine how a personalization tool could look like in practice. The purpose of a newsletter is certainly the easiest concept, and most of the respondents are familiar with this marketing tool. The experts' statements show that this group estimates that the personalization of e-commerce will have a thoroughly positive effect on the marketing and sales processes of SMEs.

Development and Operation of E-Shops

Sixty-four percent of the SMEs and 69% of expert companies responded that the Web server is run by a provider (*Web server with the provider*) (Figure 8). This means that the majority of companies has outsourced this service. It was surprising for us to see that however almost a third of SMEs operate their *own server*.

For the support of certain functions of an e-shop, such as online access to inventory or direct order processing, the seamless integration with an existing ERP system is necessary. For this reason we included a question on the current use of ERP systems. The findings show a very heterogeneous distribution of ERP systems. The high rate of responses in the category '*other provider*' (64%) reflects this situation. ERP systems are often specialized for certain sectors. *ABACUS*, *SAP (R/2 or R/3)* and *NAVISON* are the only systems which showed a certain dominance in use by SMEs. In the expert companies *SAP* and *ABACUS* dominated, resulting in 15 and 13% of responses. The heterogeneity of the systems show that the development of a personalization tool for SMEs (an original objective of our project) had to be independent from a *specific* ERP vendor.

Figure 9. Standard software vs. individual software in the e-shop field

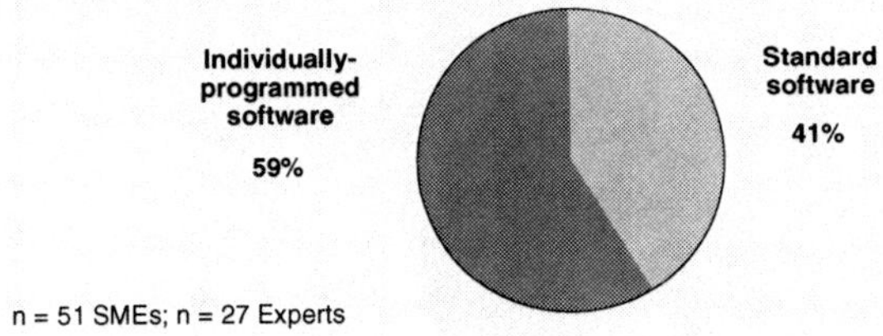

The study confirmed that online shops have not been broadly introduced by Swiss SMEs. Sixty-four percent of SMEs and 47% of the experts state that they do NOT use any e-commerce software for the communication with their customers (on the sell side). The results show that there is no market leader for e-shop software. From the companies that already have an e-shop, 59% use *individual software* and 41% *standard software* (Figure 9).

We assume that some of the respondents did not distinguish between "individually programmed software" and "individually customized standard shop solutions," so the figure of 59% might be a bit misleading. Since around the time of our survey most ERP vendors were developing their e-business solutions with selected pilot customers and then adding the e-business module to their standard product suite, we estimate that the actual number of individually programmed e-shops is a bit lower.

In the future, only 43% of the SMEs and only 31% of the expert companies intend to remain without an e-shop (Figure 10). All other companies plan to invest substantially in their e-shop in the next two years; most of these companies (15% of SMEs and 24% of experts) have opted for an investment sum ranging between US$7,800 and 39,000 per year (6,400 to 32,000 EUR).

At first sight, the study design may appear as if very little of the survey actually dealt with personalization. This has the following reason: most SMEs in Switzerland are not yet sophisticated Internet users, so we decided to phrase most of the questions indirectly, rather hinting at personalization potentials than explicitly naming them. Without using the actual word "personalization," the answers to the questions nevertheless help us in deciding the future steps of the project.

Figure 10. Investments in own online shop in the next two years

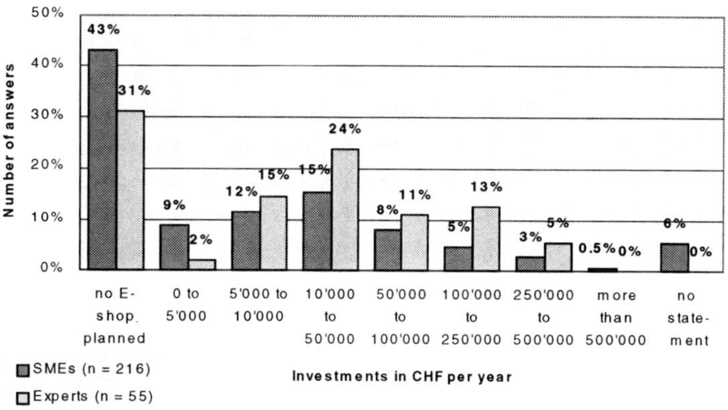

Interpretation of Findings and Future Research

Some interesting statements about the need for personalization tools in SMEs can be deduced from the findings of the survey. SMEs value very highly — independently of e-commerce — marketing and sales-related success factors: customer advisory service, delivery reliability and close customer relationships are, according to their statements, of high importance for the success of the company. In the marketing and sales area, the strengthening of customer relationships and the quality of customer information are crucial. Altogether the results show that for SMEs, addressing the customer personally is a pivotal aspect for their company's success. Wherever e-commerce applications can be used at the interface to the customer, personalization can play an important role.

The findings of the study have encouraged us to proceed with our project to develop personalization tools for SMEs. An overwhelming number of SMEs are planning to invest considerable sums in their e-commerce solutions in the next few years. Many small companies have already established their own Web sites.

The study shows that the development of personalization software is no easy undertaking. Reality shows, however, that a world of widely differing systems is being used in internal systems (ERP) on the one hand, and in e-commerce applications (e-shop software) already in use on the other hand. The operating systems used also differ greatly. Furthermore, the majority of SMEs do not operate their own Web servers, but have outsourced this task to an Internet service provider. The only possible approach is that we involve ERP solution providers who develop standard modules to extend their existing systems. In an initial project we are developing a project method for the definition of requirements for personalization of ERP-based e-commerce solutions. The project method combines a set of useful creativity tools, elements of classical project management together with a method for rapid screen design. The most important issue is to make sure that people in SMEs and ERP vendors understand each other and manage to jointly develop a new generation of SME-suitable ERP II systems which include customizable, easy-to-use personalization features. Continuing with our research, we have initiated further projects with SMEs and their respective ERP vendors where we constantly apply and refine the method.

The difficulty in the development of a software lies in the fact that SMEs are today cautious about the use of such systems, and the technical preconditions are far from optimal due to the wide difference in the systems employed. Nevertheless, many companies are planning substantial investments in this field over the next few years. All in all, the study findings have confirmed our assumption that a need for standardized, inexpensive personalization software for SMEs exists, based on existing ERP systems, or will arise within the next few years.

References

Adomavicius, G. & Tuzhilin, A. (2001). Using data mining methods to build customer profiles. *IEEE Computer, 34*(2), 74-82.

Belz, C., Bircher, B., Büsser, M., Hillen, H., Schlegel, H. J., & Willée, C. (1991). *Successful performance systems*, (orginal title: "Erfolgreiche Leistungssysteme"), Stuttgart: Schäffer Verlag für Wirtschaft und Steuern GmbH.

Buxel, H. (2001). *Customer profiling in e-commerce: Basic methodology, application problems and management implications* (original title: Customer Profiling im Electronic Commerce: Methodische Grundlagen, Anwendung sprobleme und Management-implikationen), Aachen: Shaker.

Ginsburg, M. & Weisband, S. (2002). Social capital and volunteerism in virtual communities: The case of the Internet chess club. In *Proceedings of the 35th HICSS Conference,* Hawaii.

Godin, S. (1999). *Permission marketing: Turning strangers into friends and friends into customers.* New York: Simon & Schuster.

Kimball, R. & Merz, R. (1996). *The data Webhouse toolkit: Building the Web-enabled data warehouse.* New York: Wiley & Sons.

Pennar, K. (1997, December 15). The ties that lead to prosperity. *Business Week*.

Peppers, D. & Rogers, M. (1997). *Enterprise one to one: Tools for competing in the interactive age*. New York: Ban-tam Doubleday Dell.

Schonfeld, E. (2002). eBay's Secret Ingredient, *Business 2.0*. Retrieved February 17, 2002, from *http://business2.com/articles/mag/0,1640,37743,FF.html*

Schubert, P. & Dettling, W. (2002). Extended Web assessment method (EWAM): Evaluation of e-commerce applications from the customer's viewpoint. In *Proceedings of the 35th HICSS Conference,* Hawaii.

Schubert, P. & Leimstoll, U. (2002). *Handbook Personalization of Electronic Commerce Applications* (original title: "Handbuch zur Personalisierung von Electronic-Commerce-Applikationen"), Basel: Arbeitsbericht Nr. 7 des IAB, Fachhochschule beider Basel (FHBB), 2002.

Spiliopoulou, M. (2000). Web usage mining for Web site evaluation. *Communications of the ACM (CACM), 43*(8), 127-134.

Previously published in the Journal of Electronic Commerce in Organizations, 2(3), 21-39, July - September 2004.

Chapter VII

An Interventionist Approach to E-Commerce Implementation in SMEs

David Tucker,
Manchester Metropolitan University Business School, U.K.

Anthony Lafferty,
Manchester Metropolitan University Business School, U.K.

Abstract

SMEs (small and medium-sized enterprises) make a vital contribution to the economic and social well being of most European nations. Many SMEs have invested in an e-commerce presence on the Internet. They are motivated by the potential benefits, which include increased competitiveness and efficiency. In the U.K. there are many examples of entrepreneurial SMEs that have successfully embraced e-commerce. However, there are also many more SMEs that could benefit from Web-based e-commerce but have not yet done so. This chapter sets out the main factors that are inhibiting SMEs from adopting e-commerce. It then reports on a two-year teaching company scheme (TCS) between the Manchester Metropolitan University Business School (MMUBS) and Partwell Ltd., a U.K.-based manufacturing SME. This TCS was designed to improve the competitiveness of Partwell by establishing an e-commerce Web presence. The chapter highlights the philosophy and objectives of the TCS programme and describes the process of technology transfer between Partwell and MMUBS. One of the authors became immersed in the company for the two-year duration of the project, and the data presented here are based on his experience as an initiator of change. The action learning method by which e-commerce was introduced into the company is described and the results are evaluated against contemporary technology diffusion literature. It is shown that gaining the trust of key employees at Partwell, coupled with the adoption of a soft approach to e-commerce implementation, is a critical success factor. Finally, the chapter reports on the benefits that Partwell has gained through the TCS experience.

Introduction

In the U.K., SMEs account for over 99% of the 3.7 million total businesses and for 50% of total U.K. turnover (£1 trillion). This is compared with 49% of the turnover from the 7,000 largest businesses (Small Business Service, 2003). In 2001 some 540,000 U.K. SMEs (including microbusinesses of less than 10 employees) were trading online, which is an increase of 20% from the 2000 figure of 450,000. The biggest growth in the percentage of businesses trading[1] online has been amongst microbusinesses; in the small, medium-sized, and large bands, the percentage has fallen (Dixon, Thompson, & McAllister, 2002)

However, there is an apparent reluctance for many small businesses to adopt e-commerce. A 2001 survey showed that although 77% of SMEs had an Internet connection, only 10% used the Web for selling and only 3% regarded themselves as an e-business (Figure 1).

In a survey undertaken by the U.K. Federation of Small Businesses (FSB), only 6% of the 18,500 respondents regularly used the Internet to review business opportunities or bid for work, and only 9% of respondents regularly used the Internet for e-commerce purposes (Carter, Tagg, Ennis, & Web, 2002).

A number of factors have been identified that help to explain this low uptake. The Commission of the European Communities (2002, p. 15) investigated SME barriers to B2B (business-to-business) e-commerce and found that "SMEs are constrained by having fewer resources than larger companies. This includes

Figure 1. ICT Use: All U.K. SMEs (percent, multiple responses possible)

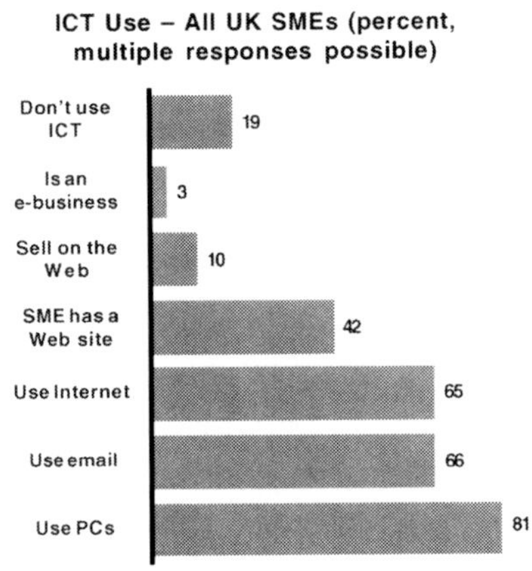

Source: SBS Omnibus Survey, Autumn 2001 (business weighted)

not only financial resources but also time and management resources. They also often have a limited capacity to take risks or engage in speculative activities."

Another factor that is often highlighted as a barrier is that small organisations encounter a bewildering variety and amount of sources of information about emerging technologies (Geisler, 1992). Often, this information comes from vendors of Internet technology and is thus not regarded as impartial. Furthermore, it has been noted that the most significant barrier to e-commerce for SMEs is that they do not perceive their products or services are suited to electronic trading (Commission of the European Communities, 2002). A 2002 survey by the Department of Trade and Industry (DTI; 2002) showed that the take-up of information and communication technologies by U.K. SMES had actually reversed. SMEs use of Web sites had declined from 1.9 million to 1.5 million. Among businesses that once had a Web site or external e-mail but decided to discontinue it, the most common reason given was that it was not used enough. Among those that had never had either facility, the main reason was that they did not see any benefit for their business (DTI).

More recent research has suggested that in the adoption of new technologies such as e-commerce, an often vital factor is the intervention of change agents who achieve positive results by gaining the trust of SMEs (Berranger, Tucker, & Jones, 2001). Trust is gained by the change agent becoming intimately involved with organisations and understanding their idiosyncrasies, objectives, and culture. Hence, the required level of trust may only be achieved after considerable time. A TCS project requires one or more individuals to become intimately involved with an organisation for a period of at least two years. Hence, a TCS provides an ideal environment in which to nurture a trusting relationship.

The Teaching Company Scheme[2]

TCS is a U.K. government-sponsored technology transfer scheme that enables firms to take advantage of the wide range of expertise available in the knowledge base. The knowledge base partner is a higher education institution or research organisation. Through TCS, partnerships are formed between U.K. companies and groups of staff, often from different disciplines, in the U.K. knowledge base organisations. The partnerships are called TCS programmes. TCS programmes focus on innovation projects that are central to the strategic development of the company partners. The projects are supervised by staff from both the company and knowledge-base partners, and implemented by recently qualified graduates (known as associates) who are recruited to the partnership.

Each TCS programme involves one or more associates, and can last two, three, or exceptionally four years. The TCS has been in operation for over 25 years and there are currently over 1,000 TCS schemes in operation that are focused (but not exclusively) on small companies.

Each TCS is essentially a collaboration between three partners: the company, the knowledge base, and the associate. Each programme is extensively defined and must have clear strategic importance to the company. The associate must be a recent graduate with a good first degree. The associate is based at the company for the duration of the project, but is employed by the knowledge base partner. Each associate is allocated an industrial supervisor (from the partner company) and an academic supervisor (from the knowledge-base partner). The associate and the supervisors meet on a weekly basis to discuss the progress of the project and to deal with any issues that may have emerged. Every three months there is a local management committee meeting at which a representative of the government attends to evaluate progress and offer advice.

Programme Benefits

Each of the participants in a TCS project is expected to gain tangible benefits from the experience.

The Company:

- business improvements
- establish new markets
- develop new products
- improve processes and quality
- consultancy from an academic
- access to specialist skills not otherwise present within the company
- continuing relationships with academic institution
- associates not on the payroll
- increase in profitability and competitiveness

The Knowledge Base:

- develop staff and reputations; relate research and teaching to business
- high-quality academic publications
- case-study material for teaching purposes
- long-term association with local industry

The Associate:

- a chance to work on a research-based project but receiving a company salary
- a chance to gain more of an understanding of the way industrial organisations work
- an opportunity to take a higher level degree
- enhanced future career prospects

The Partwell TCS

The Company

Partwell Ltd., a family-owned company established in 1979, was initially involved in cutting technology in the shoe, leather, and textile industry. As this industry slowly declined and became more competitive, the company sought new products and markets. As a consequence, they moved into industrial plastics approximately five years ago. The company's core business is still in cutting technology, although for the automotive, packaging, and fashion and textiles industries. The company also operates a lucrative sub-business that involves refurbishment and resale of press cutting machines. Historically, the market for these machines has been the U.K. During the course of this TCS programme, it has emerged that there is a significant overseas market for press cutting machines, and Partwell is actively seeking to exploit this opportunity. The company employs 23 staff and is based on one site in Blackburn, Greater Manchester, in the northwest of England.

The company's managing director (MD) has recognised that the radical changes taking place in their competitive environment demands equally radical changes within the company. He has a degree in computer science and is thus aware of the benefits that ICT could offer to the business. On his instigation, a range of ICTs was already in use at Partwell including accounting and sales order-processing systems. The MD has also invested £100,000 ($176,000) in a computer numerically controlled (CNC) machine. This was a substantial investment decision for Partwell and required significant investment in training. This is consistent with the findings of Blackburn & McClure (1988) who found that the owner's or manager's attitude, knowledge of IT, experience, and willingness to train others was often more influential than business size and sector in understanding the use of ICT in SMEs. In their classification, Partwell's MD can be seen as an enthusiast, someone who has high IT skills and a positive attitude toward IT. Similarly, the associate appointed to this TCS was a recent graduate of the BSc Business Information Technology Management programme at MMUBS and was keenly interested in exploiting e-commerce at Partwell.

The company's strategic aims are to achieve a more dominant position in the industrial plastic markets whilst seeking new markets abroad for cutting technologies. Partwell aims to raise its reputation in these markets using the extensive tacit knowledge held within the company to differentiate itself from competitors. It is recognised that to achieve such a goal, the company must review and improve its underpinning business systems. In this regard, Partwell is consistent with the typology of ICT as suggested by Southern and Tilley (2000). They distinguished between low, medium, and high users of ICT in small businesses and identified a number of endogenous (internal) and exogenous (external) factors pertinent to each type. Amongst the soft characteristics of the high user are that there is a well-articulated rationale for the use of ICT and that the owner or manager has strong perceptions of the benefits that the technology can bring.

The Situation

Partwell's product range, both traditional and new, contains a high information content. Customers do not buy products off the shelf; rather, they contact the company with a specific requirement, whether for industrial plastics or cutting tools, and the company must respond quickly and accurately to such enquiries. This ability to provide timely, accurate, and comprehensive information serves to distinguish Partwell from its competitors and is thus a source of competitive advantage. Before the commencement of this TCS project, such technical information was stored in a diverse range of media. Some was contained in the company database, more was located in numerous filing cabinets and storage boxes situated in various locations around the company premises. More significantly, the most important information was stored as tacit knowledge, held in the minds of a number of key personnel. Consequently, accessing this information was ineffective.

This situation created two major weaknesses. First, when customers contacted the company with an enquiry, if the answer required the tacit expertise of a specific individual who was not currently available, then responding to that enquiry may have taken days. Even enquiries of relatively minor complexity could meet with significant delay. Consequently, the potential customer could place an order with a rival company. Second, Partwell was highly vulnerable should a key staff member leave the organisation, taking their tacit knowledge with them and thereby removing a valuable resource.

The Solution

The TCS programme required the associate to undertake an intensive period of industry analysis. Over a six-month period of research, it was clearly established that there was a need to enable customers to interact with the company in a more effective way. The Internet was seen as an ideal way to implement this strategic objective. An Internet presence would be developed that would provide basic information about the company and its products, and would be accessible to anybody with an Internet connection. A frequently-asked-questions (FAQs) page would be added to the Web site and would provide several benefits. First, from the customer's perspective, the FAQs page would provide instant access to more in-depth technical questions. This would save the need for the potential customer to telephone or send a fax to Partwell. Also, the level of technical knowledge encapsulated in the page would serve to engender a certain level of trust amongst casual browsers. A further benefit felt within the company was that fewer low-level technical enquiries were made by telephone and fax, thus more time was available to take orders and to devise and pursue more innovative marketing strategies. The FAQs page became dynamic. The Web site allowed customers to send enquiries directly to Partwell via e-mail. If the answer to a particular enquiry was not available on the FAQs page, then once Partwell staff had researched the answer, it could be placed onto the page. Thus, a virtuous circle was established whereby the Web site became a continuously updated repository of technical knowledge. This reduces direct enquiries and allows Partwell staff more opportunity to pursue income-generating activities.

The Implementation

The decision to implement the Internet site as a marketing tool, rather than a sales medium, meant that there would be minimal effect on business processes. Enquiries received by e-mail would be dealt with in the same way as fax enquiries. With such a radical change, it was envisaged that a relatively high degree of resistance could be expected from staff. Reasons for this resistance would include fear of job losses, low levels of IT literacy leading to concern that staff would not be able to cope with the new systems, and anxiety that the new systems would add to current workloads without brining about substantial benefits to either the company as a whole or the individuals within it.

Initially, the implementation strategy for the intranet was devised by the company MD and the TCS associate. The approach was to use a Web site development tool (Dreamweaver) to create a prototype intranet. Staff would then be trained to use Dreamweaver to update pages and, most importantly, to populate the intranet with corporate knowledge. This approach was unsuccessful and two main reasons for this failure were apparent. First, Partwell staff were not consulted during the strategy-formulation stage. Thus, they felt no ownership for the intranet and were not well disposed to using it. Second, many staff had low levels of IT ability and felt intimidated by the apparent complexity of the system. This was compounded by the production of intranet user guides that contained technical jargon that was not easily understood by the majority of the staff. The net result of this approach was that the intranet did not become integrated within the company.

Having had the opportunity to reflect on the lessons learned from the initial implementation, a more appropriate approach was devised. First, an IT-skills audit was made of all Partwell staff. This revealed that most staff had some level of skill in using word processors, presentation software, and spreadsheets, whilst other staff had no IT experience. Second, a full consultation process was undertaken. The MD explained to staff the business reasons for the decision to implement an intranet and also explained how the company could benefit. Questions and criticisms were invited and as a result, some modification was made to the implementation approach. It was decided that if the system was to become useful, then it would have to be designed to capitalise on the current levels of IT knowledge within the organisation. Hence, the use of a professional development tool was abandoned. Instead, the associate designed a system whereby staff could add and update intranet pages using word-processing, spreadsheet, and presentation software. In this way, many staff were using IT applications with which they were already familiar. This had the consequence of reducing resistance to the new system and also minimised IT training costs. Another key approach was to identify specific staff members who were both highly knowledgeable about certain product areas and also well respected by other staff members. Considerable effort was expended on persuading these individuals about the tangible benefits of an intranet as well as providing them with intensive training with the new system.

The next phase was to implement a series of training days. These would involve all staff using the intranet to find answers to common customer enquiries as well as populating the KM database with new knowledge. The training days were held on Saturdays — not normal working days for the business — and all staff were paid for their participation. This approach emphasised the importance of the project. During the training sessions, the MD, the associate, and the key personnel (previously described) acted as guides and facilitators for the less-experienced staff. The sessions were conducted in an informal manner, which significantly reduced the anxiety of the staff.

Conclusion

The second approach to intranet implementation proved to be highly successful. Staff resistance to change was reduced substantially by developing the intranet based on IT with which many Partwell staff were already familiar. The identification of key staff to act as trainers was also a catalyst for change. Targeting personnel who were highly regarded by their peers to provide project support was a critical success factor. Development of the bespoke system consumed a great deal of the associate's time and energy as well as it produced a suboptimal technical solution with many bugs in the system that the associate would have to rectify. It was also recognised that full documentation of the system would be required and, again, this task would fall on the associate. Regardless of the cost of this approach, the company recognised that it would be outweighed by the strategic benefits. Producing a technically superior system that was not utilised by the staff would be disastrous both financially and socially.

In large companies, the loss of an individual is rarely disastrous. Because knowledge is shared amongst many individuals, it is possible to compensate relatively quickly. In small organisations like Partwell, the loss of key individuals can have serious long-term implications. By developing and deploying an intranet, Partwell has minimised this risk. The intranet is now used routinely within the company. Staff are continually augmenting the corporate knowledge base and are using the system to provide more efficient service to customers.

By developing an Internet presence, they have also created a global marketing presence as well as a means to promote better service to existing and potential customers. Presently, Partwell operates two Internet sites. The site http://www.pressmachines.com is dedicated to the selling of refurbished press machines. The site also enables organisations or individuals who wish to sell press machines to contact Partwell. Hence, the site provides a global supplier sourcing mechanism. The site also allows companies to submit technical questions to Partwell. Furthermore, the site enables browsers to source hard-to-find press machines. To date, the site has generated substantial interest from South Africa where there is a significant market for press machines. The site http://www.partwell.com/index.htm promotes the full range of Partwell products as well as it provides customers with extensive product and service information. The site is presently undergoing a restructuring. The aim is to provide customers with the required information as quickly and easily as possible. The design of the new site has been influenced significantly by comment from existing customers. The company is fully aware that its core knowledge is a source of competitive advantage. To make this available to everybody via the Internet would seriously disadvantage the company. Hence, this core knowledge will only be accessible to authorised Partwell staff. Partwell's field sales teams will access the information via portable computers that are password protected. In this way, the sales force becomes equipped with a means to provide an extremely comprehensive service to customers whilst on their premises. This again provides a significant factor in differentiating Partwell from its competitors.

References

Berranger, P. de, Tucker, D., & Jones, L. (2001). Internet diffusion in creative micro-businesses: Identifying change agents as critical success factors. *Journal of Organizational Computing and Electronic Commerce, 11*(3), 197-214.

Blackburn, R., & McClure (1988). *The use of information and communication technology (ICTs) in small business service firms.* Small Business Research Centre, Kingston Business School.

Carter, S., Tagg, S., Ennis, S., & Web, J. (2002). *Lifting the barriers to growth in UK small businesses*. Federation of Small Businesses. Retrieved from *http://www.fsb.org.uk/policy/lbg2002/Liftingsummary2002.pdf*

Commission of the European Communities. (2002). *Commission staff working paper. On B2B Internet trading platforms: Opportunities and barriers for SMEs-A first assessment.* Retrieved from *http://www.e-global.es/paperfree/023_commission_onb2b.pdf*

Department of Trade and Industry. (2002). *Business in the information age: International benchmarking study 2002.* Retrieved from *http://www.sbs.gov.uk/default.php?page=/research/keyresearch.php*

Dixon, T., Thompson, R., & McAllister, P. (2002). *The value of ICT for SMEs in the UK: A critical literature review.* Small Business Service Research Programme. Retrieved from *http://www.sbs.gov.uk/content/research/value_of_ICT_for_SMEs_UK.pdf*

Geisler, E. (1992). Managing IT in small business: Some practical lessons and guidelines. *Journal of General Management, 18*(1), 74-81.

Small Business Service. (2003). *Small firms: Big business. A review of small and medium sized enterprises in the UK.* Retrieved March 2003, from *http://www.sbs.gov.uk/default.php?page=/statistics/smedefs.php*

Southern, R., & Tilley, F. (2000). Small firms and information and communication technologies (ICTs): Toward a typology of ICTs usage. *New Technology, Work and Employment, 5*(2).

Endnotes

[1] The definition of trading online is made up of a number of activities. These are: (1) enabling customers to order online, (2) enabling customers to pay online, (3) using ICTs to order goods and services online, and (4) using ICTs to pay for goods and services online. In order to be counted as trading online, a business must be:

- enabling customers to order online and either (1) allowing them to pay online or (2) paying for their own supplies online; or
- using ICTs to order their own supplies, either goods or services, and either (1) allowing customers to pay online or (2) paying for their own supplies online.

[2] In July 2003, TCS became known as knowledge-transfer partnerships (KTPs).

Chapter VIII

E-Government Evolution in Ireland: A Framework for Successful Implementation

William Golden, National University of Ireland, Galway, Ireland

Martin Hughes, National University of Ireland, Galway, Ireland

Murray Scott, National University of Ireland, Galway, Ireland

Abstract

E-government provides unparalleled opportunities for governments to streamline processes and improve customer service. As a result, achieving successful citizen-centred e-government has become a key concern for many governments. This chapter analyses the Irish government's evolutionary path to the provision of successful e-government. The success factors and stages of evolution of e-government are identified and a detailed examination of how the Irish government successfully implemented its e-government strategy is presented. The lessons learned from this case provide a valuable road map for the successful attainment of citizen-centred e-government in other jurisdictions.

Introduction

Information technology has had a long association with business, first as a provider of unprecedented efficiencies and second as an element of business strategy in its own right (Porter, 2001; Venkatraman, 1994). Through the use of electronic commerce technologies, public- and private-sector companies are challenged to redesign their processes in order to achieve the benefits of increased efficiencies, cost reductions, and better customer service (Glassey, 2001; Warkentin, Gefen, Pavlou, & Rose, 2002).

The Internet is an important new technology as it provides better opportunities for companies to establish distinctive strategic positions than those offered by previous generations of information technology (Porter, 2001). It can provide opportunities for strategic advantage, cost savings, and new revenue streams (Mahadevan, 2000). Consequently, Internet technologies bring challenges for public- and private-sector companies (Earl & Bushra, 2001).

Electronic commerce can be defined as the use of the Internet to conduct commercial transactions (Mahadevan, 2000). Electronic commerce is generally conducted in three broad structures: portals, market makers, and product or service providers (Bakos, 1991; Mahadevan). The benefits of these structures to the supplier include lower costs and access to wider markets, while the advantages to the buyer are lower transaction costs, access to greater amounts of information, and convenience of purchase (Porter, 2001).

Today, governments are using the Internet to provide public services to their citizens (Gouscos, Georgiadis, Martakos, & Stamoulis, 2001; Watson & Mundy, 2001). In so doing, governments aim to form better relationships with businesses and citizens by providing more efficient and effective services (Al-Kibisi, de Boer, Mourshed, & Rea, 2001; Eyob, 2004; Layne & Lee, 2001; Warkentin et al., 2002). Governments can also use e-commerce to improve core business processes (Coulthard & Castleman, 2001; Gronlund, 2002; Lloyd, 2002).

This chapter investigates the evolution of e-government in Ireland up to the summer of 2002. A review of the literature is presented that details the recognised success factors in e-government, the stages of e-government evolution, and international e-government comparisons. A case study is presented detailing how the Irish government's e-government strategy was devised and implemented. The success of this implementation yields valuable insights into the identification and management of critical concerns during the evolvement and attainment of e-government. Cumulatively, these lessons provide a road map for the successful attainment of citizen-centred e-government. Specifically, the case details how an excess of 50 government authorities, both local and central, were brought together in order to provide a single point of access to government services.

Electronic Government

Electronic government is defined as the use of technology, particularly the Internet, as a means to deliver services to citizens, businesses, and other entities (Tambouris, 2001; Watson & Mundy, 2001) with the purpose of providing convenient access to government information and services (Brannen, 2001; Gefen, Pavlou, Warkentin, & Rose, 2002). E-government has the potential to transform not only the way in which most public services are delivered, but also the fundamental relationship between government and citizen (Burn & Robbins, 2001; Watson & Mundy).

Operational benefits of e-government include the continuous availability of service, a reduction in response time, and a reduction in error rates (Al-Kibisi et al., 2001; Detlor & Finn, 2002; Gouscos et al., 2001). These factors contribute to an increase in the efficiency of government (Coulthard & Castleman, 2001; Dearstyne, 2001; Lagroue, 2002).

Critical Success Factors of Electronic Government

Barriers to e-government include organisational, political, and technical factors as they posit threats to achieving the benefits of the integration of service delivery (Akbulut, 2002; Dawes, 1996). Redesigning services and improving their coordination are difficult tasks that are compounded in public-sector organisations as they rely heavily on consensus (Al-Kibisi et al., 2001).

Strategic Vision

Success in e-government requires strategic direction (Poon, 2002). This strategy must encourage government agencies to create a networked environment that facilitates functional integration and departmental collaboration (Akbulut, 2002; Zhang, Cresswell, & Thompson, 2002).

Technical Strategy

Implementing the correct technical strategy is essential to ensure that the operational benefits of e-government are fully realized (Al-Kibisi et al., 2001; Gant & Gant, 2001). Sinigoj (2002) argues that technological issues regarding service provision cannot be effectively implemented on a local level but need more initiative on a national level in order to be cost effective.

Integration

Traditionally, government services were provided from the government's perspective. However, e-government centralises the citizen, and thus the integration of functions is essential to successful e-government (Jupp & Shine, 2001; Lapre & van Venrooij, 2001; Watson & Mundy, 2001).

Balancing Local vs. Central Concerns

The role of local government may be threatened by the use of centralised methods of providing services (Lapre & van Venrooij, 2001). Additionally, some citizens may prefer the familiar face-to-face contact that local government provides and may continue to access services through local delivery (Gouscos et al., 2001). Thus, the roles of local and central government need to be clearly defined (Lapre & van Venrooij; Phythian & William, 2001).

Privacy and Confidentiality

Privacy, security, and confidentiality are critical concerns (Al-Kibisi et al., 2001; Kambil & Mark, 1998; Layne & Lee, 2001; Tambouris, 2001). Many citizens may feel that their privacy is threatened when personal data is stored centrally and is accessible online (Dridi, 2001). Trust and confidence must be established if the system is to be successful (Al-Kibisi et al.; Warkentin et al., 2002). One trust-building measure is to allow the user to have some control over the information stored and which government department has access to the information (Layne & Lee).

Quality Service

For citizens to conduct online transactions, the service must be convenient, time saving, and cost efficient (Al-Kibisi et al., 2001). Consequently, the issues of usability and the timely delivery of service are essential to maintaining high levels of satisfaction (Kaylor, Deshazo, & Van Eck, 2001).

E-Government Evolution

Layne and Lee (2001) have identified four stages of evolution in e-government: catalogue, transaction, vertical integration, and horizontal integration. These stages are presented in Figure 1.

Figure 1. The evolution of e-government (Layne & Lee, 2001)

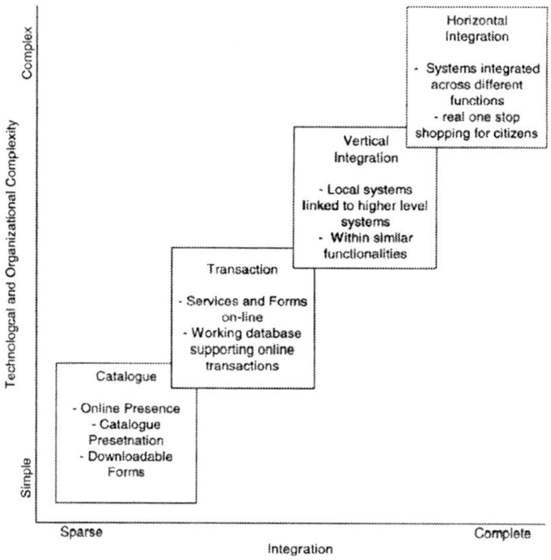

Stage 1, Catalogue: The government creates a static Web site to gain online presence. Information is catalogued for presentation to citizens and usually organised into departments. At this stage, functionality is generally limited to search facilities. In achieving Stage 1, government agencies tend to develop their Web presence on an agency-by-agency basis (Gant & Gant, 2001). Initially, this strategy can be successful as it allows the individual agency to develop its Web site quickly. However, inconsistencies, duplication of effort, and other limitations soon emerge that encourage some governments to redevelop their stand-alone sites into Web portals (Fernandes, Wilpen, & Krishman, 2001; Gant & Gant).

Stage 2, Transaction: This stage requires online interfaces for the purpose of conducting transactions. It is typically characterised by direct connections to live databases that require minimal interaction from government staff. The focus of design in this stage moves from departmental orientation to presenting a customer-focused approach. Web portals can be utilised to deliver information according to customer needs and not departmental requirements (Baker & Baker, 1999; Gant & Gant, 2001). Portals are designed like virtual agencies that cluster together the disparate services a government offers into a single entry point (Watson & Mundy, 2001). This customer-orientated approach facilitates ease of use as the customer interacts with a single point of contact, leaving the portal to communicate with the agencies that together provide the service (Al-Kibisi et al., 2001; Gant & Gant; Jupp & Shine, 2001).

Stage 3, Vertical Integration: This stage requires integration between local and central agencies that exist within the same function. It is characterised by a transformation in services and in the linking of local and central systems through the use of centralised databases. When used in conjunction with citizen identification numbers, portals can also deliver customised services enabling better customer focus by removing repetitive form filling as information about the citizen can be dynamically generated from a centralised database (Jupp & Shine, 2001). These benefits are driving portals as the centrepiece of enterprise approaches to e-government (Fernandes et al., 2001; Gant & Gant, 2001; Watson & Mundy, 2001).

Stage 4, Horizontal Integration: The final stage of evolution requires integration across not only different levels of government, but also integration across different functions of government. This type of integration means that a transaction in one agency can lead to checks against data in other functional agencies. This stage of integration supports true "one-stop shopping."

International Perspective

In a survey of European Union (EU) countries, Ireland was recently ranked best overall in online government service provision (Wauters, 2002). With an overall ranking of 85%, Ireland was considerably above the European average of 55% (Wauters, 2002). Another comparative e-government study of each member country of the United Nations (UN) revealed that of the 190 UN member states, 169 had a government Web-site presence, 84 had a national government Web site, and 36 had single-entry portals (Ronaghan, 2002). The report identifies single-entry portals as an important and accepted international standard. Classifying the 190 member states according to the Layne and Lee (2001) framework, Ronaghan argues that 97 have reached Stage 1 of the evolutionary process, 55 have reached Stage 2, 17 have reached Stage 3, and none have attained Stage 4.

Research Methodology

Exploratory research methods were used to investigate the success of both the e-government strategy adopted by the Irish government and its implementation at both local and national levels. Five in-depth interviews were conducted with three government agencies involved in the e-government project. An in-depth interview was conducted with one senior civil servant from the Department of An Taoiseach (prime minister), the governmental department providing strategic leadership to e-government initiatives in Ireland. Two in-depth interviews were conducted with members of REACH, the executive body created specifically to implement the e-government strategy. In addition, further interviews were conducted with two senior members of the Local Government Computer Supply Board (LGCSB), a public-sector company providing IS services to local government.

These interviews were conducted on site in April 2002. The interviews conducted with the LGCSB were supported by a demonstration of the technology, while the interviews conducted in the Department of An Taoiseach and the REACH agency were supplemented by access to internal documentation. Records were kept of the content of all interviews. Further clarifications and updates were obtained by e-mail and telephone contact.

Government in Ireland

Government in Ireland is conducted at two tiers: national and local levels as depicted in Figure 2. The central government consists of 17 government departments and 35 agencies such as the revenue commissioners and the court service. The local government consists of local authorities, primarily county councils or city councils, with 46 currently in operation, that are responsible for the provision of a variety of government services at a local level, and 10 health boards that are responsible for administering health services.

IS Support

IS support at both the central and local levels is provided through a combination of in-house expertise and outsourcing to the private sector. An alternative outsourcing arrangement is also available through LGCSB. LGCSB is a public-sector company whose objective is to provide local authorities with IS systems and expertise on an individual basis. The basic premise is that expertise gained in one local authority can be passed onto others. An example of such service

Figure 2. Structure of government in Ireland

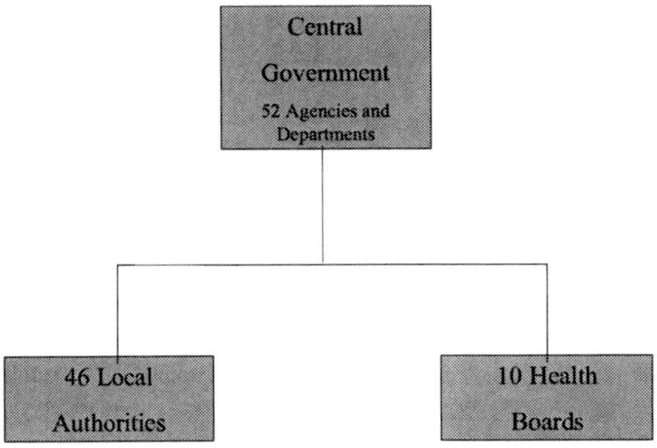

provision is the Complete Information System for Water Services led initially by one local authority. This system was subsequently installed in all local authorities by July 2000.

In response to local-authority requests, LGCSB developed electronic forms (e-forms) for use on local-authority Web sites. These forms were Web versions of the traditional paper-based forms. Users could register with their local authority, but there was no online system in place either to process the form electronically or to authenticate the individual. These initial e-forms served only to promote the accessibility of public-service forms through an electronic medium.

Road Map for E-Government

The overall strategy and corresponding implementations of the Irish government's e-government initiative are presented in Table 1.

In January 1999, the Irish government released its first action plan on the information society. The plan outlined a three-strand approach to online delivery of public services: information services, interactive services, and integrated services. The plan spearheaded the drive to make better use of the Internet for information dissemination. Government departments were required to implement Web sites, and the OASIS (Online Access to Services Information and Support; http://www.oasis.gov.ie) and BASIS (Business Access to State Information and Support; http://www.basis.ie) projects were initiated. These Web sites were to be designed to meet the entire informational needs of a client regardless of the source of the information. The action plan also introduced the

Table 1. Strategy and implementation process

Year	Strategy Formulation	Implementation
1999	First Government Action Plan for the implementation of the information society. Outlines an integrated approach to the online delivery of public services.	
2000	REACH agency established. Mandated to develop and implement a strategy for e-government. Public services broker (PSB) framework agreed on for the integrated delivery of public services, accessible from a single point.	OASIS and BASIS projects launched. E-Forms available on local-authority Web sites.
2001/2002	Second Government Action Plan: New Connections. Objectives are to radically improveme quality of service and to establish Ireland as an exemplar of international best practice The PSB endorsed and prioritized.	REACH in conjunction with LGCSB develop and launch reachservices, an interim PSB (http://www.reachservices.ie).
2002/2003	Technical specifications of PSB finalised. Implementation strategies devised.	Reachservices maintained and enhanced. Open tendering process for the construction of the PSB. Vendor-selected.
2005		Full installation of PSB.

initial concept of a portal as the possible architecture of a public-service access interface.

Toward the end of 2000, the REACH agency was officially established, its name reflecting the concept of government reaching out to its customers. REACH is an executive body with the responsibility of coordinating the central agencies responsible for implementing the e-government strategy and of providing management of the overall e-government initiative. Initially, REACH was composed of 11 members, all civil servants who were drawn from a variety of departments, and was established as an independent unit within the Department of Social and Family Affairs reporting to the Department of An Taoiseach. The concept of a portal-based PSB was adopted by REACH as the central mechanism for delivering the e-government agenda.

The framework for the PSB, as depicted in Figure 3, can be broken down into three key features: integration, multiple access channels, and data security. First, the PSB will provide a single point of access to all services of both the central and local government. The revolutionary aspect of the PSB is that service is to be provided from the customer's perspective. That is, the customer interacts with the broker and not the actual service provider, thus allowing for fully integrated services regardless of whether the provider is a local authority, of the central government, or both. Second, the PSB will make services available

Figure 3. The PSB (REACH internal documentation)

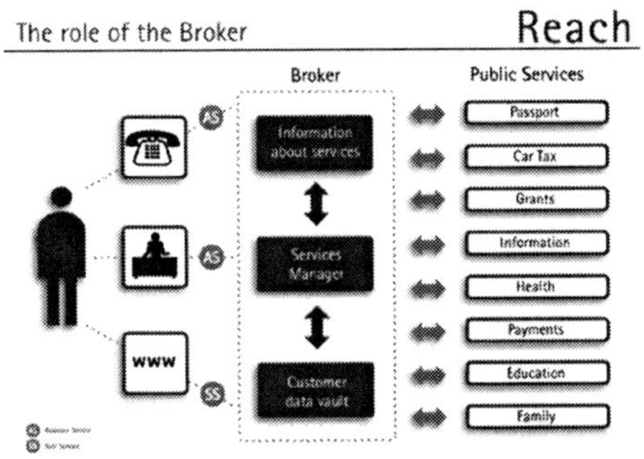

through many access channels; these include online self-service, assisted service through telephone contact centres, and one-stop shops. Finally, the PSB will provide a customer data vault that will store data relevant to his or her interaction with the government. This data will be used to facilitate online transactions and provide personalisation of the user interface and various other aids in form completion. The individual user will have authority over his or her personal data and may specify which departments may access what information. Thus, the provision of nonbasic data will be voluntary and determined by the level of interaction that the user wishes to have. For example, the storage of personal-identity photographs will be voluntary; however, if an individual intends to apply for a driver's license using the PSB, he or she will have to allow the system to hold the photograph.

Implementing E-Government

In November 2000, as an initial step in the move toward e-government, the OASIS and BASIS Web sites were launched. These Web sites provide detailed information on government services to citizens and businesses respectively. With a focus on customer requirements, these sites broke the long-standing tradition of distributing government information along functional lines.

During 2001, REACH, in partnership with LGCSB, developed an interim-level PSB. LGCSB was identified as a technical partner for two reasons: first, LGCSB had gained significant expertise through the implementation of e-forms, and second, local authorities had a tried and trusted relationship established with LGCSB. This interim service became known as reachservices and was officially launched in April 2002.

Also in April 2002, the second government action plan entitled "New Connections" was published. The main objectives of the e-government strategy were outlined as a radical improvement in quality of service to customers, major improvements in administrative efficiencies, enhanced control of fraud and abuse of publicly funded services, and finally the establishment of Ireland as an exemplar of international best practice. The government also made a commitment to have all public services capable of electronic delivery through a single point of contact by 2005.

Meeting the Challenge of Delivery

The main challenge in the development of reachservices was to have every local-authority paper-based form available online for electronic download and submission. Each of the 46 local authorities had at least 133 forms that they required to be individually customisable. This resulted in a total requirement of an excess of 5,000 forms, excluding the health boards. To meet this requirement, LGCSB developed a centrally administered system that would allow each local authority access to an electronic form builder.

The form-builder tool has a graphical user interface and is based on the idea that a generic form can accommodate any organisation for any citizen and cover any question. Figure 4 presents a representation of the form-builder application. The form builder is based on three basic entities: the organisation, the individual, and the question. It enables the local authority to create its customised form that is then uploaded onto the reachservices site.

Central to the progression of the online service provision achieved by REACH was the redevelopment of e-forms into the form builder tool accessible to the local authority through the portal reachservices. The local authorities are allocated user names and passwords allowing them access to the form builder. Each local-authority administrator can then select which e-forms are to be made available for his or her authority and can customise or edit those forms online. From a template form, the administrator creates the questions, defines what type of response the user will give, and can add whatever validation checks or mandatory fields that are required. The administrator can also remove forms for his or her local authority if necessary.

Another significant advance achieved by reachservices is citizen identification. Before using the system, the individual must register with reachservices. Part of this registration is an authentication process that is managed by the Department of Social and Family Affairs. The individual may then access the reachservices site using his or her Personal Public Service (Social Security) number and password. This is an essential feature of the process as it provides the authority with proof of the individual's identity and enables features like intelligent form filling.

Intelligent form filling allows certain fields to be populated automatically based on the information stored on each citizen. It also allows for certain questions to be

Figure 4. Representation of form builder application (LGCSB internal documentation)

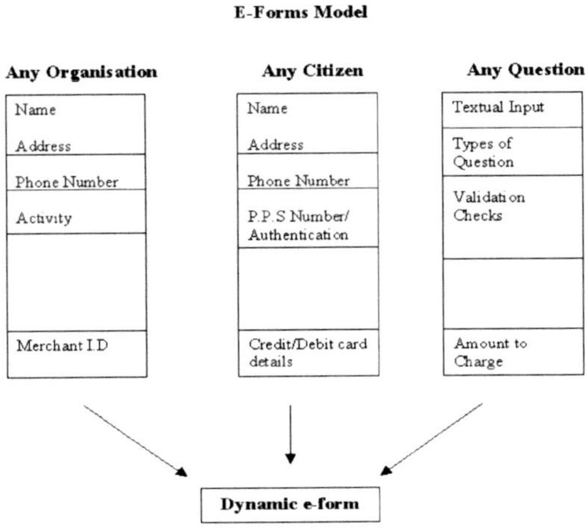

deactivated when they are not necessary. The user is also provided with the capability to save a partially completed form for completion at a later date. Visual aids are provided as means of indicating to the user which pages of a form have been fully or partially completed. When the user submits the form, it is automatically routed to the relevant authority in XML (extensible markup language) format. At present, the front-end interface is fully automated while the back-end system still relies on human interaction. Typically, when a form is received, it is printed off to a hard copy and processed manually in the same way as the traditional method.

Future Developments

The central e-government strategy is to implement a public service broker (PSB) by 2005. This broker will facilitate multiple access modes, including telephone access and one-stop shops, to all government services. Under this model, the underlying structure and departments of the central government will become less relevant to the citizen as all services will be provided in an integrated manner through the PSB. The construction of the PSB has been outsourced and is currently under development by Bearing Point. A further procurement phase is underway to locate suitable organisations to host the PSB when operational. When complete, it will act as a single point of contact to the customer by integrating services around predefined life or business events instead of presenting services around functional departments. Currently, the intention of REACH is to pilot the PSB with certain shared services, common to a number of departments and agencies, in order to initially build a critical mass of users. The scope and range of services provided through the PSB will then be gradually expanded. The fully functional PSB will also be known as reachservices and from the user's perspective, there will be a seamless transition from the initial service offering to the more sophisticated PSB.

Discussion

The immediate impact to citizens can be judged in terms of ease of access, ease of use, and efficiency. Providing a multitude of forms from individual authorities in one location gives citizens ease of access resulting in time savings. The completion of a form is greatly simplified through intelligent form filling. In addition, the submission process is simplified as it removes the need for postage or travel to the local authority, thus expediting the delivery of the service. The reachservices Web site went live in mid-April 2002 and was launched without the use of advertising in order to prevent an initial surge of activity. Nonetheless, the initial uptake rate was approximately 500 to 600 registrations per month during its first few months of operation. This volume of traffic was regarded as successful due to the subdued launch and the fact that the site only offered a fraction of the functionality ultimately intended.

Reachservices has had a 100% uptake rate by local authorities, albeit some authorities are implementing at different levels. This should be viewed in the context that the local authorities have not been mandated to participate in the reachservices project. There has also been a very high percentage in the take-up rate amongst the health boards.

Table 2 compares the achievements in this case with the Layne and Lee (2001) framework.

The development of local-authority Web sites and later the OASIS and BASIS fulfill the requirement for Stage 1, catalogue, in the Layne and Lee (2001) model. In particular, the OASIS and BASIS Web sites also represent the first evidence of a clear shift from a departmental orientation to a customer-focused orientation. Stage 2, transaction, was initially attained by the implementation of e-forms on the local-authority Web sites by LGCSB. However, enhancing the function-

Table 2. Strategy and implementation process compared to evolutionary framework

Year	Strategy Formulation	Implementation	Stage of Evolution
1999	First Government Action Plan for the implementation of the information society. Outlines an integrated approach to the online delivery of public services.		
2000	REACH agency established. Mandated to develop and implement a strategy for e-government. PSB framework agreed on for the integrated delivery of public services, accessible from a single point.	OASIS and BASIS projects launched. E-Forms available on local-authority Web sites.	Stages 1 & 2
2001/2002	Second Government Action Plan: New Connections. Objectives are to radically improve quality of service and to establish Ireland as an exemplar of international best practice. The PSB endorsed and prioritized.	REACH in conjunction with LGCSB develops and launches reachservices, an interim PSB (http://www.reachservices.ie).	Stage 3
2002/2003	Technical specifications of PSB finalised. Implementation strategies devised.	Reachservices maintained and enhanced. Open tendering process for the construction of the PSB. Vendor-selected.	Stage 3
2005		Full installation of PSB.	Stage 4

ality of e-forms was abandoned in favour of the development of reachservices. Stage 3, vertical integration, was obtained by the launch of the reachservices portal, which connected local and central systems through the use of a centralised database that maintains the authenticated data of the individual citizen. However, full vertical integration and Stage 4, horizontal integration, will only be achieved through the launch of the full PSB accompanied by authorities that focus on providing customer-focused processes.

Findings

The development of reachservices exemplifies good management, coordination, and implementation of the e-government initiative. Although this initiative is still ongoing, valuable lessons can already be drawn from this case. Collectively,

Table 3. Road map for e-government

	Stage 0 Strategy Development	Stage 1 Catalogue	Stage 2 Transaction	Stage 3 Vertical Integration	Stage 4 Horizontal Integration
Technological Infrastructure		Individual-authority Web sites. New customer-focused Web sites.	E-Forms.	Portal. Form builder. Centralised database with authentication.	PSB providing multiple access modes.
Success Factors	Develop strategy at highest level of central government. Establish entity to oversee implementation.	Central directive. Independent development. Focus on customer service.	Utilise central body of expertise to expedite development.	Identify and manage local concerns. Use familiar actors. Leverage existing expertise. Allow citizens some control over personal data. Use scalable model.	Build on experience from previous stage. Clearly define requirements. Outsource development.

these lessons amount to a road map for successful implementation of e-government as presented in Table 3.

The e-government strategy was devised and ratified by the highest possible level of central government and an independent agency established to implement this strategy. The independent agency, REACH, identified and exploited the technological expertise of LGCSB and also successfully procured a partnership with the Department of Social and Family Affairs in order to provide an authentication service. The effective management and coordination of otherwise autonomous stakeholders, combined with the right technical infrastructure and cross-departmental collaboration and integration, provided the ingredients for the provision of a successful public e-service.

Stage 1 can be achieved by directing all authorities to implement individual Web sites. This encourages the authority to become Web proficient and potentially lowers later barriers to centralised Web development. At this stage, the development of customer-focused Web sites, independent from the local authorities, as authoritative repositories of government information promotes a shift in focus from departmental orientation to customer need.

The requirements of Stage 2, transaction, can be achieved by implementing electronic forms on local-authority Web sites. This should be accompanied by authentication and payment facilities, although that was not the situation in this case. This development can be expedited by the use of an outsourcing arrangement.

Stage 3, vertical integration, can be achieved by implementing a portal strategy that provides form building, a database, and authentication services to the participating authorities. However, providing a centralised service can create tension between the central and local government. In this case, potential tension was managed by ensuring that the authority previously responsible for the service remained responsible and, furthermore, that the responsibility was made clearly visible within the portal by allowing customised forms. Customisable forms combined with the usability of the form builder and the existing relationships between LGCSB and the local authorities greatly impacted the rate of buy-in by the local authorities.

Throughout these stages, providing an easy-to-use system that is focused on the citizens' needs encourages citizen usage. Evidence from the case, in relation to registration rates, indicates that allowing the citizen some control over personal data and the use of that data helps to appease fears relating to centralising data storage.

The final stage, horizontal integration, has not yet been achieved; however, preparations are well underway and initial lessons can be drawn at this point. What is clearly evident from this case is that the gap between Stage 3 and Stage 4 is much greater than the gaps between the other stages of evolution. The successful attainment of Stage 4 will therefore require a far more sophisticated infrastructure. The design and functionality of this infrastructure can be devised from the experience gained in the earlier stages. The scale of the project at this stage will necessitate very detailed requirements specification and outsourcing of the development.

Conclusion

This case provides valuable insights into the attainment of citizen-centred e-government that cumulatively amount to a road map for successful implementation. Following the strategy formulation by the highest level of central government, a specific entity, REACH, was established with the sole purpose of implementing this strategy. REACH was therefore in a position to both identify and manage the critical success factors involved in delivering e-government. First, the most appropriate model and technical infrastructure were identified and implemented by outsourcing to leverage expertise that already existed. This use of existing expertise proved highly successful in terms of developing a robust infrastructure within a limited time frame. Second, critical concerns of local authorities were managed by using familiar actors. Third, the interactions necessary between otherwise independent agencies was successfully coordinated to ensure the delivery of a quality service. Fourth, the maintenance of a customer focus by providing a quality service through a single portal in which the citizen has control over his or her personal data contributed to a successful uptake of the system.

This case also provides strong evidence to support the evolutionary model of e-government as proposed by Layne and Lee (2001). However, it also provides evidence indicating that Stage 2 may, in some cases, be bypassed and incorporated into Stage 3. The case also suggests that the gaps between the stages greatly increase, requiring sophisticated strategies and infrastructures to obtain the latter stages. While the framework is useful in identifying the stages of evolution, it provides little support for how to evolve. Evidence from this case suggests that the road map for success may be constituted as follows. Develop a strategy at the highest level of government and establish an entity with the sole purpose of implementing this strategy. Implement an appropriate model initially by leveraging existing expertise. Once the model has been proven successful, outsource its full implementation. Encourage local buy-in through the use of familiar actors and by maintaining the role of the authority. Encourage citizen buy-in by the provision of high-quality service in a convenient manner that is nonthreatening to individual privacy concerns.

References

Akbulut, A. Y. (2002). An investigation of the factors that influence electronic information sharing between state and local agencies. In *Proceedings of the Eighth Americas Conference on Information Systems*.

Al-Kibisi, G., de Boer, K., Mourshed, M., & Rea, N. (2001). Putting citizens on-line, not inline. *The McKinsey Quarterly, 2*, 64.

Baker, S., & Baker, K. (1999). Portals to paperless prosperity. *Journal of Business Strategy, 20*(6), 32.

Bakos, J. Y. (1991). A strategic analysis of electronic marketplaces. *MIS Quarterly, 15*(3), 295.

Brannen, A. (2001). E-government in California: Providing services to citizens through the Internet. *Journal of State Government, 74*(2), 6.

Burn, J. M., & Robbins, G. (2001). Strategic planning for e-government. In *Proceedings of the Seventh Americas Conference on Information Systems.*

Coulthard, D., & Castleman, T. (2001). Electronic procurement in government: More complicated than just good business. In *Proceedings of the Ninth European Conference on Information Systems.*

Dawes, S. (1996). Interagency information sharing: Expected benefits, manageable risks. *Journal of Policy Analysis and Management, 15*(3), 377.

Dearstyne, B. W. (2001). E-Business, e-government & information proficiency. *Information Management Journal, 34*(4), 16.

Detlor, B., & Finn, K. (2002). Towards a framework for government portal design: The government, citizen and portal perspectives. In A. Gronlund (Ed.), *Electronic government: Design, applications and management* (pp. 99-119). Hershey, PA: Idea Group Publishing.

Dridi, F. (2001). Security for the electronic government. In *Proceedings of the First European Conference on E-Government* (pp. 99-111).

Earl, M., & Bushra, K. (2001). E-commerce is changing the face of I.T. *MIT Sloan Management Review*, 64-72.

Eyob, E. (2004). E-Government: Breaking the frontiers of inefficiencies in the public sector. *Electronic Government, 1*(1), 107-114.

Fernandes, D., Wilpen, G., & Krishman, R. (2001). ServiceNet: An agent-based framework for one-stop e-government services. In *Proceedings of the Seventh Americas Conference on Information Systems.*

Gant, J. P., & Gant, D. B. (2001). Web portals and their role in e-government. In *Proceedings of the Seventh Americas Conference on Information Systems.*

Gefen, D., Pavlou, P. A., Warkentin, M., & Rose, G. M. (2002). Egovernment adoption. In *Proceedings of the Eighth Americas Conference on Information Systems.*

Glassey, O. (2001). Model and architecture for a virtual one stop public administration. In *Proceedings of the Ninth European Conference on Information Systems.*

Gouscos, D., Georgiadis, P., Martakos, D., & Stamoulis, S. (2001). Re-orientating information systems for customer centric service. In *Proceedings of the First European Conference on E-Government.*

Gronlund, A. (2002). Electronic government: Efficiency, service quality and democracy. In A. Gronlund (Ed.), *Electronic government: Design, applications and management* (pp. 23-50). Hershey, PA: Idea Group Publishing.

Jupp, V., & Shine, S. (2001). Government portals: The next generation of government online. In *Proceedings of the First European Conference on E-Government* (pp. 217-223).

Kambil, A. G., & Mark. (1998). Public access Web information systems: Lessons from the Internet EDGAR project. *Communications of the ACM, 41*(7), 91.

Kaylor, C., Deshazo, R., & Van Eck, D. (2001). Gauging e-government: A report on implementing services among American cities. *Government Information Quarterly, 18*(4), 293-307.

Lagroue, H. J. (2002). The impact of e-government initiatives: Louisiana's "express lane" license and vehicle registration system. In *Proceedings of the Eighth Americas Conference on Information Systems.*

Lapre, L., & van Venrooij, A. (2001). Bridging the gap between citizen and administration. In *Proceedings of the First European Conference on E-Government* (pp. 247-259).

Layne, K., & Lee, J. (2001). Developing fully functional e-government: A four stage model. *Government Information Quarterly, 18*(2), 122.

Lloyd, R. M. (2002). Electronic government. *Business & Economic Review, 48*(4), 15.

Mahadevan, B. (2000). Business models for Internet-based e-commerce. *California Management Review, 42*(4), 55-69.

Phythian, M. J. T., & William, G. K. (2001). Progress in electronic service delivery by English district councils. *International Journal of Public Sector Management, 14*(7), 569.

Poon, S. (2002). ESDLife of Hong Kong e-government application with an e-business spirit. In *Proceedings of the Eighth Americas Conference on Information Systems.*

Porter, M. (2001). Strategy and the Internet. *Harvard Business Review, 79*(3), 63.

Ronaghan, S. (2002). *Benchmarking e-government: A global perspective-Assessing the UN member states.* United Nations Division for Public Economics and Public Administration & American Society for Public Administration.

Sinigoj, A. (2002). Goriska e-region a new vision that can be accomplished by educating citizens and improving e-security. In *Proceedings of the 15th Bled Electronic-Commerce Conference.*

Tambouris. (2001). European cities platform for online transaction services: The euro city project. In *Proceedings of the First European Conference on E-Government.*

Venkatraman, V. (1994). IT-enabled business transformation: From automation to business scope redefinition. *Sloan Management Review, 35*(2), 73.

Warkentin, M., Gefen, D., Pavlou, P., & Rose, G. M. (2002). Encouraging citizen adoption of e-government by building trust. *Electronic Markets, 12*(3), 157.

Watson, R. T., & Mundy, B. (2001). A strategic perspective of electronic democracy. *Communications of the ACM, 44*(1), 27.

Wauters, P. (2002). *Web based survey on electronic public services.* Cap Gemini Ernst and Young.

Zhang, J., Cresswell, A. M., & Thompson, F. (2002). Participants' expectations and the success of knowledge networking in the public sector. In *Proceedings of the Eighth Americas Conference on Information Systems.*

Chapter IX

E-Taxation: An Introduction to the Use of TaxXML for Corporate Tax Reporting

Vikramaditya Pant, Villanova University, USA

M. Susan Stiner, Villanova University, USA

William P. Wagner, Villanova University, USA

Abstract

Online tax systems are rapidly replacing paper-based tax reporting systems. Promising many advantages over the traditional method of hard copy tax filing, these systems promise faster process, lower costs and increased efficiency. Using a specific language from the Extensible Markup Language family called TaxXML, TIGERS, a government subcommittee for the establishment of electronic taxation standards is looking to revolutionize the way government administers taxation. TaxXML draws upon the concepts and constructs of basic XML and utilizes tax-related vocabularies to create a standardized and systematized framework of electronic tax preparation and reporting. Having said that electronic tax reporting is advantageous over traditional paper-based reporting, there are further advantages of using a TaxXML-based electronic system than one that is engineered using non-standard proprietary technologies. While it is still in its early stages of development, it is unclear how hard the government will impose this technology onto the industry and also how the industry will react to this new technology. This paper will provide some background for the study of TaxXML and will suggest why TaxXML is a very significant development in the realm of online tax systems.

Introduction

The Internal Revenue Service (IRS) is the federal government agency charged with collection of taxes for the nation. Under the U.S. Constitution, the power to impose and collect taxes is given to Congress[1]. Congress delegated power to the IRS. The IRS is most often associated with the collection of income tax levied on individuals, corporations, estates and trusts. In addition, the IRS collects excise tax, estate tax[2], gift tax[3], and generation-skipping transfer tax[4]. The IRS also collects social security and Medicare taxes on behalf of the Social Security Administration[5].

In fiscal 2001, the latest year for which figures are available, the IRS collected $2,128,831,182,000 in gross revenue. According to the IRS, it cost 41 cents for every $100 of revenue collected. The IRS continually strives to reduce the costs of revenue collection, eliminate the paper on which records are kept and diminish the storage space necessary to handle the business of taxes in the U.S. Simultaneously, the IRS constantly tries to improve the quality of data it processes. One new initiative involves the use of TaxXML for online filing of taxes. This paper will examine this new initiative as it applies to corporate tax reporting.

There are two types of corporations for federal tax reporting purposes: C, or regular, corporations and S corporations. They have different tax characteristics that are declared in the respective subchapters of the Internal Revenue Code (Code) that contains the tax rules for these business entities. These are summarized in Table 1.

In addition to one of the two varieties of the Form 1120, corporations use forms such as Form 941 (Employer's Quarterly Federal Tax Return) and Form 940 (Employer's Annual Federal Unemployment (FUTA) Tax Return), among others, to declare federal taxes.

Limited Liability Corporations, or the LLCs, can choose to file their taxes as a regular corporation or as a partnership. They don't have a dedicated tax area because they can fit in existing tax structures.

Table 1.

Corporation	Tax-Stage		Federal Tax Form	Status Validity
	Corporation	*Shareholder*		
C	Yes	Yes	Form 1120	In all states
S	No	Yes	Form 1120S	Not in all states

Electronic Tax Reporting and TaxXML

E-Taxation Technology

Electronic Tax Reporting refers to the process of filing tax reports and compatible supporting documentation to a taxation authority using a computer or another electronic device over publicly switched or dedicated telephone lines or via the Internet. Mostly used by individuals, corporations are now beginning to take up this method of tax reporting. E-filing was created by the Internal Revenue Service in 1986. The late 1980s saw a move from entirely paper-based tax processing to a process that incorporated the telephone for transmitting information from simple tax returns or wire transfer to make tax payments. Today some individuals can file simple income tax returns over the Internet, and some types of taxes are filed on magnetic media and the payment is automatically remitted by the taxpayer's bank. In order to have a more robust and complete transfer of certain kinds of information, a specialized vocabulary of the Extensible Markup Language (XML) family is being developed.

The rate of change is accelerating and businesses are adopting electronic tax technologies at an increasing pace. As per IRS estimates, the estimated "Electronically filed partnership returns" will rise to approximately half a million returns for 2008 as opposed to the roughly 29,000 returns that will be filed for fiscal year 2006. The visionaries will seize the new opportunities afforded by the use of XML. They will stumble occasionally, but will overcome the difficulty. This is an increase of around 13 times regarding the electronic filing of taxes for businesses between these six years.

In the early days of electronic filing, such reporting involved the entering of information on electronic tax forms and then the submission of these forms to the IRS in a batched format over a telephone. With the advent of the Internet, electronic filing has evolved from just a peer-to-peer terminal-based service to one that allows for real-time tax reporting over the World Wide Web.

Online filing was engendered in 1995 by the combined efforts of the IRS and various tax preparation services. Online filing refers to the process of filling and submission of the tax forms on the World Wide Web. This is done in one of two ways. Comparatively non-complex forms are filled out and submitted directly using a generic Web browser such as Internet Explorer or Netscape Communicator in a manner similar to "surfing the Web." This method is referred to as the "Online e-File" method. Here the documents are created and transmitted over popular Internet mediums such as Hypertext Markup Language (HTML) for document creation and TCP/IP (Transfer Control Protocol/Internet Protocol) for transmission. HTML is a language in the family of Standard Generalized Markup Language (SGML). HTML is most commonly used for creation of Web pages on the World Wide Web. Since these electronic forms are created by and reside at the tax authority's computers, the filer accesses them remotely over the Internet, and the tax authority is able to process the documents.

More complex forms are filled out from within proprietary software[7] that results in output that is compatible to governmental requirements. This method is referred to as the "Upload Data" method. Here too the transmission is done using a more secure version of the TCP/IP; however since the documents are created at the filer's/service provider's computer(s), they need to ensure that the documents are in the format that the computers at the tax authority can process. These documents may be created asynchronously (prepared over time and then submitted at once after the preparation is complete). Table 2 distinguishes between these two approaches to electronic tax reporting.

Earlier, there was no standardized method of architecting software that allowed for the creation of a common data interchange mechanism for electronic tax reporting. Also, there was no inexpensive method for developing such software, as everything from the groundwork to the accouterments needed creation individually for different software. These costs were transferred over to the customers, making the software pricey and often times incompatible with one another. Since these software applications were created to "get the job done" by any means necessary, and that meant that as long as the software package conformed to the tax schematic it could be created in any programming language and could use any kind of data format to deliver the tax information the tax

Table 2. Comparison of online e-Filing vs. uploading

	Online e-File	**Upload Data**
Form Location	Server Side [Tax Authority]	Client Side [Tax Filer]
Software Interface	World Wide Web Forms	Application's User Interface
Software Provider	IRS/Tax Authority	Software Developer
Report Preparation	Synchronous	Asynchronous
Usability	Relatively simple tax forms	Complex tax forms
Delivery Route	TCP/IP [Over the Internet]	Private Network [To a Virtual Private Network]

authority. Clearly this method was cumbersome because every software developer attempted to "re-invent the wheel" within the framework of the tools and resources available to them.

With the variety of computer software platforms and architectures today, it is impossible for any tax authority to allow for eclectic methods of electronic tax information submission. Nowadays, the IRS releases a schematic regarding the acceptable data types and transport mechanisms and different software vendors[8] adapt their software to generate output that is compliant with the rules[9]. This is where the power of XML as a device independent, platform independent data interchange language can be truly harnessed.

SGML and Markup Technology

Standard Generalized Markup Language, or SGML, is a system for organizing and tagging elements of a document. In SGML, the tags encapsulate the informational portions of a document rendering the data separate from the presentational information. A "tagged" document is created using rules outlined in a dictionary file regarding the definition and uses of the tags and the data within them. A "tagged" document can be interpreted using the dictionary file that was referenced at the time of document creation. A style sheet can be used to render the data using the presentational guidelines specified in the design template. The same data can be displayed in multiple ways by using different style sheets. The International Organization for Standards (ISO) created SGML in 1986. New languages in the SGML family are constantly being developed and HTML and XML are both parts of the SGML family.

Currently, HTML forms lack complexity because HTML is basically a presentational markup language and not a data-interchange markup language. Therefore this method is only useful for businesses for filing comparatively simplistic and recurring tax forms such as Form 1098 (Mortgage Interest Statement) and Form 4136 (Credit for Federal Tax Paid on Fuels). The difference between a presentational markup language and a data-interchange markup language is that the tags in a presentational markup language such as HTML only declare the render/data display attributes of information contained within them in one specific way. A data-interchange markup language such as XML (based on the SGML family) uses its tags to define the meaning, significance, and used of the information enveloped by the tags. This difference is a big reason for the limitations presented by the use of the HTML alone in creating and transporting tax forms because the forms vary greatly in their elemental compositions (tax items) and interpretational methodologies (use of the data)[10]. One generic set of presentational rules is inadequate to the "interpretation" of complex tax forms because data display guidelines do not define the significance, use or meaning of the data. Following are two snippets of portions of financial statements from two years from an organization. The first is in the HTML format and the latter in the XML format.

```
<p>Financial Statements<br>
Income Statement<br>
2002<br>
Revenue $5,000,000<br>
COGS $3,500,000<br>
Gross Profit $1,500,000<br>
2003<br>
Revenue $4,500,000<br>
COGS $4,000,000<br>
Gross Profit $500,000</p>
```

HTML-based representation does not support the separation of data from its presentational information and the data is mixed in with its field's name along with the presentational information. Consequently, computer applications are unable to process complex information presented in this format as numbers and words don't have any connectivity (other than being on the same line) and the numbers don't signify their purpose.

```
<Financial Statements>
<Income Statement>
<2002>
<Revenue>$5,000,000</Revenue>
<COGS>$3,500,000</COGS>
<Gross_Profit>$1,500,000</Gross_Profit>
</2002>
<2003>
<Revenue>$4,500,000</Revenue>
<COGS>$4,000,000</COGS>
<Gross_Profit>$500,000</Gross_Profit>
</2003>
</Income_Statement>
```

XML-based representation is very definitive in declaring what each number denotes. There is no presentational information in the file containing the data as a separate style sheet can be applied to the data at the time of presentation.

XML, XML Vocabularies, and XML Schema/Namespace

XML or Extensible Markup Language is a family of meta-languages. A meta-language, as the name suggests, is "above and beyond" a regular language because it allows for the creation of new languages based on its own attributes, methods and guidelines.

XML allows for the exchange of data between computers regardless of configurations, platforms or operating systems. It also allows for data to be transferred to computers from devices such as telephones, personal digital assistants, faxes, etc. This ability of communicating data seamlessly has led to the creation of many industry and application specific XML-based languages. Since February 1998 when XML was recommended by the World Wide Web Consortium (W3C), close to 300 new XML languages have been created. Chemical Markup Language (used for transferring chemistry formulae and chemical information) and VoiceXML (used for voice-based data input/output) are two examples of the many XML-based languages being used today. Each week, roughly two to three new XML languages are created. XML, according to the World Wide Web consortium:

"...is primarily intended to meet the requirements of large-scale Web content providers for industry-specific markup, vendor-neutral data exchange, media-independent publishing, one-on-one marketing, workflow management in collaborative authoring environments, and the processing of Web documents by intelligent clients... The Language is designed for the quickest possible client-side processing consistent with its primary purpose as an electronic publishing and data interchange format." (W3C Press Release, 199811)

To get the meaning, use and significance of the data contained within XML documents, there needs to be a dictionary file that is used to encode/decode the information present in the XML documents. One XML language differs from another in that the dictionary it uses is different. Theological Markup Language, or ThML, uses a different dictionary than Mathematical Markup Language, or MathML, because it needs to define different types of data in different ways for different uses. XML dictionaries are also known as XML vocabularies because they differentiate one XML language from another. Every XML based language has its own unique vocabulary. DTDs or Document Type Definitions were the

XML dictionaries of the past and these days XML schemas with wider scope are used in their place. XML schemas are very explicit and detailed set of instructions regarding the attribute types used in an XML document. This collection of clear definitions ensures that there is no difference in the meaning of the data contained in an XML document between the time of its creation and its subsequent interpretation. A process called "validation" is executed after an XML document is created to ensure that the document conforms to the XML schema that it uses.

An XML namespace is a unique collection of XML element names that is referenced by a Uniform Resource Identifier. This is a repository of the details regarding the tags used in XML documents as elements and attributes. Since an XML document can have element types and attributes that have the same name but come from different sources, there needs to be a way of differentiating between them for their proper usage. An example of this is that an XML document might contain an attribute named "Employee" that it references in the first instance from a book publisher and in another instance from an airline pilot. Clearly the two different "types" of employees will have very different attributes and here namespaces can be used to differentiate the attributes of one from another. This one further extension of XML vocabularies because by specifying the exact dictionary to use minor differences within a particular vocabulary can be utilized. This applies in the realm of corporate tax reporting in that a company that owes taxes in many states can prepare its XML based tax returns using the authorized tax schema while at the same time implement marginal differences between tax procedures in the different states via specific namespaces.

Also, an XML document might contain an attribute name "Employee_ Specialization" twice with the first use referring to the term from a hospital vocabulary and the second from a law firm vocabulary. This ability of uniquely identifying the dictionary to be used enables unlimited flexibility in an XML document. This relates to corporate tax reporting by way of the fact that a company might include a certain item in its returns as a deduction however the percentage of that amount that the company may write off might differ based upon the charter of that company (non-profit vs. for-profit). Namespaces allow for the accurate handling of the data in that scenario by the return creator referencing the location of the relevant tax XML vocabulary.

TaxXML

Extensible Markup Language is very significant in the realm of tax reporting in general and corporate tax reporting in specific. This is because it allows for a standardized data distribution framework for the dissemination of tax information from a company to the government or vice-versa.

TaxXML is the XML vocabulary that is related to tax reporting. It is presently in a developmental stage, but given the encompassing nature of such a standard, a modular approach is being taken regarding its preparation. The tax schemas for the different tax forms are being developed one-by-one so as to enable the thorough trialing and testing of each form individually. The schema for generating and handling the IRS forms 1120, 1120S and 941 have already been created. When the first schemas were being created, Form 1120 was selected because it is the primary corporate tax reporting form and it represents about 85% of all the tax elements at the IRS. If the TaxXML-based electronic version of this form works successfully then other forms that utilize common elements and attributes can derive those from the schema of Form 1120. Only common elements that withstand testing within Form 1120 are being incorporated into the new forms that are being developed. Form 1120 was also used as one of the first candidates because there are many common elements between this form and Form 1040 (for Personal Income Tax reporting). The success of deploying 1120 on the TaxXML system will enable the creation of TaxXML based documents for personal income tax reporting as well. The schemas for forms 1041, 1065 and 990 are presently under development as they share quite a few common elements with Form 1120.

According to the XML think-tank XML Cover Pages:

"Tax XML is an initiative to research and analyze personal and business tax reporting & compliance information, represented in XML, to facilitate interoperability in a way that is open, flexible and international in scope. The products of Tax XML will include a vocabulary of terms, a repository of artifacts including XML templates, documents exchanged for tax compliance, best practices, guidelines and recommendations for practical implementation. It will focus on developing a common vocabulary that will allow participants to unambiguously identify the tax related information exchanged within a particular business context." (XML Cover Pages, 2001[12])

The government as well as industry and academic research groups are following the development of TaxXML because the creation of a standardized electronic tax-reporting medium can impact the financial management of businesses in a big way.

The governmental research and development group that is working on the creation of the TaxXML standard is called Tax Information Group for ECommerce Requirements Standardization or TIGERS. TIGERS is a sub-group within the Government Subcommittee that develops tax standards known as the Tax Information Interchange or "Task Group 2." TIGERS is a part of the American National Standards Institute ASC X-12 (Accredited Standards Committee, X12-

Government Subcommittee). It has been synthesized to discuss the state and future of business practices and corporate standards in relation to tax data formatting and exchange. Most of the major technical formats and standards for electronic tax reporting are developed and maintained by TIGERS. The XML based Tax vocabulary that TIGERS is developing will be one that will be used by all federal, state and local authorities for electronic tax governance. This vocabulary will standardize and systematize all electronic taxation related technologies. As per XML Cover Pages:

"A current [2001-11] TIGERS effort is to examine the possible use of eXtensible Markup Language (XML) in tax administration and its standardization. One of the emphases of TIGERS is to review opportunities for consistency in state and federal filing processes. Individual tax authorities should use available guidelines, formats and codes for each tax application they are putting in place, and seek TIGERS guidance in implementation, strictly limiting 'customization.' This will benefit all trading partners and reduce their cost." (XML Cover Pages, 2001[13])

From a corporate tax reporting standpoint, different parties that have an incentive in the development of the TaxXML standard at TIGERS are shown in Table 3.

TIGERS is working on a project that might bring about one of the most dramatic and positive changes to the Internal Revenue Service. A standard such as TaxXML has the potential to redefine the methods that the government utilizes for tax administration.

Methodologies of TaxXML Implementation

According to Dr. Glenda Hayes of MITRE, TIGERS is engaged in researching the three main methods of electronic tax reporting via TaxXML (Hayes, 2001). Each of these methods is different it its level of control. Control refers to the degree of security in the representation and transport of data marked up using TaxXML. It is the extent of encryption that is sought in the implementation of the TaxXML standard. These methods are:

XBRL-based "Open" method: XBRL is a standard for marking up the accounting information of a business's financial reports. This is a very flexible approach to implementing TaxXML as the data is marked up using a schema founded on an open standard that passes over the Internet as a plain text file. This is the most

Table 3.

Group	Implication
TIGERS	TIGERS has been chartered with the tax of standardizing an electronic tax reporting system. The success of TIGERS will depend, for the most part, on the efficacy and popularity of the TaxXML standard. TaxXML holds the potential of revamping the entire framework of electronic tax reporting through all governmental agencies.
Corporations	Companies will need to report their taxes in TaxXML within the rules established by TIGERS. There will be no scope for "creativity" in tax reporting as the elements and attributes being used will be explicitly detailed in the definitions within the TaxXML schema. Tax reports will need to be prepared within a strict regime that will minimize the scope for fraud.
Vendors	The schema for TaxXML that is finalized at TIGERS will dictate the way in which the computer software will be engineered and used. With a pre-described foundation of the technology to be used for the development of such software, there will be the scope for far greater inter-operability between electronic tax reporting software.
International Tax Agencies	Taxation agencies of foreign governments will likely choose to be compatible to the TaxXML standards developed at TIGERS because that will enable them to integrate with the American tax system and also help them optimize their own tax systems.

seamless approach to integrating TaxXML components into pre-existing corporate accounting packages.

EDI-based: Using this method the taxes are encrypted with a moderate level of security. Since there is the process of encoding the returns before they are readied for filing and decoding, this method is slightly harder to integrate into an existing accounting software. The advantage of this approach is the increased certainty that tax filing are going directly to an electronic data interchange set up by the tax administration authority over a secure connection.

Direct method: This is the strictest method for deploying TaxXML. Here every component of the filing is strongly encrypted. Data is only passed over secured connections. Authenticity and integrity of the filings is maintained by validation of the document to the schema and authentication of the transport mechanism for conveying the tax returns. This is the most resources intensive method of implementing TaxXML due to the immense computing requirements of the coding and decoding of the tax filings. Microsoft Strawman is an encryption project that is being considered by TIGERS for possible implementation in such an approach to TaxXML implementation.

Figure 1 relates to trade-off between the deployment simplicity and level of security in the filings.

Conclusion

The IRS has the goal of achieving 80% of federal tax and returns and information to be filed electronically by the year 2007[14]. This paper has surveyed a number of competing methodologies for electronic tax filing. Of these we have concluded that TaxXML is one of the most promising. In a few scenarios the IRS has stipulated certain guidelines forcing the adoption of electronic filing by corporations. It requires filers with over a certain number of tax documents to file using magnetic media, or optionally, online. The success of this initiative depends largely on getting corporations to move to this new format.

There are numerous advantages of filing taxes electronically from a business standpoint. E-filing has some explicit benefits such as extended filing periods and instant refunds while others are intrinsic such as the enhancement of the overall business process at an organization. For businesses to adopt the process of electronic filing *en-masse* it is important for the tax administrators to standardize the data interchange medium. TaxXML is ideally suited for enabling this.

The TaxXML framework has benefits that electronic tax filing systems based on other technologies do not. For instance, as soon as a tax document encoded using

Figure 1.

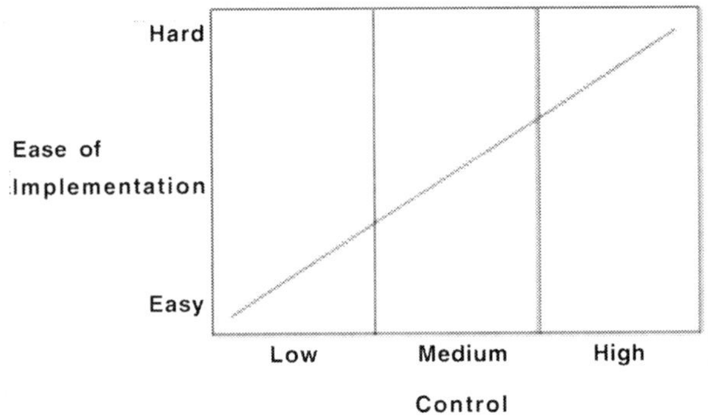

TaxXML is submitted to the tax authority, the document is checked for validity and authenticity (via the TaxXML schema) and an acknowledgment receipt can be issued to the filer almost instantly. Since every valid TaxXML document will be free of structural anomalies, the tax administrator can expeditiously process the document and reduce the cost of tax administration.

Another advantage that TaxXML- based systems have is that since most of the state and local tax elements are derived from federal forms, the taxes for multiple levels of administrations (federal, state, local) can be prepared at once cognizant of the differences that might exist between the protocols.

The creators of TaxXML are working to optimize the tax administration mechanism in America. When there are no more challenges presented to them by the use of XML for generating and processing tax information, they will move on to the next paradigm shift. As the visionaries advance, they will leave behind a cadre who experience significantly less upheaval, but who will deepen and broaden the uses to which the new process is put. In the end the use of XML as a tax planning and compliance vehicle will be as commonplace as using a telephone is today.

References

AICPA. (2002). *New XML-based standard now being used in financial statements.* Retrieved from *http://www.aicpa.org/pubs/cpaltr/may2002/newxml.html*

Hayes, G. (2001). XML schema activities at IRS, *MITRE Report.*

Meta Group. (2001). September 2001 report.

MITRE. (1999). MITRE supports tax administration modernization. *MITRE Report.* Retrieved from *http://www.mitre.org/pubs/showcase/irs-july99/index.html*

TaxXML. (2002). TaxXML development resource page. Retrieved from *http://www.taxadmin.org/fta/edi/xmldev.html*

TIGERS Homepage. (2002). *Tax Information Group for EC Requirements Standardization (TIGERS).* Retrieved from *http://www.taxadmin.org/fta/edi/1205ann.html*

Vasarhelyi, M. A. (2002). *Essentials of Xbrl: Financial reporting in the 21st century,* Indianapolis, IN: John Wiley & Sons.

Wagner, W., and Hilken, R. (2003). *Introduction to applied XML for business,* Prentice-Hall.

W3C. (1998). The World Wide Web Consortium issues XML 1.0 as a W3C recommendation. *W3C Report.*

XML Cover Pages. (2002). US Internal Revenue Service and SGML/XML for tax filing. *XML Cover Pages Report.* Retrieved from *http://xml.coverpages.org/irs.html*

XML Cover Pages. (2001). TIGERS work group releases draft XML schemas for electronic income tax submission. *XML Cover Pages Report.* Retrieved from *http://xml.coverpages.org/ni2001-11-15-a.html*

Endnotes

[1] U.S. Constitution, Art. 1, Sec. 8

[2] This is tax paid by the estate of a deceased person of some means for the privilege of giving his or her property to someone, to an institution such as a foundation, to a trust or to a charity such as the Red Cross after the person's death.

[3] This is tax paid by a person of modest or more means for the privilege of giving his or her property to someone or a favorite organization while the person is still alive.

[4] This is the tax paid by a person of significant means who gives his or her property to a person two or more generations younger than the giver. The gift can occur either while the property owner is alive or after the owner's death. The tax is punitive in both intent and effect.

[5] IRC § 1401(a)

[6] According to a Data Release by the IRS titled "Projections of Returns to Be Filed in Calendar Years: 2001-2008." This report is accessible at http://www.irs.gov/pub/irs-soi/08rs01pr.pdf.

[7] Sample listing of such proprietary software can be found at the Texas Comptroller of Public Accounts office Web site (http://www.window.state.tx.us/taxinfo/etf/etf.html)

[8] An updated list of software vendors that are authorized by the IRS for providing electronic tax reporting services/software is available at the IRS website at http://www.irs.gov/efile/lists/0,,id=100422,00.html.

[9] The latest list of rules for the creation and transportation of forms is available at the IRS website for use by software developers at http://www.irs.gov/taxpros/providers/article/0,,id=101145,00.html.

[10] Tax items can have many sub-components and the same items may need to be interpreted differently given the nature of the entire tax filing in

totality. For instance, a certain kind of an expense might be considered a deduction based on the type of the company (non-profit, for-profit) and also the percentage of deduction (if applicable) might depend on the fulfillment of other criteria demonstrable in other portions of the filings.

11 http://www.w3.org/Press/1998/XML10-REC

12 Source: xml.coverpages.org (2001).

13 Source: xml.coverpages.org (2001).

14 The IRS Restructuring and Reform Act of 1998, P.L. 105-206 § 2001(a) (7/22/1998).

Previously published in the Journal of Electronic Commerce in Organizations, 2(1), 29-41, January-March 2004.

Chapter X

Online Consumer Trust: A Multi-Dimensional Model

Felix B. Tan, Auckland University of Technology, New Zealand

Paul Sutherland, The University of Auckland, New Zealand

Abstract

Consumer trust is widely heralded as an essential element for the success of electronic commerce, yet the concept itself is still clouded in confusion by the numerous definitions and points of view held across multiple disciplines. It is the aim of this paper to synthesise the viewpoints from across the disciplines and bring them together in a multi-dimensional trust model. It is hoped that in doing so, these broad assortment of views will highlight the true underlying nature of trust in the online environment. From these multiple disciplines, three dimensions of trust emerged: dispositional trust, institutional trust and interpersonal trust, each bringing its own influencing factors into the overall intention to trust. From this model emerged the notion that the consumer as an individual is central to the understanding of trust, and in turn that the individual's personality and culture form the foundation for the development of trust.

Introduction

There is increasing acceptance that consumer trust is a key foundation for electronic commerce success. If the consumer cannot develop some sense of confidence in the vendor's competence, predictability, benevolence and integrity, then they are likely to abort the purchase and simply look elsewhere for a more trustworthy alternative (McKnight & Chervany, 2002; McKnight, Cummings, & Chervany, 1998; Tan & Theon, 2001).

Much of the literature surrounding trust in electronic commerce looks to substitute trust by focusing solely on the aspects of consumer privacy and security (Belanger, Hiller, & Smith, 2002; Benassi, 1999; Dekleva, 2000; Huberman, Franklin, & Hogg, 1999). The literature also tends to lack a firm definition of trust and therefore often causes further confusion by presenting the belief that trust is a simple factor that can be explained by addressing these vendor specific factors. This does not however address the issue of trust as a whole and simply serves to look to deal with addressing the symptoms rather than the underlying issue.

The lack of scope in the Information Systems literature has been highlighted in Gefen (2002) where it was stated that there was a "need to establish the dimensionality of trust as it is applied to MIS topics and in doing so to recognise that although trust may occasionally be unidimensional as found by some research, it may also be multi-dimensional depending on the circumstances." He went further stating that in addressing trust automatically as a one-dimensional construct, researchers may be oversimplifying their study, which in turn may prevent them from revealing the whole story (Gefen, 2002). However, as with much of the literature surrounding trust, Gefen (2002) addressed the attributes of trust rather than the nature of trust as a whole.

To further research in the field of electronic commerce, it is necessary to widen the research scope and bring in additional perspectives from outside of the information systems literature. Webster and Watson (2002) highlighted the need for information systems literature for this widened scope, when they commented: "IS is an interdisciplinary field straddling other disciplines, you often must look not only within the IS discipline when reviewing and developing theory but also outside the field". This viewpoint is highly relevant in addressing the issue of trust, as it has long been theorised and argued across many disciplines. It is therefore necessary to take into account the numerous perspectives these disciplines attach to the topic of trust.

Taking a holistic view of trust that encompasses multiple disciplines is somewhat rare in research into trust in the electronic environment, yet it has the potential to yield the greatest insights into the underlying factors at work within the consumers' mind in their assessment of an electronic retailer. Borrowing from the fields of psychology, sociology, marketing and management, as well as information systems, we can help to create a better understanding of the true nature of trust online.

The purpose of this paper is therefore to present a multi-dimensional insight into the nature of consumer trust online. We will firstly look to synthesise a broad literature base surrounding trust in relation to electronic commerce, and then look to identify gaps and inconsistencies in the current literature. These gaps will then be addressed through the development of a multi-dimensional trust model that can be applied to gain an insight into this commonly misunderstood construct and provide a better understanding of the true nature of trust.

Although the formation of trust holds similarities across differing business forms, this paper's scope has been narrowed to focus primarily on the B2C (business-to-consumer) environment.

Literature Review

What is Trust?

Before we delve too deeply into the nature of trust, we first need to form a clear idea of just what trust is. Literature that fails to take this step often ends up causing further confusion and debate amongst researchers rather than adding to the knowledge base. The lack of a widely accepted definition has been highlighted by numerous researchers (Belanger et al., 2002; Bigley et al., 1998; Lee & Turban, 2001; Lewis & Weigert, 1985; Yoon, 2002), but most clearly in Hosmer (1995), where it was stated that "there appears to be widespread agreement on the importance of trust in human conduct, but unfortunately there also appears to be equally widespread lack of agreement on a suitable definition of the concept."

If we turn to dictionary definitions of trust, we are still not much further from the confusion. The Oxford dictionary holds 17 definitions for the word trust, whereas Webster's holds 18. Selections of the most relevant definitions from these publications are shown in Table 1.

From these dictionary definitions it is apparent that similar words are repeatedly appearing, words like reliance, confidence, integrity, faith, risk and hope. The diversity of the definitions indicates the diverseness of the topic, yet researchers often try to narrow the scope of trust so it will fit into their empirical research. This is a valid form of research if the narrowed scope is adequately explained and reasoned, but it needs to be made clear just where the research boundaries

Table 1. Dictionary definitions

Oxford Dictionary	*Webster's Dictionary*
Confidence in or **reliance** on some quality or attribute of a person or thing, or the truth of a statement.	Assured resting of the mind on the **integrity**, veracity, justice, friendship, or other sound principle of another person; **confidence**; **reliance**.
To accept or give credit to without investigation or evidence.	To **risk**; to venture **confidently**.
The condition of having **confidence** reposed in one or of being entrusted with something.	To place **confidence** in; to **rely on**, to confide, or repose **faith**, in; as, we can not trust those who have deceived us.
The quality of being trustworthy; fidelity, **reliability**; loyalty, trustiness.	
Confident expectation of something; **hope**.	

begin and end. This is illustrated in a large body of research surrounding trust in Information Systems literature which often leads people to the conclusion that addressing consumers' privacy concerns and setting up a safe shopping cart is sufficient to deal with the issue of trust online, while in reality this only addresses a singular dimension.

It is important to note that these definitions are focusing on identifying the attributes of trust rather than defining trust itself. This idea needs to be emphasised, as it is a point of much confusion in the literature, whereby researchers look to address these attributes alone rather than the construct of trust as a whole.

If we turn to the trust literature for a definition, we narrow the scope somewhat further as seen in Table 2. From those articles that clearly define the attributes of trust, we can see that the majority are centred on the ideas of competence, predictability, benevolence and/or integrity. Competence is the belief in the other parties' abilities, skills and expertise within the certain domain. It is the thought that the other party will be able to accomplish the expected level of service. Benevolence is the belief that the other party wants to do good for the customer and is not solely looking to make a profit. Predictability focuses on the belief in the other parties' consistent behaviour. Integrity is the belief that the other party will act in an honest fashion and adhere to an accepted set of principles or standards. McKnight and Chervany (2002) notes that predictability and integrity are similar, yet they differ as integrity is a value-laden attribute whereas predictability is not.

Across the literature there is a growing acceptance of Mayer et al. (1995) which presented the attributes of ability (competence), benevolence and integrity as central to the concept of trust. As seen in Table 2, this combination of attributes has been the most commonly grouped assortment in literature (Cheung and Lee, 2001; Gefen, 2002; Lee and Turban, 2001). This line of thinking has also been further built upon in more recent research, which adds predictability to Mayer's identified attributes (McKnight and Chervany, 2002). Tan and Theon (2001) held a similar view, but described the attributes of trust slightly differently, naming them as competence belief, dependence belief, disposition belief and fulfilment belief, which can be translated into the same attributes as noted above.

Defining Trust

Now that we have a clearer understanding of the attributes that make up trust, we can start to incorporate the situational instances in which trust becomes important. There is a general widespread agreement across the literature on the conditions needed for trust to exist. Risk plays a central role in the fostering of trust and is a

Table 2. Attributes of trust identified in literature

Author	*Attributes of Trust*			
	Competence	***Benevolence***	***Predictability***	***Integrity***
Cheung and Lee (2001)	x	x		x
Deutsch (1958)	x	x		
Doney and Cannon (1997)		x		x
Gefen (2002)	x	x		x
Lee and Turban (2001)	x	x		x
Mayer et al. (1995)	x	x		x
McKnight and Chervany (2002)	x	x	x	x
Nöteberg et al. (2003)				x
Ratnasingham and Pavlou (2003)	x	x	x	
(Rousseau et al. (1998)		x		
Sirdeshmukh et al. (2002)	x	x		
Tan and Theon (2001)	x	x	x	x

prerequisite for trust to arise as an issue, i.e., if there is no risk, then the consumer is not forced to make an assessment of trustworthiness (Deutsch, 1958; Mayer et al., 1995).

The most commonly accepted definition amongst the recent research on trust has taken a similar view to that of Mayer et al. (1995), incorporating vulnerability into their central definition of trust (Gefen, 2002; Lee and Turban, 2001; Rousseau et al., 1998; Tan and Theon, 2001). This definition holds that trust is a "willingness to be vulnerable," i.e., when the consumer allows themselves to be vulnerable, they are taking a risk (Mayer et al., 1995). Rousseau et al. (1998) builds on this central idea of vulnerability, presenting that "trust is a psychological state comprising the intention to accept vulnerability based upon positive expectations of the intentions or behaviour of another". The centrality of vulnerability in trust definitions can be traced back to Deutsch (1958), where it was presented that the consumer "perceives that he will be worse off if he trusts and his trust is not fulfilled than if he does not trust". The consumer therefore would be allowing themselves to be vulnerable while holding the hope that the other party will deliver on their promise.

Putting Trust in Perspective

In identifying vulnerability as the central situational feature of trust, we can see the importance this holds in the electronic commerce setting. This vulnerability is magnified in the online situation due to the nature of the Internet. In the traditional physical environment, consumers' attitudes and behaviours are often affected by intrinsic cues gathered from the physical surroundings such as lighting, colour, music and store layout (Bitner, 1992). When the consumer is faced with risk, they look to make a trust-based assessment of the other party by looking to gather further information. This information search can take numerous forms, be it gathering intrinsic cues from situational surroundings, recalling past experiences in similar situations or looking for other external sources like personal recommendations from others (Koernig, 2003).

As a product offering moves from being a highly tangible to an intangible offering such as a "pure service," the greater the degree of associated consumer risk. The more intangible the product, the greater the influence the cues hold on the consumers' purchase decision as there are fewer physical aspects for consideration (Bitner, 1992; Zeithaml, 1988).

As the Internet does not allow the consumer to gather the same range of intrinsic cues as traditional physical shopping does, the perceived risk is magnified and therefore an assessment of trustworthiness needs to be made by the consumer. It is the dimensions involved within this assessment of trust that is the focus of this research, as the true underlying nature of the subject is still unclear and the point of much confusion. To try and provide a clearer picture of trust, it is necessary to look across the disciplines and look at the differing dimensions of trust.

Dimensionality of Trust

As mentioned earlier, trust has been addressed across numerous fields and different conclusions have been reached. The field of psychology holds the view that trust is a personality-based trait, which is a deep-rooted feeling or belief that is shaped by the individual's life experiences. These life experiences mould the individual's disposition to form trust in general (as seen in McKnight and Chervany, 2002) and is commonly referred to as dispositional trust.

In stark contrast, sociology holds the view that trust is a social structure which is situationally constructed. Lewis and Weigert (1985) describes trust as being "applicable to the relations among people rather than to their psychological states taken individually" and therefore theorise that trust does not exist in the individual, but rather is the collective property of the groups involved. In the electronic commerce context, this dimension has been labelled as institutional trust.

The social psychology perspective offers another view, which presents trust in terms of the expectations and willingness of one party in regards to another, as well as the associated risks this brings along with it (Lee & Turban, 2001). This perspective focuses on forming trust in another specific party and is often referred to as interpersonal trust.

The differing views currently evident within trust research are illustrated in Table 3. The literature has been categorized by the dimensions it covers, be it directly or indirectly. It also indicates the field the research originates from, with the information systems literature grouped further into broad and focused categories. Broad IS literature borrows ideas from diverse fields whereas focused IS literature does not look far outside of its own discipline and tends to hold a narrow scope. From Table 3 we can see that only five (out of 22) papers covered directly addressed all three dimensions of trust.

From the literature covered, only six articles directly (and three indirectly) addressed the individual's disposition to trust. This indicates a large gap in the research into trust, as the consumers themselves are being overlooked. The disposition to trust is fundamental in the formation of trust, i.e., if the individual holds a low disposition to trust, they find it hard to develop a sense of trust in general and therefore would likely find it difficult to trust an online retailer.

Ten articles acknowledged trust at the institutional level and one did so indirectly. This also presents additional research opportunities as the institutional or sociological viewpoint has been somewhat overlooked by trust research.

Table 3. Dimensional concepts identified in literature

Author	Concepts Identified			Field of Research
	Dispositional Trust	Institutional Trust	Interpersonal Trust	
Belanger et al. (2002)			X	IS focused
Cardholm et al. (2000)			X	IS focused
Cheung and Lee (2001)	X	X	X	IS broad
Dekleva (2000)			X	IS focused
Doney and Cannon (1997)	*	X	X	Marketing
Earp et al. (2002)			X	IS focused
Gefen (2002)			X	IS broad
Hosmer (1995)	X	X	X	Management
Huberman et al. (1999)			X	IS focused
Lee and Turban (2001)	X	X	X	IS broad
Lewis and Weigert (1985)		X		Sociology
Malhotra and Murnighan (2002)			X	Management/ Psychology
Mayer et al. (1995)	X		X	Management
McKnight and Chervany (2002)	X	X	X	IS broad
Naquin and Paulson et al. (2003)		X	X	Psychology
Nöteberg et al. (2003)			X	IS focused
Ratnasingham and Pavlou (2003)		X	X	IS focused
Rousseau et al. (1998)	X	X	X	Management
Tan and Theon (2001)	*	X	X	IS focused
Van Den Berg and Van Lieshout (2001)			X	IS/ Accounting
Wang et al. (1998)			X	IS focused
Yoon (2002)	*	*	X	IS focused

As expected, all except one article addressed the interpersonal trust dimension, the one that did not was a sociology-based article which held a highly focused view (Lewis & Weigert, 1985). Also noteworthy is the sole focus of the majority of information system literature, which often only addressed a single dimension of trust. This viewpoint is usually focused on the issues surrounding online consumer privacy and transactional security. As noted by Gefen (2002), by addressing trust automatically as a one-dimensional construct, the researcher may be oversimplifying the problem and therefore failing to address the issue of trust as a whole.

Conceptual Trust Model

Now that a trust has been defined and explained, we can look to integrate the construct further into the electronic commerce arena to offer additional insights into the nature of trust online. From the review of the literature, online consumer trust can be looked at as a three-dimensional construct that encompasses the consumer (dispositional trust), the vendor (interpersonal trust) and the Internet (institutional trust). These dimensions help explain the forces at work in electronic commerce, thereby illustrating that the consumer, the Internet and the vendor all bring their own issues into the overall assessment of trust.

However within these dimensions themselves, there are additional inter-relationships that are indicated by the proposed model shown in Figure 1. From this we can form the view that dispositional trust is the primary foundation to the development of trust and the associated outcomes.

Dispositional Trust

Dispositional trust refers to an individual's ability and willingness to form trust in general. This dimension is driven by the field of psychology, which describes

Figure 1. Multi-dimensional trust model

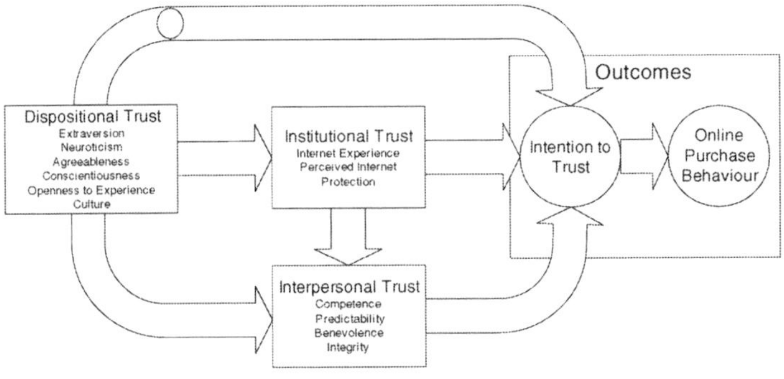

dispositional trust as a personality trait that is formed through an individual's lifetime.

Individuals first have their own upbringing and cultural issues which moulds their persona and their overall disposition to trust. If individuals typically find it hard to trust in general, they are not likely to find the Internet a comfortable place to conduct business due to the non-personal nature and the relatively high levels of trust required. On the other hand, individuals that finds it easy to trust will likely hold little reluctance in considering purchasing online. This disposition to trust could be looked upon as the necessary foundation in the formation of trust, as it is a prerequisite for the other dimensions of trust.

The concept of the personality is the subject of much debate amongst psychologists, but the five factor trait theory is one of the most accepted models (Costa, McCrae, & Dye, 1991; Goldberg, 1990, 1992; Olson & Suls, 2000). This model contends that an individual's personality can be described through five factors: extraversion, neuroticism, agreeableness, conscientiousness, and the openness to experience.

Extraversion refers to the individual's level of focus on the outside world. Extraverted personalities are said to be socially outgoing and are generally more careless and quick to change views. From this personality trait we can propose that extraversion leads to a higher disposition to trust.

Neuroticism is described as encompassing emotional instability, pessimism, fear and low self-esteem (Olson et al., 2000). An individual holding a neurotic personality is likely to hold high levels of anxiousness and view themselves as vulnerable (Costa et al., 1991). From this research we take the view that a neurotic individual would likely find it difficult to trust in general, and form the proposition that neuroticism leads to a lower disposition to trust.

Conscientious personalities are said to be dutiful and responsible, always carefully deliberating situations and usually on the side of cautiousness. From this cautious deliberation we propose that conscientiousness leads to a lower disposition to trust.

Openness to experience is characterised by open-mindedness as opposed to conservatism and traditionalism (Costa et al., 1991; Olson et al., 2000). This open-mindedness leads individuals to accept new experiences. We therefore propose that openness to experience leads to a high disposition to trust.

From these five factors that are said to encompass an individual's personality, agreeableness is of particular importance as it is this aspect of the personality which is said to "influence the self-image and help to shape social attitudes and philosophy of life" (Costa et al., 1991). Agreeable personalities are said to hold an optimistic view of human nature and generally believe people to be honest, decent, and trustworthy.

It could also be suggested that culture also plays a part in the disposition to trust, as some cultures may be more trusting in general and therefore hold a higher disposition to trust. Research into the issue of culture is quite widespread, yet there is very little that addresses the issue in relation to the formation of trust. Much of the literature on culture builds on the work done by Hofstede (1980), which groups culture into two broad categories: those that are thought to be individualistic vs. those that are seen as collectivistic cultures. These two groups are thought to act differently, think differently and most importantly in relation to work on trust, make judgements differently. For example, advertising messages emphasising personal benefits are most suited to those cultures that are individualistic, whereas a different focus of family benefits would be necessary to appeal to collectivist cultures (Han & Shavitt, 1994). It was found that in general, western countries were primarily individualistic, whereas East Asian countries tended to be more collectivist (Triandis, 1989). Taking these findings in account, it can be proposed that culture has an impact on the individual's disposition to trust, where collectivist cultures hold a lower disposition to trust and individualistic cultures are the opposite.

Institutional Trust

Institutional trust takes into account the sociology viewpoint that trust is a social structure that is situationally constructed. This dimension draws on the idea of forming trust in the Internet as a whole, and therefore trusting the technology. If consumers hold a fear of technology or the Internet, they are likely to not look towards the Internet as a shopping medium. It is therefore necessary to consider this viewpoint if we want to understand trust.

It is at this institutional level that the individual's perception of the regulatory, legal and technical environment comes to fruition (McKnight & Chervany, 2002). If individual do not believe the Internet offers adequate regulatory, legal or technical protection, they are unlikely to hold a high level of institutional trust in the Internet as a shopping medium. It is therefore proposed that perceived Internet protection has an impact on the level of institutional trust.

The institutional dimension also needs to take into account the individual's Internet experience, as previous experiences carry considerable weight when making judgments about a situation. These experiences carry more significance than any assumptions an individual could make about a situation without experiencing it personally beforehand (McKnight & Chervany, 1998). If an individual is familiar with the Internet and has used it on a regular basis, he is likely to hold a higher level of institutional trust in the medium than a person who has never used the Internet before. It is, therefore, proposed that the Internet experience increases the level of institutional trust and consequently, a lack of Internet experience decreases the level of institutional trust.

As shown in Figure 1, it is proposed that institutional trust is reliant on dispositional trust, such as if individuals have difficulty in forming trust in general, it is likely they will also have difficulty in developing trust in the Internet as a shopping medium.

Interpersonal Trust

Interpersonal trust focuses on the trust formed in another specific party. In this case, it is the assessment by the consumer in regards to the trustworthiness of the electronic vendor.

As discovered earlier when covering the literature definitions of trust, the attributes of competence, predictability, benevolence and integrity are found to be the cornerstones of developing trust in another party. We therefore need to address these issues at the Interpersonal level, as this is the dimension in which trust is formed in a specific other.

In addressing competence, consumers assess whether vendors have the appropriate abilities, skills and expertise to satisfy their needs. Predictability takes into account the vendor's perceived reputation for providing a consistent service. Integrity is the belief that the internet vendor will act in an honest fashion and adhere to an accepted set of principles or standards. When looking at benevolence, the consumer makes a judgement on whether the vendor is focused on making a fast profit or has the customer's best interests in mind.

Each of these attributes of interpersonal trust are measured by the consumer's impression of the internet vendor, drawn from previous experience or gathered from outside sources of information. These outside sources can take the form of friends and family that have shopped at the site before and relay their experiences, therefore transferring their assessment of trustworthiness to the consumer. It can also take the form of third party sites whereby internet users post feedback about particular vendors and shopping experiences. These third party assessments can prove a valuable trust builder in the online environment, as it provides the consumer with additional information that can help foster trust at this interpersonal level.

Online privacy and security issues are also evident in this interpersonal dimension. The effectiveness of third party privacy and security seals of approval have been widely commented on (Belanger et al., 2002; Benassi, 1999; Dekleva, 2000). Such policies and third-party endorsements have been found to have a positive effect on trust within this dimension enhancing the vendor's trustworthiness, particularly the attributes of integrity and competence. However, it is also important to note that the third party themselves must also be trusted by the individual before the trustworthiness endorsement can be transferable.

As seen in Figure 1, interpersonal trust relies on other dimensions of trust. First, dispositional trust is necessary foundation, as if the individual has trouble forming trust in general they are also likely to find it hard developing trust in a specific party. It is therefore proposed that interpersonal trust is reliant on dispositional trust.

In turn, institutional trust is also thought to have an impact on interpersonal trust online. If the individual is inexperienced with the Internet or does not believe there are adequate regulations protecting them online, their interpersonal trust assessment of the online vendor will also be affected. It is therefore proposed that institutional trust has a positive effect on the degree of interpersonal trust.

Overall Intention to Trust

The concept of overall intention to trust is the outcome of the consumers online trust assessment, which takes into account the levels of dispositional, institutional and interpersonal trust. We can view this intention to trust as the construct of trust in its fullest form, as it encompasses the multiple dimensions which are evident in the development of trust.

This overall intention is the willingness of the consumer to depend on the vendor. Relating this back to the definition of trust developed earlier, it is the willingness for consumers to make themselves vulnerable to particular Internet vendors after they have taken into account the various aspects attributed within each dimension. It is proposed that this overall intention to trust takes into account dispositional trust, institutional trust and interpersonal trust.

Online Purchase Behaviour

Online purchase behaviour is the anticipated result of the overall intention to trust. This behaviour, however, is not the sole result of the intention to trust, it also takes into account other factors such as relative price, speed of delivery and product availability, which are all outside the scope of this paper.

In the context of electronic commerce transactions, this purchase behaviour depends on the consumer holding an overall intention to trust the particular vendor, such as if this overall level of trust is not evident, consumers will likely shop elsewhere with vendors they hold a greater degree of trust in. It is, therefore, proposed that online purchase behaviour depends on the consumer holding a level of overall trust (intention to trust) in the vendor.

Discussion

The aim of this paper was to synthesise the current literature on trust from a broad range of disciplines and develop a model to better explain the underlying nature of the construct of trust. It is hoped that from this conceptualisation, information systems researchers will recognise that trust in electronic commerce is not a simple single-dimensional issue, but rather a broad and complex construct that operates on multiple dimensions.

A differing viewpoint was presented, whereby the individual consumer was seen to be the most central aspect. This is an important change in research perspective, as it is the consumers themselves that are making the trust-based assessments and, therefore, it is the consumers that need to be looked upon as the central figures in the electronic commerce environment. It is rare for this view to be taken, as typically literature on electronic commerce is written from the vendor's perspective, highlighting aspects that need to be taken to improve the success of an electronic commerce venture.

This consumer-centric viewpoint does not mean that this research holds no value for e-commerce practitioners — it is first necessary to comprehend the issue before we can adequately address it. Once this underlying nature of trust is fully understood, the focus can be shifted to developing methods for practitioners to address the aspects of consumer trust that are found to be influential.

By identifying the nature of trust and the dimensions involved, this paper has provided a conceptual foundation for future research into trust in electronic commerce. Now that the numerous definitions of trust have been synthesised and addressed, research can progress by adopting the definition provided by Mayer et al. (1995). This definition was found to be the most appropriate and also the most widespread classification, whereby trust was defined as the willingness of the consumer to be vulnerable.

Within the construct of trust itself, three-dimensional elements were identified to have an impact on the overall intention to trust. From these dimensions and their interactions, 19 propositions were uncovered for future research. Table 4 summarises the research propositions formed from our conceptualisation of trust in the online environment. The relevant literature identified for each proposition is the theoretical grounding for each proposition.

The dispositional trust propositions cover a large gap in current trust research, as the individual consumer's personality has not been previously represented in the literature. The addition of these personality traits however presents some problems in trying to empirically formulate the propositions into a quantifiable manner, as they are dealing with relatively high-level concepts. The literature listed for the personality-based propositions is psychology based research whereby the five facets of

Table 4. Future research propositions

Proposition	Relevant Literature	Previous Research
Dimension: Dispositional Trust		
Proposition 1: Extraversion leads to a higher Disposition to Trust.	Costa, McCrae, & Dye, 1991; Goldberg, 1990, 1992; Olson & Suls, 2000)	No
Proposition 2: Neuroticism leads to a lower Disposition to Trust.	Costa, McCrae, & Dye, 1991; Goldberg, 1990, 1992; Olson & Suls, 2000)	No
Proposition 3: Conscientiousness leads to a lower Disposition to Trust.	Costa, McCrae, & Dye, 1991; Goldberg, 1990, 1992; Olson & Suls, 2000)	No
Proposition 4: Openness to Experience leads to a higher Disposition to Trust.	Costa, McCrae, & Dye, 1991; Goldberg, 1990, 1992; Olson & Suls, 2000)	No
Proposition 5: Agreeableness leads to a higher Disposition to Trust.	Costa, McCrae, & Dye, 1991; Goldberg, 1990, 1992; Olson & Suls, 2000)	No
Proposition 6a: Consumers from collectivist cultures hold a lower Disposition to Trust. Proposition 6b: Consumers from individualistic cultures hold a higher Disposition to Trust.	(Han et al., 1994; Hofstede, 1980; Triandis, 1989)	No
Dimension: Institutional Trust		
Proposition 7a: Perceived Internet Protection increases the level of Institutional Trust. Proposition 7b: Perceived lack of Internet Protection decreases the level of Institutional Trust.	(McKnight and Chervany., 2002)	Yes
Proposition 8a: Internet Experience increases the level of Institutional Trust. Proposition 8b: Lack of Internet Experience decreases the level of Institutional Trust.	(McKnight and Chervany., 1998)	Yes
Proposition 9: Institutional trust is dependent on the consumer holding a Disposition to Trust		No
Dimension: Interpersonal Trust		
Proposition 10: The perceived Competence of the Internet Vendor increases the level of Interpersonal Trust.	(Belanger et al., 2002; Cheung and Lee, 2001; Doney and Cannon., 1997; Gefen, 2002; Lee and Turban, 2001; McKnight and Chervany., 2002; McKnight et al., 1998; Rousseau et al., 1998)	Yes

the personality (extraversion, neuroticism, agreeableness, conscientiousness and openness to experience) were identified. Each of these five personality factors was proposed to have an impact of on the individuals ability to form trust in general (dispositional trust). The propositions dealing with the effect culture has on an individual consumer's disposition to trust is also another area which is lacking in research. Cultural

Table 4: Future research propositions (cont.)

Proposition	Relevant Literature	Previous Research
Dimension: Interpersonal Trust		
Proposition 10: The perceived Competence of the Internet Vendor increases the level of Interpersonal Trust.	(Belanger et al., 2002; Cheung and Lee, 2001; Doney and Cannon., 1997; Gefen, 2002; Lee and Turban, 2001; McKnight and Chervany., 2002; McKnight et al., 1998; Rousseau et al., 1998)	Yes
Proposition 11: The perceived Predictability of the Internet Vendor increases the level of Interpersonal Trust.	(McKnight and Chervany., 2002; McKnight et al., 1998)	Yes
Proposition 12: The perceived Benevolence of the Internet Vendor increases the level of Interpersonal Trust.	(Belanger et al., 2002; Cheung and Lee, 2001; Doney and Cannon., 1997; Gefen, 2002; McKnight and Chervany., 2002; McKnight et al., 1998; Rousseau et al., 1998)	Yes
Proposition 13: The perceived Integrity of the Internet Vendor increases the level of Interpersonal Trust.	(Belanger et al., 2002; Cheung and Lee, 2001; Doney and Cannon., 1997; Gefen, 2002; Lee and Turban, 2001; McKnight and Chervany., 2002; McKnight et al., 1998; Rousseau et al., 1998)	Yes
Proposition 14: Interpersonal Trust is dependant on an individual's Disposition to Trust.		No
Proposition 15: Institutional Trust increases the level of Interpersonal Trust formed.	(McKnight and Chervany., 2002; McKnight at al., 1998)	Yes
Outcome: Overall Intention to Trust		
Proposition 16: Dispositional Trust increases the Overall Intention to Trust.		No
Proposition 17: Institutional Trust increases the Overall Intention to Trust.		No
Proposition 18: Interpersonal Trust increases the Overall Intention to Trust.		No
Outcome: Online Purchase Behaviour		
Proposition 19: Online Purchase Behaviour is dependant on the consumer holding a level of trust (Intention to Trust) in the Internet Vendor.		No

differences have been found in numerous examples between individualistic cultures as opposed to those from collectivistic cultures (Han et al., 1994; Hofstede, 1980; Triandis, 1989). From these differences collectivist cultures have been found to form tightly coupled groups, which may also mean that collectivist cultures have trouble forming trust in general (dispositional trust) compared to those individuals from individualistic cultures.

At the institutional level, the ideas of perceived Internet protection and the impact of Internet experience and their association with trust, have been previously identified but have yet to be empirically tested (McKnight and Chervany, 2002; McKnight et al., 1998). The dependency of institutional trust on the individual holding a disposition to trust has not been previously identified or researched.

The interpersonal dimension has been widely covered in trust literature, with the attributes of competence, predictability, benevolence and integrity and their impact of interpersonal trust being widely identified (Belanger et al., 2002; Cheung and Lee, 2001; Doney & Cannon, 1997; Gefen, 2002; Lee & Turban, 2001; McKnight & Chervany, 2002; McKnight et al., 1998; Rousseau et al., 1998) and even empirically tested (Gefen, 2002; Lee & Turban, 2001; Sirdeshmukh et al., 2002).

The conceptualised outcomes of the overall intention to trust and the online purchase behaviour have been touched upon in other contexts, but not in the domain of trust research. It is therefore necessary for further research to be carried out to explain how these outcomes are reached and the relationship they hold with each of the dimensions of trust. It was seen as important to break up the overall intention to trust and the online purchase behaviour, as trust is not the single issue that leads the consumer to purchasing. It was, however, proposed that the purchase behaviour is dependant on consumers holding this intention to trust, such as if they do not trust the electronic vendor they will likely shop elsewhere.

The propositions formulated provide direction for future work into the nature of trust in the electronic commerce environment. Few of these core dimensional relationships have been covered in previous research in the electronic commerce domain, meaning that some empirical testing will need to be carried out to assess the validity of the proposed impacts and relationships.

Conclusion

The importance of trust in the electronic commerce setting is widely acknowledged, yet the concept of trust itself is still the point of much confusion. Firstly, an agreement on the fundamental definition of trust has not been formed, which means that research can in fact be measuring different things depending on the viewpoint the researcher adopts. It was therefore necessary for a synthesis of the trust-related literature to uncover the commonly identified attributes of trust that define the necessary foundations for trust. The attributes of competence, predictability, benevolence and integrity were uncovered from the literature and were later used to form the basis of interpersonal trust.

The concept of trust itself was defined as a "willingness to be vulnerable" on the part of an individual. This willingness was then proposed to be dependant on not only the singular interpersonal dimension that the majority of literature takes, but rather also encompassing individuals own disposition to trust and their faith in the Internet as a whole, as seen in the institutional dimension. These additional dimensions have not been widely covered in trust literature, as they have only recently emerged in a handful of articles.

The dimensions of trust were then conceptually modelled to illustrate the relationships and the underlying nature of trust as a complete construct, rather than a singular concept, which is the view taken by the majority of ecommerce trust literature. This conceptual model can be used to assist the understanding of trust and also provide a foundation for future research into the construct of trust.

The conceptualisation also raised new research questions into the topic of trust in electronic commerce, presenting the idea that the individual's disposition to trust is a necessary prerequisite for the formation of trust in the online environment. This disposition to trust not only has an impact on the overall level of trust, but is also necessary in the development of trust within the institutional and interpersonal dimensions. This viewpoint has not been raised in previous research, and therefore requires further study to validate. The dispositional trust dimension was said to embody individuals' personality traits and also their culture. Research from the field of psychology provided the groundwork for the five factors that are said to characterise an individual's personality and also the foundation for future research into this dispositional dimension.

New questions were also raised within the institutional dimension of trust, whereby the individual's Internet experience and the amount of perceived internet protection were said to impact the level of institutional trust formed.

It is hoped that this research has helped remove some of the confusion surrounding the topic of trust in the online environment whilst also providing a foundation for future research. From this conceptualisation information systems researchers will hopefully recognise that trust in electronic commerce is not a simple single-dimensional issue, but rather a broad and complex construct that operates on multiple dimensions.

References

Belanger, F., Hiller, J., & Smith, W. (2002). Trustworthiness in electronic commerce: the role of privacy, security, and site attributes. *Journal of Strategic Information Systems*, 11, 245-270.

Benassi, P. (1999). TRUSTe: An online privacy seal program. *Communications of the ACM.*, *42*(2), 56-59.

Bigley, G., & Pearce, J. (1998). Straining for shared meaning in organization science: Problems of trust and distrust. *Academy of Management Review, 23*(3), 405-421.

Bitner, M. (1992). Servicescapes: The impact of physical surroundings on customers and employees. *Journal of Marketing*, 56, 57-71.

Cardholm, L., Karlsson, S., & Karvonen, K. (2000). Trusted e-business, (userstudy 2000), 1-21. Helsinki: Helsinki University of Technology.

Cheung, C., & Lee, M. (2001). Trust in internet shopping: Instrument development and validation through classical and modern approaches. *Journal of Global Information Management*, *9*(3), 23-35.

Costa, P., McCrae, R., & Dye, D. (1991). Facet scales for agreeableness and conscientiousness: A revision of the NEO personality inventory. *Personality and Individual Differences*, 12, 887-898.

Dekleva, S. (June, 2000). Electronic commerce: A half empty glass? *Communications of AIS*, *3*(18).

Deutsch, M. (1958). Trust and suspicion. *Journal of Conflict Resolution*, 2, 265-279.

Doney, P., & Cannon, J. (April, 1997). An examination of the nature of trust in buyer-seller relationships. *Journal of Marketing*, *61*, 35-51.

Earp, J., Antón, A., & Jarvinen, O. (2002). A social, technical and legal framework for privacy management and policies. Paper presented at the *Eighth Americas Conference on Information Systems*.

Gefen, D. (2002). Reflections on the dimensions of trust and trustworthiness among online consumers. *ACM Special Interest Group on Management Information Systems*, *33*(3), 38-53.

Goldberg, L. (1990). An alternative "description of personality": The big-five factor structure. *Journal of Personality and Social Psychology*, *59*(6), 1216-1229.

Goldberg, L. (1992). The development of markers for the big-five factor structure. *Psychological Assessment*, *4*(1), 26-42.

Han, S., & Shavitt, S. (July, 1994). Persuasion and culture: advertising appeals in individualistic and collectivistic cultures. *Journal of Experimental Social Psychology*, *30*, 326-350.

Hofstede, G. (1980). *Culture's consequences*. Newbury Park, CA: Sage.

Hosmer, L. (1995). Trust: The connecting link between organizational theory and philosophical ethics. *Academy of Management Review, 20*(2), 379-403.

Huberman, B., Franklin, M., & Hogg, T. (1999). Enhancing privacy and trust in electronic communities. In *Proceedings of the First ACM Conference on Electronic Commerce,* Denver, Colorado.

Koernig, S. (2003). E-Scapes: The electronic physcial environment and service tangibility. *Psychology & Marketing, 20*(2), 151-167.

Lee, M., & Turban, E. (2001). A trust model for consumer Internet shopping. *International Journal of Electronic Commerce, 6*(1), 75-91.

Lewis, D., & Weigert, A. (1985). Trust as a social reality. *Social Forces, 63*(4), 967-985.

Malhotra, D., & Murnighan, J. (September, 2002). The effects of contracts on interpersonal trust. *Administrative Science Quarterly, 47*, 534-559.

Mayer, R., Davis, J., & Schoorman, F. (1995). An intergrative model of organizational trust. *Academy of Management Review, 20*(3), 709-734.

McKnight, D., & Chervany, N. (2002). What trust means in e-commerce customer relationships: An interdisciplinary conceptual typology. *International Journal of Electronic Commerce, 6*(2), 35-59.

McKnight, D., Cummings, L., & Chervany, N. (1998). Initial trust formation in new organizational relationships. *Academy of Management Review, 23*(3), 473-490.

Naquin, C., & Paulson, G. (2003). Online bargaining and interpersonal trust. *Journal of Applied Psychology, 88*(1), 113-120.

Nöteberg, A., Christiaanse, E., & Wallage, P. (2003). Consumer trust in electronic channels. *e-Service Journal, 2*(2), 46-67.

Olson, B., & Suls, J. (2000). Self-, other-, and ideal-judgments of risk and caution as a function of the five-factor model of personality. *Personality and Individual Differences*, 28, 425-436.

Ratnasingham, P., & Pavlou, P. (2003). Technology trust in Internet-based interorganizational electronic commerce. *Journal of Electronic Commerce in Organizations, 1*(1), 17-41.

Rousseau, D., Sitkin, S., Burt, R., & Camerer, C. (1998). Not so different after all: A cross-discipline view of trust. *Academy of Management Review, 23*(3), 393-404.

Sirdeshmukh, D., Singh, J., & Sabol, B. (January, 2002). Consumer trust, value, and loyalty in relational exchanges. *Journal of Marketing, 66*, 15-37.

Tan, Y., & Theon, W. (2001). Toward a generic model of trust for electronic commerce. *International Journal of Electronic Commerce*, *5*(2), 61-74.

Triandis, H. (July, 1989). The self and social-behavior in differing cultural contexts. *Psychological Review*, *96*, 506-552.

Van Den Berg, R., & Van Lieshout, J. (2001). Finding symbolons for cyberspace: addressing the issue of trust in electronic commerce. *Production Planning & Control*, *12*(5), 514-524.

Wang, H., Lee, M., & Wang, C. (1998). Consumer privacy concerns about Internet marketing. *Communications of the ACM*, *41*(3), 63-70.

Webster, J., & Watson, R. (2002). Analyzing the past to prepare for the future: Writing a literature review. *MIS Quarterly*, *26*(2), xiii-xxiii.

Yoon, S. (2002). The antecedents and consequences of trust in online-purchase decisions. *Journal of Interactive Marketing*, *16*(2), 47-63.

Zeithaml, V. (1988). Consumer perceptions of price, quality, and value: A means-end model and synthesis of evidence. *Journal of Marketing*, 52, 2-22.

Previously published in the Journal of Electronic Commerce in Organizations, 2(3), 40-58, July - September 2004.

Chapter XI

A Customer Relationship Management System to Target Customers at Cisco

Rahul Bhaskar, California State University - Fullerton, USA

Abstract

This case describes the implementation of an Internet empowered Customer Relationship Management (CRM) at Cisco Systems Inc. After describing the organizational background of Cisco, the case takes the student into the issues that the executives faced after the market crash in 2001. John Chambers, Cisco CEO, and his team decided to strengthen Cisco's relationship with the customers so that the company could emerge stronger when the markets recovered. Questions are raised as to the implementation of technology and supporting processes in a company that traditionally had not considered CRM as its core marketing strategy.

Introduction

A project was undertaken at Cisco to implement a CRM system called Customer Insight. In addition to the implementation of the information system, processes were formulated by actively involving marketing and sales managers. The goal of this combined initiative (system and processes) was to provide marketing personnel with the marketing knowledge and contact intelligence required for creating and implementing marketing strategies and CRM related processes. The CRM system was implemented using the distributed technology using multi-agent system. The system provided a single repository for each theater that supported the quantifiable and measurable needs of marketing functions. Data from different source systems were "cleaned," "de-duped," and integrated into one data mart. Missing data was also replaced with the best possible alternative information. Processes were established to use this information effectively at local, regional and corporate levels. The system was made available via the Internet and, in the first phase, used a repository of customer data from the 25 most important systems across the company. An error-reporting module was implemented simultaneously to make it easy for people to report any issues. It was determined that one of the critical success factor for such a system was a guaranteed turn around time with any issue so that users feel encouraged to contribute their information to the system. The system was implemented in North America and some parts of Europe first. In Europe localization using local language and local laws was implemented.

Organizational Background

The history of Cisco is not atypical for a company in Silicon Valley. The company was founded by Stanford University husband and wife team Leonard Bosack and Sandra Lerner and their colleagues in 1984. Bosack developed technology to link his computer lab's network with his wife's network in the graduate business school. Anticipating a market for networking devices, Bosack and Lerner mortgaged their house, bought a used mainframe, put it in their garage, and got friends and relatives to work for deferred pay. They sold their first network router in 1986. Originally targeting universities and aero-space, the company expanded in 1989 to include large enterprises. Short of cash, Cisco turned to Venture capitalist Donald Valentine of Sequoia Capital, who bought a controlling stake and became chairman. He hired John Morgridge of laptop maker GriD systems as the president and CEO. Cisco had a head start in the market as the market in network routers ripened in the late 1988. Sales leapt from $1.5 million in 1987 to $20 million in 1989. The company went public in 1990.

With competition increasing, Cisco began expanding through acquisitions. Purchases included networking company Crescendo Communications (1993) and ATM switch maker LightStream (1995). More than any other high-technology firm in history, Cisco has built its dominant position by acquisitions.

In 1995, EVP, John Chambers succeeded Morgridge as president and CEO, and Morgridge became chairman. The company continued its acquisitive ways. Market success against the competition was based upon the quality of the firm purchased, successful integration, and rapid next generation product introduction. Table 1 shows companies acquired by Cisco in 2000-2001. Total number of companies Cisco acquired between 1993-2001 was more than 70 for over $36 billion. Without these acquisitions it could not have maintained an annual growth in revenues and profits of over 30% from 1987 through 2000.

Cisco's success is especially remarkable as acquisitions in the information technology industries have a long history of failure. To understand how remarkable this success has been, it is only necessary to examine Cisco's competitors. These include Nortel, Juniper, Ericsson, and Lucent. They also acquired aggressively, but they had to record multi-billion dollar losses from failed acquisitions. For example, Lucent purchased Ascend Communication for $20 billion. In 2001, Lucent recognized multi-billion dollar losses from failed acquisitions including Ascend Communications, and its total market capitalization had fallen to less than $25 billion — a drop of more than 30% drop.

John Morgridge (1995) described the successful Cisco strategy in the following statement: "At the time, we made our first acquisition we had a wonderful asset in the form of a channel to sell, install, and service products for global market. As a result, there was tremendous leverage in acquiring a product that met the market requirement and to put it through our channels. We can take [a new product] and leverage it very dramatically. To a large degree, that has been our strategy with most acquisitions." The main reason for Cisco's success was its strategy to retain employees at all costs in the acquired company (Mayer & Kenney, 2004). As a reference, some of the major events between 1998-2000 are shown in Table 2. Some of Cisco's acquisitions in 2000-2001 are shown in Table 1.

Cisco has continued with the "acquisition and development" strategy throughout its existence. It has been able to achieve its overall objective defined by John Chambers, "to be No. 1, No. 2 or (not) compete; to have 50 percent share in every market, as an objective; and never to enter a market where we cannot get at least a 20 percent share right off the bat." The following table captures some highlights during Cisco's stellar growth during 1998-2000.

As shown in the Table 1, Cisco had acquired companies and products that the rapidly expanding telecom market needed. All the newly created companies in

Table 1. Some acquisition by Cisco 2000-2001 ("Business Summary")

Company	Month, Year	Product
Allegro Systems Inc.	September, 2001	Virtual Private Network Acceleration
Auroranetics	August, 2001	Chips for Fiber-Optic Routing
ExiO Communications	February, 2001	Wireless Telephony
Radiata	February, 2001	Chipsets for Wireless Networks
Active Voice	February, 2001	Internet Protocol Based Messaging
CAIS Software Solution	December, 2000	Internet Service Management SW
PixStream	December, 2000	Digital Media Management Systems
Vovida Networks	November, 2000	Voice over Internet Protocol SW
IPCell Technologies	November, 2000	Voice and data access integration
IP Mobile	September, 2000	Wireless Networking Software
NuSpeed Internet Sys	September, 2000	Storage-area network
Komodo Technology	September, 2000	Voice over Internet Protocol
Netiverse	September, 2000	Content Acceleration Tech
HyNEX	September, 2000	Asynchronous Transfer Mode Access
Qeyton Systems	June, 2000	Optical Networking
ArrowPoint	June, 2000	Content Networking Technology
Seagull	July, 2000	Silicon for terabit routers
PentaCom	June, 2000	Metro Internet Protocol network
InfoGear Technology	June, 2000	Information appliance software
SlightPath	May, 2000	Network element management
JetCell	May, 2000	Wireless telephony
Atlantech tech	May, 2000	Network Element Mgmt SW
Aironet Wireless Communication	March, 2000	Wireless Local-Area Network
Growth Networks	March, 2000	Internet Switching Fabrics
Altiga Networks	March, 2000	Virtual Private Network
Compatible Systems	March, 2000	VPN
Perelli Optical Systems	February, 2000	Optical Networking
Internet Engineering Group	January, 2000	Optical Networking SW
Worldwide Data Systems	January, 2000	Consulting and Engineering Services

this market were eager to build new networks using Cisco "next generation" networking gear. But many of the new telecom companies were poorly managed and had weak business plans. Therefore, they failed to meet their earning targets. As these telecom companies failed, the demand for Cisco's telecom products plummeted. Chambers and his managers failed to anticipate the telecom market crash and forecast lower demand for their company's products in 2001. On April 16, 2001 Cisco announced layoffs of 8,500 employees and announced that fiscal third quarter sales will fall 30%. Stock price tumbled to $17.20 from a high of about $75.00. Cisco's quarterly revenues for 2001 are shown in Table 3.

Table 2. Major events in 1998-2000 ("Business Summary")

Time Period	Event	Stock Price
Fall of 1998	CEO John Chambers shocks a group of telecom executives declaring that voice calls will be free and transmitted over the Net.	mid to high teens
January 10, 2000	Cisco wows Wall Street by closing its books in a single day, using its online system.	$54.91
March 27, 2000	Cisco market cap reaches $550 billion.	$80.06
November 6, 2000	Cisco beats analyst's earning estimates by a penny a share for the 13th consecutive quarter. Despite rumblings of a capital-spending slowdown, the company urges analysts to raise their revenue and profit estimates.	$55.13

Table 3. Quarterly revenue (2001)

Quarterly Revenue 2001	Amount
Quarter 1	$6.5
Quarter 2	$6.7
Quarter 3	$4.7
Quarter 4	$4.3

Setting the Stage

In 2001, Cisco offered end-to-end connectivity solutions (Table 4). It manufactured and sold networking and communications products and provided services associated with that equipment and its use. Its products were used by large enterprises as well as small and medium-sized businesses. Cisco provided broad line of products that transported data, voice and video within the building or across the world. Customers could customize networks according to their needs. These products could be used individually or in combination with other products to formulate solutions.

As shown in the Figure 1, Cisco conducted its business globally and was managed geographically in four areas: the Americas, Europe, the Middle East and Africa (EMEA), Asia Pacific (APAC) and Japan. They were further divided into three

Table 4. Cisco's product offerings ("Business Summary")

Products	Features
Routing	Cisco's routing products had features to increase security of transmissions and increase efficiency. It also offered storage networking products. These offered customers variety of options in accessing and interconnecting storage networks that can be shared and managed globally.
Switching	The Cisco's switching products allowed users to migrate from traditional shared LANs to fully switched networks. The products were based on various known technologies including Ethernet, gigabit Ethernet, token rings, and asynchronous transfer mode.
Access	Cisco offered various access products. These included Asynchronous and Integrated Service Digital Network (ISDN) remote access routers, dial-up access servers, wireless and digital subscriber line technologies and cable universal broadband routers.
IP Telephony	Cisco's IP telephony products used a single IP infrastructure for transmission of data, voice and video traffic to deliver IP voice and integrated communications.
Internet Network Services and Security	Cisco offered products that allowed network managers to improve their services. This was achieved by architectural consistency by using industry standards.
Optical Networking	Cisco uses optical technology such as dense wave division multiplexing (DWDM) and coarse wave division multiplexing (CWDM) to scale optical bandwidth as high-bandwidth applications, such as gigabit Ethernet and storage.
Network Management Software	Cisco offered its own suite of software that became standard in the market.
Service	Cisco offered technical maintenance, and consultative services.

major business units: enterprise level business unit, small- and medium-enterprise business unit, and service provider business unit.

Each organizational unit had its own marketing department. For example, Americas had an enterprise-marketing department, medium and small business marketing department, and a service provider-marketing department. Similarly EMEA, APAC, and Japan had their marketing departments organized into decentralized units. This organizational structure worked really well under the acquisition strategy where it gave marketing responsibilities to the acquired organizations as they were expected to know their customers and were close to them. Depending upon the size of its customers and

Figure 1. Cisco organization showing theaters

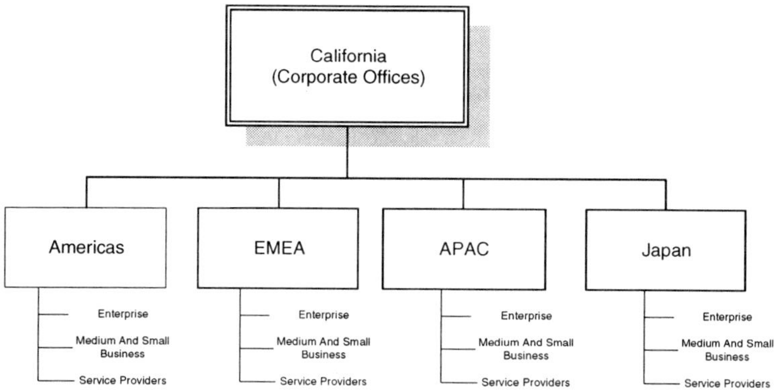

geography, the acquired company was loosely tied to an appropriate business unit within Cisco.

In addition to the marketing at the enterprise, small and medium business, and service provider department levels, Cisco had marketing departments at the corporate level in the four different geographical areas. These departments were expected to align the different marketing strategies of all the business units within their geographical region into an overall marketing strategy. The North American corporate marketing department was responsible for worldwide marketing in addition to its geographical marketing responsibilities. Due to the geographical distances and rapid growth through acquisition, corporate marketing departments were not very successful in meeting their marketing objectives. Each of these departments had a vice president level executive in charge. Overall, Keith Fox, Executive Vice President, was responsible for Cisco World Wide marketing.

In January 2001, the marketing departments across Cisco marketed products to more than 15 million contacts in 5 million organizations. The corporate marketing department of Cisco classified these customers into two categories:

- *Business Decision Makers (BDM)*: These included the president, the chief executive officer, the chief financial officer of a company and any personnel in the job classes of customer support, marketing, product management, purchasing, sales, teachers, educators, attorney, or lawyers.
- *Technical Decision Makers (TDM)*: These included the chief technology officer, the chief information officer, or the vice president — information systems of a company or any personnel in the job classes of IT manager, IS/MIS, IS networking, Webmasters or IS applications.

These customer segmentations were targeted using direct as well as indirect marketing methods. Indirect marketing included activities such as television advertisements and billboard advertisements.

For direct marketing, there was a heavy reliance on externally produced customer name lists (provided by trade journals and private companies), as the internally available customer data did not allow proper targeting of the customers.

The ultimate purpose of all these marketing activities was to identify customers (called leads) who will buy Cisco products. This was managed through a legacy lead management system. This system, named Response Management System (RMS), was an outsourced oracle database. Cisco paid about $1 million per year for the maintenance and running of the system to the outsource company. Due to the dependence for the data on the outsourcing company, the marketing campaigns and their management had to be done using the resources of this external company.

Any responses to the marketing campaign shown by the customers were received using varied communication mediums (Web, mail, e-mail, telephone, etc.). These responses were received by Cisco directly or through the medium of the outsource company in the form of reports.

Case Description

In 2001, for the first time in its history, Cisco was struggling to grow its revenue base. It shook the markets, as Cisco was hailed a master of everlasting growth in telecom equipment and the shining light of the new economy management. John Chamber and his team were convinced that to face the challenge of changed reality, plummeting revenues and a strong competition from companies like Lucent, Juniper, Nortel and so forth, they had to change the way Cisco did business. They knew that the overall business strategy had to be altered to meet the new realities. A key foundation of this strategy was to be in a close relationship with the customers. This strategy would then give Cisco an insight into the needs of the customer and accurately predict the demand forecast that had caused the sequence of events in 2001. Looking at the competitive landscape and cash flow of the company, they knew that the best policy would be to position the company to take market share from the competition ("Cisco Price Premiums") by using an Internet empowered Customer Relationship Management (CRM).

The senior management was aware of the CRM technology being successfully used at other companies like HP, Dell, and Proctor and Gamble. Dell had been able to use the customer relationship technology to dynamically change the products it offered and the prices it charged from the customer. HP, after receiving feedback from its customers, using this technology, had undertaken an extensive program to overhaul its marketing program for its printers division. Proctor and Gamble was using the prior interaction history with the customer in all its communications to create brand loyalty. In all these cases, marketing automation using the latest information technology (e.g., OLAP) tools had enabled these companies to achieve a close one-to-one relationship with their customers.

At Cisco, during the days of 30% growth per year, marketing and supporting information technology functions were considered cost centers and were not an integrated part of the core strategy (of acquisition and development). In the new era of slump in the market and the changed competitive landscape, these functions were being considered imperative for Cisco to broaden its brand loyalty and customer base.

Corporate marketing departments in each of the geographical regions were given the responsibility to use the marketing automation information technology such as online analytical processing to establish Internet empowered CRM that will support the overall strategy of establishing one-to-one relationship with the customer and thus help Cisco come out of the slump stronger than its competitors. It was decided that the North America corporate marketing would spearhead this effort, as they were well placed within the headquarters complex in San Jose, California.

There were many concerns, however, with this approach:

1. This was a new way of thinking for Cisco. Although managing customer relationship at every level of the company seemed an obvious policy in the new environment, Cisco — particularly North American operational departments like finance and manufacturing, had traditionally not done a good job of knowing and using the information about Cisco customers to establish a one-to-one relationship with them and address their needs. Although the sales department had an established setup to collect information about Cisco's customers they used this information for a very limited purpose.
2. Another cause of concern was that the development and maintenance of the major customer database was outsourced. There was not much expertise in-house to design, develop and maintain an in-house custom database system.
3. Another challenge that the marketing management executive team had to face was that in order to reach customers and build a one-to-one relationship with each one of them, they had to dismantle all the marketing programs being done in various groups in North America and consolidate them within an umbrella of corporate marketing group under one vice president. As shown in Figure 2, their research had shown that they needed to have an automated marketing IT system that:

Figure 2. Aims of the new Internet-based customer relationship management

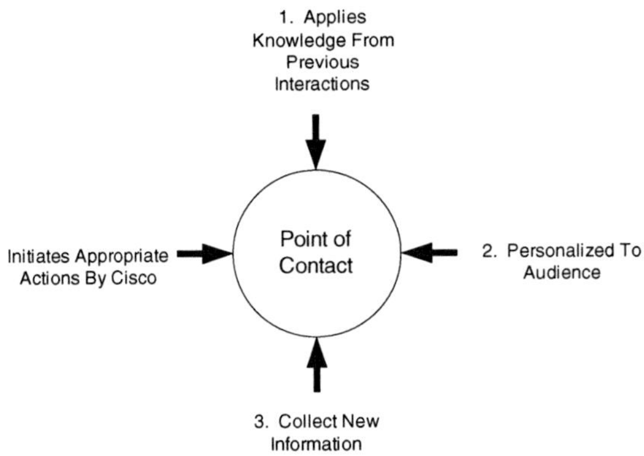

1. Supported application of knowledge from previous interactions
2. Supported sending messages that were personalized to the target audience
3. Supported collecting new information
4. Supported initiating appropriate responses from Cisco

Cisco marketing team wanted to make the Internet as the hub of interaction with the customer. To them, Cisco's brand image required that most of the interaction with the customers be via the Internet. To achieve this, it was decided that the customized information technology system that is developed must be tightly integrated with the Cisco's Internet site.

In the present process, to produce lists of customer leads, everything had been tried including outsourcing the whole operation. Cisco had outsourced the whole operation of maintaining a customer database. This customer database was used to produce the list of customers for targeting. The lists of customers were produced using the information available in this database. On analysis some managers had found that this information was not accurate and reliable. Cisco was spending about $1 million on this database for maintenance and occasional additions.

An analyst could produce a list of customers to be targeted, based on certain criteria from this database. A list was produced using the process shown in Figure 3.

Figure 3. Current processes of producing customer list

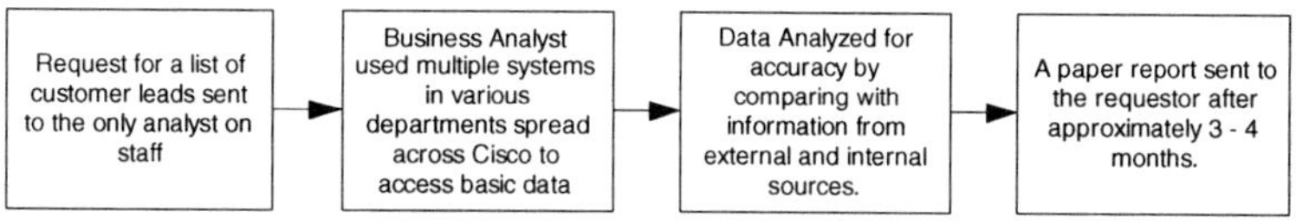

This way of producing a list was contrary to the direction in which Cisco with new market realities wanted to move but there were challenges to move to a new process supported by information technology.

Senior executives charged with the CRM initiative knew that it would not be simple to change this process overnight. They were aware of the fact that the use of information technology will take a central part to any solution they decide. To come up with the best strategy, they started meeting different stakeholders.

Current Challenges

As the senior executives started to meet the stakeholders ("Management Update") — the junior marketing management, business analysts in the marketing department and information technology personnel — they realized that there were issues that needed to be resolved before the CRM initiative could be undertaken. They knew that they had to make some tough choices to make the Internet the hub of interactions with the customer. The Chief Financial Officer (CFO) was unlikely to allow an overall funding for such a project without a considerable evidence of the benefits of implementation of a Web based CRM solution (Brooks, 1975). For a successful implementation of the system, all the stakeholders needed to be on board with the solution. Moreover, there were other issues related to data and processes that needed to be resolved prior to any implementation.

Multiple Databases Held Customer Information

Cisco had marketing databases with overlapping aims. Growth in the initial years resulted in tremendous pressure on managers to employ whatever means they had available to increase the company's output. There was no coordination across departments to implement systems that held customer information for

CRM related activities. It was obvious from a report by the Chief Technology Officer (CTO) that this was a critical challenge. In his report, the CTO reported that there were more than 400 databases that held customer information. He spoke to a group of senior managers in a meeting: "To integrate these databases to produce information useful for CRM will be a Herculean task."

Incomplete or Incorrect Data and Poor Maintenance of the Databases

Marketing databases that were being maintained had missing data, rendering them useless for decision-making. Senior management understood the reason for it. They were aware that throughout the beginning years of the company every manager had an unlimited choice to implement a database to support her immediate needs. Marketing systems and databases to support them were created without much thought to the long-term maintenance and improvements. Most of the time, only the initial needs were used as the primary drive to design and implement the system and its supporting databases. After this initial use, the systems and their databases were neglected or maintained poorly by teams of people who did not understand their initial purpose. This had caused many databases with empty fields or erroneous data. Also, there were no data standards followed in these databases — a simple term like "customer" could mean different things in different departments.

Process of Collecting Customer Information not Uniform

The process of collecting information about customers and using it was not uniform across the company. The present process to collect information about customers had gone through at least three major changes by 2001. The company had invested millions of dollars in the systems and online line transaction processing software like Business Objects®. This system allowed managers to create a list of customers based on a restricted set of criteria. This system was the front end of a database that was maintained and serviced by an outsourcing company at a cost of $100,000 per month. A decision had to be made on whether to improve the present system or replace it.

Irrespective of the solution chosen, a significant investment needed to be made for additional IT staff — perhaps six to eight employees in each theater. Should these new employees be permanent or temporary? Moreover, any new employees would need to be trained before any results could be expected. That could cause unpredictable delays. The question facing the management was how to overcome these challenges.

References

Brooks, F. P. (1975). *The mythical man-month.* Reading, MA: Addison Wesley.

Business summary (financial summary of Cisco). Retrieved from *http://finance.yahoo.com*

Cisco price premiums: Best practices breakdown. (December, 2002). Version 10 (research study). San Francisco: Gartner.

Management update: How Cisco uses real time webcasts to gain competitive advantage. (March 2003). Version 5 (research study). San Francisco: Gartner Research.

Mayer, D., & Kenney, M. F. (2004). *Economic action does not take place in a vacuum: Understanding Cisco's acquisition and development strategy.* Unpublished manuscript, UC - Davis, Davis, CA.

Previously published in the Journal of Electronic Commerce in Organizations, 2(4), 63-73, October - December 2004.

Chapter XII

E-Government and Social Exclusion: An Empirical Study

Liz Lee-Kelley, University of Surrey, U.K.

Thomas James, University of Surrey, U.K.

Abstract

In the U.K., central government's vision is to deploy all local government services electronically by 2005. Yet recent government and commercial statistics have indicated a widening gap between those who are e-literate and those who are not. This study examines the possibility of social exclusion from e-government implementation. Anchored on two questions: (1) What are the factors influencing the adoption of e-government initiatives? and (2) Is the implementation of e-government likely to result in the social exclusion of certain groups in the community? The study sampled members of the public from two local authorities in the U.K. to investigate their dispositions towards the new offering of online government services. The results found that unlike previous research, basic demographic characteristics do not appear to be related to Internet (or e-government) use. This could be a consequence of new and improved technologies reducing access barriers. However, there were clear indications that language, ethnicity, cognitive computer skills and a positive personal attitude towards online transactions are the key drivers for e-government adoption. Of concern is the existence of a hard core of non-users, which will require a proactive policy to provide the relevant facilitating conditions to promote use and experience. This study contributes to a better understanding of the factors required for effective online public services delivery and the ways to direct resources into increasing Internet literacy and use.

Introduction

The declining cost of Internet access facilitated by cheaper computers and emergence of digital television, Wireless Application Protocol (WAP) phones and more recently, Broadband connection, is lowering the access barriers to the Internet. For example, by March 2002, 38% of all U.K. households (9.3 million homes) logged on to the Net regularly. This has led to a rapid awakening by governments around the world to its potential (World Market Research Centre, 2001). One of them is the U.K. government. Its stated objective is an integrated, responsive and high quality online local government service delivery by 2005 (DETR, 2001a, 2001b).

E-government has been defined in a number of ways, with some scholars perceiving it as a fundamental transformation of government and governance at a scale not witnessed before (EzGov, 2000a). For others it is the use of technology to enhance the access to and delivery of public services to benefit the community, business partners and employees (Deloitte Research, 2000a). Yet a recent report by Continental Research (2002) indicated that penetration is restricted to affluent households and white-collar workers with blue-collar workers and adults aged over 65 having little or no access to the Internet. Additionally, the *Guardian* newspaper (July 3, 2002) suggested that even a £600 PC is beyond the means of many. This implies the possibility of sections of the community being excluded and not benefiting from online services offered by the government ("e-government"). Possible barriers such as a lack of familiarity and high access cost may be preventing lower economic groups (socio-economic groups C2, D and E) to go online. On the other hand, the office environment is the main training ground for higher income, white-collar households (A, B & C1) to go online. In addition, Bucy's (2000) research on Internet adoption has highlighted that apart from socio-economic status, demographic characteristics and family structure are also important variables influencing Internet access. As e-government adoption is dependent on Internet use, it is vital to investigate the apparent penetration disparity.

This study is anchored on the questions: (1) What are the factors influencing the adoption of e-government initiatives? (2) Is the implementation of e-government likely to result in the social exclusion of certain groups in the community? The research will sample members of the public (collectively as "citizens") from two local authorities in the U.K. (Tunbridge Wells and Medway) to investigate their disposition towards the new offering of online government services. The results from the study will inform public policy on whether e-government is really an effective delivery channel for public services and to elicit ways to direct resources into increasing Internet literacy and use.

The Rationale for E-Government

The perennial challenge for any local authority has been the delivery of high quality services at an affordable cost. Delivering services via the Internet seems a logical way to be cost effective and to increase value to the user. It reduces the need for replication of information by different departments. The pull/push technology of the Internet along with its inclusive principle is an effective medium to cope with large volume enquiries. It allows the community to serve themselves at their own convenience. Additionally, there is a potential of linking communities locally, nationally and globally. This technology-enabled openness and accessibility should also encourage greater interest and participation in the process of governance and policymaking (Csetenyi, 2000).

The main U.K. objectives, found in the framework set out by the Central IT Unit (2000), are the offer of public services based on choice, access, inclusion and quality of information use. The ultimate goal is a seamless delivery of all government services through a single, common inter-departmental database and interface in which citizens can directly access services from any department (Harman & Brelade, 2001). Customer-centric portals may be used to deliver interactive content and transactional applications such as electronic review and payment of licences and taxes. However, although Internet use is growing rapidly, there is a gulf between people who are "e-literate" and those who do not have access to technology and/or are daunted by its use (Continental Research, 2002), leading Woolgar (in Ward, 2000) to caution against an indiscriminate belief in the technological revolution as a universal panacea for social change. Digital divide cannot be rectified completely through general physical access to computer technology alone, since online information sources require a certain level of cognitive ability or Internet literacy (Hofstetter, 1998). Resource constraints and attitudinal orientations on the part of local authorities have resulted in varying forms and substance of e-government, leading Wong (2000) to suggest a six-stage process of e-government implementation: information publishing, two-way transactions, multi-purpose portals, personalised portals, clustering of common services, and full enterprise transformation. The speed at which a government moves through the stages will depend on the degree of resistance to change by government employees, the funding available, the legal environment and most importantly, the rate of adoption by the target users. As a result, most governments are still at the first stage of establishing a presence on the Internet (Turban et al., 2002), with few offering real-time, true two-way interactions (Socitm, 2002). Given the U.K. government's ambitious mission of full online local government services by 2005, this implies an urgent need to locate the reasons for the competency gulf, to identify the segments of the population that are excluded or are simply not ready for active participation in e-governance, to understand the challenges facing the government in transitioning beyond the first stages of e-government and to formulate strategies to overcome the penetration barriers.

E-Government Acceptance

As e-government is a new innovative communication method, insight to the perceptions of citizens on the usefulness and user-friendliness of e-government processes should be central to the government's objective of providing real-time services around citizens' lifestyles. Completing Web-based official forms can be less embarrassing than having to furnish personal information at a face-to-face meeting. It also allows the citizen to retain his "dignity" when asking for financial assistance. For example, someone who has lost his/her job and has to sign on for a job-seeker's allowance may find it a degrading or demoralising experience, thus further affecting his/her already dented self-confidence. Electronic delivery of this social service is likely to be perceived as both useful and easy-to-use, provided the forms are well designed and access to the Internet is made publicly available.

Citizens need to be convinced that e-government is an equal or better alternative to traditional methods. Hence, the value-proposition of online public service offerings must be communicated to the users. Thompson et al. (1994) and Jiang et al. (2000) concluded in their studies that prior experience and facilitating conditions are significantly related to the utilisation of personal computers. Learned behaviour from prior exposure to a new technology (i.e., the Internet) and the acquisition of Internet-related skills over time are key determinants of further use. If facilitating conditions such as access, assistance and training are not easily available to the technology user, then Internet utilisation may not occur.

Additionally, the longer an individual has adopted the Internet, the more likely he is to continue using it. Since Internet use is a key factor in the adoption of e-government, their findings are relevant when defining e-government acceptance. Indeed the question of how to encourage and monitor extended utilisation of e-government is critical to the success of the e-government project.

Social Access and Accessibility

Concern has been growing steadily over the widening knowledge gap as technologies serge forward (Tichenor et al., 1970). Hofstetter suggests (1998) that online resource utilisation requires a certain level of cognitive ability or Internet literacy. The commercialisation of the Internet further raises questions not only about information benefits, but also about social and technical access to the technology. For e-government to succeed, accessibility is a key issue for policy makers. Technological access refers to the physical availability of computer hardware and software, while social access refers to the mix of professional knowledge, economic resources and technical skills required for effective use of information and communication technologies (Kling, 1999a). In practice, social access is the ability of diverse organisations and people to actually use the services offered by e-government, and it is crucial if e-government were to move from pilot projects into widespread use. As government services come online, issues relating to both forms of access become more important (Demchak et al., 1997). This is particularly so, since Internet use is correlated with an individual's demographic characteristics such as income, education and location (Anderson et al., 1995).

Four groups of people have been identified by McConnaughey and Lader (1998) as lagging behind the national average: the rural poor, the rural and city minorities, young households (below the age of 25) and female-headed households. Therefore, there is little point in embarking on e-government projects if it is destined to provide greater access to those who already have no trouble accessing the services. However, Hofstetter (1998) cautions against providing universal physical access without addressing social access issues such as user-friendly systems design, support and training. Less experienced or competent users may back away from online media altogether when faced with technical difficulties and unfamiliar terminology and processes (Kiesler et al., 1997) without the requisite support systems in place. In order to fulfil its potential, the Internet (and hence, e-government) has to become omnipresent in society as with telephones and electricity (Holmes, 2001). The government needs to look beyond the standard home-own or business-available PC to find viable alternatives to allow even the most technophobic of citizens to benefit from the e-government transformation. This is particularly pertinent since a recent report by e-Mori (2002) had highlighted the widespread ownership of mobile phones (63%) by even the less well-off DE social group. However, running parallel services is likely to add to the cost and complexity of government (Jupp, 2000). Over time, total social access to e-government may well be a better predictor of adoption than the availability of suitable equipment (Bucy, 2000).

Research Model and Hypotheses

This study extends on existing research by investigating the factors that may limit successful e-government implementation. It also aims to explore the possibility of e-government leading to social exclusion for certain groups in the community. Therefore, the research is based on the following research hypotheses that:

1. There is a relationship between a citizen's demographic characteristics and his utilisation of e-government services.
2. Facilitating conditions affect a citizen's willingness to use e-government services.
3. A citizen's willingness to adopt e-government is related to his prior experience and knowledge of the Internet.

The proposed research model (Figure 1) is adapted from the literature's argument for the importance of prior experience and facilitating conditions (e.g., Hofstetter, 1998; Thompson et al., 1994; Jiang et al., 2002) and individual demographic characteristics (e.g., Anderson et al., 1995; Bucy, 2000) as key factors in Internet adoption and ultimately, e-government use. Facilitating conditions and prior experience are used to assess citizens' perceptions of social accessibility and their cognitive ability in using the Internet. The focus of this study is the perceived usefulness and ease-of use of online government services and, as such, the facilitating conditions have been limited specifically to matters of access, assistance and training availability, and to length of time using the Internet, cost of access and cognitive Internet skills. This research will also add to the demographical discourse by the inclusion of two specific variables — ethnicity and language. England is a multi-national society and many of its communities are not English. As U.K. e-government Web sites are in English and constructed so that citizens may "pull" relevant information through the search process, this may impede those who do not have a good command of the

Figure 1. This study's model on e-government adoption

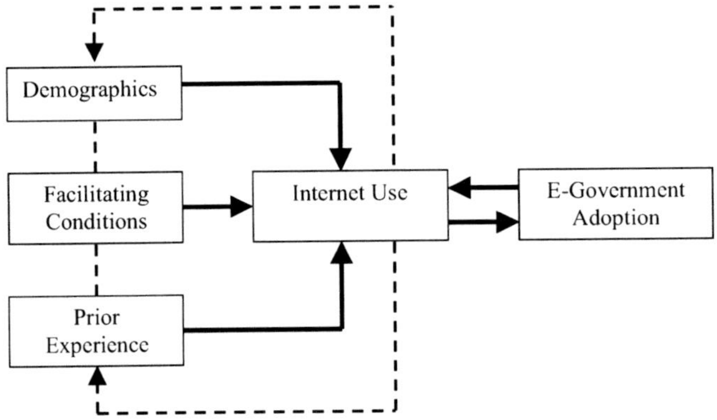

English language or adequate cognitive skills to negotiate their way around the Internet. It is imperative to understand if e-government initiatives, despite their inclusive objective, will in fact result in the exclusion of certain social groups.

Internet use is the intervening variable between the independent variables of demographics, facilitating conditions and prior experience, and the dependent variable, e-government adoption. The results from the study will inform public policy on whether e-government is really an effective delivery channel for public services and elicit ways to direct resources into the most important areas of Internet use.

Methods

The survey instrument. The questionnaire was divided into three sections. Section one consisted mainly of dichotomous nominal scale questions focusing on the respondent's frequency of Internet use and confirmation of e-government utilisation. The questions on the respondent's self-assessment of his/her computer skills and identification with the government's vision for online services were anchored on a five-point Likert scale ranging from strongly disagree (point 1) to strongly agree (point 5). Section two questions were also anchored on a five-point Likert scale ranging from strongly disagree (point 1) to strongly agree (point 5), covering:

1. Facilitating conditions identified as physical availability of hardware and software to access the Internet, support availability (assistance and training), perceived ease of access to information and services.
2. Prior experience identified as length of time of Internet use, cognitive skills, confidence level and affordability.

Finally, Section three focused on the respondents' demographical characteristics — gender, age, education, profession, income level, whether English is the respondent's first language, and ethnic background.

The sample. The researchers had located the local authorities of Medway and Tunbridge Wells for this research because, while situated next to one another, there are marked differences in the general income levels of the two local authorities (Office of National Statistics, 2001, 2002). Unemployment in Medway was reported at 5% of the workforce and only 1.1% for Tunbridge Wells (Medway Council and Tunbridge Wells Borough Council). The population for this research consisted of all citizens aged 16 and above in the two regions of Medway (189,000) and Tunbridge Wells (81,000). As the specified population of Medway was about 2.3 times that of Tunbridge Wells, sampling was done proportionately. The survey was conducted on the High Streets of the five towns in Medway — Chatham, Gillingham, Rochester, Strood and Rainham. Every fifth citizen passing the interviewers was approached. The survey was concluded when the desired number of respondents was obtained. Likewise, within the Tunbridge Wells area, the towns were Tunbridge Wells, Cranbrook, Paddock Wood, and Hawkhurst.

Two hundred and seventy completed questionnaires were collected in the summer of 2002. Eight questionnaires were incomplete or had numerous errors making them unusable, yielding a net of 262 responses with 180 (68.7%) from Medway and 82 (31.3%) from the Tunbridge Wells area. Table 1 shows the demographical characteristics of the sample respondents. The profiles of the respondents from the two target regions reflected the Office of National Statistics' (2001) report.

In the Tunbridge Wells area, most of those approached who were willing to give their time to the survey were aged between 25 and 45 (47.6%) and educated to higher certificate ("A") level. Nearly one in three was educated to university level. There was a 50 to 50% split between white-collar (ABC1) and blue-collar (C2DE) workers. Of the 68.3% earning less than £30,001, over half came from the socio-economic group C2 alone. In contrast, the Medway respondents were generally younger, less well educated and earned less than the respondents from the Tunbridge Wells area. The split between white and blue collar was one to

Table 1. Demographical characteristics

Characteristics	Tunbridge Wells (n=82)		Medway (n=180)	
	Frequency	**Percentage**	**Frequency**	**Percentage**
Gender				
Male	42	51.2	85	47.2
Female	40	48.8	95	52.8
Age				
16-24	9	11.0	38	21.1
25-45	39	47.6	96	53.3
46-65	30	36.6	41	22.8
65+	4	4.9	5	2.8
Highest level of				
education	13	15.9	44	24.4
Secondary	38	46.3	78	43.3
Higher	25	30.5	55	30.6
Undergraduate	6	7.3	3	1.7
Postgraduate				
Socio-economic				
group	18	22.0	12	6.7
AB	23	28.0	45	25.0
C1	27	32.9	49	27.2
C2	9	11.0	42	23.3
D	5	6.1	32	17.8
E				
Annual Income (£)				
Below 10,000	3	3.7	5	2.8
10,001-20,000	23	28.0	74	41.1
20,001-30,000	30	36.6	84	46.7
30,001-40,000	19	23.2	14	7.8
40,001-50,000	5	6.1	3	1.7
Over 50,000	2	2.4	0	0

two; 21.1% were below 25 years old. Two thirds (67.7%) did not have a university degree and over 90% earned less than £30,001.

Results

Results on the relationship between a citizen's demographic characteristics and his willingness to use e-government services (Table 2): The findings for

Table 2. Chi-square demographical characteristics of Tunbridge Wells and Medway

	Tunbridge Wells			Medway		
Characteristic	Chi-square value	Degrees of freedom	Associated significance	Chi-square value	Degrees of freedom	Associated significance
Gender	0.758	1	0.384	1.220	1	0.269
Age	2.363	3	0.500	4.907	3	0.179
Education	5.104	3	0.164	3.033	3	0.387
Socio-economic group	9.638	4	0.047*	1.866	4	0.760
Annual income	6.120	5	0.295	3.648	4	0.456
Language	4.209	1	0.040*	17.183	1	0.000*
Ethnic group	10.424	4	0.034*	14.512	4	0.006*
Computer skills	27.809	4	0.000*	22.444	4	0.000*
E-government vision	24.121	4	0.000*	24.447	4	0.000*

* *significant at 0.05 level (or lower)*

Tunbridge Wells indicate that the demographical factors of age, gender, education and income level are not associated with an individual's adoption of e-government. However a citizen's socio-economic status, language and ethnic background, computer skills and his/her belief in the e-government vision are significantly related to his/her willingness to utilise e-government services. In Medway, only language, ethnic group, computer skills, and e-government vision are related with e-government use. It appears that an individual's socio-economic status is not associated with his/her willingness to use e-government. It is possible that the form and/or content of e-government offered by the two local authorities may differ so that one is perceived to be more inclusive than the other. Alternatively, as well over 80% of the Medway population earned between £10,001 and £30,000 with a majority of them aged below 45 years old, there might have been less of a socio-economic divide than those from the relatively greater affluent and more mature Tunbridge Wells area. Language and ethnic background in Medway appear to be more significant or critical relative to those in Tunbridge Wells in the utilisation of e-government. This could be a result of the higher concentration of immigrants in the Medway towns.

Results on the relationship between facilitating conditions and a citizen's willingness to use e-government services (Table 3): Forty-six respondents from the Tunbridge Wells area and 76 from the Medway have used the Internet to access government information and services online. In Tunbridge Wells, the

Table 3. Pearson correlation for facilitating conditions and attitudes towards e-government services

Facilitating conditions	Tunbridge Wells e-government use (n=46)	Medway e-government use (n=76)
Internet is available – Pearson correlation	0.428**	0.289*
Sig. (2 tailed)	0.024	0.011
Assistance & training – Pearson correlation	0.316*	0.382**
Sig. (2 tailed)	0.033	0.001
Ease of access – Pearson correlation	0.546**	0.200
Sig. (2 tailed)	0.000	0.083
Expressed willingness – Pearson correlation (e-government use)	0.313*	0.124
Sig. (2 tailed)	0.034	0.284

* *Correlation is significant at the 0.05 level (2-tailed)*

** *Correlation is significant at the 0.01 level (2-tailed)*

results indicate that Internet availability, assistance availability and expressed intention to use public services online are related with actual Internet utilisation. Not surprisingly, the strongest correlation is between ease of information access and Internet use, accounting for nearly 30% of the score variances ($r^2 = 0.298$, $p < 0.01$), indicating that prolonged use will occur given easy and convenient access. In Medway, the results are less positive, with ease of access and expressed intention for accessing public services online showing no significant associations with Internet use. Evidence of a relationship exists between assistance availability ($r^2 = 0.146$, $p = 0.01$) and Internet use and Internet availability and Internet use ($r^2 = 0.084$, $p < 0.05$). It is possible that the main constraint for the citizens from the Medway area is getting physical access in the first instance.

A multiple regression analysis was conducted to determine the strength of correlation between dependent (utilisation of e-government services) and independent variables (facilitating conditions). Table 4 depicts the results.

Consistent with the findings in Table 3, the aggregate facilitating conditions in Tunbridge Wells are found to influence citizens' attitudes towards e-government acceptance; 34.9% of the variance in the utilisation of e-government is explained by the aggregate facilitating conditions. Of the four attributes, ease of access makes the largest contribution in explaining the willingness to use e-government.

Table 4. Multiple regression for facilitating conditions and e-government utilisation

Attribute	Tunbridge Wells			Medway		
	R Square Value	Sig.	Beta	R Square Value	Sig.	Beta
Facilitating conditions	0.349	0.001	-	0.175	0.008	-
Internet is available	-	0.159	0.219	-	0.590	0.073
Assistance is available	-	0.873	0.024	-	0.020	0.319
Ease of access	-	0.017	0.388	-	0.227	0.142
Expressed willingness	-	0.422	0.116	-	0.792	0.031

This appears not to be the case in the Medway towns. Although not statistically significant, the most likely predictors for internet use are Internet availability and intention to use e-government services, if available and accessible.

Results on the relationship between a citizen's willingness to adopt e-government and his past experience and knowledge of the Internet: Pearson correlation is used to examine the association between a citizen's previous experience, knowledge, economic situation and technical skills and his/her willingness to access public services online. Table 5 shows the multiple regres-

Table 5. Multiple regression for prior experience and utilisation of e-government services

Prior experience and knowledge	**Tunbridge Wells e-government use (n=46)**	**Medway e-government use (n=76)**
Used Internet for long time – Pearson correlation	0.361*	0.287*
Sig. (2 tailed)	0.014	0.012
Internet skills are high – Pearson correlation	0.431**	0.409**
Sig. (2 tailed)	0.003	0.000
Confident using Internet – Pearson correlation	0.710**	0.427**
Sig. (2 tailed)	0.000	0.000
Internet is affordable - Pearson correlation	0.467**	0.120
Sig. (2 tailed)	0.001	0.302

* *Correlation is significant at the 0.05 level (2-tailed)*

** *Correlation is significant at the 0.01 level (2-tailed)*

sion results for Tunbridge Wells and Medway for prior experience and utilisation of e-government services.

Both Tunbridge Wells and Medway Pearson correlation coefficients show that there is a large correlation between past experience and e-government adoption. In Tunbridge Wells, confidence using the Internet makes the largest contribution in explaining the utilisation of e-government. In Medway, there is medium correlation with Internet skills and confidence using the Internet. Both variables are significant at the 0.01 level. There is small correlation regarding a citizen's length of time using the Internet, training availability and Internet affordability, and the use of e-government. The variable concerning the length of time a citizen has used the Internet is significant at the 0.05 level. Further regression analyses confirmed that past experience is a strong predictor of e-government use in Tunbridge ($r^2 = 0.566$, $p < 0.01$) as well as Medway ($r^2 = 0.271$, $p < 0.01$).

Discussion

Contrary to Bucy's (2000) research, many of the basic demographic characteristics such as gender, age, education, and annual income do not appear to influence a citizen's utilisation of the Internet and willingness to adopt e-government. Unlike previous technical innovations, the Internet (and e-government) may now be accessed via a variety of compatible technologies such as Broadband, WAP phones, digital television, affordable computers, and competitive access and line costs. Hence, this increasing technical accessibility means people of differing age, education and spending power are able to find ways to get online. In time, prolonged use will occur given convenient and economical access. However, other demographic factors, namely, language, ethnicity, level of computer skill and belief in e-government, have been found to influence e-government use. U.K. citizens who are not fully conversant in the English language find it difficult to use the English e-government Web sites which do not offer the option of alternative languages. They are likely to opt for continuing face-to-face interactions, preferring to rely on interpreters to overcome any communication difficulties. This implies that many citizens from ethnic minority groups are not likely to use e-government, despite physical access availability. Different cultural beliefs may also implicate e-government adoption. In the more affluent Tunbridge Wells area, socio-economic status is significantly related to the willingness to adopt e-government but not so in Medway. A possible explanation to this discrepancy is given by Bucy (2000) who suggests that citizens from higher socio-economic groups tend to transfer their information acquisition to new media (such as the Internet) more quickly than those at the lower end. Tunbridge Wells with its even split of white and blue collar workers is more likely to demonstrate such a characteristic than the less well off, largely blue-collar citizens in Medway.

Jiang et al.'s (2000) assertion that experienced computer usage reduces the cognitive dissonance associated with the Internet (and therefore, e-government) finds support in this study. Certainly, apart from language and ethnicity, computer literacy is found to influence a citizen's use of e-government. Citizens with high computer skills will be comfortable using the Internet which in turn instills confidence and understanding in the use of e-government. In addition, a citizen's identification with the U.K. central government's vision of e-government is likely to strengthen his/her perception of the usefulness of e-government services whether in a near or long-term basis. However in reality, this positive attitude has been slow in translating into practice since at the time of the study, Internet access in Tunbridge Wells is only 56% and in Medway 42%. There remains a hard core of non-users who are unlikely to use the Internet in the near future — the main reasons could be a lack of access to a computer and/or lack of confidence in trying it out and language difficulties. This finding is especially relevant in Medway with its younger, less well educated and less affluent population. To succeed, the government needs to attend to the needs of the citizens and to convince them that e-government is a better alternative to traditional methods. Public access limitations may be overcome by local authorities encouraging Internet cafes, access in libraries and other public buildings and conveniently sited Internet kiosks. Charities in partnership with multinationals are collecting and upgrading old PCs for wheelchair bound citizens. To increase home access, local authorities could work with the charities to extend that service. The provision of a public hotline to assist with difficulties in accessing e-government would be very useful. Addressing the technical access needs of the less e-literate is a first step towards building cognitive skills and confidence.

This study has found that in affluent areas, facilitating conditions are significant components of Internet penetration. In non-affluent areas the main determinants are more fundamental — that of physical access and assistance. In Tunbridge Wells, the most important condition allowing access to e-government is the ability to navigate around information and services on the Internet. If citizens are unable or find it difficult to locate a service, they are not likely to use that service again. This is logical given the wealthier segments of the population are increasingly time poor and income rich. For affluent areas, local authorities need to concentrate on enhancing the e-government surfing experience. In Medway less experienced Internet users are likely to use e-government provided that help is readily at hand. In addition, as identified earlier, citizens from ethnic minority groups such as Asian/Chinese, Black Afro/Caribbean, Black African, and non-U.K. white are less likely than U.K. white to adopt e-government. For the providers of e-government, not only will ease of access and ease of use issues need addressing, sensitivity to language and ethnic differences is just as critical to encourage e-government use. Web design is therefore vital. Managers should develop Web sites which allow for a variety of languages to be displayed. The languages displayed will be determined by the ethnic make-up of the area and the Web sites should be designed to take into account different cultures. Terminology which may be acceptable to one ethnic group may not be acceptable to another. Local authorities need to increase the awareness of e-government and communicate its benefits to citizens to raise awareness and identification with the central government's vision of citizen empowerment. With the exception of affordability, the results in this study support Thompson et al. and Jiang et al.'s suggestion that prior experience is an important factor for people's use of the Internet. The findings indicate that the Internet is a technology which becomes more user-friendly over time as use creates and extends cognitive skills and confidence. This implies that citizens with growing Internet skills are likely to increase their participation of Internet-based activities such as e-government. With the assurance of assistance and training availability, citizens are likely to develop their Internet skills through practice, knowing they can seek help and advice when required.

Another interesting observation is that respondents from the more affluent Tunbridge Wells citizens appear to be more concerned with the affordability of the Internet than the less well-off Medway respondents. This has significant implications in the possibility of exclusion for certain groups of citizens — either by choice in the case of the cost-conscious citizens or through economic limitations for those who would have liked access but cannot afford it in the first instance. Hence, while Internet use in general is increasing, there is still a gulf between citizens who are e-literate and those who do not have access to the technology and those who are wary of the cost of access. In order to reduce social exclusion, local authorities have a definite role to play to address the physical access issues such as making access local and economical, and providing the means for citizens to improve their Internet skills. Therefore in conclusion, the results show that there is a social-economic and ethnic divide in Internet and e-government penetration. Until the issues of awareness creation, value identification and physical and social access are addressed, it is unlikely that local authorities will find it beneficial to progress beyond the basic pilot stage of information publishing and limited two-way transactions.

Limitations and Future Research

As the study was conducted in the comparatively affluent region of the South-East of England and the subsequent limited number of ethnic minority responses, a larger-scaled study across the U.K. regions would be required in order to ensure findings are truly generalisable across the U.K. population. While insights are drawn and inferences made on the role of perceived usefulness, the study has its locus primarily on examining the influences of two of the constructs from Jiang et al.'s e-commerce user behaviour model — facilitating conditions and prior experience — and on Bucy's assertion that demographics are related to new technology acceptance. The attributes of facilitating conditions and prior experience are tested on a general basis assuming there is no difference between demographic groups. In addition, the importance of security, privacy and trust issues on Internet use were deliberately excluded in this study to keep the survey instrument tightly focused on citizens' perceptions of the usefulness and social accessibility of online government services. Future research extended to include the direct and/or indirect impact of these factors on e-government adoption should yield a broader account for the apparent reluctance in participation. It is also worth noting the cultural influences of a multinational audience and their willingness to adopt and utilise information technology. In the context of cross-governmental initiatives, this can be an important factor. The authors would also encourage further research into the specific attributes of perceived usefulness and to test for differences between demographic groups to establish a more holistic picture of the determinants of e-government use. For example, facilitating conditions and prior experience may be tested against each individual ethnic group (U.K. white, Asian/Chinese, etc.) or for each socio-economic group to determine e-government use.

References

Anderson, R. H., Bikson, T. K., Law, S. A., & Mitchell, B. M. (1995). Universal access to e-mail: Feasibility and societal implications, *RAND*. Retrieved from *http://www.rand.org/publications*

Bucy, E. P. (2000). Social access to the Internet. *Harvard International Journal of Press/Politics, 5*(1), 50-61.

Central IT Unit. (2000). Implementing e-government. Retrieved from *http://www.citu.gov.uk*

Continental Research. (2002). Huge gap in Internet class/age divide must be addressed for the government's "UK Online" initiative to succeed (Internet report). Retrieved from *http://continentalresearch.com/reports/reports/internet.htm*

Csetenyi, A. (2000). Electronic government: Perspectives from e-commerce. *DEXA 2000, 260*(6), 294-298.

Deloitte Research. (2000a). At the dawn of e-government: The citizen as customer. Retrieved from *http://www.deloitte.com/dt/cda/doc/content/e-gov~1.pdf*

Demchak, C. C., Frilis, C., & LaPorte, T. M. (1997). Governance in an information age: Early patterns of global diffusion of the Web and openness across public agencies. Retrieved from *http://www.cyprg. arizona.edu/CyGovN97.htm*

Department of Environment, Transport and the Regions, DETR. (2001a). *e-Government: Delivering local government online, milestones and resources for the 2005 target,* London, The Stationery Office Limited.

Department of Environment, Transport and the Regions, DETR. (2001b*). e-Government: Delivering local government online, guidelines for preparing implementing electronic government statements.* London, The Stationery Office Limited.

e-Mori. (2002). Technology Tracker. Retrieved from *www.e-mori.co.uk/tracker.html*

EzGov. (2000a). Realizing E-Government. Retrieved from *http://www.ezgov.com/downloads/realizing.pdf*

Harman, C. & Brelade, S. (July-August, 2001). Knowledge, e-government and the citizen. *Knowledge Management Review, 4*(3), 18-23.

Hofstetter, F. T. (1998). *Internet Literacy.* Boston: Irwin/McGraw-Hill

Holmes, D. (2001). *e.Gov: E-business strategies for government.* London: Nicholas Brealy Publishing.

Jiang, J. J., Maxwell, K. H., Klein, G., & Lin, B. (2000). E-commerce user behaviour model: An empirical study. *Human Systems Management, 19*(4), 265-276.

Jupp, V. (June, 2000). Implementing e-government: Rhetoric and reality. *Andersen Consulting Insights, 1*(2), 1-32.

Kiesler, S., Kraut, R., Mukho-padhyay, T., & Scherlis, W. (June, 1997). HomeNet overview: Recent results from a field trial of residential Internet use. Retrieved from *http://homenet.andrew.cmu.edu/progress/overview8697.html*

McConnaughey, J. W. and Lader, W. (1998). *Falling through the Net II: New data on the digital divide.* Washington, D.C., National Telecommunications and Information Administration.

Medway Council. (n.d.). Retrieved from *http://medway. gov.uk*

Office for National Statistics. (2001). Retrieved from *http://www.statistics.gov.uk/neighbourhood*

Office for National Statistics. (2002). Adults who have used the Internet by their characteristics: Individual Internet access. Retrieved from *http://www.statistics.gov.uk/statbase/xsdataset.asp?More=Y*

Society of Information Technology Management (SOCITM). (February, 2002). Better connected 2002? A snapshot of all local authorities websites, Northampton, U.K. Retrieved from *http://www.socitm. gov.uk/Public/insight/publications/Better+Connected+02.htm*

Thompson, R. L., Higgins, C. A., & Howell, J. M. (1994). Influence of experience on personal computer utilisation: Testing a conceptual model. *Journal of Management Information Systems, 1*(1), 125-143.

Tichenor, P. J., Donohue, G. A., & Olien, C. N. (1970). Mass media flow and differential growth in knowledge. *Public Opinion Quarterly, 34*(2), 159-170.

Tunbridge Wells Borough Council. (n.d.) Retrieved from *http://www.tunbridgewells.gov.uk/plan/c16htm*

Turban, E., King, D., Lee J., Warkentin, M., & Chung, H. (2002). *Electronic commerce: A managerial perspective 2002.* NJ: Pearson Education Inc.

Ward, M. (2000). The Revolution Will Be Postponed, BBC News Online. Retrieved from *http://news.bbc.co.uk/1/hi/sci/tech/1048532.stm*

Wong, W. Y. (2000). *At the dawn of e-government,* New York: Deloitte & Touch.

World Markets Research Centre. (2001). Global e-government survey. Retrieved from *http://worldmarketsanalysis.com/pdf/e-govreport.pdf*

Previously published in the Journal of Electronic Commerce in Organizations, 1(4), 1-16, October - December 2003.

Chapter XIII

From Seeking Information to Transacting: The Impact of Web Site Quality on E-Taxation

Stuart J. Barnes, Victoria University of Wellington, New Zealand

Richard Vidgen, University of Bath, U.K.

Abstract

As government organisations have begun increasingly to communicate and interact with citizens via the Web, providing services has demanded acute understanding of the requirements of users and appropriate tailoring of solutions. In this chapter, we examine the results of a survey of the quality of a Web site provided by the U.K. government. The site is that of the Inland Revenue (IR). The survey was administered directly after the launch of a new system to enable the online submission of self-assessed tax returns. The instrument, E-Qual, draws on previous work in Web site usability, information quality, and service interaction quality to provide a rounded framework for assessing e-government offerings. The metrics and qualitative comments provide some detailed insights into the perceptions of users who attempted to interact with the online taxation system. The results point to specific areas in need of development on the Web site, which are found to be consistent with initiatives launched recently by the Inland Revenue.

Introduction

The implications of Web-based services have now moved well beyond e-commerce and are being felt in many other areas of organisations. One such area is electronic government. Since the late 1990s, substantial government services have been provided via the Web in countries such as the U.S., the U.K., New Zealand, Australia, Portugal, Italy, Malaysia, and Singapore. Digital government has huge potential benefits. The government transcends all sectors of society and not only provides the legal, political, and economic infrastructure to support other sectors, but also exerts considerable influence on the social factors that add to their development (Elmagarmid & McIver, 2001). E-government thus has the potential to profoundly transform people's perceptions of civil and political interactions with their governments. Even though we may see further convergence of e-commerce and e-government services (Kubicek & Hagen, 2001), unlike e-commerce, e-government services must, in most societies, be accessible to all. Through the Web, expectations of the service levels that e-government sites must provide have been raised considerably (Cook, 2000).

This research utilises the E-Qual method (previously called WebQual) to assess the quality of a specific national Web site provided by the U.K. government. The Web site is that of the Inland Revenue (IR), a site relating to U.K. tax policy and administration. E-Qual was developed originally as an instrument for assessing user perceptions of the quality of e-commerce Web sites. The instrument has been under development since the early part of 1998 and has evolved via a process of iterative refinement in different e-commerce and e-government domains (e.g., see Barnes & Vidgen, 2001a, 2001b, 2002). Most recently, the instrument has been used in areas of the U.K., New Zealand, and cross-national governments. The method turns qualitative customer assessments into quantitative metrics that are useful for management decision-making. Typically, the tool allows comparisons to be made for the same organisation over time or between organisations in an industry.

The Web application examined in this research includes transaction-based interaction via the submission of self-assessed tax returns. While e-government can provide communication, transaction, and integration of administrative services, many countries are not making extensive use of the Web. A study by the Cyberspace Policy Research Group (CyPRG) suggests that the 1999 global average score for information transparency is less than 50%, and for interactivity it is less than 25% (La Porte, Demchack, & Friis, 2001). Although there appears to be less progress with transaction-based services, a Gartner Research (2001) survey of European countries showed that the demand by citizens for information massively outweighs the demand for interactivity. The research reported here focuses on this important issue, drawing specific attention to the perceptions of interactive e-government Web site users. The chapter also includes a comparison of the conclusions of this research with the developments made by IR (independently of this study) and launched in an enhanced Web site in the second half of 2003.

The structure of the chapter is as follows. In the next section we describe the background to the research and the methodology used. The chapter then reports the quantitative and qualitative data findings respectively, which are then discussed and interpreted. Conclusions are drawn in the last section.

Research Context and Methodology Used

In this section, we review e-taxation initiatives, provide some background to the specific study outlined in this chapter, and give an explanation of the specific methodology adopted for evaluating the e-government Web site of the U.K. IR.

E-Taxation Initiatives

Steyeart (2004) has analysed the U.S. Internal Revenue Service (IRS) as part of a wider investigation into the performance of electronic government services. One of the case-study dimensions used was conversion efficiency, defined as the "process by which a shopper becomes a buyer, or moves from individual government service provision to electronic self-service" (p. 370). Stayeart used the American Customer Satisfaction Index (ACSI) and visitor time to assess conversion. In 2002 the ACSI for electronic filing was 78 vs. 53 for paper filing. This commendable score is reflected by the IRS's Web site's high ranking in surveys such as keynote.com and can be attributed to one-stop filing, instant acknowledgement, online and secure refunds, and flexible payment options. Stayeart concludes that the IRS e-government service is successful since it achieves the double benefit of reduced filing time for taxpayers and increased processing efficiency for the IRS.

Aside from information provision, a major part of the U.K. IR Web site is the launch of a self-assessment facility for tax returns, first used for the 1999 to 2000 financial year to submit returns by April 5, 2001. Thus, the site provides a high degree of interactivity and the possibility for transactions. The online self-assessment facility is a major part of the IR's £200 million e-strategy (HMSO, 2001) aimed at delivering 50% of services electronically by December 31, 2002. In addition, the long-term aims are to provide all services electronically by December 31, 2005, by which time the take-up of services should be 50%. However, according to Steve Marsh from the Office of the e-Envoy, the level of access to Web-based services in 2003 was 70% and would rise to only 80% by 2005 ("No thanks, we prefer shopping," 2003). Lee-Kelley and Kolsaker (2004) compared the U.K. and Singapore approaches to e-government and noted that Singapore had made 95% of services available online as compared to 70% in the U.K. They also note that U.K. citizens are ambivalent to e-government services and that usage rates have been declining in some areas. Lee-Kelley and Kolsaker argue that "[a]s in business, e-services must offer a clear value proposition to draw people online." The proposed benefits for taxpayers of using the self-assessment service in the U.K. are accuracy, convenience, confirmation of submission, and faster processing of any tax refunds (HMSO, 2002). While it is difficult to predict confidently the savings achievable, the department estimates that when take-up reaches 50% across all activities, this might enable efficiency savings equivalent to some 1,300 posts. This, of course, depends on U.K. online tax filing having an acceptable value proposition as perceived by U.K. citizens.

Background to the Research Project

A project to evaluate the quality of the U.K. IR Web site (http://www.ir.gov.uk) was initiated in the early part of 2001 by the Tax Management Research Network, a consortium of academic and taxation practitioners, and carried out with the support and cooperation of the IR.

The evaluation of the IR Web site was undertaken using the E-Qual instrument, developed at the University of Bath, and was carried out during the period of August 1 through September 30, 2001. In this report we present the results of the evaluation of the IR Web site using quantitative results produced through analysis of the E-Qual data. The quantitative analysis is supplemented by qualitative comments of the respondents to provide triangulation of the results and a deeper insight into user attitudes. Information is also included about the development of the Web site by the IR in order to contextualise the findings and to provide a comparison with actual subsequent developments.

Previous Experiences with the Evaluation Instrument

A review of the literature on Web site evaluation revealed no comprehensive instruments aimed specifically at e-government Web applications. Therefore, at the request of the IR, we adopted the E-Qual instrument, adapting the format for interactive and noninteractive users. By adapting a previously developed and validated instrument, benefits accrue in the form of improved validity, the ability to compare results from previous studies with the current study, and a movement toward building a cumulative tradition of research (Malhotra & Grover, 1998; Straub & Carlson, 1989).

E-Qual is based on quality function deployment (QFD), which is a "structured and disciplined process that provides a means to identify and carry the voice of the customer through each stage of product and or service development and implementation" (Slabey, 1990). Applications of QFD start with capturing the "voice of the customer": the articulation of quality requirements using words that are meaningful to the customer. These qualities are then fed back to customers and form the basis of an evaluation of the quality of a product or service. E-Qual differs from studies that emphasise site characteristics or features (Kim & Eom, 2002), which are used as part of later processes in QFD. In the context of E-Qual, Web site users are asked to rate target sites against each of a range of qualities and to rate each of the qualities for importance. Although the qualities in E-Qual are designed to be subjective, there is a significant amount of data analysis using quantitative techniques, for example, to conduct tests of the reliability of the E-Qual instrument.

E-Qual has been under development since 1998 and has undergone numerous iterations. The development of E-Qual is discussed fully elsewhere (see Barnes & Vidgen, 2001a, 2001b, 2002, in press). E-Qual 4.0, as shown in Table 1, draws on research from three core areas:

- *Information quality* from mainstream IS research. A core part of the E-Qual instrument, from Version 1.0, was the quality of online information. The questions developed in this segment of E-Qual build on literature focused on information, data, and system quality, including Bailey and Pearson (1983), Strong, Lee, and Wang (1997), and Wang (1998).
- *Interaction and service quality* from marketing, e-commerce, and IS service-quality research. Bitner (1990, p. 72) adopts Shostack's (1985) definition of a service encounter as "a period of time during which a

consumer directly interacts with a *service*," and notes that these interactions need not be interpersonal; a service encounter can occur without a human-interaction element. Bitner also recognises that "many times that interaction *is* the service from the customer's point of view" (p. 71). We suggest that interaction quality is equally important to the success of e-businesses as it is to bricks-and-mortar organisations (and possibly more so given the removal of the interpersonal dimension). In Version 2.0 of the instrument, we therefore extended the interaction aspects by adapting and applying the work on service quality, chiefly SERVQUAL (Parasuraman, 1995; Parasuraman, Zeithaml, & Berry, 1985, 1988; Zeithaml, Berry, & Parasurman, 1993; Zeithaml, Parasuraman, & Berry, 1990) and IS SERVQUAL (Kettinger & Lee, 1997; Pitt, Watson, & Kavan, 1995, 1997; Van Dyke, Kappelman, & Prybutok, 1997).

- *Usability* from human-computer interaction. In WebQual 4.0, the usability dimension draws from literature in the field of human-computer interaction (Davis, 1989, 1993; Nielsen, 1993) and more latterly Web usability (Nielsen, 1999, 2000; Spool, Scanlon, Schroeder, Snyder, & DeAngelo, 1999). Usability is concerned with the pragmatics of how a user perceives and interacts with a Web site. Is it easy to navigate? Is the design appropriate to the type of site? It is not, in the first instance, concerned with design principles such as the use of frames or the percentage of white space, although these are concerns for the Web site designer who is charged with improving usability.

Notwithstanding, we have used quality workshops at every stage of E-Qual's development to ensure that the qualities were relevant, particularly where they relate to pre-Internet literature and new organisational or industrial settings, such as e-government.

In addition to the applications of specific versions of E-Qual for electronic commerce in business-to-consumer and consumer-to-consumer settings (see Barnes & Vidgen, 2001a, 2001b, 2002), the instrument has also been used in several other e-government areas. Most recently, the instrument has been used to evaluate the following:

- The Forum for Strategic Management Knowledge Exchange (FSMKE), a site relating to international tax policy and administration provided by the Organisation for Economic Cooperation and Development (OECD). The FSMKE Web site was first evaluated in April to May 2001 and then, following a Web site redesign exercise, the new site was reevaluated in the period of July to September 2001. In our sample we collected data from a variety of FSMKE members, including the U.K., Australia, Canada, Japan, and the Netherlands. The multistakeholder analysis of the Web site redesign in this case helped to enhance understanding of how quality is perceived differently among different groups rather than treating all site users as a homogeneous group. The perspectives of the range of international members emphasise the importance of a full understanding of how different users interact with the site when attempting redevelopment; an improvement for one group might be perceived as a lessening in quality for another group.

- The Alcohol Advisory Council (ALAC) of New Zealand and Alcohol Concern in the U.K. ALAC is a government-funded, crown-owned entity whose primary objective is "to promote moderation in the use of alcohol and to develop and promote strategies that will reduce alcohol related problems for the nation." Alcohol Concern is a registered charity, partly funded by the government, and the national voluntary agency on alcohol misuse. It plays a key role in promoting and advising on the development of national alcohol policy and in promoting public awareness of alcohol issues. The ALAC site was benchmarked against its U.K. equivalent, Alcohol Concern, to provide a comparison and to give insight into potential differences in perceptions of Web site quality that are associated with cultural aspects. The results show that the New Zealand respondents rated the ALAC site considerably higher than its U.K. counterpart, Alcohol Concern, with overall WebQual indices of 71% and 61% respectively. In contrast, the U.K. respondents viewed the Alcohol Concern site more favourably in relative terms with WebQual indices of 70% (Alcohol Concern) and 68% (ALAC). The findings lend some early evidence for differences of perception that are culturally based with associated implications for Web site design in organisations that are operating in more than one geographic region.

Design of the Evaluation

The standard E-Qual instrument, previously called WebQual, contains 23 questions (Barnes & Vidgen, 2002). These are shown in Table 1. Three of the questions relate to personal information and making transactions:

- Question 17: It feels safe to complete transactions.
- Question 18: My personal information feels secure.
- Question 22: I feel confident that goods/services will be delivered as promised.

These three questions are relevant to respondents using the self-assessment facilities of the IR Web site, but not to those who are using the site for information-gathering purposes only. By self-assessment, we are referring to the online submission of tax returns that have been processed by the taxpayer using the self-assessment guidelines. The interaction questions were qualified with the instruction to "please tick n/a if you have not used the Internet service for self-assessment or the Internet service for PAYE [pay as you earn]." This allows the data set to be divided between information gatherers and interactors.

The survey of Web site quality for the IR was conducted using an Internet-based questionnaire. The home page of the questionnaire had instructions and guidelines for completion of the instrument. From the home page, the user opens a separate window (control panel) containing the Web site qualities to be assessed. The control panel allows the user to switch the contents of the target window between the instruction page, the IR Web site, and the quality dictionary. The online quality dictionary is linked to the question number, allowing the respondent to get a definition for any particular quality. Users were asked to rate the IR site for each quality using a scale ranging from 1 (*strongly disagree*) to 7 (*strongly agree*). Users are also asked to rate the importance of the quality to them, again using a 1 (*least important*) to 7 (*most important*) scale. Open comments were encouraged, and a remarkably high proportion of respondents (65%) took the effort to provide an additional comment on the site.

The evaluation resulted in 420 usable responses. Demographic and other respondent information are shown in Table 2. The respondents were typically

Table 1. The E-Qual questionnaire

Category	Questions
Usability	1. I find the site easy to learn to operate
	2. My interaction with the site is clear and understandable
	3. I find the site easy to navigate
	4. I find the site easy to use
	5. The site has an attractive appearance
	6. The design is appropriate to the type of site
	7. The site conveys a sense of competency
	8. The site creates a positive experience for me
Information Quality	9. Provides accurate information
	10. Provides believable information
	11. Provides timely information
	12. Provides relevant information
	13. Provides easy-to-understand information
	14. Provides information at the right level of detail
	15. Presents the information in an appropriate format
Service Interaction	16. Has a good reputation
	17 It feels safe to complete transactions
	18. My personal information feels secure
	19. Creates a sense of personalisation
	20. Conveys a sense of community
	21. Makes it easy to communicate with the organisation
	22. I feel confident that goods/services will be delivered as promised
OVERALL	23 Overall view of the Web site

Table 2. Respondent demographics and experience

Question	Response	Frequency (%)
Sector	Agent or accountant	15.5
	Pensioner	3.7
	Small employer	5.0
	SME (small to medium-sized enterprise)	12.3
	Student	2.9
	Other	60.6
Sex	Male	71.4
	Female	28.6
Age	Under 26	11.1
	26 to 35	23.1
	36 to 45	28.5
	46 to 55	25.9
	Over 55	11.4
Internet Experience	Less than 6 months	1.8
	6 months to 1 year	3.6
	1 to 2 years	8.2
	2 to 3 years	18.6
	More than 3 years	67.9
Internet Usage	Less than once a month	0.3
	Once a month	0.3
	Once a fortnight	0.3
	Once a week	11.5
	Two or three times a	2.6
	Once a day	11.8
	More than once a day	73.7
IR Usage	Less than every 3 months	39.4
	Once every 3 months	11.4
	Once a month	13.6
	Once a week	13.6
	Two or three times a	12.0
	Daily	10.1

highly experienced and intensive users of the Internet, although not intensive users of the IR Web site. The majority of respondents were male (71%) and of a working age. Ten percent use the IR site daily. Agents and accountants comprised 15.5% of respondents, while 60% categorised themselves as "other."

Analysis and Discussion of Quantitative Results

This section reports on the results of the survey using a variety of statistical methods for data analysis.

Discussion of Summary Data

The data were analysed according to the degree of interaction of the user. The questionnaire asked respondents to answer Questions 17, 18, and 22 only if they had had full interaction with the site, such as the online submission of a tax return. Data collected are summarised in Tables 3 and 4. Note that at this stage, we have not presented any categories for the questions (this is discussed follows). The importance scores give the average importance ranking for each question and for each group ("Interact" refers to those who answered Questions 17, 18, and 22, where $n = 264$, and "No Int." to those who did not, where $n = 156$) based on all of the responses. In addition, the per-question average scores for each of the classifications ("Interact" and "Do Not Interact") is given along with the standard error of the mean.

Interactive Users

Referring to Table 3, we see some interesting patterns in the data. In terms of the importance ratings of particular questions, there are some useful groupings to note. Overall, those questions considered most important, for example, above the upper quartile of 6.10, are all about ease of use, safety of personal information, and accurate, trusted, and pertinent content. Here we find, in descending order of importance, Questions 9, 10, 4, 13, 18, and 12. At the other end of the spectrum, those questions considered least important, that is, below the overall 5.36 lower quartile, are based around reputation and the look and feel of the site in terms of user empathy and site design. Specifically, Questions 20, 5, 19, 6, 16, and 8 are in ascending order of importance. Other questions are in between, and the median is 5.93.

The results suggest that there are specific priorities in the qualities demanded from the IR Web site by users. Getting easy access to "good" information appears paramount, while certain other aspects that may be important for some commercial sites, such as design aesthetics and building a networked community experience for users to return to, are not so important. Interestingly, reputation is not considered important, presumably because the IR is a known government body.

Noninteractive Users

For the users who did not interact fully with the IR Web site (Questions 17, 18, and 22 are excluded), the resultant data on site quality yield some similar importance rankings. However, there were some changes in priorities for questions. In the upper quartile range (6.39 and above), Question 11 (timely

Table 3. Summary of the data: mean, standard error (St. Err.), and standard deviation (St. Dev.)

No.	Description	Importance (Interact)			Interact			Importance (No Int.)			Do Not Interact		
		Mean	*St. Err.*	*St. Dev.*	*Mean*	*St. Err.*	*St. Dev.*	*Mean*	*St. Err.*	*St. Dev.*	*Mean*	*St. Err.*	*St. Dev.*
1	I find the site easy to learn to operate	6.02	0.10	1.60	3.87	0.14	2.24	6.11	0.09	1.10	5.05	0.13	1.66
2	My interaction with the site is clear and understandable	5.99	0.10	1.58	3.88	0.13	2.11	5.99	0.09	1.08	4.91	0.13	1.60
3	I find the site easy to navigate	6.07	0.09	1.53	3.85	0.14	2.23	6.26	0.08	0.97	4.76	0.14	1.76
4	I find the site easy to use	6.15	0.09	1.50	3.84	0.14	2.33	6.27	0.08	0.95	4.91	0.14	1.72
5	The site has an attractive appearance	4.35	0.11	1.82	4.36	0.11	1.74	4.07	0.13	1.54	4.66	0.11	1.33
6	The design is appropriate to the type of site	4.73	0.11	1.72	4.60	0.11	1.85	4.84	0.13	1.59	5.24	0.12	1.48
7	The site conveys a sense of competency	5.63	0.10	1.67	4.29	0.14	2.20	5.51	0.12	1.50	5.16	0.12	1.50
8	The site creates a positive experience for me	5.28	0.11	1.83	3.44	0.14	2.20	4.99	0.14	1.65	4.20	0.14	1.77
9	Provides accurate information	6.36	0.08	1.31	4.90	0.13	2.05	6.56	0.09	1.14	5.60	0.12	1.45
10	Provides believable information	6.19	0.09	1.43	5.15	0.12	1.95	6.61	0.07	0.84	5.92	0.10	1.17
11	Provides timely information	5.99	0.10	1.51	4.70	0.13	2.02	6.48	0.08	0.97	5.34	0.13	1.56
12	Provides relevant information	6.11	0.09	1.51	4.76	0.13	2.01	6.55	0.08	0.95	5.34	0.14	1.67
13	Provides easy-to-understand information	6.13	0.09	1.46	3.98	0.13	2.10	6.30	0.09	1.08	4.95	0.13	1.58
14	Provides information at the right level of detail	5.87	0.09	1.48	4.20	0.12	1.98	6.19	0.09	1.07	4.70	0.13	1.57
15	Presents the information in an appropriate format	5.69	0.09	1.47	4.52	0.12	1.96	5.82	0.10	1.22	5.09	0.12	1.42
16	Has a good reputation	5.24	0.13	1.91	3.97	0.16	2.12	5.34	0.14	1.60	4.93	0.14	1.48
17	It feels safe to complete transactions	6.04	0.11	1.64	4.90	0.14	2.07	6.42	0.50	1.73	-	-	-
18	My personal information feels secure	6.12	0.11	1.58	5.02	0.13	1.97	6.45	0.55	1.81	-	-	-
19	Creates a sense of personalisation	4.55	0.12	1.87	3.32	0.12	1.90	3.70	0.15	1.62	3.20	0.15	1.61
20	Conveys a sense of community	3.73	0.13	2.00	2.93	0.11	1.75	3.01	0.15	1.69	2.87	0.14	1.57
21	Makes it easy to communicate with the organisation	5.59	0.11	1.70	3.45	0.13	2.04	5.36	0.14	1.66	3.69	0.15	1.77
22	I feel confident that goods/services will be delivered as promised	5.86	0.11	1.66	3.87	0.14	2.20	6.22	0.66	1.99	-	-	-
23	*Overall rating of the site*	-	-	-	*3.79*	*0.13*	*2.17*	-	-	-	*5.09*	*0.12*	*1.46*

Note: n = *420; interactive users = 264; noninteractive users = 156*

Table 4. Weighted (Wgt.) scores and E-Qual indices: interactive (I) and noninteractive (NI) users

No.	Description	Max. Score (I)	Interact		Max. Score (NI)	No Interaction		Difference
			Wgt. Score	*EQI1*		*Wgt. Score*	*EQI2*	*(EQI2 - EQI1)*
1	I find the site easy to learn to operate	42.14	23.41	56%	42.80	31.46	74%	-18%
2	My interaction with the site is clear and understandable	41.92	23.61	56%	41.95	30.08	72%	-15%
3	I find the site easy to navigate	42.51	23.77	56%	43.82	30.48	70%	-14%
4	I find the site easy to use	43.06	23.89	55%	43.91	31.41	72%	-16%
5	The site has an attractive appearance	30.43	19.56	64%	28.52	19.79	69%	-5%
6	The design is appropriate to the type of site	33.12	22.65	68%	33.86	26.55	78%	-10%
7	The site conveys a sense of competency	39.42	24.77	63%	38.57	29.79	77%	-14%
8	The site creates a positive experience for me	36.98	18.87	51%	34.95	22.08	63%	-12%
9	Provides accurate information	44.50	31.89	72%	45.95	37.76	82%	-11%
10	Provides believable information	43.30	32.90	76%	46.27	39.74	86%	-10%
11	Provides timely information	41.94	29.23	70%	45.38	35.08	77%	-8%
12	Provides relevant information	42.79	30.24	71%	45.88	35.86	78%	-7%
13	Provides easy-to-understand information	42.91	25.01	58%	44.11	31.81	72%	-14%
14	Provides information at the right level of detail	41.08	25.42	62%	43.33	29.65	68%	-7%
15	Presents the information in an appropriate format	39.84	26.39	66%	40.71	30.45	75%	-9%
16	Has a good reputation	36.69	22.36	61%	37.35	27.43	73%	-12%
17	It feels safe to complete transactions	42.26	30.67	73%	44.92	-	-	-
18	My personal information feels secure	42.81	31.90	75%	45.18	-	-	-
19	Creates a sense of personalisation	31.84	16.00	50%	25.91	13.31	51%	-1%
20	Conveys a sense of community	26.12	12.25	47%	21.06	10.30	49%	-2%
21	Makes it easy to communicate with the organisation	39.12	19.80	51%	37.49	20.54	55%	-4%
22	I feel confident that goods/services will be delivered as promised	41.00	23.23	57%	43.56	-	-	-
	TOTALS:	***865.76***	***537.81***	***62%***	***875.49***	***533.59***	***72%***	***-10%***

Note: n = *420; interactive users = 264; noninteractive users = 156*

information) replaces the missing Question 18, giving yet greater emphasis on information quality. At the other end of the scale, questions below the lower quartile (5.28) are identical, although the ordering is slightly different; that is, the least important questions again refer to soft issues of empathy and aesthetics. The picture for interactive and noninteractive users is therefore remarkably similar, with the key difference relating to the security of personal information (Question 18) for interactive users.

Weighted Scores and the E-Qual Index

The unweighted scores in Table 3 give an idea of the strengths and weaknesses of the IR site as perceived by the respondents in raw terms. Weighted results serve to accentuate these differences in the direction of user priorities. These are shown in Table 4.

One key aim of this approach is to achieve some overall quality rating for the Web site so that we can benchmark the perceptions of site users. The total scores make it difficult to give a standard benchmark for the Web site, especially since Questions 17, 18, and 22 are omitted from the responses of noninteractive users. One way to achieve this is to index the total weighted score for each site against the total possible score in that time period (i.e., the total importance for all questions answered multiplied by 7, the maximum rating for a site). The result is expressed as a percentage. A summary of these calculations and totals is given in Table 4.

Overall, we can see quite clearly that the interactive users benchmarked well below the noninteractive users (62% and 72% respectively), a difference of 10 points in the E-Qual Index (EQI). Even more remarkable is that the evaluations of interactive users rated consistently below that of noninteractive users for all questions, with differences ranging from one to 18 points. The major areas of difference between interactive and noninteractive users are shown in Table 5. The largest differences relate to usability (Items 1, 4, 2, 3), followed by competency and understandable information.

To see the bigger picture, it is useful to assess how perceptions of quality differ. To this end, the next section uses reliable subgroupings obtained from previous applications of E-Qual and applies them to the analysis of the IR data set.

Analysing the Differences in Perceptions

The data indicate differences in perceptions in terms of E-Qual site quality. Here we examine where these perceived differences have occurred and consider the

Table 5. Differences between interactive and noninteractive users

Question		Difference
1	I find the site easy to learn to operate	-18%
4	I find the site easy to use	-16%
2	My interaction with the site is clear and understandable	-15%
3	I find the site easy to navigate	-14%
7	The site conveys a sense of competency	-14%
13	Provides easy-to-understand information	-14%

overall shape of the evaluation of the IR site. Previous research for E-Qual has led to a number of valid and reliable question subgroupings (Barnes & Vidgen, 2002). Briefly, they can be explained as follows:

- Usability (Questions 1 to 8). Qualities associated with site design and usability; for example, appearance, ease of use and navigation, and the image conveyed to the user. Usability and design provide two subcategories in the data.
- Information quality (Questions 9 to 15). The quality of the content of the site. The suitability of the information for the user's purposes, for example, accuracy, format, and relevancy.
- Service quality (Questions 16 to 22). The quality of the service interaction experienced by users as they delve deeper into the site, embodied by the subcategories trust and empathy, including items such as reputation, security, personalisation, and communication with the site owner.

These categories provide some useful criteria by which to assess the perceptions of site users. Using the question groupings, we can build a profile of a user group that is easily compared to others. We are now in a position to examine the considerable differences in perceptions of interactive and noninteractive users on the E-Qual Index.

As a starting point, the data were summarised around the questionnaire subcategories. Then, similarly to the E-Qual Index in Table 4, the total score for each category was indexed against the maximum score (based on the importance ratings for questions multiplied by 7). Figure 1 is the result, which rates the two sets of users with these criteria. Note that the trust category is limited to Question 16 for the users who do not interact. Furthermore, the scale has been adjusted to between 40% and 80% to allow for clearer comparison. Clearly, the users who do not interact with the site have higher perceptions in all aspects, although the general pattern of site ratings is similar for all users.

Figure 1. Radar chart of E-Qual subcategories for user groups (note the gap between interactive and noninteractive users)

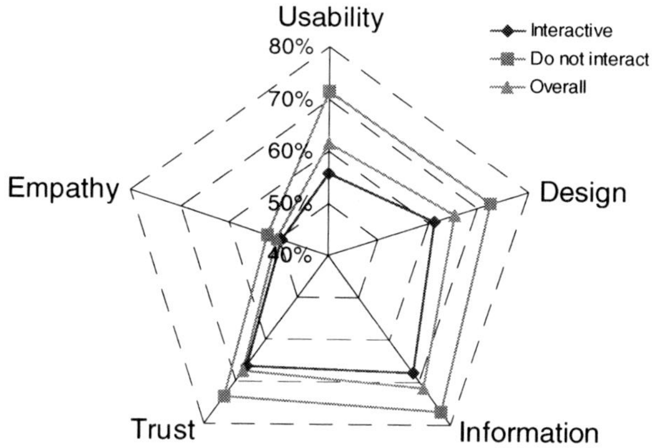

In absolute terms, for users who do not interact, all site categories rate quite highly at between 72% and 77%, except for empathy (52%). Although this category also rates lowest in importance, it does indicate an opportunity for building relationships with users. For interactive users, empathy, usability, and design rate lowest (at 49%, 56%, and 61% respectively), with information (68%) and trust (66%) the best rated scores.

Figure 1 demonstrates that the biggest subcategory differences in perceptions are in usability and design: 16% and 11% respectively. Close behind is information quality at 9%. The most similar quality perceptions were for empathy, a difference of just 3%. Apparently, interaction with the IR site severely affects perceptions of usability and design (as identified in Table 5). This finding is further explored in the comments of site users below.

Qualitative Results

At an interpretive level, many of the features drawn out in the quantitative findings are supported in the qualitative data drawn from the open comments of respondents. This also adds richness and helps to explain the *why* behind some of these patterns in the quantitative data.

As indicated in Figure 1, numerous areas were open to criticism in the IR Web site, particularly by interactive users. Out of the 420 responses received, there were 274 comments, representing 65% of the respondents. Below we present some of the user comments. These are largely in an unadulterated format to give a richer qualitative context to the E-Qual survey, although they have been grouped into pertinent areas of response.

In terms of site design and usability, difficult navigation, links, and password access appeared to be the most common complaints, and there were very large volumes of feedback in this area. Comments included the following (reproduced verbatim):

Getting to the PAYE [pay as you earn] Self Assessment forms is not easy — can't we have one BIG button? I have to trawl through pages of stuff I'm not interested in to find it — or am I blind? Can't I have a "go back to your form log in" button like I do with travel sites? Oh, and I'm still waiting for my ID weeks after registering — I've mailed the help desk.

An opportunity lost! This is the least intuitive website I have ever visited. One can go around in circles for days! You have to be very lucky to find and submit your Self Assessment forms on-line!!

On page cto/pa6 it says "if you know what forms you need, click here" and you then get taken only to form IHT 200. I knew I wanted IHT 205 and 206. But it took me hours to get them. And it's very irritating we can't send you an e-mail without coming to this point!!

Link to the DMG (tax credits manual) is broken — no easy way to report this and very, very annoying.

Links often missing, even when found on your own search, content and structure seems to change on a random basis!!

This site is very unhelpful when it comes to the most important parts of my entry: my UTN [UTR: unique tax reference] and what the passwords were. I used this system last year and it was fine. This year it is a total shambles, as is the IR when it comes to informing people of changes to the logging in system. I have tried 3 times without success to register my return and am now in the situation that I cannot do so before the deadline.

I only wish to access the site to submit my self-assessment. I have already started to compile the return on the IR site but now cannot find it. There is the

Government Gateway that I can't remember seeing before. I can't log in with the user ID I have used just some months ago. I don't find the site easy to navigate at all. In fact I would find filling in the form on paper both quicker and easier I think. I had to phone up for the UTR [unique tax reference] as it was not printed on the demand sent to fill in my tax return. I think I am looking for a button that simple says "Fill in/submit your tax return". Sorry to be so negative about the web site.

I find it hard to locate specific information and have limited success with the search engine which, after a long wait, often returns an "unavailable page" which doesn't really tell me if there are no matches or if there is a problem with the site.

Positive responses to site design and navigation tended to be associated with those who had not attempted sophisticated interaction such as the submission of self-assessment forms. There were much fewer of these responses, largely because open comments typically came from those who had a poor experience in interaction. Comments included the following:

Thank you for having such a wonderful web site where I was able to come and get some much-needed information regarding SMP. My company is located in the USA and this is a new experience for me.

A good site — nice and easy to navigate and to find what you want.

Very Useful in the short time I have used it. Particularly useful for downloading forms and I am sure that when the filing of SA [self-assessment] documents by agents becomes operational will prove very popular.

The content provided was generally considered to be of high quality. Most of the critical comments regarded the need for further information, or greater detail:

The web site is good, giving easy access to important information. I'd like to more information and forms being made available and also you may possibly consider putting some tax education facility on the web so that the interested amateur may learn and also so that students may learn. Let me end by saying THANK YOU for all the hard work that goes into this site. I appreciate it.

Overall — reasonably good site — could be more detailed in some areas dealing with Employers matters.

Overall a good site but a pain not having all the leaflets available in the PDF format. Having the manuals in this would be good also, as having each section on a different page is very poor. It makes it more difficult to look for information.

Generally good, but I couldn't find detailed information on transfer of principal private residence and letting CGT [capital gains tax] reliefs on transfer of a property between husband and wife.

Several comments criticised the quality of information, including the accuracy, currency, ease of understanding, and format:

The site is next to useless. One has to know Revenue terminology to stand even half a chance of finding relevant information.

I found a couple of inflexibilities & some inaccuracies (over treatment of pension relief) in online SA Form. Also form does not allow enough space for appending comments (255 word limit).

It's excellent to have a definitive reference for tax info. The online forms are excellent although the PDF format has dire usability.

Information needs updating, for instance, rates from April 1999 are no use, currents rates needs to be shown and updated. I believe that emailing enquiries to the local tax office would be useful and less time consuming.

Frustrated by having to search for so long for information. Also that most of the PDF files have last year's figures. It would be most convenient if leaflets could be ordered centrally through the website (for business). The site looks good and works quickly. Perhaps it's just the nature of the business that makes the experience frustrating.

Have now written to MP [member of parliament] over lack of response to complaint of factually incorrect information about "requirement" for Windows operating system to use SA Return service.

Basically I can't easily ever find what I'm looking for, search engine hopeless, can't easily get to what I want to know. HATE PDF — so slow and often causes problems.

The Web site should be updated for changes to telephone numbers etc.

I have 21" monitor and I could not get the text to the size needed to for me to see it get it sorted please.

However, there were also numerous comments from users praising the informative nature of the site:

Probably the most useful and informative site I visit on a regular basis.

Excellent, informative web site.

This site is very informative; I find out more from here than I do from my local IR. Thank you.

The web site is good, giving easy access to important information. I'd like to more information and forms being made available and also you may possibly consider putting some tax education facility on the web so that the interested amateur may learn and also so that students may learn. Let me end by saying THANK YOU for all the hard work that goes into this site. I appreciate it.

Charity sector — good to find plenty of info in downloadable PDF format.

Easily found info on IT allowances that I required.

Thank you for having such a wonderful web site where I was able to come and get some much needed information regarding SMP. My company is located in the USA and this is a new experience for me.

From a service perspective, one of the key problems appears to be communicating with the organisation:

Apart from this survey I can't find any way of contacting the IR via e-mail.

All I want to do is to ask a simple question, i.e. are there any circumstances under which the allowance restriction is not deducted from a person's personal allowance. Please reply as soon as possible to the above address. P.S. It would be helpful if you had an e-mail address on your web page.

1) Why doesn't the IR deal with queries on line? I appreciate that this is not going to be suitable for all detail queries but you could answer simple questions that don't require detail of an individual's case. Most web sites have this facility now. The reason that I am completing this form is really to communicate a specific point — see below. 2) You need to make sure that your Internet site is consistent with your other communications. You've just sent me my Tax Calculation and the accompanying document SA354 said that I could find details of how to pay my tax due at: www.inlandrevenue.gov.uk/howtopay/self-assessment.htm. I used this address and got a statement saying that the page longer exists (and no reference to where I could now find the information). It's unacceptable customer service to tell me where I can find information if you don't actually have the information there. I have gone through the route that you communicated and have not got the information that I need.

Requires e-mail facility to get more detailed answers; other than that a good, helpful site.

Have you considered offering a mailing list to advise of updates to the site? I'd be particularly interested in one for the Pension Schemes Office.

More communication links required. All tax offices should have email links.

The other key customer-service issues centre on the ability of the IR site to provide what is promised or expected (partly linked to the difficulty in the submission of returns), and the ability of users to receive a personal service (partly linked to the previous communication issue):

Has not resolved the issue or my reason for visiting your page.

As a complete beginner to taxation, I came to this site expecting to be able to find some kind of "beginner's guide to tax" — a simple explanation of taxation rules that will help me deal with my own budget during my first few months in employment.

I would like to see an easy comparison chart showing how much tax I should pay for an income of £xxx pounds and then have NI contributions split out. I know the are a lot of different factors but the ability to get quick easy and basic information will allow me to make sound judgement as to if I feel that I have been over or under charged tax contributions and decide to subsequently get in touch with IR.

Why can't we just ask questions by e-mail? I have an important but non time-critical question and the answer cannot be found on the site. Why can't I just send an email? It's a generic question with no personalisation component (Is the Industrial CASE portion of the income of a PhD research student taxable?), and would be ideal for email response. Site needs this kind of better interaction if you really want it to feel like "community."

Discussion

Overall, the qualitative data provide an interesting triangulation with the quantitative results of the E-Qual survey. In particular, it helps to explain why there were such radically different perceptions among users who attempted online submission of self-assessed tax returns (interactors) and those that were largely concerned with finding certain information (information seekers). Typically, the quality of the user experience was significantly less for those users who attempted deeper site interaction.

Specifically, the survey showed that users who access the site for information-gathering purposes are significantly more satisfied (EQI = 72%) with the service than those who attempted to interact through self-assessment (EQI = 62%). The major areas of difference relate to usability, navigation, understandable information, and communication. The conclusion we draw from this is that the self-assessment interaction damages respondents' perceptions of the IR Web site. This downgrading of user-perceived quality relates to all aspects, including trust and information quality.

Based on the qualitative data, the two key problems determining the differences in perceptions among information seekers and interactors appear to be the following:

- *Usability of the online self-assessment facility.* Open comments supplied by respondents suggest that the self-assessment interaction is complicated by the need to leave the IR site to register for a user ID at the government gateway. The delivery of a password by post creates a delay that can be compounded by the user not being able to locate his or her unique tax reference (UTR), possibly requiring a further telephone call. Once the user has registered, it is not immediately apparent how to find the self-assessment forms on the site (hence the comment that a "big button" is needed on the home page to take the user directly to the forms). All in all, the respondents found the self-assessment process to be cumbersome.
- *Communicating with the organisation.* The second major area of concern was with contacting the IR electronically. Many respondents wished to e-mail the IR with queries but could find no way of doing so via the Web site. The IR does not enter into e-mail correspondence due to concerns about security and privacy, a situation that is unlikely to be resolved until there is widespread adoption of digital certificates and a public-key infrastructure. This issue is compounded by the problems experienced when users attempted online self-assessment. Users based overseas are particularly keen to communicate by e-mail due to telephone costs and time-zone differences. This lack of accessibility creates further frustration; some respondents resorted to e-mailing the E-Qual survey e-mail address because it was the only e-mail address they could find.

Other areas of concern regarding the site included the accuracy and currency of information (and links), the availability of specific information or online facilities for use by the user (such as online tax calculation or ready reckoner), and the format of information (typically via difficulties with PDF [portable document format]). However, these other areas were typically not specifically related to the use of the online self-assessment facility, being largely shared by interactive and noninteractive user groups.

Summary and Conclusion

This research has examined an important area of development for digital government: online taxation systems. It focuses on the experiences in the U.K. surrounding the introduction of an online facility for self-assessed tax returns, specifically, in evaluating the quality of the associated Web site using E-Qual. E-Qual is a method for assessing the quality of an organisation's electronic offering. The E-Qual Index gives an overall rating of a Web site that is based on user perceptions of quality weighted by importance. Within E-Qual, five factors are used: usability, design, information, trust, and empathy. The quantitative data is typically supplemented by qualitative comments from respondents. In applying the method, we have found a distinct and consistently different rating of the site between two user groups: information seekers and interactors. The latter group involves those who attempted to engage in online self-assessed tax returns, and who typically rated the quality of the site much lower than those who merely sought information. Key problems affecting the perceptions of the interactive users are the usability of the self-assessment facility and the difficulty in communicating with the organisation.

The findings of this research demonstrate the early difficulties experienced by one government department in establishing an online, interactive e-government service. Such difficulties go well beyond those in establishing information transparency, which in most examples appears much easier to achieve (Barnes & Vidgen, in press; La Porte et al., 2001). The core areas of difficulty in providing e-government services in this case study appear to be usability (especially in accessing and submitting a return), empathy, and personalisation (particularly in understanding the needs of the individual taxpayer, providing easy delivery of the required services, and providing a means for personal contact, should the need arise). The same issues are also likely to be important as other government departments move toward electronic delivery of interactive services.

The latest information from the IR shows that there was a major increase in take-up in the year that ended on April 5, 2003, when 329,420 users accessed the system to submit their tax return. High take-up of the IR's e-services depends on taxpayers finding some clear benefit for themselves in dealing with the IR in that way. The benefits for taxpayers of using the self-assessment Internet service are an assurance that the return is arithmetically correct, convenience, confirmation that the return was received, and faster processing of any tax refunds (HMSO, 2002). However, taxpayers expect further added value from completing their tax returns electronically. Internet users typically look for a time saving, such as a simplified form or being able to rely on the department completing many of the questions from existing data on the taxpayer's behalf. Take-up of the Internet service for self-assessment will only improve significantly once online forms offer further added value to customers (HMSO).

The research findings suggest that usability (rated only 56% for interactive users) has been a major issue that requires attention. This finding is also borne out in indicative information about submission experiences. The proportion of successful attempts for first-time submission reached 44% on average between April and September 2001, and it improved further to an average of 70% for the quarter ending in December 2001 (HMSO, 2002). At one stage, the revenue even asked customers to avoid using the service between 7 and 11 p.m., when most people would want to use it, in an effort to help the system cope (Contractor UK, 2002). According to *The Economist* ("No thanks, we prefer shopping," 2003), "As anyone who has tried to use the IR's website to calculate and submit their income tax return will testify, badly designed and bug-ridden sites are likely to make users nostalgic for the old-fashioned, paper-based approach."

The second major finding is the need for empathy and personalisation in the delivery of services (empathy rated lowest of all categories, at only 49% for interactive users). Recent developments at the IR also support these findings; the IR is currently moving from its existing arrangements for taxpayers to file a tax return toward a portal environment offering secure personalised services, such as the option for taxpayers to view their account as well as the facility to file a tax return electronically.

The new developments by the IR implemented in the second half of 2003 support the findings about usability and the need for greater empathy and personalisation. This is especially evident in the redevelopment of the IR's online tax return and the full integration of secure services within the site. Although the IR is constantly evaluating both its Web site and the services hosted, it will take time and resources to fully redesign existing services. Simplification of the form would require legislative change and drawing on data stored elsewhere in the department to complete many of the questions on behalf of users, which would further require new software to link existing computer systems (HMSO, 2002).

The implementation of online taxation reported here is thus characterised as the automation of paper forms; to create an effective online taxation service, a business process redesign approach will be needed, which will involve the cost and pain typical of such transformational and cross-functional initiatives.

A considerable volume of both quantitative and rich qualitative data has been collected through the research programme outlined in the chapter. This is the first in a series of studies of online e-government taxation focusing on the U.K. Further research is planned to follow up this phase of data collection with additional phases. Specifically, we wish to conduct further detailed interviews with site users to ascertain in more detail their experiences with the site and perceptions of quality for online taxation systems.

References

Bailey, J. E., & Pearson, S. W. (1983). Development of a tool for measuring and analyzing computer user satisfaction. *Management Science, 29*(5), 530-544.

Barnes, S. J., & Vidgen, R. T. (2001a). An evaluation of cyber-bookshops: The WebQual method. *International Journal of Electronic Commerce, 6*(1), 11-30.

Barnes, S. J., & Vidgen, R. T. (2001b). *Assessing the quality of auction Web sites.* Proceedings of the Hawaii International Conference on Systems Sciences, HI.

Barnes, S. J., & Vidgen, R. T. (2002). An integrative approach to the assessment of e-commerce quality. *Journal of Electronic Commerce Research, 3*(3), 114-127.

Barnes, S. J., & Vidgen, R. T. (in press). Measuring Web site quality improvements: A case study of the Forum on Strategic Management Knowledge Exchange. *Industrial Management and Data Systems.*

Bitner, M. (1990). Evaluating service encounters: The effects of physical surroundings and employee responses. *Journal of Marketing, 54*, 69-82.

Contractor UK. (2002). *Revenue problems continue as self-assessment site fails to cope.* Retrieved December 31, 2002, from *http://www.contractoruk.co.uk/article687.shtml*

Cook, M. E. (2000). *What citizens want from e-government.* Retrieved August 9, 2001, from *http://www.ctg.albany.edu/resources/htmlrpt/e-government/what_citizens_want.html*

Davis, F. (1989). Perceived usefulness, perceived ease of use, and user acceptance of information technology. *MIS Quarterly, 13*(3), 340-351.

Davis, F. (1993). User acceptance of information technology: System characteristics, user perceptions, and behavioral impacts. *International Journal of Man-Machine Studies, 38*, 475-487.

Elmagarmid, A. K., & McIver, W. J. (2001). The ongoing march toward digital government. *IEEE Computer, 34*(2), 32-38.

Gartner Research. (2001). *E-government: What are citizens really looking for?* London: Author.

HMSO. (2001). *Inland Revenue e-strategy.* London: Author.

HMSO. (2002). *E-revenue.* London: Author.

Jarvenpaa, S. L., Tractinsky, N., & Vitale, M. (2000). Consumer trust in an Internet store. *Information Technology and Management, 1*(1), 45-71.

Kettinger, W., & Lee, C. (1997). Pragmatic perspectives on the measurement of information systems service quality. *MIS Quarterly, 21*, 223-240.

Kim, E. B., & Eom, S. B. (2002). Designing effective cyber store user interface. *Industrial Management and Data Systems, 102*(5), 241-251.

Kubicek, H., & Hagen, M. (2001). Integrating e-commerce and e-government: The case of Bremen Online Services. In J. Prins (Ed.), *Designing e-government.* The Hague, Netherlands: Kluwer Law International.

La Porte, T., Demchak, C., & Friis, C. (2001). Webbing governance: Global trends across national-level public agencies. *Communications of the ACM, 44*(1), 63-67.

Lee-Kelley, L., & Kolsaker, A. (2004). E-government: The "fit" between supply assumptions and usage drivers. *Electronic Government, 1*(2), 130-140.

Malhotra, M., & Grover, V. (1998). An assessment of survey research in POM: From construct to theory. *Journal of Operations Management, 16*(4), 403-423.

Nielsen, J. (1993). *Usability engineering.* San Francisco: Morgan Kaufmann.

Nielsen, J. (1999). User interface directions for the Web. *Communications of the ACM, 42*(1), 65-72.

Nielsen, J. (2000). *Designing Web usability.* IN: New Riders Publishing.

No thanks, we prefer shopping. (2003, January 2). *The Economist.*

Parasuraman, A. (1995). Measuring and monitoring service quality. In W. Glynn & J. Barnes (Eds.), *Understanding services management.* Chichester: Wiley.

Parasuraman, A., Zeithaml, V. A., & Berry, L. (1985). A conceptual model of service quality and its implications for future research. *Journal of Marketing, 49*, 41-50.

Parasuraman, A., Zeithaml, V. A., & Berry, L. (1988). SERVQUAL: A multiple-item scale for measuring consumer perceptions of service quality. *Journal of Retailing, 64*(1), 12-40.

Pitt, L., Watson, R., & Kavan, C. (1995). Service quality: A measure of information systems effectiveness. *MIS Quarterly, 19*(2), 173-187.

Pitt, L., Watson, R., & Kavan, C. (1997). Measuring information systems service quality: Concerns for a complete canvas. *MIS Quarterly, 21*, 209-221.

Shostack, G. (1985). Planning the service encounter. In J. Czepiel, M. Solomon, & C. Surprenant (Eds.), *The service encounter.* Lexington, MA: Lexington Books.

Slabey, R. (1990). *QFD: A basic primer. Excerpts from the implementation manual for the three day QFD workshop.* Transactions from the Second Symposium on Quality Function Deployment, Novi, MI.

Spool, J., Scanlon, T., Schroeder, W., Snyder, C., & DeAngelo, T. (1999). *Web site usability: A designer's guide.* San Francisco: Morgan Kaufmann.

Stayaert, J. C. (2004). Measuring the performance of electronic government services. *Information and Management, 41*(3), 369-375.

Straub, D. W., & Carlson, C. L. (1989). Validating instruments in MIS research. *MIS Quarterly, 13*(2), 147-169.

Strong, D., Lee, Y., & Wang, R. (1997). Data quality in context. *Communications of the ACM, 40*(5), 103-110.

Van Dyke, T., Kappelman, L., & Prybutok, V. (1997). Measuring information systems service quality: Concerns on the use of the SERVQUAL questionnaire. *MIS Quarterly, 21*, 195-208.

Wang, R. Y. (1998). A product perspective on total data quality management. *Communications of the ACM, 41*(2), 58-65.

Zeithaml, V. A., Berry, L., & Parasuraman, A. (1993). The nature and determinants of customer expectations of service. *Journal of the Academy of Marketing Science, 21*(1), 1-12.

Zeithaml, V. A., Parasuraman, A., & Berry, L. (1990). *Delivering quality service: Balancing customer perceptions and expectations*. New York: The Free Press.

Chapter XIV

The Strategic Importance of E-Commerce in Modern Supply Chains

Peter R. Gibson, University of Wollongong, Australia

Janet Edwards, Loughborough University, U.K.

Abstract

Considering some aspects of the motor industry as an example, this paper outlines strategic opportunities for e-commerce-enabled supply chains and, hence, greatly improved responses to customers. The authors demonstrate that there will be resulting strategic advantage for firms that become enabled to take a further step of making changes to their much wider manufacturing process philosophies. The developed knowledge associated with these changes will not be easily copied by competitors, and as such, provides the basis for a sustainable competitive advantage for those firms that are able to lead the way with the enabling technology of e-commerce in supply chains. However, leadership and change management are identified as key issues requiring further investigation.

Introduction

This paper discusses the importance of e-commerce with respect to supply chains. It outlines the present imperative for supply chain managers to recognise a strategic opportunity for Internet-based technology in establishing cooperative partnering relationships and collective decision making amongst cooperating supply chain players. This provides a view of mutual strategic benefit to all supply chain players with enhanced customer service and is illustrated in terms of, for example, reduced work in progress, faster response times and enhanced customisation (e.g., greater potential for "Build to Order" in the motor industry). The paper has the objective of demonstrating that a supply chain view of e-commerce can be beneficial from an overall business-wide and business-to-business point of view, rather than the somewhat narrower context sometimes presented elsewhere. E-commerce-enabled supply chains require cultural changes. For example, adversarial relationships that currently offer more powerful players short-term gains can be transformed into a collective strategic advantage for committed supply chain partners. Some of the elements of this change are introduced as areas requiring further research.

Supply Chain Management (SCM) is becoming an increasingly strategic issue in manufacturing and service industries across the world. Major multinationals, for example motor manufacturers, are beginning to realise that real competitive advantage can be obtained by achieving improved effectiveness from local and international supply chain business relationships (Horner & Thompson, 2003). Further, it is becoming clearly demonstrated that the knowledge used by a firm to improve this efficiency is unique to a particular supply chain and is therefore very difficult for competitors to imitate (Robertson et al., 2001), in their own situations, thus developing a degree of sustainability in the competitive advantages created. However, it has been suggested that most published work in research and practice is biased towards e-commerce in sales and marketing (Van Hoek, 2001), and the wider strategic benefits from fully integrated supply chains that utilise e-commerce are ignored (Davidrajuh, 2003; Fraser et al., 2000; Reynolds, 2000).

There can be little doubt that the most significant enabler of improved supply chain management efficiency is business-to-business (B2B) e-commerce. In general, e-commerce has provided a means of achieving fundamental changes in the structure, management and operations of organisations (Dertouzos, 1997; McLaren & McLaren, 1999; Meyer & Taylor, 2000). The basis of strategic advantage from supply chains may well be proven to be dependent on a firm's capacity to use the Internet to integrate and synchronise supply chain activities, particularly to enable transparent, collaborative and connected decision-making processes among those positioned within the chain. Indeed, it is quite likely that the concept of supply chain itself is becoming outmoded and that the idea of supply networks (Overby & Min, 2001; Robertson et al., 2001) will become the norm. There is also little doubt that international trade between supply chain partners and outsourcing as a result of strategic emphasis on core competencies are increasing at a pace not experienced before. This adds more complexity to supply chains and is further evidence for the need to clearly understand the significance of strategic advantage from supply chain business networks.

Supply Chain Management (SCM)

A supply chain encompasses all activities associated with the flow of materials, information and services from raw material supplies, through product or service processing facilities and warehouses to the end customer. Supply chains include end-to-end processes that create and deliver these products, information and services (Turban et al., 2002). In the motor industry, for example, this also involves sourcing and procurement of raw materials and parts, assembly and production, inventory management, order fulfilment, distribution, transportation and final delivery. The success of supply chain management requires efficient co-ordination and decision making (Chopra & Meindle, 2001). The decision phases in a supply chain are design, planning and operational, depending on the time frame applied.

There are two different ways to view the processes performed in a supply chain, which are the cycle view and the push/pull view (Chopra & Meindle, 2001). The cycle view is a series of cycles, respectively named customer, replenishment, manufacturing and procurement cycles. Each is performed at the interface between two successive stages in the supply chain. The four process cycles are vital when considering operational decisions. These specify the roles and responsibilities of each member of the supply chain and the desired outcome of each of the above processes. In the push/pull view, the pull processes are initiated by an actual customer order and the push processes are initiated and implemented in expectation of customer orders. An example of a supply chain that uses pull processes is Dell Computer. This enables one of the key strategic initiatives of modern supply chains, which is Build to Order (BtO) and thus provides a cornerstone of Dell's strategic position. Build to Order is an idea the motor industry would prefer to get much closer to with the aim of enhanced customer satisfaction. Today's situation, where mostly uniform vehicle products are offered, is a direct outcome from Henry Ford's "any colour you like as long as it is black." This in turn resulted from a very simplistic and inflexible view of supply chain management. E-commerce allows all of this to be changed, thus providing greater potential customisation.

Western manufacturing industry traditionally has been riddled with supply chain inefficiencies due to conflicting player interests and market power at the different stages of the supply chain. Large powerful players, whether suppliers or receivers, have tended to use their power to encourage the less powerful players to bend to their needs rather than the needs of the overall entity. This has resulted in a lack of coordination and harmony and hence distorted information moving among the supply chain partners at different stages. An example of this might be that a car manufacturer produces different models and various options for each model. Extensive product variation makes it difficult for the company to coordinate the exchange of information with its multiple suppliers and dealers, and so they tend to dictate their requirements to those further down the chain. Several organisations have experienced this "bullwhip" effect, in which fluctuations in orders increase as they move up the supply chain from retailers, through wholesalers and manufacturers, to suppliers. This results in a distortion of information within the supply chain. Different stages have a different estimate of what is the actual demand (Chopra & Meindl, 2001). This is one problem where Internet-based e-commerce can offer significant improvements by removing gaps in communication and maintaining a focused view of the service received by the final customer. The unpredictability of supply and demand and the need to stay connected with the supply chain partners has made Internet-enabled SCM tools vital for competitive organisations (Au & Ho, 2002; McGuffog & Wadsley, 1999). However, in order for this to work successfully, the players have to first agree that customer service is in fact an imperative. This management issue cannot be underestimated and is discussed later.

E-Commerce, B2B Developments, and Supply Chain Management

In today's competitive business environment, integrating business functions through improved supply chain relationships between trading partners is vital. Unlike the past, where manufacturers were the drivers of supply chain management activities (i.e., "pushers"), in terms of how, when, where and which products were to be manufactured, customers are now the drivers of the supply chain processes (i.e., "pullers"). This is in terms of demanding tailor made, differentiated, quality products that can be delivered in a cost-effective way. In today's supply chain management, organisations need to address complex interdependencies and create an extended enterprise that looks beyond its manufacturing plants (Supply Chain Council, 2002). All internal and external trading partners, i.e., wholesalers, distributors, transporters, raw material and service providers, software and infrastructure providers are vital players in the supply chain management.

The Internet and the role of leading edge technology such as B2B e-commerce is, to a large extent, creating opportunities in the optimisation and synchronisation of supply chains (Pawar & Driva, 2000). People and operations of an organisation can exist anywhere that computers and the Internet services can reach and effectively interact, with powerful business, research, visualisation and decision-making tools available. B2B tools facilitate integration and synchronisation of the supply chain functions through collaboration, either by "clicks and mortar" (part physical and part Internet) or by fully automating the supply chains to enable internal and external trading partners to electronically conduct their business activities. The take-up and choice of the options and the extent to which exploitation of the opportunities and advantages offered by B2B e-commerce may progress, will depend on various factors within the organisation and the supply chain.

Anderson and Lee (2000) indicate the potential of the Internet and B2B tools to transform and enhance supply chain management functions by the three steps of integration, collaboration and synchronisation. However, it is important to note that the practice of e-commerce in supply chain management started in the late 1970s through the use of Electronic Data Interchange (EDI), which has since substantially replaced telephone and paper-based communications and transactions (Min & Galle, 1999). The Internet revolution gave rise to the World Wide Web (Murillo, 2001), which has enabled organisations to perform more B2B supply chain activated processes such as:

- Flow of information across the supply chain partners to assist in the decision making processes;
- Negotiation of prices and contracts with the trading partners and suppliers;
- Order placement, order fulfilment including order tracking;
- Logistics management, warehouse management, transport and delivery to the end user; and
- Financial transactions between the trading partners in the supply chain.

Supply chain management has a wide scope but the focus of this paper is on the opportunities e-commerce can offer to improve supply chain efficiencies by the use of B2B e-commerce tools in specific areas such as:

- The emergence of B2B e-marketplaces and exchanges as the facilitator of various market mechanisms and new business models;

- The integration of the supply chain via B2B e-commerce tools, between trading partners for transparency, real-time visibility and smooth flow of vital information and how this impacts cycle time and lowers inventory leading to collaborative supply chain management and synchronisation of the supply chain functions; and
- The Internet enables the Build to Order concept. The concept radically changes supply chain functions to building products driven by the demand in real time and actual customer orders.

B2B e-commerce activities are usually conducted along the supply chain of an organisation and its suppliers. The relationships between businesses are best understood in the supply chain context. It is imperative to understand that the emergence of B2B e-commerce has two types of impact on supply chains:

1. Aggregation of suppliers and buyers.
2. Facilitation of information exchanges in businesses and their supply chain relationships (*The Economist*, 2000).

The main characteristic of B2B e-commerce is that organisations attempt to automate the trading process in order to improve it, the transactions are conducted electronically between the businesses and their supply chains over the Internet, intranets, advanced extranets, Internet-based EDIs or Virtual Private Networks (VPN). The key driver of B2B e-commerce is its ability to offer distinct competitive advantage through the automation of business processes (Au & Ho, 2002; Elliman & Orange, 2000; McGuffog & Wadsley, 1999; Liu & Zhang, 2002; Leonard & Cronan, 2002).

B2B applications play the role of supply chain enablers in organisations to enhance the supply chain management functions of coordination, order generation, order fulfilment, distribution of products, services and information.

The access to information offered to organisations via B2B applications as identified by Handfield and Nichols (1999) pertains to:

- *Product*: sales history, prices, specification;
- *Customer*: sales history and forecasts;
- *Supplier*: product line and lead times, sales terms and conditions;
- *Product*: process capacities, commitments, product plans;
- *Transportation*: carriers, lead times, costs;

- *Inventory*: inventory levels, carrying costs, locations;
- *Supply chain*: key contacts, partners roles and responsibilities, schedules; and
- *Process*: description, performance measures, quality, delivery time, customer satisfaction.

Key B2B Entities

The key entities in B2B e-commerce as identified by Turban et al. (2002) are:

- *Buying and selling*: organisations with procurement management or marketing management perspectives;
- *Electronic intermediaries*: third party service providers like exchanges and supply chain service eHubs (the scope of the service can be extended to order fulfilment);
- *Trading platforms*: pricing negotiation protocols such as auctions and payment services;
- *Logistic providers*: packaging, storage, deliveries and other logistics required for transactions;
- *Network platforms*: Internet, intranets, extranets, VPNs;
- *Protocols of communication*: EDI or XML; and
- *Back end integration*: connecting to ERP systems, databases and functional applications.

The impact of B2B e-commerce has initiated the implementation of various B2B application tools to contribute data to support various functional areas such as:

- Improving the time to market of products and services;
- Enhancing developed and engineered productivity by providing collaboration interactions across product development process;
- Creating an environment that supports exponential scalability; and
- Reducing costs while improving quality.

The functional areas that tend to exist in supply chains are sales and marketing, product planning, finance, human resources, design, engineering, work in progress, purchasing, planning, manufacturing and field services. (Lambert & Cooper, 2000; Stevens, 1989). Those traditionally having strongly vertical-operating philosophies can be linked to operate horizontally. In so doing, it is clear that communication efficiency and hence business processes can be linked more seamlessly. However, it has to be recognised that this change will be inhibited unless functional vertical management accepts behavioural change that could mean relinquishing their traditional (vertical) hierarchical philosophies. E-commerce enables a much more integrated, seamless supply chain in this way. The goal of many supply chains is to achieve just that, through horizontal integration of functional areas. Prior to this type of supply chain thinking, enabled by e-commerce, these horizontal linkages were not possible. Significant cost savings of 3 to 5% have been reported as a result of fairly unsophisticated integration of chain linkages of this type (Berger & Deutsche Bank, 2000). Further evidence comes from case studies where electronic commerce has been implemented from a strategic stance and substantial benefits are reported (Power & Sohal, 2002).

Two typical source areas of cost savings in supply chains enabled by e-commerce are:

1. Procurement of direct materials that go into the product or service and indirect materials. Online procurement initiatives have the potential to radically re-engineer order processing.
2. Order to delivery. Customers are increasingly demanding Build to Order rather than buying "off the shelf." Reductions in lead times enabled by e-commerce make this much more viable.

Collaborative Commerce

A major benefit of B2B e-commerce is collaborative commerce where an Internet-based system is used for communication, design, planning, information sharing and information discovery. These activities are conducted between and among the supply chain partners. Collaboration can be achieved between and within organisations via collaborative platforms that can help in communication between subsidiaries and supply chain partners via e-mail, message boards, chat rooms and online corporate data access. The potential enablers of this are advanced extranets that can link the various trading partners, leading to tight integration, better collaboration, speedy communication and better visibility across the supply chain. The "portal" is a technology infrastructure that is emerging as a critical integration mechanism within an organisation, among its suppliers, distributors and virtual integration partners. The vital feature of portals as an integration platform is the incremental nature in which they can be implemented. Most exchanges include their own portals (Reddy, 2001).

SCM and Improvement by Utilising B2B E-Commerce Tools in Motor Industry

The prominent potential savings that can be made by utilising B2B in supply chains in the motor industry can be summarised as follows:

- Many industries have a need to overcome obvious inefficiencies, such as insufficient connectivity between product processes and assemblers, the various tiers of supply chain partners and the customers.
- Lack of timely accurate data between the supply chain partners, distributors and retailers results in excessive levels of inventory.
- Product or service development and design changes often take several weeks to filter through the supply chain via traditional methods that involve time-consuming face-to-face meetings, faxes and approvals.
- Insufficient real time access to information held within the supply chain on customer buying preferences and actual purchases results in supply chain inefficiencies.
- Excess inventory pile up due to poor demand forecasting and under-utilised or over-capacity processing facilities.
- High logistics costs due to last minute transportation and shipping and hence far less than optimal transport or inventory costs.

The availability of customer data has the ability to overcome various inefficiencies such as excess inventories, poor capacity utilisation, and higher transportation and distribution costs. This is because supply chain partners will tend to produce too little or too much due to a lack of real-time information. Romano and Passiante (2001) consider the "organisational proximity" that may be achieved through e-commerce supply chain management. Global companies have begun to use B2B e-commerce tools to initiate these changes to overcome some of the problems. A wide range of initiatives for e-procurement and other business functions via the creation of e-marketplaces and exchanges have been initiated. For example the Internet's open architecture has tremendous potential for free flow of information between the various supporting tiers of a supply chain. Systems are being developed to automate various processes that currently entail human interaction. Processes such as procurement, production, planning and various other business functions are becoming much more efficient through automation and the creation of new business models via the Internet.

Internet-Enabled Integration of Entire Supply Chains

Internet-enabled B2B technology has the ability to communicate large amounts of information with greater speed to supply chain partners, resulting in the efficient connectivity, integration and synchronisation of several processes. In many industries, restructuring of the entire supply chain adds value, in terms of transforming the entire structure of the existing participants of the value chain and the synchronisation of the various activities such as product development, manufacturing, sales and marketing.

Real-time connectivity will increase among tier 1 suppliers and the lower tiers through data sharing in areas of engineering and design change. This could reduce the typical time required for design changes (Berger & Deutsche Bank, 2000). The integration of data sharing is vital at the development stages of the product and the availability of this data through Internet-based platforms or the exchanges developed.

EDI was used in the automotive industry between the supply chain partners when massive amounts of data were to be shared between them. However, the limitations of EDI were apparent in that it only facilitates point-to-point flow of data, is expensive, needs costly updating of programs and requires a dedicated server. Further, each supplier had to deal with many EDI systems, which made it impractical and time consuming. The Internet-enabled standardised tools and XML-based technology is cost effective. For example, the B2B integration server of webMethods.com used by SAP in their B2B solutions has created a "supply chain renaissance" that has led and will continue to lead to significant cost reductions (Baker et al., 2002). The Internet and the broadband data networks are providing cost-effective communication platforms to enable supply chain partners to integrate their existing legacy systems efficiently and quickly. This is important for reducing order-to-deliver time (Conway, 2000).

Supply Chain Management Software (SCM)

The introduction of "off-the-shelf" SCM software packages has enhanced communication between the various tiers of the supply chain and has created opportunities for supply chain partners in areas of inventory management, quality management and the capability to speedily address any incompatibility issues within the supply chain tier levels. The transparency of information on availability of competitive prices across various tiers of the supply chain and the automation of varied functions and processes are beginning to save revenue and time. Logistics and manufacturing, enhanced with SCM technology modules, provides a wide range of functionalities and features for production, planning processes, actual real-time data sharing along the supply chain, production scheduling and inventory. According to Conway (2000) efficient B2B supply chain management would bring substantial savings to the tier 1 suppliers, manufacturers and assemblers. Organisations that add value based on supply chain management knowledge, e.g., engineering expertise, will be competitively ahead of organisations that add value only through product or service processing and should therefore achieve inimitable, sustainable competitive advantages.

Demand Forecasting

A known actual market demand is vital to efficient supply chain management in the motor industry and elsewhere but is currently full of inefficiencies in terms of matching actual market demand of customer preferences to manufacturing or service capacities. This results in loss of profits and inefficient production scheduling. By integrating the supply chain processes through connected information systems, B2B tools have the capacity to improve planning and demand forecasting (Arntzen & Shumway, 2002).

Integration and Synchronisation

The key impact of B2B e-commerce is on its ability to offer rapid, cost effective, asynchronous communication in complex supply chains, such as those in the motor industry. Efficient communication and integration would synchronise various activities between the motor manufacturers and their supply chains. The current supply chain model compartmentalises clear responsibilities among different layers. All players from OEMs (Original Equipment Manufacturers), suppliers, dealers to service providers follow a linear structure; the tier 1 and 2 suppliers deal with OEMs and the tier 3 and 4 suppliers deal with tier 1 and 2 suppliers (Conway, 2000; Berger & Deutsche Bank, 2000). In a complex supply chain, as in the automotive industry, this model involves paper-based processes and clearly outlined individual functions among the trading partners. B2B e-commerce enables the automobile manufactures to outsource and extract more functions, without trade-offs of the inefficiency related to limited communication and integration with suppliers (Berger & Deutsche Bank, 2000). Integration of technology, knowledge, product development, design, engineering and synchronising these functions along the supply chain via B2B initiatives is the main focus and has resulted in reductions in tangible assets.

The impact of B2B e-marketplace/exchange has the potential to transform supply chains into a comprehensive connected system. There are issues that need to be resolved such as organisational and cultural changes (considered later in this paper), in terms of completely moving away from manual processes to Internet-based supply chain functions. The investment in technology at the lower tier of the supply chain is a major concern, if complete integration is to be achieved. As per the Berger & Deutsche Bank (2000), enterprise resource planning for a fully integrated system will enable communication through the entire supply chain and connection to front-end data on customer demand. The result will be reduced inventory and efficient planning. The online connectivity provided by e-marketplaces will speed up production and reduce the time for delivery resulting in low inventories for processes, dealers, retailers and suppliers. The e-marketplace enables more buyers and sellers to conduct business at lower prices or derive better prices for their products, thus eliminating high processing costs used in traditional purchasing.

The automation of various processes and functions through e-marketplaces will enable rapid identification of suitable vendors and will include bidding processes, purchase orders, proposal streamlined accounts payable and receivable processes by providing a connection between the procurement, account and the ERP systems. This will provide an interface with each other to overcome hurdles in management of inventory and production capacity (Min & Galle, 1999; Tarn et al., 2002). Exchanges or e-marketplaces can in fact create a global market for components and various services. This offers the potential to be a catalyst for standardisation of many business functions that would result in global integration of supply chain systems. This global marketplace is enabling purchases of industry-standardised products and services. As customer tastes change and taking into account various economic and political factors, many companies have gone through major restructuring to stay competitive and have realised the importance of product and service standardisation and simplification in their supply chain processes (Warkentin et al., 2001). However, whilst standardisation will simplify the supply chain problems, B2B has the potential to allow greater degrees of complexity, and hence BtO in the motor industry could become a reality.

E-Commerce and BtO in Motor Industry

Build to Order concepts were not really possible prior to e-commerce-enabled supply chains. Build to Order capacity is becoming an increasingly important strategic requirement for many businesses; Ford and General Motors have announced ambitious plans (using B2B Internet-based tools) to shift the automobile market globally, from the traditional ways of buying largely from the dealers' inventory to the Build to Order systems. Here customer orders initiate the car building process, and the customised automobile is delivered to a customer's doorstep in days. The Build to Order concept is attempting to imitate the success of computer vendor strategies such as Dell Computer's direct-selling model. There are clear-cut advantages from the BtO model in areas of customer service, logistics, inventory and marketing costs. The growth of BtO in vehicle manufacturing will probably gain ground in a slow evolutionary manner, as manufacturing a vehicle is a more complex task that manufacturing a computer. As high inventory levels are reduced, profits may temporarily be affected if customers cannot be serviced. The enormity of changes to business cultures, structures and practices should not be underestimated here. For example, changes to vehicle dealer networks and relationships with manufacturers will potentially generate very radical restructuring in the industry because dealers become less essential.

The development of a BtO model essentially requires electronic integration between an organisation and its trading partners across the supply chain by interconnections between information systems. The impact is increased real-time visibility among the supply chain partners that results in synchronisation of their functions, thus reducing cycle time and inventory. The entire supply chain's goal in a BtO model changes to building products as per actual demand from the customer versus against building products on forecast for future demand. (In other words, an emphasis on "pull" processes).

E-commerce initiatives taken by large motor manufactures in developing BtO capabilities have come in the form of hub and portal architecture, integrating internal systems that electronically commune with supply chain and key trading partners. Dell Computer has successfully implemented Build to Order and has created a direct sales model via B2B e-commerce. The key success of Dell's strategy is supply chain simplification and pull processes. This results in low inventories and ensures that design defects are not introduced into a large quantity of stock products. The supply chain is facilitated with sophisticated exchange of information and provides real-time data to suppliers on the state of the demand. Further suppliers are able to access their components inventory status at the manufacturing plants, along with their daily production requirements. However, it could be argued that BtO in the motor industry, whilst not introducing defects in a large quantity of products might in fact result in many different defects in a large quantity of products, due to the increasingly individual nature of sequential procurement processes. Tang and Lu (2002) discuss an internet/extranet/intranet system that is able to integrate quality information in these situations as a way to alleviate this potential risk.

The application of Build to Order concept in the automobile industry would deliver a vehicle to a customer based upon their specifications, preferences and needs quickly and effectively, on demand and in real time, versus the current prevalent systems where customers are persuaded to purchase what is in stock and available "off the shelf." Currently, ordering a custom-made vehicle means a long waiting period. Further, the purchase of products online by customers would enable manufacturers and service providers to compile large amounts of data on consumer preferences that could serve as an important tool for product design and development purposes. This points to massive implications for cultural change in the motor industry. Questions in relation to the current role of sales persons and dealers, and how they will integrate into the new system, must be considered. While it is likely that car buyers will value more customisation in the specifications of their vehicles, some may see that the elimination of sales advice and the dealer premises (both of which currently add very significant costs) in fact lead to more commoditisation of the vehicle market. In buyer behaviour terms, this would not be desirable. However, this does point to the need to develop new marketing strategies. At present dealers fulfil two major functions. First, they provide an inventory function for the manufacturers. In an enabled supply chain, the need for this function can be substantially reduced due to the greater applicability of Build to Order. There would still be a need for distribution of the completed product, which could be an opportunity to take further advantage of relationship marketing, perhaps involving personal delivery and home marketing. Many could substantially reduce their retailing premises as a result. Second, they provide advice and customer service. In order to avoid the commoditisation of the market, this function will need considerable reengineering. There are many potential solutions, not the least of which might involve greater use of e-marketing. Large in-roads have already been made in vehicle sales in this area (Forester Research, 1998).

Change Management Issues in the Implementation of E-Commerce in Supply Chains

Some industries, particularly in the manufacturing sector, have traditionally moved at a very slow pace. In order to embrace the Internet, the restructuring process will need attention in many areas, including procurement, product design and distribution. Organisational change is often a challenge in adapting to a new technology. If people (and the way their traditional vertical accountability and authority are organised) throughout supply chains do not adapt to the potential offered by the Internet and B2B technology, the savings expected by this change will continue to remain unrealised (Reynolds, 2000; Au & Ho, 2002; Croom, 2001).

Historically many firms have legacy systems and cultures that are customised and extensive. Integrating and synchronising communications thoroughly is a challenging and slow process. Industry will require end-to-end integration and reengineered internal processes to be compatible and integrate with the front-end processes of B2B to realise any substantial savings (Fraser et al., 2000; Croom, 2001). The implementation of BtO will require a platform concept, modular product architecture, and flexible manufacturing processes (Berger & Deutsche Bank, 2000). Changing the internal processes of the entire supply chain will require major restructuring. This transition is a long cumbersome process in a complex and multiple-tiered supply chain. Reengineering and restructuring involve large investments. Lower tier supply chain partners may not find large amounts of investment within their reach. This could result in a lack of vital B2B participants in the supply chain. Of possibly even greater concern are the cultural and change management issues that would inevitably become an issue in the motor industry for example, which has a well-established pattern of organisational behaviour. Traditionally, the assembler holds the balance of power in the industry. Using this power, they are able to manipulate suppliers further down the supply chain by, for example, using price as a bargaining factor in setting off one supplier against another. If this culture is allowed to prevail in an e-commerce B2B-enabled supply chain, there will be little achieved, other than automation of the supply limitations that currently exist. Some have already begun to discuss this issue, putting forward Business Process Reengineering and restructuring models (Lui & Lin, 2001; Liu & Zhang, 2002). However, this and, in particular, the area of inter-organisational processes are undoubtedly areas that will require much further research. Smith (2000) expresses further caution. In addition to this, many motor organisations have tended to be hierarchical and autocratic/consultative in management style and hence there will inevitably be a degree of resistance to technical change. McIvor and Humphreys (2002) have discussed some of the issues involving the development of a culture of trust. It is argued that a culture change is required in order to establish real partnerships through which information can be exchanged to the mutual benefit of all supply chain participants. Towill (1997) probably best describes the main issue by raising the question of leadership. The paper talks of the term "predator" who is "the supply chain leader with vision, drive and determination to re-engineer the entire supply chain so as to satisfy end-customer needs" (p. 37). Clearly, further work is still needed in this area.

Real network power comes from strong ties among every partner in the supply chain, with a multiplicity of links reaching in all directions. Enhancing the value of the entire network by adoption of B2B could potentially offer competitive advantage. However, value is as difficult to create as it is to duplicate, and unless industry strives towards enhancing the value of the network it has already created, its goal of long-term B2B solutions will not be realised (Kanter, 2001). The transparency of the flow of real information in the entire supply chain is a major change management issue. A standard set of protocols and code of shared conventions is required to be adopted by the participating supply chain organisations to enhance the constant flow of real-time information of all processes and functions. Internet-based systems make this more readily achievable. However, the change management issues may actually bring in a whole new dimension for consideration because behavioural changes in inter-firm, rather in addition to intra-firm communication, will become an issue.

Legally, many questions remain unanswered in relation to B2B e-commerce in regards to buying and selling online. Various other issues such as tariffs, trade barriers, and customs and excise rules of different countries and the global operations of online exchanges in relation to tax have to be scrutinised. Further, B2B exchanges introduce a certain level of collaboration among business partners and competitors; as a result in both cases, antitrust and competition laws must be considered. B2B technology's success lies in its flexibility and performance. There are various issues that need to be resolved such as systems security standards and communication protocols, vendor selection and coordination, telecommunications and bandwidth insufficiencies, content management and outsourcing issues (Turban et al., 2002; Min & Galle, 1999).

Conclusion

As businesses become comfortable in adopting an e-commerce culture, B2B e-business will explode within supply chain networks. Forrester Research (1998) indicated that customers used the Internet to select two million cars and light vehicles, and this figure was to rise to four million in 2003-2004. The realisation of a BtO program will depend greatly on a pull system that addresses customers' requirements and also gears customers to accept mix and match configurations and the options that Internet-based BtO provides. Transformations will be required in adapting to B2B tools to meet the demand for online business and this would rest on the supply chain functions of pull processes, coordination of material movements of inbound and outbound warehousing, manufacturing work centres and quality control. B2B e-commerce is vital in achieving this. Success would largely be attributed to the focus and efficiencies achieved in the implementation of the "back-end" applications such as the SCM, restructuring various processes, together with the front-end applications.

An online e-procurement model would simplify and improve processes such as ordering, order processing, order accuracy, access to lower prices of materials, etc. This model can offer easy-to-use functionality based on the Web browser interface. In the motor industry, online catalogues maintained by the manufactures and the supplier of preferred supplier products supported by authorisation tools and other relevant data are examples of the e-commerce-derived e-procurement cost-effective purchasing power. However, while these potential benefits have been postulated for some time (Sheldon, 1994), it is clear that achieving the wider strategic advantage still has some distance to go (Warren & Hutchinson, 2000; Reynolds, 2000 & Van Hoek, 2001; Robertson et al., 2001).

This paper has clearly illustrated the potential for strategic advantage from a more cooperative and participatory view of supply chain management. Modern thinking in e-commerce, and in particular B2B, has been shown to be a key enabling factor in making this potentially achievable. Competitive advantage can be achieved because individual supply chains tend to be unique to particular organisational groups, and so it is difficult to quickly imitate competitors' supply chain e-commerce strategies. Some clear cases, for example, movement towards Build to Order in the automotive industry, where there are substantial potential benefits to customers, have been illustrated. However, the paper has also highlighted areas for further research in terms of the cultural adaptation and adoption of the e-commerce technology to existing supply chains. There is a need for process redesign to overcome established structural and cultural issues. The views of Gattorna et al. (1991) are still clearly reflected: "A pragmatic, market-based approach is needed which is repeatedly proven by practical applications and relies on identifying and accepting the differing objectives and styles of other supply chain members, and clustering these seemingly disparate groups into their 'natural logics'"(p. 5). This and the findings of this paper, tend to suggest that supply chain players will require better alignment before the full strategic potential of e-commerce, involving B2B technologies, can be achieved. However, this alignment is clearly an area where there is much potential for further research. As Gattorna et al. (1991) state: "The fundamental weakness in traditional supply-chain management thinking is that of trying to change the behaviour of everyone involved by exhorting them to create and maintain shared vision and strategy" (p. 5). The issue of supply chain management leadership is going to prove crucial if e-commerce is to be truly successful in this setting. Towill's (1997) supply chain "predator" is clearly going to prove a crucial factor. The issues are probably not going to be the e-commerce B2B technology, but its leadership and implementation.

References

Anderson, D. L. & Lee, H. (2000). *The Internet-enabled supply chain: From the "first click" to the "last mile."* Retrieved from *http://www.manufacturing.net/scm/contents/pdf/anderson_lee_wp.pdf*

Arntzen, B. C. & Shumway, H. M. (January, 2002). Driven by demand: A case study. *Supply Chain Management Review*, 34.

Au, K. F. & Ho, D. C. K. (2002). Electronic commerce and supply chain management: Value-adding service for clothing manufacturers. *Integrated Manufacturing Systems, 13*(4), 247-255.

Baker, G., Hensley, R., & Reismen, L. (2000). *Supply chain innovation in the new economy* (white paper). Arthur Andersen Automation.

Berger, Roland, Strategy Consultants, & Deutsche Bank. (2000). *Automotive e-commerce: A (virtual) reality check*. Retrieved from *http://www.rolandberger. com/documents/1907009/RB_B2B_Automotive.pdf*

Chopra, S. & Meindl, P. (2001). *Supply chain management: Strategy planning and operations*. Englewood Cliffs NJ: Prentice Hall.

Conway, D. G. (2000). Supplier affiliated supply chain backbones. *Information Systems Frontiers, 2*(1), 57-64.

Croom, S. (2001). Restructuring supply chains through information channel innovation. *International Journal of Operations and Production Management, 21*(4), 504-515.

Davidrajuh, R. (2003). Realizing a new e-commerce tool for formation of virtual enterprise. *Industrial Management and Data Systems, 103*(6), 434-445.

Dertouzos, M. (1997). *What will be: How the new world of information systems will change our lives*. San Francisco: Harper Edge.

The Economist. (March 30, 2000). The real long term impact of IT and the NET. *The Economist*.

Elliman, T. & Orange, G. (2000). Electronic commerce to support construction design and supply-chain management: A research note, *International Journal of Physical Distribution and Logistics Management, 30*(3/4), 345-360.

Forrester Research. (1998). Retrieved from *http://www.forrester.com/ER/Research/Report/Summary/0,1338,11127,00.html*

Fraser, J., Fraser, N., & McDonald, F. (2000). The strategic challenge of electronic commerce. *Supply Chain Management, 5*(1), 7-14.

Gattorna, J. L., Chorn, N. H. & Day, A. (1991). Pathways to customers: reducing complexity in the logistics pipeline. *International Journal of Physical Distribution and Logistics Management, 21*(8), 5-11.

Handfield, R & Nicols, E. (1999). *Supply Chain Management*. Englewood Cliffs, NJ: Prentice Hall.

Horner, G. & Thompson, D. (2003). The contribution of Internet technology in achieving lean management within British automotive supply chains. *Inter-*

national Journal of Services Technology and Management, 4(1), 42-52.

Kanter, R. M. (2001). *Evolve: Succeeding in the digital culture of tomorrow.* Boston: Harvard Business School Press.

Lambert, D. M. & Cooper, M. C. (2000). Issues in supply chain management. *Industrial Marketing Management,* 29, 65-83.

Leonard, L. N. K. & Cronin, T. P. (2002). A study of the value and impact of electronic commerce: Electronic versus traditional replenishment in supply chains. *Journal of Organizational Computing and Electronic Commerce, 12*(4), 307-327.

Liu, Y. & Lin, J. (2001). Network supply chain management about transforming a traditional business into e-enterprise. *Industrial Engineering Journal, 4*(2), 14-17.

Liu, J. & Zhang, S. (2002). An inter-enterprise workflow model for supply chain and B2B e-commerce. *High Technology Letters, 8*(2), 51-55.

McGuffog, T. & Wadsley, N. (1999). The general principles of value chain management. *Supply Chain Management,* 4, 218-225.

McIvor, R. T. & Humphreys, P. K. (2002). Electronic commerce: Supporting collaborative buyer-supplier relations? *International Journal of Services Technology and Management, 3*(2), 192-207.

McLaren, B. J. & McLaren, C. H. (1999). *E-commerce business on the Internet.* OH: South Western Publishers.

Meyer, A. & Taylor, P. (2000). E-commerce an introduction. *Computing and Control Engineering Journal, 11*(3), 107-108.

Min, H. & Galle, W. P. (1999). Electronic commerce usage in business-to-business purchasing. *International Journal of Operations and Production Management, 19*(9), 909-921.

Murillo, L. (2001). Supply chain management and the international evolution of e-commerce: Infrastructure, institutional and complementary assets determinants. *Industrial Management and Data Systems, 101*(7), 370-377.

Overby, J. W. & Min, S. (2001). International supply chain management in an Internet environment: A network-oriented approach to internationalization. *International Marketing Review, 18*(4), 392-420.

Pawar, K. S. & Driva, H. (2000). Electronic trading in the supply chain: A holistic implementation framework. *Logistics Information Management, 13*(1), 21-32.

Power, D. J. & Sohal, A. S. (2002). Implementation and usage of electronic commerce in managing the supply chain: A comparative study of ten

Australian companies. *Benchmarking: An International Journal, 9*(2), 190-208.

Reddy, R. (2001). *Supply chains to vertical integration.* McGraw-Hill.

Reynolds, J. (2000). E-commerce: A critical review. *International Journal of Retail and Distribution Management, 28*(10), 417-444.

Robertson, P. W., Gibson, P. R. & Flanagan, J. T. (2001). Supply chain integrated logistical processes: Achieving the key logistical process linkages required to deliver optimal supply chain performance. In *Proceedings of the 12th Annual Conference of the Production and Operations Management Society*, Orlando, March 30-April 2 (pp. 1-13).

Romano, A. & Passiante, G. (2001). New sources of clustering in the digital economy. *Journal of Small Business and Enterprise Development, 8*(1), 19-27.

Sheldon, D. (1994). Shaping up for the information revolution. *Logistics Information Management, 7*(4), 15-18.

Smith, M. (2000). The visible supply chain. *Intelligent Enterprises, 3*(16), 44-50.

Stevens G. C. (1989). Integrating the supply chain. *International Journal of Physical Distribution and Materials Management, 19*(8), 3-8.

Supply Chain Council. (2002). *SCOR, part 1: An introduction to the supply chain operations reference model.* Retrieved from *http://www.ebizq.net/topics/eai/features/1769.html*

Tang, X. O. & Lu, Q. L. (2002). Intranet/extranet/Internet-based quality information management system in expanded enterprises. *International Journal of Advanced Manufacturing Technology, 20*(11), 853-858.

Tarn, J. M., Yen, D. C. & Beaumont, M. (2002). Exploring the rationales for ERP and SCM Integration. *Industrial Management and Data Systems, 102*(1), 26-34.

Towill, D. R. (1997). The seamless supply chain-the predator's strategic advantage. *International Journal of Technology Management* (special issue on strategic cost management), *13*(1), 37-56.

Turban, E., Lee, J., King, D. & Chung, H. M. (2002). *Electronic commerce: A managerial perspective.* Englewood Cliffs, NJ: Prentice Hall

Van Hoek, H. (2001). E-supply chains: Virtually non-existing. *Supply Chain Management, 6*, 21-28

Warkentin, M., Bapna, R., & Sugumaran, V. (2001), E-knowledge networks for the inter-organizational collaborative e-business. *Logistics Information, 14*(1-2), 146-163.

Warren, M., & Hutchinson, W. (2000). Cyber attacks against supply chain management systems: A short note. *International Journal of Physical Distribution and Logistics Management, 30*(7/8), 710-716.

Previously published in the Journal of Electronic Commerce in Organizations, 2(3), 59-76, July - September 2004.

Chapter XV

On E-Markets in Emerging Economy: An Indian Experience

Ashis K. Pani, XLRI, Jamshedpur, India

Amit Agrahari, XLRI, Jamshedpur, India

Abstract

MetalJunction.com is a joint venture of TISCO (Tata Iron & Steel Company) and SAIL (Steel Authority of India), the steel makers contributing more than 60% to the India's total steel production. The case illustrates how an organization(s) can use information technology to spin off key processes such as procurement and selling. Since its first year of operations, MetalJunction.com generated substantial savings for TISCO and SAIL. The case also supports the argument that the business context in emerging economies is significantly different from developed economies; hence, setting up a successful B2B marketplace may require the creation of basic services that are taken for granted in developed economies.

These days Indian dot.com companies are having a tough time because of the dot.com burst, the 9/11 terrorist attack, and the sluggish American economy. However, Mr. Viresh Oberoi, MD, of MetalJunction.com has enough reasons to celebrate. His firm not only survived the dot.com bloodbath, but also generated substantial profit from the very first year of operations. Total transaction value in financial year 2003 to 2004 has touched Rs 21.35 billion ($427 million).

The Background

Before moving to MetalJunction.com, Oberoi spent his entire career with TISCO. He has extensive knowledge of the Indian iron and steel industry, which is nearly a century old. Established in 1907, TISCO is the first integrated steel plant in Asia. Today, India is the 10th largest producer of steel in the world with SAIL and TISCO contributing over 60% to India's total steel production. SAIL is the largest steel conglomerate in the country and the world's ninth largest steel maker. On the other hand, TISCO is the second lowest cost producer in the world after the South Korean steel giant POSCO. SAIL and TISCO differ considerably in ownership pattern, processes, governance structure, and organization culture. SAIL is a government-of-India undertaking whereas TISCO is a private-sector organization. However, during the dot.com boom, these two fierce competitors realized the immense potential of the Internet and information technology, and entered into a joint venture to launch MetalJunction.com Private Limited.

The Inception

It was the year 1999, the year when the dot.com boom was at its peak and e-commerce was the new buzzword doing the rounds. It was the time when Dr J.J. Irani, MD, of TISCO and Mr. Arvind Pande, chairman of SAIL, had a spate of offers to join domestic and international e-commerce platforms for the steel industry. Rather than joining any ill-conceived dot.com, SAIL and TISCO independently set up internal e-commerce task forces to study various e-commerce models that had sprung up during the dot.com boom of the late 1990s. These two task forces came to identical conclusions: that while e-commerce is definitely the way forward, it would make more business sense for two or three of the largest players in a similar industry or region to come together and consolidate their e-commerce plans on a common platform. Thus, MetalJunction.com was born.

The Organization

MetalJunction.com is not a neutral marketplace between buyers and sellers. It is a selling and procurement service provider. It has two separate divisions that provide these services operating under two different URLs (uniform resource locators), namely, http://www.metaljunction.com and http://www.commercejunction.com. Thus, it tries to create value across the entire value chain except manufacturing (Figure 1). The organization has its head office at Kolkata and regional offices across India (Appendix A). MetalJunction.com currently offers three services, namely, procurement services, selling services, and channel finance services. Insiders feel that the company has potential business of over Rs 50 billion (approximately $1 billion) a year. Figure 2 shows the potential value that MetalJunction.com can realize as a percentage of sales.

Figure 1. Process innovation across the entire supply chain

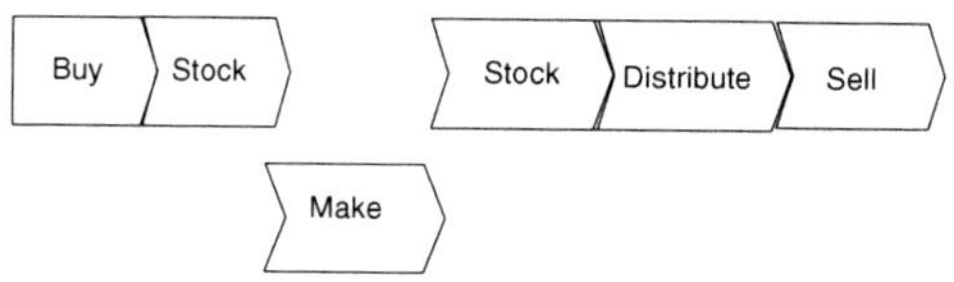

Figure 2. Potential impact of e-commerce (% of sales)

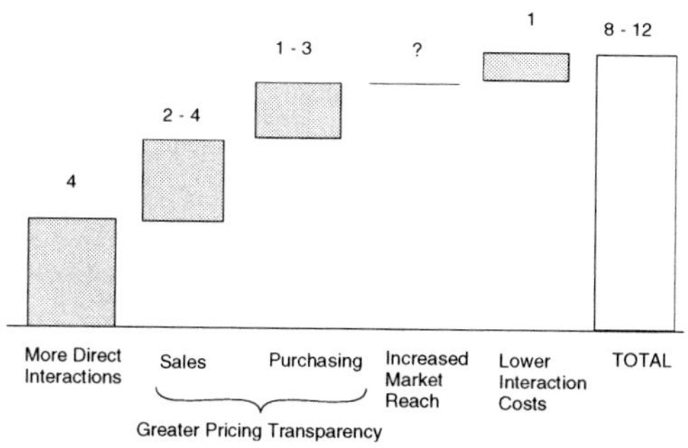

Note: Impact of increased market reach could not be quantified

Setting the Stage

After the dot.com burst, companies providing procurement and selling services had to reinvent themselves to survive and grow in line with market needs. Corporations around the world, SAIL and TISCO included, realized that in a world without boundaries, certain regions and people with distinct competencies would be more efficient than others. Outsourcing, therefore, is the visible trend in the world today. Companies are outsourcing manufacturing activities, customer services, back-office operations, and a whole host of other activities either because there is someone else who can do the same thing for less or there is a specialist in the activity who can do the same thing better.

Globally and in India, companies have recognized that an Internet marketplace and bulletin-board services would not serve the real needs of companies. What companies were really looking for was a complete solution that embraces technology, the Internet, and most importantly, specific industry domain expertise. This lead to the emergence of specialists for procurement and selling services who are typically called procurement service providers (PSPs) and selling service providers (SSPs). Their scope of work envisages the entire procurement process and selling and fulfillment processes of companies, and emphasizes the importance of an online solution backed with a strong off-line presence. Taking these clues from the industry, MetalJunction.com organized itself to become a specialist service provider rather than just another B2B (business-to-business) auction site. It owns the entire selling and procurement

Figure 3. Graphical representation of MetalJunction.com architecture

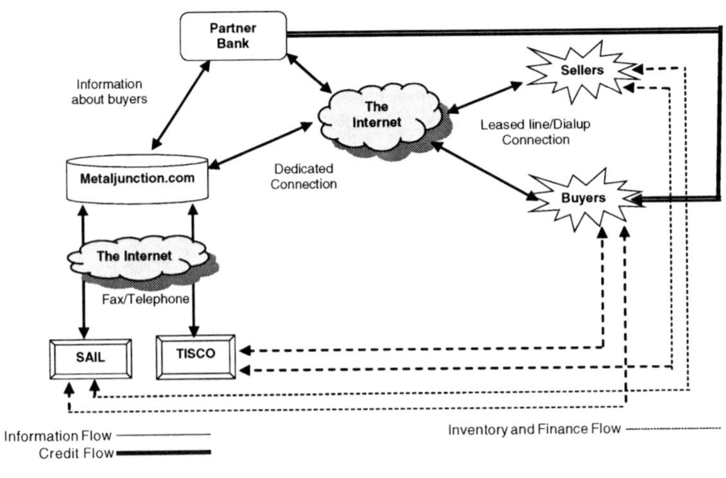

process. Clients (TISCO and SAIL), for a fee, hire the procurement and selling services. MetalJunction.com charges different fees for different services offered. Fees range from a low of 0.1% to a high of 7.5% of goods sold or procured. However, no fee is charged to client's channel partners (buyers using e-selling or suppliers using e-procurement). To avail, e-selling and e-procurement services clients do not even need to be Web enabled. They do not even need an ISP (Internet service provider) connection or a Web browser. However, their channel partners need to have Internet connectivity. A graphical representation of the overall architecture is provided in Figure 3.

Case Description

Prior to the use of IT in an interorganizational information system, it was believed that investments to increase the level of explicit coordination with suppliers would result in increased risk to a firm. Consequently, buyer firms have traditionally avoided this increased risk by becoming vertically integrated or by underinvesting in coordination. Clemons and Row (1992) have shown that IT can lower the cost of coordination without necessarily increasing the risk associated with a greater level of explicit coordination. Malone, Yates, and Benjamin (1987) have suggested that the increasing adoption of IT will lead to a greater degree of outsourcing and hence less vertically integrated firms. Moreover, since search costs are reduced, firms will rely more on search, leading to the emergence of e-markets. Using MetalJunction.com, TISCO and SAIL could spin off key processes of procurement, selling, and channel finance. This resulted in substantial savings and process improvement for them.

E-Procurement

In procurement, MetalJunction.com has delivered on two critical elements, namely, saving on the current market prices and arresting rising price trends. It takes complete ownership of the procurement process, right from preparing the request for quotations (RFQ) to identifying, validating, and training new suppliers to conducting the e-sourcing event. The competitive bidding brought in by the online e-sourcing event ensures that the leanest suppliers are identified, which has brought about substantial savings in procurement (Table 1). In some cases, MetalJunction.com has conducted an e-sourcing event within 24 hours from the generation of the RFQ. This reduction in cycle time means that clients do not have to maintain high inventory levels. For some products, for which prices are

Table 1. Savings in procurement for financial year 2002 to 2003

Category (All figures in $; Rs 50 = $1, approximately)	*Value Procured*	*Actual Savings over Last Procured Price*	*% Savings*
Chemicals	4,056,600	647,700	15.97%
Electrical Consumables	3,350,320	355,060	10.60%
Explosives	2,712,000	75,460	2.78%
Ferro-Alloys	481,800	5,700	1.18%
General Consumables	2,939,880	254,760	8.67%
Instruments	2,124,740	497,840	23.43%
Logistics	7,732,000	449,720	5.82%
Mechanical Consumables	1,883,200	244,400	12.98%
Nonferrous Metal, Iron Metallics	8,467,200	0	0.00%
Petroleum By-Products	1,686,920	166,380	9.86%
Pharmaceuticals	21,820	0	0.00%
Refractories	3,570,760	44,420	1.24%
Total	39,027,240	2,741,420	7.02%

volatile, it has created a standing RFQ for 1 year, and the price is determined on a monthly basis through an online e-sourcing event.

Savings are calculated as a reduction achieved in online price over the immediately preceding off-line procurement price. In some cases, though, there is no savings over the preceding price; the price was lower than current off-line prices.

In financial year 2002 to 2003, TISCO procured materials and services totaling Rs 902.5 million ($18.05 million) through MetalJunction.com. The savings accrued by TISCO from these procurements were to the tune of Rs 53.7 million ($1.07 million) or approximately 5.96%. Savings have been as high as 23.43%, but in some cases savings have been marginal or there have been none at all. However, procurement through CommerceJunction.com has brought in more competition and has ensured that prices were either reduced or arrested. SAIL has procured caustic soda, welding electrodes, transformer coils, lamps and fittings, pipes, and stone bricks worth Rs 520 million ($10.4 million) through online bidding in financial year 2002 to 2003.

In the financial year 2003 to 2004, TISCO procured material worth Rs 2.41 billion ($48.2 million), whereas SAIL procured material worth Rs 1.71 billion ($34.2 million) through MetalJunction.com. The total savings for SAIL and TISCO from e-procurement has been 10.45%, which was approximately double as compared to savings in 2002 to 2003.

E-Selling

In e-selling, MetalJunction.com takes ownership of the client's selling process for standard or commoditised products and by doing so, it delivers benefits such as an increase in realizations by selling further down the value chain and bringing in efficiencies in the selling and distribution value chain. E-selling leads to disintermediation, which allows direct end users an equal opportunity to compete with larger buyers (traders or distributors). This happens as e-selling enables the breakup of large quantities into small lots through automation without increasing workload on human resource (In conventional selling, due to expensive labor-oriented paperwork, manufacturers prefer bulk buyers and are prepared to offer quantity discounts). Smaller lots ensure wider participation, especially from end users. This enables end users to buy material at lower prices than they used to from traders while ensuring that the client organization earns higher realizations. Both buyer and client organizations gain by sharing erstwhile traders' margins. TISCO gained 1.69% to 23.07% immediately on migrating from off-line to online selling. For SAIL, the price increases were in the range of 4.66% to 18.21%. E-Selling also results in reduced cycle time. The speed with which an e-selling event can be created and communicated to the buyer community ensures stock can be sold immediately on generation.

During the financial year 2002 to 2003, TISCO sold 221,259 MT and has aggregated Rs 2.91 billion ($58.2 million). In 2003 to 2004, the total transaction value was Rs 4.03 billion ($80.6 million). Some of the products that TISCO sold through MetalJunction.com were HSM defectives, HSM POR, GP coils, LP defectives, prime billets, and various secondary products. In financial year 2002 2003, SAIL sold prime products worth Rs 500 million ($10 million) through the forward auction mechanism. The total transaction value in 2003 to 2004 was Rs 5.26 billion ($105.2 million). The major items sold were HR coils and plates, IU (industrial use) rails, structures, MS plates, and other items. It also sold secondary steel worth around Rs 80 million ($1.6 million) through the e-commerce route, generating additional revenue over 5% for the different items.

Financial Services

The business context in emerging economies differs significantly from developed economies. Hempel and Kwong (2001) argued that there is a fundamental difficulty in applying the Western best practices in e-commerce to Asian economies because of differences in business and cultural assumptions. Like any other emerging economy, India also lacks financial, legal, and physical infrastructures necessary to develop successful e-marketplace. For instance, unlike in a developed economy, credit terms in India are quite stringent and the banking process is characterized by bureaucratic delays. Major banks are lagging far behind in Internet revolution, with a large number of branches still working without any kind of automation.

The Indian banking industry was nationalized in the early 1970s to ensure credit regulation. The aim was to ensure credit availability for priority sectors such as agriculture, infrastructure, power, and so forth. However, the nationalization scheme backfired, with banks accumulating huge nonperforming assets (NPAs). In the early 1990s, private operators were once again allowed in the banking industry. These private-sector banking companies penetrated rapidly in urban areas, but they have no branches in rural and semi-urban areas, where the majority of SAIL and TISCO's channel partners operate. A lack of organized finance forced SAIL and TISCO to sell on credit basis, hence increasing their working capital requirements. In some cases, intermediators purchased from SAIL and TISCO on cash basis and sold it to end users on credit basis. However, disintermediation by MetalJunction.com threatens to remove these traditional credit sources from the scene.

To solve this infrastructural problem, MetalJunction.com launched online channel finance for its clients (SAIL and TISCO). There is a tripartite agreement between the bank, MetalJunction.com, and MetalJunction.com's clients (SAIL and TISCO). The bank agrees to provide clean credit to channel partners of MetalJunction.com's clients without collateral from channel partners and, in the event of default, without recourse to the client. The bank assesses the risk on the basis of the financial soundness of MetalJunction.com's client and the relationship (dependency factor) of the channel partner with the client. The client company provides a comfort letter to the bank assuring the bank that, in the event of default by the channel partner, it will cease further supplies until all payments are cleared. MetalJunction.com acts as the facilitator between bank, client, and channel partners, and assists the bank in assessing the risk in the distribution channel. MetalJunction.com has also created an online interface that can integrate banks' online platforms to the client company's ERP system. Channel partners can access their sales orders online, make a finance request online through MetalJunction.com's interface, and make payments online to the client through the same interface.

Past experience with channel finance says that it brings efficiencies by reducing a client's working capital requirements by enabling it to sell on cash basis while providing the channel partners a source of organized finance at competitive interest rates. Besides the above services, MetalJunction.com is also offering fulfillment services such as e-collection in association with Standard Chartered, HDFC, and Citibank. The amount of finance that has been arranged is Rs 2.62 billion ($52.4 million) in 2002 to 2003, and Rs 7.61 billion ($152.3 million) in 2003 to 2004. The number of channel partners availing of this service has grown to 58 (only for TISCO). So far, SAIL has not availed this service.

The Environment

Currently, a total of six specialized steel-trading sites are functional in the country. If everything goes well, then e-commerce will account for around 20% of the total steel traded in the country in next three years. According to an estimate in December 2002, around 3% of the total volume of steel is traded online, whereas the international standard is around 10%. Industry observers predict a dot.com shakeout and suggest that critical attributes for survival are liquidity, credibility, and financial health. Oberoi thinks that MetalJunction.com is clearly aligned with its clients, improving their processes and committed to deliver value to them.

Current Challenges

Though the first year's result looks quite impressive and the future is filled with opportunities, Oberoi can see some challenges ahead. Some of them are discussed in the following paragraphs.

Value Generation and Retention for Channel Partners

So how does this result in value creation? Oberoi knows this is the most crucial question any organization has to answer. For his company, the task is still more difficult as the value has to be created for client companies as well as their channel partners. The commonly observed phenomenon in B2B markets is that the initiator takes all. However, he thinks that in e-procurement, suppliers prefer bidding online rather than participating in the tender process. The reason for this is greater transparency in the online procurement process because the rules are predefined and the L1[1] price is known to all participants. Since the time required for negotiation is cut down to just an hour or so, it frees their time to develop new business. Furthermore, as online procurement is rarely maverick buying despite margins coming under pressure, the suppliers' order-book position is more secure. Though channel partners seem to enjoy some benefits, MetalJuction.com wants to ensure that all these benefits are not bargained away by powerful clients (SAIL and TISCO). Oberoi needs some ways to ensure long-term, tangible benefits for channel partners so that they will keep using MetalJunction.com.

Insufficient Integration

Though MetalJunction.com covers a sufficiently wide breadth of the partner base, the level of business integration is still low. Tuunainen (1999) suggests that integration is the key to realize maximum value from e-procurement systems. How can MetalJunction.com increase integration among its participants? Should it offer services such as order tracking and a payment gateway?

Is the Auction Model Sustainable?

Before the advent of the Internet, the auction model was used for the price discovery of nonproduction goods such as fine art and land. Steel can be produced in bulk and the marginal cost of production is known. Does that mean the auction model is not suitable for MetalJunction.com? Oberoi's experience in the Indian steel market suggests that the market price of steel is not determined by the cost of production alone, but by the market dynamics of demand, availability, and stocking cycles. The auction model can reach the length and breadth of a geographical region and can ensure that at any given point in time, material goes to the region that is willing to pay the most for it. However, since the worldwide steel industry is having an overcapacity, will it not be a good idea to sell as much as possible to as many people as possible, and not just sell to a selected few through online sales?

In the case of procurement, the auction model can take care of one attribute only (mainly price). As far as managing other attributes such as lead time and quality, MetalJunction.com collaborates with the material-management group (procurement team) of the client. If technocommercial bids are necessary before a supplier participates in the auction, MetalJunction.com and the client undertake them jointly. All elements of delivery schedule, lead time, and quality are predefined. In case the commodity is of a strategic nature in which quality is essential, only the client's existing supplier panel is allowed to participate, or new suppliers are allowed to participate with the caveat that if they are the L1 bidder, only a small part of the order, for testing purposes, will be placed on them in the first cycle of procurement. Depending on the nature of the procurement, the request for quotation is designed with all the rules predefined. On acceptance of all the terms, suppliers are allowed to participate in the price-bidding event. MetalJunction.com also identifies and validates new suppliers for its clients; however, the decision of allowing the new supplier to participate rests with the client. Hence, except for price, all other attributes are determined before the auction begins. Can there be some way to have multiattribute negotiation? If, at the end of the day, it is the lowest price that matters, then what are suppliers' incentives to invest in innovation and relation-specific assets?

Threat of Reintermediation

The disintermediation in the steel industry can create a substantial chunk of value. The traditional intermediaries are medium-sized companies with extensive knowledge about products and end users. As proposed by Chircu and Kauffman's (2000) IDR framework, can we see reintermediation by traditional intermediaries equipped with e-commerce capability? How can MetalJunction.com counter such reintermediation threats?

Future Plans

In financial year[2] 2002 to 2003, the first year of operations, services were offered only to founding companies. From financial year 2003 to 2004, the plan was to extend selling services beyond steel into the industry domains of minerals, nonferrous metals, and ferro-alloys. In e-procurement, the plan is to extend services horizontally across all verticals. The short-term future (two-year) plans also include global sourcing for Indian clients and selling materials from India to buyers in contiguous countries. MetalJunction.com also plans to market financial services as a stand-alone product to industries that have large distribution networks and other corporations across industry verticals. MetalJunction.com has tied up with banks to offer two different products depending on the nature and relationship of the original equipment manufacturer (OEM) with its client. One product is for large OEMs and the second product is for small and medium OEMs. These products will be rolled out in Quarter 2 of financial year 2003 2004. MetalJunction.com has also tied up with banks to offer pre- and postshipment finance to suppliers with whom clients have placed a purchase order. These products will be rolled out in Quarter 2 of financial year 2003 to 2004.

The sky outside the Tata center is now clear and the atmosphere inside is filled with enthusiasm and hope for the future. With such a good performance in the very first year of operation, Oberoi and his team is all set to take on the current challenges and leverage the Internet to change the Indian steel industry.

Acknowledgment

The authors would like to thank Mr. Viresh Oberoi, MD, CEO, and Mr. Linus Lobo, head of marketing and content at MetalJunction.com, for their valuable support in data collection and case development.

References

Chircu, A. M., & Kauffman, R. J. (2000). Reintermediation strategies in business to business electronic commerce. *International Journal of Electronic Commerce, 4*(4), 7-42.

Clemons, E. K., & Row, M. C. (1992). Information technology and industrial cooperation: The role of changing transaction costs. *Journal of Management Information Systems, 9*(2), 9-28.

Hempel, P. S., & Kwong, Y. K. (2001). B2B e-commerce in emerging economies: I-metal.com's non-ferrous metals exchange in China. *Journal of Strategic Information Systems, 10*(4), 335-355.

Malone, T. W., Yates, J., & Benjamin, R. I. (1987). Electronic markets and electronic hierarchies. *Communications of the ACM, 30*(6), 484-497.

Tuunainen, V. K. (1999). Opportunities of effective integration of EDI for small business in the automotive industry. *Information and Management, 34*(6), 361-375.

Endnotes

1 L1 price is the lowest price bid in the e-sourcing event for procurement. H1 price is the highest price bid in the e-selling event.

2 The financial year in India starts on April 1. The financial year 2002 to 2003 was MetalJunction.com's first year of operation.

Appendix A

The Organization

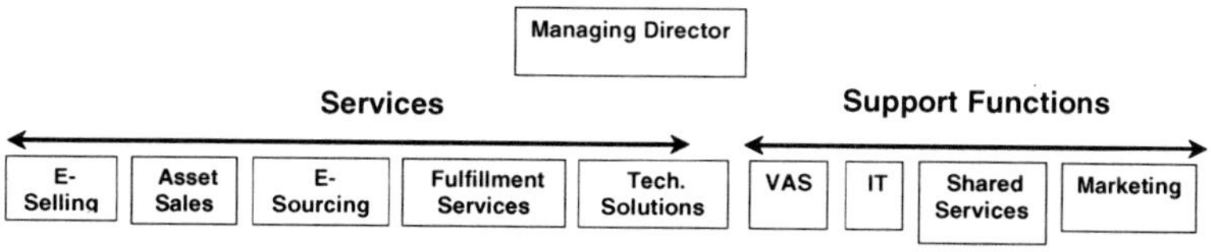

Technological Solutions — Designing, building, marketing, and customizing technological solutions

VAS — To develop and implement value-added services

IT — Information technology

Shared Services — HR, administration, finance, secretarial, and legal

Marketing — Content, business development, marketing

Number of employees — 42 executives

Corporate Headquarters — Kolkata

Regional Presence in India — Bombay, Delhi, Chennai, Bhilai, Bokaro, Durgapur, Rourkela, Jamshedpur

Share Holding — 50:50 by TISCO and SAIL

MetalJunction.com's Revenue since Inception

Period	Q1FY02-03	Q2FY02-03	Q3FY02-03	Q4FY02-03	Q1FY03-04	Q2FY03-04	Q3FY03-04	Q4FY03-04
Revenue (Rs)	899.8	1027.5	1674.2	2876.7	2813.0	4089.0	5107.5	9226.2
Revenue ($)	17.996	20.55	33.484	57.534	56.26	81.78	102.14	184.52

All figures are in millions.

Chapter XVI

An E-Government Model

Sushil K. Sharma, Ball State University, USA

Jatinder N.D. Gupta, The University of Alabama in Huntsville, USA

Abstract

Electronic government (e-government), the ability for government to provide access to services and information twenty-four hours a day, seven days a week, is an emerging force today. There are several models that attempt to explain the way in which e-government has evolved or is evolving. This paper presents an overview of a few important government models and frameworks.

Introduction

Electronic government (e-government) refers to the delivery of national or local government information and services via the Internet or other digital means. It is defined as the use by government agencies of information technologies (such as wide-area networks, the Internet, and mobile computing) that have the ability to transform relations with citizens, businesses, and other arms of government (Venkatachalam, Shore, & Sharma, 2003). These technologies can serve a variety of different ends: better delivery of government services to citizens, improved interactions with business and industry, citizen empowerment through access to information, or more efficient government management (Larsen & Rainie, 2002; Margetts & Dunleavy, 2002; World Bank Group, http://www1.worldbank.org/publicsector/egov/definition.htm). E-government, the ability for government to provide access to services and information 24 hours a day, seven days a week, is an emerging force today. The purpose of e-government is to provide an e-portal, "a one-stop Internet gateway," to major government services by the streamlining, simplification, and integration of services of various government agencies (Sharma & Gupta, 2002, 2003). Heeks (2001) describes e-government as i-governance or integrated governance since it integrates both the processing and the communication technologies, and since it integrates people, processes, information, and technology in the service of achieving governance objectives (Bertucci, 2003; Bollier, 2003; Heeks).

The e-government concept is under implementation at the federal or provincial/state level in many countries. Governments have taken the initiative and are intent on applying e-commerce tools and techniques to the business of governing (Dearstyne, 2001; Grönlund, 2002; Howard, 2001). Federal, state, and local governments, under pressure to deliver services more efficiently at lower cost, are recognizing e-commerce as an attractive option both commercially and politically. E-government has the greatest potential to revolutionize the performance of government and revitalize the democracy by speeding transactions, increasing efficiency, and bringing people closer to the government (Sharma & Gupta, 2002, 2003). All OECD (Organisation for Economic Cooperation and Development) member countries have already embarked on an e-government revolution, offering government information and services online, although the quantity and range varies considerably (Carey, 2004; Coleman & Gotze, 2002; Organisation for Economic Cooperation and Development, 2001, 2003). For example, the government Web portals of the United States and Norway provide a single entry point to access hundreds of public Web sites (United States, http://www.firstgov.gov; Norway, http://www.norge.no). Worldwide, many initiatives have been taken to create electronic states in order to increase the efficiency of the government and its services. Such projects include the Intelligent Island: Concept of Singapore, Golden Bridge Project of China, Multimedia Super Corridor of Malaysia, Access America of the USA, and Government Direct of the U.K. (Gurstein, 2000; Harris, 2002; Hunter & Jupp, 2001). As e-government principles and practices have been applied in the past few years, this chapter presents an overview of a few important e-government models and frameworks that have been evolved or are evolving.

E-Government Models

This chapter may use e-government, e-governance, and e-democracy in many places, so it is worthwhile to define these terms at the beginning and make the distinctions between them. E-government constitutes the way public-sector institutions use technology to apply public administration principles and conduct the business of government. This is government using new tools to enhance the delivery of existing services. E-governance is the movement of governments online to electronically deliver their services and programs, provide government information, and interact with the citizen. This is the formation of new relationships, and includes the private sector along with citizens and other levels of government. E-democracy is about how the citizen interacts with the government or influences the legislative or public-sector process. It is all about participatory democracy. This is the shift from representational democracy to participatory democracy (Riley, 2003a, 2003b, 2004; Riley & Riley, 2003).

There are several models that attempt to explain the way in which e-government has evolved or is evolving. The first step into the e-government or online-government world is a basic Web presence. Accenture ("E-government leadership: Engaging the customer," 2003) describes three levels of online delivery capability before the final stage of service transformation. The word transformation is important. The previous three levels are essentially about automation: that is, taking existing processes and computerising them with little or no change. These processes typically exist within a single government department, ministry, or agency. One aspect of transformation is that online service transcends organisational boundaries by integrating departmental silos ("E-government leadership").

The United Nations Public Administration Network defines e-government as "a permanent commitment by government to improve the relationship between the private citizen and the public sector through enhanced, cost-effective and efficient delivery of services, information and knowledge" (Durrant, 2002). There have been various e-government models that have been documented in literature. We are picking three main models of Layne and Lee (2001), Moon (2002), and Sharma and Gupta (2003). Layne and Lee support the stages-of-growth model being applied to e-government, and they define e-government as "government's use of technology, particularly web-based Internet applications, to enhance the access to and delivery of government information and services to citizens, business partners, employees, other agencies and government entities." Layne and Lee propose a four-stage evolutionary progression through the stages of the growth-management model. The Layne and Lee four-stage model consists of cataloguing, transaction, vertical integration, and horizontal integration. The cataloguing stage is the one in which governments establish an online presence. The Web site is usually one on which government information is made available. In the second stage, transaction, government customers are permitted to enter into transactions online, such as paying license fees and fines. The third stage, vertical integration, is one in which local, state, and federal agencies engaged in fulfilling the same customer need or function are linked together so as to form a seamless service. The final stage of their model, horizontal integration, is applied to break down the boundaries between functional silos within government.

Moon (2002) proposed other stages of the growth model. Moon defined e-government as including the use of technologies to "improve citizen access to government information, services and expertise to ensure citizen participation in and satisfaction with the government process" (United Nations & American Society for Public Administration, 2001). Moon proposed a five-stage model, with stages named information dissemination or cataloguing, two-way communication, service and financial transactions, vertical and horizontal integration, and political participation. Moon's Stages 1 and 2 are extensions of Layne and Lee's (2001) Stage 1. His Stage 3 is Layne and Lee's transaction stage. The two stages of vertical integration and horizontal integration that Layne and Lee had in their model have been concatenated into one stage by Moon. Moon has a fifth stage that recognizes the political dimension of e-government.

Sharma and Gupta (2003) define e-government as the process of transacting business between the public and government through the use of automated systems and the Internet network, more commonly referred to as the World Wide Web. Sharma and Gupta's e-government framework not only includes stages of the growth model like Layne and Lee, but also contains evolutionary stages that are needed to achieve the e-government stage and the delivery channels of e-government. The details of the framework are given in Figure 1.

Sharma and Gupta (2003) have devised their framework in different layers.

Layer 1: Networks and Technical Infrastructure

The logical first layer that is needed for an e-government is network and technical infrastructure in the form of private and public data communication network infrastructure, servers, and so forth. A large number of local-area networks (LANs) form an intranet and extranet to offer e-government services. The government is the media gateway between the city or state and the citizens that promotes the exchange of information and services. E-government would enable all city, state, or federal services and information to be accessed through the Internet. At this layer, these network systems should be secured enough to offer e-government services. Firewalls, encryption, anti-network-intrusion sys-

Figure 1. A framework for an e-government

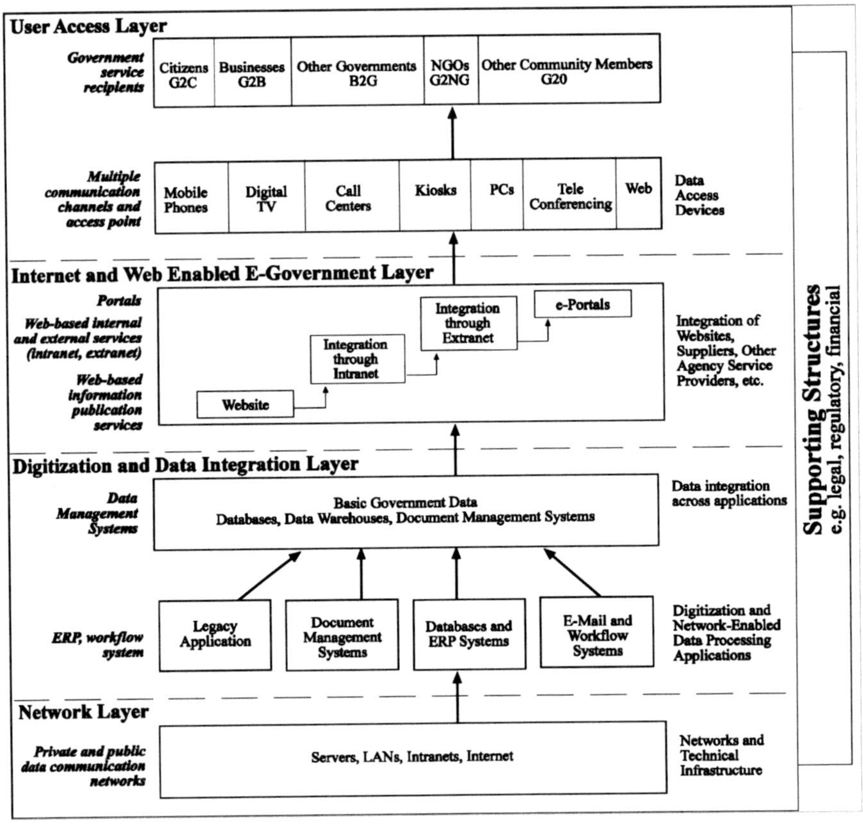

tems, and so forth are security measures that need to be implemented to protect systems from any breach or attack. Once the country has a private and public data communication network infrastructure, services can be provided from e-enabled locations within and across national borders.

Layer 2: Digitization and Data Integration

Once the basic network infrastructure in the form of private and public data communication networks is in place, then the next step requires a digitization and data integration layer consisting of legacy data applications, ERP (enterprise resource planning), a workflow system, document-management systems, and other data-management systems. At this layer, the emphasis would be to convert manual forms (data on paper) to digitized data. The digitization of data could involve data of GIS solutions wherever available in the fields of land-records management, watershed management, master-plan preparation, revenue collection, documents registration, tourism-facility management, agricultural-input management, hospital and health management, state-plan preparation, law and order administration, and various other government departments. At the data-digitization and data-integration layer, federal and state agencies are required to provide public access to nonconfidential government databases in whatever formats the user requests. Also at this layer, many document technologies like imaging document management and work-flow technologies, ERP systems, e-mail, and groupware systems are integrated to achieve structure and efficiency for document management. This integration will maximize the return on investment and will prepare the government for ERP, customer-relationship management, and e-business solutions built into e-government (Knapp & Sanders, 2000). At this layer, the digitization and integration of data may also result in much reengineering of various government processes (Miranda, 2000).

Layer 3: Internet- and Web-Enabled E-Government Service

Once the digitization and data integration is achieved at the data digitization and data integration layer, the stage is set for making the digitized and integrated data Internet and Web enabled so that government users can access the data and services using Internet technology. Internet- and Web-enabled e-government service allows citizens access to services, information, group discussions, decision-making opportunities, and new ways to transact business with the government anywhere and anytime. Many federal, state, and local governments are all striving to meet citizens' rising expectations for easy, fast, secure, and accurate interactions.

Internet- and Web-enabled e-government service can be attained by moving through four developmental stages as shown in Figure 2. Stage 1 is establishing Web sites to provide static information about various government services. The first stage involves more use of the Web by governmental departments and agencies to offer information about themselves to citizens and the use of Web sites for two-way communication. Stage 2 is extending the Web site to full integration with intranet applications that facilitate the gathering, processing, and sharing of data within and across many federal and state governmental agencies. Stage 3 is setting up an extranet integration with the Web site that connects governments to business partners, suppliers, and other public and private

Figure 2. Four stages of Internet- and Web-enabled e-government layer

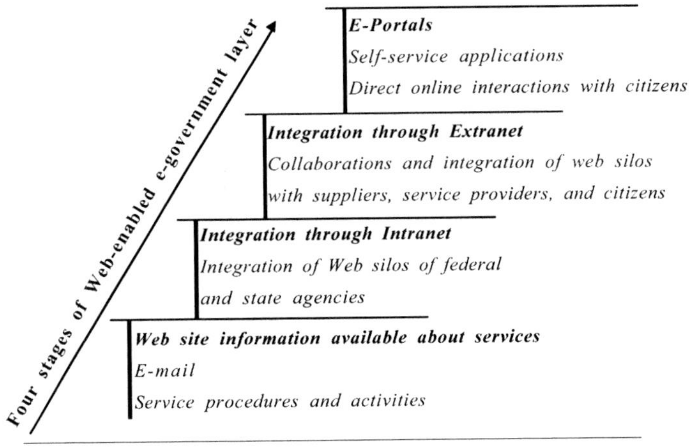

agencies. In this step, the intranet integration that is achieved in the previous step would be extended into extranet applications. This would require the integration of many Web silos and would provide collaboration across enterprises for offering online services. Stage 4 is creating an e-portal for offering self-service e-government applications. Stage 4 integrates various government Web sites both at the federal and state level to facilitate the formal and quantifiable exchange of information, and the establishment of a portal that combines all government services and offers a path to them based on need and function.

With more citizens on the Net, an e-portal would provide an opportunity for creating an e-community through the use of various newsgroups and other bulletin-board services, and would offer direct online interactions with citizens. It will be a challenging task for governments to transition federal information services from legacy systems to more advanced, integrated global systems in the form of e-portals.

At the e-government portal stage, the government delivers interactive services to citizens. This stage of e-government is increasingly interactive, allowing governments to use information-technology tools to engage citizens in the development of policies, programs, and services. Merely attaining this stage of developing an e-government portal would not be sufficient to offer e-government services. E-government implementation would require many changes at the governmental and cultural level for its full exploitation. Providing citizens with a single point of access to government information and Web enabling government payments are the critical initial goals of many governments (Watson & Mundy, 2001). For comprehensive e-government to develop, it is necessary for profound changes to take place in the culture, processes, and relationships that define the government as an entity.

Layer 4: User Access

One would feel that once the Internet- and Web-enabled e-government-service layer is complete, the e-government framework is complete. However, we argue that while developing Internet- and Web-enabled e-government service, the government should also be concerned about how various users of government services would receive these services. Citizens and other government-service recipients can access various Web-enabled e-government services through multiple communication channels and access points. While the Web-enabled e-government-service layer creates different offerings to citizens through various systems, the user access layer opens these services to the public at anytime from anywhere on the globe with the required security and trust. The user access layer should support all-purpose personal communicator systems geared to societies on the go, including multifunction cell phones, e-mail capability, PCs (personal computers), Web surfers, fax, video and television, picture phones, AM/FM radios, call centers, and global positioning systems.

The designer of an e-portal should ensure that citizens or other users of government services are able to access services from anywhere at anytime and on any device like a personal digital assistant, cellular phone, and any other Internet-enabled embedded system. The general public has the maximum stake in how its government functions. Therefore, the e-government model should ensure that citizens are able to easily access the government services using any device. The common citizen should be able to participate in political discussions to express his or her viewpoints and should be able to get many of the services through a self-service mode of the e-government framework.

Supporting Infrastructure Layer

The framework for e-government is incomplete if it is not supported with the required legal and regulatory infrastructure. The support infrastructure includes an integrated network for banks and financial institutions to serve as an automatic clearinghouse, and a legal and regulatory framework to support payments online and protect privacy. Security must be a top priority during the creation of a support infrastructure for an e-government (Rohleder & Jupp, 2003).

Conclusion

The current research on e-government briefly outlined above shows that ICT and Internet technologies are increasingly moving into a civil societal domain that is multidimensional and requires new forms of research, management, and learning. Since the mid-1990s, governments around the world have been taking extraordinary efforts to make services and information available over the Web. E-government implementations have been helping to improve service delivery and offer greater transparency and accountability in governance systems. The first wave of e-government projects has focused primarily on the following four categories: the setting up of a national and global information infrastructure, digital delivery of government service to citizens, internal organisational reform, and digital procurement including the realization of electronic commerce. Many of the objectives have been achieved, demonstrating how information technology can enhance productivity in both public and private governing and managing systems. E-government projects in most countries are realized through setting up government Web sites, mostly in the form of an integrated government Web portal or a separate and independent government-agency Web site. While a considerable number of e-government projects of these types in the United States and elsewhere have mounted in scope and cost, still many of these e-government projects do not account for many important measures of e-government implementations that are significant in the full scope of an e-government framework. There is also no hard evidence to date to indicate that e-democracy processes have had any significant impact on governments (Watson & Mundy, 2001). However, as citizens are using the Internet and wireless communications to share information and knowledge amongst each other, a hesitant conclusion can be made that such capabilities are contributing to the democratic process as the capacities and potentialities of an informed citizenry are growing. The idea of an informed citizenry is still a limited one, confined to those who have direct interests in government policies or programs, are educated, and have the wherewithal to access and use the available tools to share this information (O'Siochru & Constanza-Hock, 2003; Surman & Reilly, 2003; Taylor, 2004; Taylor & Marshall, 2004).

Acknowledgments

Some material in this paper is taken from our earlier publication: Sharma, S. K., & Gupta, J. N. D. (n.d.). Building blocks of an e-government: A framework. *Journal of Electronic Commerce in Organizations, 1*(4), 34-48.

References

Bertucci, G. (2003). World public sector report 2003: E-Government at the crossroads. United Nations. Retrieved March 2004, from *http://unpan1.un.org/intradoc/groups/public/documents/un/unpan012733.pdf*

Bollier, D. (2003). The rise of Netpolitik. How the Internet is changing international politics and diplomacy: A report to the 11th annual Aspen Institute Roundtable on Information Technology. Aspen Institute. Retrieved March 7, 2004, from *http://216.181.117.89/index.asp?bid=1290*

Carey, K. (2004). Boosting take up means ensuring access for all. Paper presented at the *E-Government Bulletin Practical Ways to Boost Take-Up of E-Government Services Seminar*, London. Retrieved March 2004, from *http://www.electronic-government.com/takeup.htm*

Coleman, S., & Gotze, J. (2002). Bowling together: Online public engagement in policy deliberation. Hansard Society. Retrieved March 2004, from *http://www.bowlingtogether.net/about.html*

Dearstyne, B. W. (2001). E-business, e-government & information proficiency. *Information Management Journal, 35*(4), 16-24.

Dutta, S., & Jain, A. (2003). The networked readiness index 2003-2004. In S. Dutta, B. Lanvin, & F. Paua (Eds.), Global information technology report 2003-2004. New York: Oxford University Press. Retrieved March 2004, from *http://www.weforum.org/site/homepublic.nsf/Content/Global+Competitiveness+Programme%5CGlobal+Information+Technology+Report*

E-government leadership: Engaging the customer. (2003). *Accenture.* Retrieved from *http://www.accenture.com/xd/xd.asp?it=enweb&xd=industries\government\gove_capa_egov.xml*

Grönlund, Å. (2002). *Electronic government: Design, applications and management.* Hershey, PA: Idea Group Publishing.

Gurstein, M. (2000). *Community informatics: Enabling communities with information and communications technologies.* Hershey, PA: Idea Group Publishing.

Harris, R. (2002). Research partnerships to support rural communities in Malaysia with information and communication technologies. In J. Lazar (Ed.), *Managing IT/community partnerships in the 21st century.* Hershey, PA: Idea Group Publishing.

Heeks, R. (2001). *Understanding e-governance for development: I-Government working paper series.* Institute for Development Policy and Management, University of Manchester.

Howard, M. (2001). E-Government across the globe: How will "e" change government? *Government Finance Review, 17*(4), 6-9.

Hunter, D., & Jupp, V. (2001). E-Government leadership: Rhetoric vs. reality-Closing the gap. Accenture. Retrieved March 2004, from *http://www.accenture.com/xdoc/en/industries/government/final.pdf*

Larsen, E., & Rainie, L. (2002). The rise of the e-citizen: How people use government agencies' Web sites. Retrieved April 2004, from *http://www.pewinternet.org*

Layne, K., & Lee, J. (2001). Developing fully functional e-government: A four stage model. *Government Information Quarterly, 18*, 122-136.

Margetts, H., & Dunleavy, P. (2002). Cultural barriers to e-government. In *Building public services through e-government*. London: Comptroller and Auditor General.

Moon, M. J. (2002). The evolution of e-government among municipalities: Rhetoric or reality? *Public Administration Review, 62*(4), 424-433.

Organisation for Economic Cooperation and Development. (2001). Engaging citizens in public policy-making: Information, consultation and public participation (PUMA policy brief no. 10). Paris: Author.

Organisation for Economic Cooperation and Development. (2003). *The e-government imperative*. Paris: Author.

O'Siochru, S., & Constanza-Hock, C. (2003). Global governance of information and communication technologies: Implications for transnational civil society networking. Social Science Research Council. Retrieved March 2004, from *http://www.ssrc.org/programs/itic*

Pinder, A., & Hewitt, P. (2002). UK on line annual report 2002. Retrieved March 2004, from *http://www.e-envoy.gov.uk/Home/Homepage/fsen*

Riley, T. B. (2003a). E-Government vs e-governance: Examining the differences in a changing public sector climate. Commonwealth Centre for E-Governance. Retrieved March 2004, from *http://www.electronicgov.net/pubs/index.shtml*

Riley, T. B. (2003b). The information society: The role of information in the emerging global e-government, e-governance and e-democracy environments. Commonwealth Centre for E-Governance. Retrieved March 2004, from *http://www.electronicgov.net/pubs/index.shtml*

Riley, T. B. (2004, February 12-13). Report on E-Democracy Seminar Brussels. Retrieved March 2004, from *http://www.electronicgov.net/pubs/research_papers/brussels/brussels.shtml*

Riley, T. B., & Riley, C. G. (2003). E-Governance to e-democracy: Examining the evolution. Commonwealth Centre for E-Governance. Retrieved March 2004, from *http://www.electronicgov.net/pubs/index.shtml*

Rohleder, S. J., & Jupp, V. (2003). E-Government leadership: Engaging the customer. Retrieved March 2004, from *http://www.accenture.com/xd/xd.asp?it=enweb&xd=industries5Cgove_capa_egov.xml*

Sharma, S. K., & Gupta, J .N. D. (2002). Transforming to an e-government: A framework. In *Proceedings of the Second European Conference on E-Government* (pp. 383-390).

Sharma, S. K., & Gupta, J. N. D. (2003). Building blocks of an e-government: A framework. *Journal of Electronic Commerce in Organizations, 1*(4), 34-48.

Surman, M., & Reilly, K. (2003). Appropriating the Internet for social change: Towards the strategic use of networked technologies by transnational civil society organizations. Retrieved March 2004, from *http://www.ssrc.org/programs/itic*

Taylor, W. (2004). *Building smart communities for the information age: Putting people at the centre of the information society*. COIN Internet Academy, Central Queensland University.

Taylor, W., & Marshall, S. (2004). Community informatics systems: A meeting place for useful research. In P. Day & D. Schuler (Eds.), *Community practice in the network society: Local action/global interaction*. London: Routledge.

United Nations & American Society for Public Administration. (2001). *Global survey of e-government*. New York: Author.

Venkatachalam, A. R., Shore, B., & Sharma, S. K. (2003). Customization of e-government systems: A global study. In *Proceedings of the Fourth Annual Global Technology Management (GITM) World Conference* (pp. 96-98).

Watson, R. T., & Mundy, B. (2001). A strategic perspective of electronic democracy. *Association for Computing Machinery, Communications of the ACM, 44*(1), 27-30.

Chapter XVII

Beauty is More than Skin Deep: Organisational Strategies for Online Consumer Risk Mitigation in Apparel Retailing

Mary Tate, Victoria University of Wellington, New Zealand

Beverley G. Hope, Victoria University of Wellington, New Zealand

Brent Coker, Victoria University of Wellington, New Zealand

Abstract

Buying and selling clothing can be a stressful and risky business for both consumers and retailers, even without the complications of e-commerce. Yet recent figures from the U.S. and from Korea show an increase in online sales of apparel. In this chapter we investigate the reasons for this through examination of the literature and research of best practice in a successful Australasian multichannel e-tailer. The chapter is organised in four sections. First we describe the apparel industry, and then we examine online shopping risks and their consequences, paying particular attention to consumer risks and consequences in the apparel industry. Next we present a set of organisational strategies that can mitigate customer perceived risk and conclude with six key strategies for success in online apparel retailing.

Introduction

The Apparel Industry

Research shows that apparel purchases are declining as a percentage of overall consumer spending. In 1993, households spent on average 6% of their total expenditures on apparel, but by 2003 this had dropped to 4% while expenditure on entertainment and dining out had remained stable or increased (Gardyn, 2003).

There are a variety of potential explanations for the changes in apparel spending. One explanation is the increases in industry competition and offshore manufacturing leading to lower per-unit costs. Where these are passed on, consumers are able to purchase the same quantity of apparel for a smaller percentage of their total expenditure. Lower prices, and hence reduced total expenditure, is supported by the movement to more casual clothing. The most regularly worn items for both men and women by 1999 were jeans, t-shirts, other casual shirts, casual slacks, and running or tennis shoes (Setlow, 1999).

More formal items, such as business suits, dress shoes, and jackets or blazers, had fallen significantly in popularity over the period between 1990 and 1999.

Compared to previous decades, it is increasingly difficult to make generalisations about the buying patterns of apparel customers. A Belgian study of the retail

Table 1. Six most regularly worn apparel items

Women	Men
Jeans	Jeans
Blouse or shirt	T-shirt
T-shirt	Sports shirt
Running or tennis shoes	Running or tennis shoes
Shorts	Casual shoes
Casual slacks	Slacks

Source: Setlow (1999)

apparel industry found that while apparel retailers might target market niches, customers cannot easily be categorised (Danneels, 1996). Even those who can afford to buy quality, high-fashion, high-priced clothing, and who do so on occasion, will also regularly patronise discount stores:

Many people tend to switch segments: there are some people who buy an expensive coat yet who go to cheap sites to buy T-shirts. The customer's only criterion is, "what do I need it for?...Do I really need something fancy?" (Danneels, p. 46)

This has led to the conceptualisation of the apparel market as consisting of "clothing moments" rather than market segments comprised of specific groups of people:

Society as it evolves now suggests the idea of "clothing moments," rather than a specific group of people. In the morning people get dressed to go to school or work, more formal and neat. After five o'clock, when back home, people dress more casually, this is another moment. (Danneels, p. 46)

Danneels' (1996) study found that almost the entire population, with all its diversity, was a potential customer for any clothing retailer depending on the particular clothing moment the purchaser had in mind. This poses considerable challenges to retailers in developing customer intimacy.

Price is a major factor in apparel purchasing, even for the more expensive, fashionable items. This is evidenced by the popularity of the off-price store model where high-quality, brand-name apparel is sold at 20 to 75% off the regular retail price. Off-price retailing is estimated to account for up to 10% of apparel and retail sales in the U.S. (Rogers, 1983). As early as 1983, it was suggested that the popularity of this model was being driven by value-conscious consumers with a desire to stretch their disposable income (Rogers). More recently, the explosion of popularity in online auction sites for apparel companies disposing of excess stock reflects this trend.

A major difficulty in the apparel industry of many countries is the nonstandardisation of sizes or the use of out-of-date standards (Gardyn, 2003). For example, the sizing system for women's clothing in the U.S. is based on a 1941 study that obtained measurements from a small sample of mostly young, white women in the military. Since then, people in many Western countries have become larger overall, with the average dress size increasing from size 8 in 1985 to size 14 in 2003. Today, some informal industry standards exist, but these are not uniformly adopted. Each apparel company has its own proprietary sizing system based on an average fit model. But in an era of increased ethnic diversity, average may be insufficient. For example, in the U.S. there are increases in Asian and Hispanic communities, populations that are, on average, smaller and several inches shorter than their white counterparts. Similarly, in New Zealand, increases in Asian and Pacific immigration have increased the heterogeneity with respect to body shape and size. An initiative based on three-dimensional imaging is underway to gain a better understanding of the diversity of body types in the U.S. When complete, this will inform the clothing industry, but at present it is still at an early stage (Gardyn).

The findings regarding the importance of sizing are supported by a consumer survey conducted by Price Waterhouse Coopers (as cited in Discount Store News, 1999), in which an "adequate selection" in the customer's size was a major criterion for a person deciding where to shop in the U.S. Another study by NPD Fashionworld (Gardyn, 2003) showed that quality, value, size, and assortment are the most desired apparel attributes, with the lowest price being also important for mass-merchant shopping.

A picture emerges of apparel as a challenging retail environment. Retailers are selling to a more physically diverse group of customers who display more varied buying patterns and spend proportionately less on apparel than previously. They are united by their preference for more casual styles, increasing price consciousness, and the need for convenience and one-stop shopping. Customers' price sensitivity, even when purchasing high-fashion and brand-name items, may partly explain the declining share of consumer spending allocated to apparel. The "anywhere, anytime" value proposition of the Internet would seem to offer the potential to meet apparel buyers' demands for convenience and one-stop shopping (Goersch, 2002).

Table 2. Desired apparel-purchasing attributes

	Department-Store Shoppers*	Mass-Merchant Shoppers*
Quality	54%	43%
Value	47%	49%
Size	35%	36%
Assortment	33%	26%
Brands	25%	19%
Lowest prices	24%	37%
Returns	22%	22%
Convenience	21%	26%
Style	21%	17%
One-stop shopping	19%	25%

*Percentage of shoppers ranking the attribute among their three most important purchasing attributes

Source: NPD Fashionworld (as cited in Gardyn, 2003)

The requirements of Internet apparel customers are likely to be similar to those of face-to-face apparel customers: quality, value, size, assortment, brands, price, returns, and convenience. Brown and Iorio (2000) found that the most important requirements of online apparel buyers were a liberal return policy, instant help, promotions, and a wide selection. Privacy has also been cited as a possible reason people buy apparel online. Some categories of apparel, particularly underwear and intimate apparel, are popular online because people like the opportunity to try them on in their own home ("Shopping Spree: Labels Launch Online Sales for Customers," 1999). However, some additional expectations revolving around trust and virtual experiences might be expected in online transactions.

In summary, studies investigating the requirements of apparel buyers on the Internet suggest that their priorities and requirements are similar to those of apparel buyers using other channels. However, buying apparel over the Internet offers the potential to address customer issues of adequate product selection, sizing, privacy, and convenience.

Online Shopping Risks

Consumer risk has been the subject of research since the 1960s. An early definition posits that purchasing is, by its nature, a potentially risky activity because purchasing "will produce consequences which [a consumer] cannot anticipate with anything approaching certainty...some of which...are likely to be unpleasant" (Bauer as cited in Lim, 2003). Many subsequent studies have confirmed that uncertainty and perceived risk are important influences on consumer behaviour, particularly for remote shopping (see, for example, Dowling & Staelin, 1994; Verhage, Yavas, & Green, 1990).

Research into perceived risk in e-commerce is characterised by conflicting or incomparable definitions. A comprehensive review of this literature leading to a model that distinguishes between risk sources and consequences is provided by Lim (2003). Sources are external factors that expose the customer to risk, while consequences are the types of losses the consumer may suffer.

Sources of risk (external factors) are classified into four types:

- Consumer risk: caused by social pressures
- Technology risk: arising from the Internet and related technologies
- Product risk: related to product suitability and performance
- Vendor risk: arising from the reliability and responsiveness of Internet vendors

Consequences (losses consumers may suffer) are classified into eight types:

- Financial risk: the possibility of monetary loss arising from online shopping
- Performance risk: the possibility that products will not perform as expected or will not have the anticipated life span
- Physical risk: the possibility that products will be harmful to the health
- Privacy risk: the possibility that information about the consumer will be captured without authorisation and used inappropriately
- Psychological risk: the possibility of mental stress as a result of purchasing behaviour
- Social risk: the possibility that others will perceive online shopping behaviour negatively
- Time-loss risk: the possibility that people will lose time in waiting for order fulfillment, returning goods, or in actual shopping activity

There is a many-to-many relationship between the sources and consequences of online shopping risk. For example, a vendor (source) may create a financial consequence through misuses of credit-card data, a time-loss consequence through poor logistical processes, or a privacy consequence through the on-selling of personal data such as an e-mail address. Similarly, a financial consequence may originate with the vendor (as above), with the technology (e.g., when there is inadequate security), or with the product (e.g., where it is found to be inappropriate for the intended purpose or is faulty). Table 3 shows the relationship between risk sources and consequences as identified by Lim (2003).

The current research focuses on vendor and product sources. We exclude consumer risk, which is a weak construct not supported by previous research. Its only hypothesized consequence is social risk: the possibility that others will perceive online shopping behaviour negatively. We also do not examine technology risk in this study. Technology risk is significant but has been widely discussed in other contexts. Furthermore, the solutions to technology risk are often industry-wide, with the contribution of the individual e-commerce vendors limited to selecting which of the currently available technology offerings they will deploy. In this study, we are concerned with the organisational responses that may differentiate major players in the field; hence, we focus on vendor and product sources.

Vendor risk is associated with the capability and trustworthiness of the vendor. The importance of this factor is reinforced in many studies of e-commerce strategy that have found vendor brand and reputation for service delivery and recovery to be essential for e-commerce success (Barua, Konana, Whinston, &

Table 3. Risk sources and consequences for consumers

Consequence	Source of Risk			
	Technology	Vendor	Consumer	Product
Financial	√ X	√ X	X	√ X
Performance	X	√ X	X	√ X
Social			√	
Physical		√		√
Psychological	√ X	√ X	X	√ X
Time-loss	√ X	√ X	X	√ X
Privacy	√	√		

Source: Lim (2003)
Check marks indicate associations identified by Lim. Rows marked with X's represent consequences mitigated by organisational responses identified in this research.

Yin, 2001; Ghoshal & Gratton, 2002; Goersch, 2002; Kaufman-Scarborough & Lindquist, 2002; Lee & Whang, 2001). Breakdowns in any aspect of vendor competency have the greatest potential for negative customer consequences. Our study concentrates on successful vendor strategies for addressing some of the obstacles and risks of apparel purchasing on the Internet, so this construct is central to the study.

Product-related risk arises from characteristics of the product rather than the processes or actions of the vendor. If the product is not what is expected, the customer can potentially lose time and money, and experience frustration and stress. As apparel seems to be an inherently risky purchase, with many of the risks exacerbated in an e-commerce environment, we also focus on organisational strategies to reduce product risk.

Some consequences are more commonly identified in the literature than others, with the strongest support being found for financial and performance risk. Also significant in previous empirical studies on risk were: time-loss risk (Festervand & Snyder, 1986) and privacy risk (Miyazaki & Fernandez, 2001; Nyshadham, 2000; Tan & Teo, 2000).

The current research considers financial, performance, time loss, and psychological consequences. We include psychological consequences because psychological stress appears to be closely associated with adverse financial consequences and time loss. Furthermore, there is a stronger psychological and emotional dimension to apparel purchases than many other product categories (Hammond & Kohler, 2002). We exclude social, physical, and privacy consequences. Social consequences are not included because they are related to the consumer, not the vendor or product, which are the focus of this study. We do not consider physical consequences because we believe their occurrence in apparel purchasing is rare, and the consequences, should they occur, are likely limited. We also do not consider privacy consequences. Although the probability of their occurrence in the apparel industry is likely similar to that in other industries, the strategies used to ameliorate them will also be similar and are well-reported elsewhere.

In summary, we are concerned with organisational responses to mitigate sources and consequences of risks that are particular or strong in the apparel industry. These include vendor and product risks, and financial, performance, time loss, and psychological consequences.

Online Shopping Risks for Apparel Buyers

Research has found that the easiest products to sell online include digitised products, low-cost products, commodities, and functional or clearly defined products (Turban & King, 2003). This is understandable. Digitised products offer immediate delivery and no time-loss consequence (and no delivery costs), low-cost products offer reduced financial consequences, and commodities and functional goods have less performance consequences.

The most challenging products to sell online are high-touch or high-experience goods because the purchaser of these items relies on the overall effect rather than objective information (Zeng & Reinartz, 2003). The consumer may use multiple senses to assess high-touch goods; that is, they may wish to touch a product to feel its texture or quality, taste a sample, listen to the sound output, or see the product to gauge its size, impact, true colour, or fit with an intended space. The lack of the ability to sense high-touch products decreases the potential of the Internet as a shopping channel and increases the customer's perceived risk (Chen & Dubinsky, 2003; Lim, 2003; Miyazaki & Fernandez, 2001).

Apparel is considered a high-touch good. A particular aspect of apparel as a high-touch good is the issue of fit. Clothing sizes vary greatly between manufacturers in any market and, on occasion, across product lines of a particular manufacturer. This intensifies the product-induced performance and time-loss risks in Internet apparel purchases because the customer cannot try an item for fit before ordering. Purchasing globally exacerbates this risk enormously. One of the authors, a Caucasian in the upper quartile of height and weight in her home country but certainly not exceptional in any way, discovered recently she could not buy anything in Shanghai unless it was XXL (extra, extra large). So, product risk is a considerable deterrent to purchasing apparel over the Internet.

Vendor risk is also important in Internet apparel retailing because the lack of a face-to-face interaction diminishes trust, and the pay-before-delivery aspect induces psychological anxiety. We believe that vendor and product risk are closely intertwined in apparel retailing. Confidence in and experience of the vendor mitigates product risk. Knowledge of the vendor's normal product fit, quality, and image veracity diminish product-induced risk (Tate, Coker, & Hope, 2004). A strong service record from the vendor and excellent service-recovery processes also diminish perceived product risk (Tate et al.).

In face-to-face retailing of apparel, quality vendors reduce risk and increase sales through personal selling. This involves identifying customer needs and helping the customer to find products that meet those needs. In remote retailing, personal selling has been difficult to achieve and has acted as an obstacle to sales (Schneider & Perry, 2001). To make purchase decisions remotely, consumers rely on nonsensory evaluations such as word-of-mouth recommendations or cognitive associations with past purchase experiences. In our study, we find that new Internet technologies and organisational practices can mitigate this risk.

In summary, both product and vendor are significant risk sources when buying apparel on the Internet. The potential risk to the customer of the product not being delivered, not fitting, or not meeting expectations in some other respect can lead to adverse performance, time-loss, financial, and consequent psychological stress. This can present a potent deterrent to purchasing apparel online over and above the general e-commerce risks arising from technology and privacy issues.

Increases in Online Apparel Sales

Despite the risks in selling apparel remotely, apparel sales have increased in both Western and Eastern cultures. One explanation is the increase in the use of the Internet in general and online shopping in particular. In consumer surveys, one fifth of respondents included convenience and one-stop shopping among their three most important requirements for apparel shopping (Table 2), and online shopping offers anytime, anywhere shopping experiences to meet this need. Convenience coupled with rich information provisioning and search capabilities offset some of the risks in online shopping. Although information is not a primary determinant in apparel purchasing, it can play a role. Many successful apparel e-tailers provide detailed sizing information, allowing the customer to evaluate the likelihood of fit without having to try on the product. Many also provide current stock levels and size and colour availability, offering the potential to save a wasted trip to the mall. In this respect, online apparel shopping has the potential to diminish product-induced time loss and psychological risks (Gardyn, 2003).

Another factor that may be driving the increase in apparel sales on the Internet is the increasing participation of women in e-commerce, given that women are the major buyers of apparel for themselves and for their families. Figure 1 shows the number of male and female buyers for the 10 most commonly sold items on the Internet. Books (greatest number of buyers), apparel (4), toys (5), and clothing and accessories (8) all had more female than male buyers, while gender balance of buyers for other products, except computer software, was close to even. Previous Internet and online purchasing experience has been shown to be important antecedents of trust and willingness to purchase online (Corbitt, Thanasankit, & Yi, 2003; Jarvenpaa, Tractinsky, & Vitale, 2000; Miyazaki & Fernandez, 2001), so we might expect even more women online in the future. As the participation of women on the Internet and in e-commerce increases, women's buying preferences will be increasingly reflected in e-commerce sales.

A further factor that may be contributing to increases in online apparel sales is the "showroom effect." The showroom effect occurs when customers use physical stores to browse for and try products before searching online for specific products at a cheaper price (Reynolds, 2002; Steinfield, Bouwman, & Adelaar, 2002). Opportunities for the showroom effect increase as more stores adopt a multichannel strategy incorporating some combination of physical store, catalogue, Internet, contact centre, and mobile commerce. Research indicates that around one third of consumers use a combination of the Internet, catalogues, and stores to do their purchasing, and that these consumers spend more than

Figure 1. Number of e-commerce buyers by product category (United States, 2003)

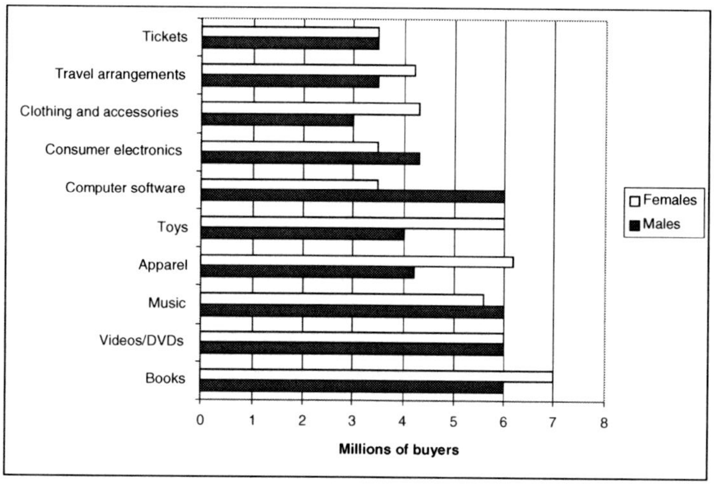

Source: Based on "Retail February 2003 Data Overview: A Gender Analysis of Online Shopping Behaviors" (2003)

Table 4. Most popular U.S. apparel and beauty Web sites: Week ending March 9, 2003

Rank	Firm	Purchases	Product	Channels
1.	OldNavy.com	339,000	Apparel	Retail Store/Internet
2.	Gap.com	329,000	Apparel	Retail Store/Internet
3.	VictoriasSecret.com	327,000	Apparel	Catalogue/Retail/Internet
4.	LandsEnd.com	272,000	Apparel	Catalogue/Retail/Internet
5.	Youravon.com	258,000	Beauty	-
6.	LLBean.com	250,000	Apparel	Catalogue/Retail/Internet
7.	Spiegel.com	246,000	Apparel	Catalogue/Retail/Internet
8.	Mary Kay	238,000	Beauty	-
9.	Chadwicks.com	226,000	Apparel	Catalogue/Internet
10.	Blair.com	200,000	Apparel	Catalogue/Retail/Internet

Source: Nielsen/NetRatings (Greenspan, 2003)

consumers who purchase from physical stores only and are more loyal ("Multi-Channel Retail Report 2.0," 2001; "RIP: The Online Consumer, 1998 to 2003," 2003). We posit that the increase in multichannel shopping may provide a partial explanation for the increased sales of apparel over the Internet. This is supported by sales figures for apparel Web sites in the U.S., where the majority is multichannel retailers (Table 4).

A particular advantage in apparel e-tailing seems to accrue to organisations with catalogue selling origins. Table 4 shows that most (75%) of online apparel Web sites include mail-order catalogues in their channel mix. In our experience, the catalogue operation has almost invariably preceded the establishment of an Internet channel for selling apparel. Experienced catalogue retailers have robust logistics-management systems and a track record of service delivery (Lee & Whang, 2001; Tate, Coker, & Hope, in press-a). This simplifies the shift for the vendor to online selling. In addition, it is relatively easy to transfer catalogue customers to the Internet because these customers are accustomed to purchasing apparel remotely, and they find Internet shopping to be a close substitute (Ward, 2001). Research has shown that previous adoption by customers of remote retail purchase using telephone or mail-order shopping also reduces the perceived risk of buying online (Miyazaki & Fernandez, 2001).

In summary, the increase in apparel sales over the Internet reflects both the general increase in Internet use and the particular impact of the buying preferences of female customers who are increasingly participating on the Internet and in e-commerce. Within this overall trend, some organisations have been more successful than others. Many popular and successful apparel e-tailers have a multichannel strategy with catalogue origins. These organisations have developed the skills and competencies to successfully allay common customer anxieties about buying apparel online. In the next section, we examine some effective organisational responses to managing the sources of risk in apparel e-commerce.

Organisational Strategies to Mitigate Risk

In this section, we offer a series of organisational strategies that can mitigate the sources and consequences of risk for online apparel customers. As noted earlier, the sources and consequences of risk have a complex many-to-many relationship. There is a similar complexity between risks and organisational strategies to mitigate them. One organisational strategy may contribute to mitigating several risks, and one risk may be diminished by several organisational strategies.

To illustrate the organisational strategies we describe, we use examples from a successful apparel e-tailer in New Zealand, supplemented with examples from other organisations. The New Zealand e-tailer, which we will call Buywell, is a very successful multichannel apparel and home-goods retailer serving the Australasian market. Buywell commenced business as a catalogue company in 1978 with just two employees. Today it has 650 staff and 500,000 customers with significant expansion anticipated following the recent purchase of a major Australian direct-marketing company. In recent years, the product range has diversified to include men's and boys' wear, lingerie, footwear, houseware, and oversized clothing, but women's wear continues to account for most of Buywell's total sales.

Buywell expanded into a multichannel organisation with the addition, first, of a free-call contact centre, then six physical retail outlets followed in 1998 by an Internet channel. Buywell's current channel mix includes a mail-order catalogue, an Internet Web site, a contact centre, and six physical retail stores located in New Zealand. Despite the introduction of physical stores, Buywell continues to sell mostly through remote channels, with most sales arising from catalogues supported by a contact centre, though Internet sales are increasing.

In the discussion and recommendations that follow, we make the assumption that the organisations of interest are genuine, ethical organisations desirous of staying in the industry for the long term. These organisations would not intentionally defraud customers, violate their privacy, or make promises they have no intention of keeping. In other words, the strategies and recommendations are not aimed

Figure 2. Strategies to mitigate consumer risk and develop customer loyalty

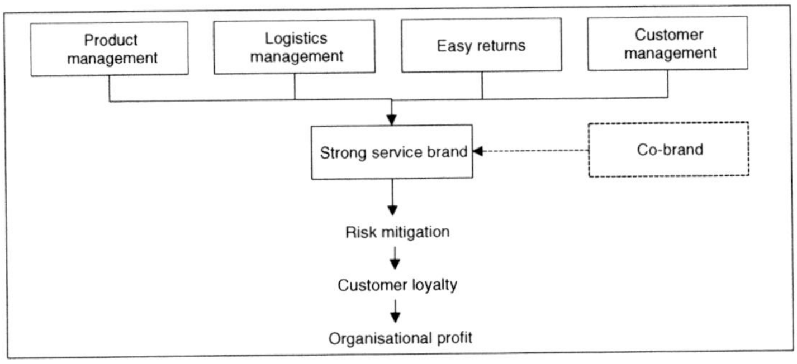

at stopping bad companies from misbehaving, but rather to help good companies avoid online pitfalls and establish a brand image of reliability and service quality in e-commerce apparel sales.

We discuss six organisational strategies that contribute to reducing customer-perceived risks in apparel buying online. When these are employed successfully, organisations can build a trusted online presence that leads to customer loyalty, retention, repeat business, and profitability (Figure 2).

The strategies focus on product, logistics, returns, and customer management to provide a strong delivered service brand. Where a firm does not have the expertise or resources to emulate these management processes, they can gain the advantages through co-branding with a successful e-tailer such as Buywell.

Product Management

Product management in apparel involves getting the sizing right, being consistent in that sizing, and providing customers with realistic expectations about sizing, fabric, and style.

Buywell requires it suppliers to provide garments made to their measurements: measurements that are matched to the body shape of their target market. So, there is a good initial likelihood of fit. In a market where sizing of women's apparel is extremely inconsistent, this offers confidence in the remote buying experience. The marketing manager explains:

I can be a size 10 in one retail store, an 8 in another store, or a 12 in another. Whereas at Buywell, we work really hard [on sizing consistency] and decrease returns by doing that. Our size 10 is this size waist, this size hips — and that's for New Zealanders. So we have "Buywell measurements."

Product consistency begins with supplier selection and the ordering process, and continues through to the imaging processes. It extends to all aspects of the garment. With respect to ordering, the channel campaign manager explains:

[Our buyers] go to a manufacturer who will create a sample for us. When the buyers receive the sample, they will say "yes," "no," "change this," "change that," "the fit's OK" or "needs to be bigger," "smaller," or whatever. The sample goes back...[until] we are happy with the sample size or colour.

The marketing manager describes part of the catalogue-production process:

We have an established relationship with an imaging company. They are the ones who make sure our images are accurate. And we have a strong relationship with our printer as well. Sometimes I will watch a run coming of the press and check that the colours at the printers are accurate...And we'll have samples of the clothing styles in every colour, so the imaging company can compare—they can grab the garment and put it against the image.

Detailed pictures of fabric texture are provided alongside images of the garment in catalogues:

We might get a texture that's waffle. [The reader] can't tell from the image. So we do a close-up to show the type of material. That reduces the return rate.

Internet Web sites have the capability to extend product-information provision to the extent that it becomes a virtual experience for customers. Many apparel Web sites now offer the customer the choice of larger garment images or fabric swatch images to show colour and texture. Showing a photo of the selected garment on a model that resembles the customer (e.g., larger size models for larger-sized garments) also offers a more realistic virtual experience. Some online apparel e-tailers, such as Lands' End, have experimented with allowing the customer to build an interactive virtual model of their own measurements to try garments on. Research has found interactive images to be positively associated with willingness to return to online stores (Fiore & Jin, 2003). However, it is possible that bandwidth and response-time limitations may limit the effectiveness for customers in some geographical areas. We noted that only the larger online apparel retailers included interactive imaging capability, possibly due to high development costs.

In combination, these processes mitigate product-performance risk, especially for repeat customers who may, as a result of experience, have a higher likelihood of fit than they do when shopping face to face. Reduced performance risk leads to reduced time loss and psychological risk.

In summary, careful attention to quality and consistency in product development, manufacturing, and imaging mitigates perceived product-performance risk. High-quality virtual experiences can reduce product-performance risk by setting realistic expectations.

Logistics Management

Logistics management and order fulfillment is an expensive yet critical operation for e-commerce retailers (Lee & Whang, 2001; Pyke, Johnson, & Desmond, 2001). If the organisation gets it right, the firm develops a reputation for reliability, risks from time loss diminish, and service brand improves; if they get it wrong, service brand falls and sales will drop. The seasonal, fashion-sensitive nature of apparel means reliable and speedy order fulfilment is essential. The logistics manager commented:

Buywell is where it is today because it delivers on the customer service promise. The company grows because it has consistently delivered what it has said it will deliver.

However, sometimes simply doing what you have promised is not enough. Buywell's management is responsive to the personal, emotional aspects of apparel purchasing, especially to the fact that apparel is often purchased as a gift. Although they would not have put it in these words, they were sensitive to the psychological risks for customers and are prepared to go to some lengths to reduce them. The marketing manager commented:

[The owners] keep their eye on customers the whole time, and they will break the rules for a customer.

The distribution manager provided some examples of going the extra mile in order fulfillment for a special occasion:

[An] example which occurred quite a lot, even after our Christmas cut-off dates, was when customers would phone and say, "Oh I know it's late but..." They would really like something. We would set up, particularly for Australia, a bit of a relay in terms of getting that product to the customer. One [customer] was living in Perth. We actually got somebody to pick up her parcel from the airport and deliver it in person — outside of the normal distribution network. She was very happy, and she's going to be a customer for a long time. We tend to go that extra mile at Christmas time when it really matters.

In summary, reliable, timely, first-time order fulfillment and a track record of delivery on logistics promises is the entry-level service standard for apparel e-commerce. Apparel e-tailers also need to be sensitive to the perceived psychological risk of apparel purchasing and be prepared to make an extra effort to mitigate it, especially at high-profile times such as the Christmas period.

Returns

A liberal return process is an essential requirement of online apparel customers. Buywell's channel campaign manager commented that "if it wasn't for our returns policy we would have dug our own grave." Buywell has streamlined their return process to make it as simple as possible for customers:

In New Zealand we do something we call Easy Returns. To send an item back [the customer] needs only to affix a sticker that we send to them. They don't need to go the post office to pay for anything. Just put a sticker on and post it and we debit their account $3.00.

As well as providing a service to customers, Buywell also uses the return process as a source of market intelligence:

On our returns form we have a section where people say why they are returning the item. Obviously, if 80% of people are saying the product is too long, we have a problem. So, comments are always analysed.

The easy return policy reduces the perception of financial, time-loss, and performance risk associated with the product. This in turn reduces psychological stress. Buywell's channel campaign manager noted that to reduce uncertainty about product performance, many customers order a range of different products with the intention of returning those that do not meet expectations in some respect such as colour or size.

Researcher: "So do you find that quite a lot of people buy things that they don't intend to keep? Is that common?"

Buywell: "Yes, people will buy a size 10 and a size 12 in the same style and same colour, or three size 10s in a black, white, and blue because they don't know what colour they want."

In summary, a liberal return policy can reduce customer perception of risk on several levels. The customer becomes confident they will not have a frustrating, stressful, time-wasting experience in returning products, and money spent will be refunded.

Customer Experience Management

Face-to-face vendors rely on personal selling to reduce product risk. This involves understanding customer needs and helping customers find products to meet these needs. The lack of opportunity for personal selling can be a limitation in selling high-touch goods remotely (Schneider & Perry, 2001). However, having knowledgeable, helpful staff available in real time decreases the perception of risks originating with the vendor and, more importantly, allows personalised merchandising that assists the customer to quickly identify a product that meets his or her requirements (reducing time-loss risk), reduces anxiety about buying the wrong product (reducing product-performance risk), and provides a positive and affirming apparel shopping experience (reducing psychological risk).

Some companies are using online chat to assist customers, but Buywell's support processes are based primarily on telephony. Customer service representatives (CSRs) can access portable racks around the walls of the call centre containing all the apparel offered in the current catalogues. A customer can seek an opinion from a CSR as to size or colour match. The marketing manager explained:

So, when a customer calls, the CSR can be proactive and say, "Hey, it's not exactly that colour, it's a little lighter (or darker). Do you still want it?" Or, "This size 10 is actually larger than a normal size 10. You may want to go down a size."

Figure 3 shows a Buywell CSR interacting with one of the authors (a customer) about a product characteristic (in this case, colour), thereby reducing perceived product-performance risk. The customer has a catalogue image of two products she is contemplating on purchasing, though a Web-site image could have served the same purpose. The concern relates to the veracity of the colour reproduction.

Figure 3. Remote personalised selling using telephony at Buywell

CSR: This is Buywell, how may I help you?

CUST (customer): I'm interested in some of the homeware: one of the bedspreads. Catalogue Number 4968. [slight pause] This is just an enquiry at this stage.

CSR: That's no problem. Now, that's the tulip pattern?

CUST: Yes. Now, I'm also interested in some ready-made curtains to go with the bedspread. You have a couple that I think might be suitable. I was looking at the red, and possibly the blue.

CSR: OK. Just let me check those products. I'll be back in a minute. [pause while the CSR gets the curtains and duvet fabric from the walls of the call centre] Hello. I have them here. Have you got the picture in front of you?

CUST: Yes.

CSR: You can see there are two sorts of flowers. There's one that's slightly more pink, and another that's red with an orange centre. [slight pause] The red curtains are a perfect match to the red flowers with the orange centre—exactly the same shade. I think you would be quite happy with that. Let's have a look at the blue. [slight pause] The blue is not so good. It's rather a grey sort of blue. It's not really the same colour. But the red is a very good match.

CUST: Thank you very much. I need to check the dimensions of the window before I can order.

CSR: Thank you.

In the online image, it appears that a duvet cover and some ready-made curtains intended for a child's room would be a good match. However, the customer is not completely confident so she telephones Buywell.

Lands' End, another apparel company, uses a wider range of technology in combination to personalise selling remotely. In the second example (Figure 4), the same author-customer had become frustrated with online searching, which was not producing the selection she was looking for. She decided to try the online chat to assist in searching for the product. The Lands' End live assistant identified a suitable product and sent the relevant Web page. The personalised help was easy to access, reasonably fast, and did not require any preregistration process. In this example, we see that the Lands' End live representative reduced the time-loss risk for the customer by rapidly directing her to a product that met her requirements. The instant, professional assistance she received also provided reassurance that reduced the psychological risks of her online shopping experience.

Some e-commerce sites use recommendation engines as a substitute for personal selling by CSRs or online-chat assistants. These engines employ data mining and artificial intelligence techniques to identify and extract associated products in a customer-data warehouse. Associations are based on the current

Figure 4. Personal selling through online chat at Lands' End

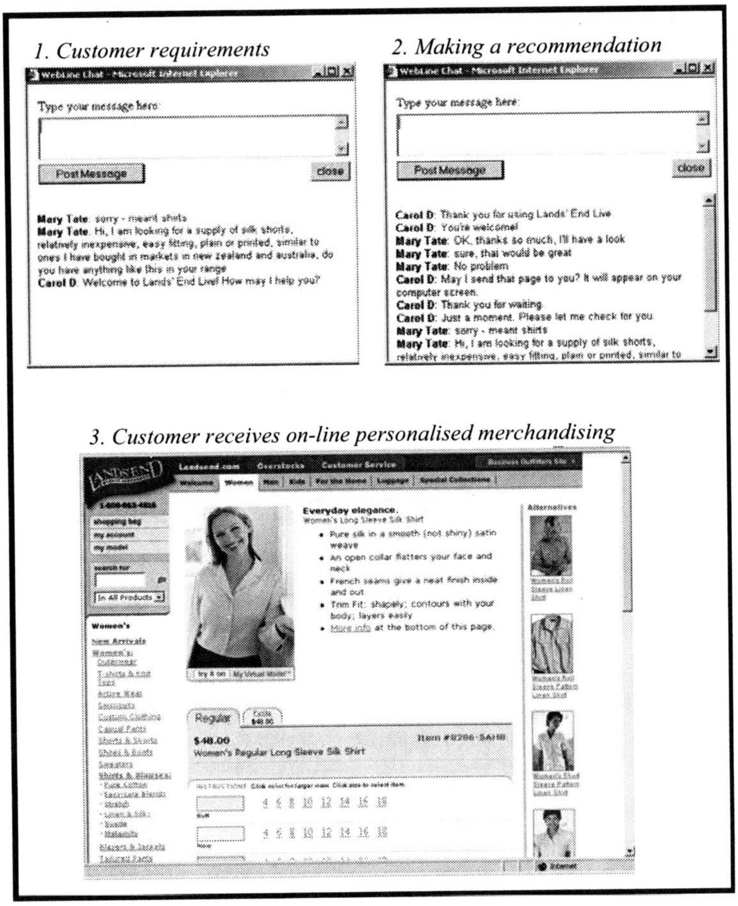

and other customers' purchasing patterns, and recommendations are presented online. Amazon.com is the leading example of this strategy. One of the authors (a customer) has purchased books on human-computer interaction and usability from Amazon.com in the past. Every time she visits Amazon.com, the latest publications in this area are recommended, with links to additional related publications that were purchased by other customers with similar interests (Figure 5).

We have not seen this strategy used by apparel e-tailers. Two factors seem to argue against its use in apparel sites. First, current recommendation-engine technologies would have difficulty in recognizing and reacting to the nuances of customers' requirements for specific clothing moments. Second, recommendation engines work best with commodity or high-specificity products such as

Figure 5. Recommendation engine at Amazon.com

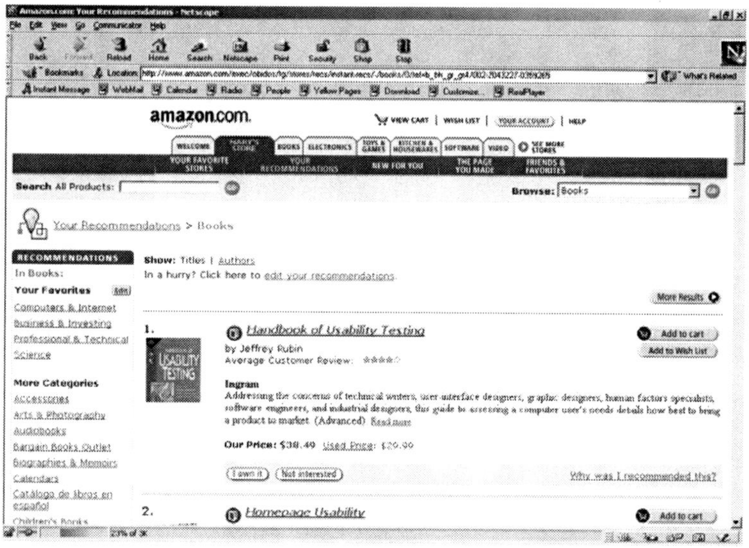

books. Apparel, being a high-touch good, requires the use of human senses to assess quality. The online CSR can act as a proxy for the customer using his or her touch and sight to help the customer develop a judgement of value or quality. The marketing manager at Buywell highlighted the value of the CSRs:

The Web site isn't as good as the old CSR. CSRs can give information like the true colour of [an item of clothing] or quality. A CSR can also tell the customer if two items of clothing go together. Now, how much of that can you put onto a Web site? With a CSR [the customer] can have a conversation.

Despite this, many apparel Web sites will recommend products that complement those the customer is currently browsing, reducing the customer's performance risk. The Australasian children's wear retailer JK Kids Gear offers a "complete the look" service on its Web site (Figure 6).

In summary, the most successful apparel e-tailers do not rely on automated tools and processes to assist their customers to find what they want and reassure them about quality. Leading e-tailers offer instant help in the form of personalised selling over the phone or in online chat to reduce the time-loss and performance risks to customers. Indirectly, the availability of helpful, professional staff also contributes to increased confidence in the vendor.

Figure 6. Web site recommendations for apparel at JK Kids Gear

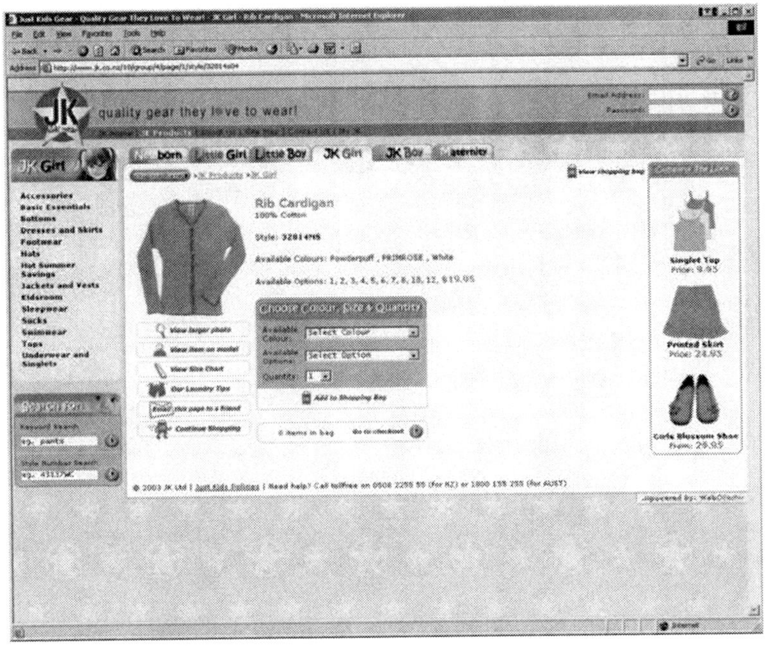

Building a Service Brand

Excellence in product, logistics, and customer management coupled with an easy return policy serves to develop a strong service brand. Many researchers have suggested a strong brand is essential for apparel e-tailing success given the plethora of unknown companies and the inherent risks of online shopping (Brown & Iorio, 2000; Cuneo, 1999; Goersch, 2002; Willcocks & Plant, 2001).

Building a service brand requires building trust with customers. The trust literature suggests that customer trust may relate to psychological characteristics such as an individual disposition to trust, or to external factors such as suitable legislation and controls (McKnight, Cummings, & Chervany, 1998). In addition, trust in an Internet store is influenced by the reputation of the store, defined as the extent to which buyers believe a selling organisation is honest and concerned about its customers (Jarvenpaa et al., 2000). Creating a trusted reputation requires a commitment to "a long term investment of resources, effort, and attention to customer relationships" (Jarvenpaa et al.). This suggests that organisations with a track record of online service quality are more likely to have a good reputation, which contributes to greater trust and lower perceived risk by online customers.

Some studies suggest the benefits of a brand established with physical retail outlets can be readily transferred to the Internet (Bahn & Fischer, 2003; Goersch, 2002; Reynolds, 2002; Willcocks & Plant, 2001). Under this view, promotion of the brand name, logo, colours, and slogans across multiple channels contributes to greater customer recognition and trust resulting in an increased likelihood of success (Goersch). This type of brand may be termed a presented brand, and its impact can be temporary. A presented brand may diminish vendor risk, particularly with respect to financial consequences, but if service quality in the new Internet-based channel is unsatisfactory, delivered brand will be weak. It is a combination of presented and delivered brand that comprises service brand and, of these, delivered brand is the stronger need in online environments. As Berry (2000) notes, "A presented brand cannot...rescue a weak service." The delivered brand sustains long-term sales through good experiences at every touch point the customer has with the company (Chernatony, Drury, & Segal-Horn, 2003).

Buywell has extremely loyal customers, with a retention rate of around 70% from year to year. The general manager is emphatic that a major reason for this is its customer service philosophy, the "Buywell Way," they call it, and their service brand. The marketing manager elaborates:

A lot of customers trust us with their credit card details. They think, "Oh, that's Buywell, they're OK." We're not a fly-by-night company...We're here to stay...I think it's the experience that the customer has...Are we consistent? Is our brand delivery consistent?

A strong service brand, based on a track record of e-commerce service delivery and word-of-mouth recommendations, is the best way of increasing trust and reducing perceived vendor risk. But this does not happen by chance; it is an aggregation of several strategies and competencies pursued consistently over time. Building a strong service brand in apparel e-tailing requires excellent internal systems, particularly in logistics management, a liberal return policy, and strong product and customer-experience management.

Co-Branding and Partnerships

The competencies and organisational resources required to provide a strong service brand are many. On the logistics side, an organisation needs a warehouse and distribution centre, managed relationships with carriers and postal services, and sophisticated internal processes that ensure accurate, on-time delivery. For customer management, a remote customer-support centre is essential, and this needs to be backed by a comprehensive customer database and staff trained both in the use of technology and in the organisation's quality culture.

Not every organisation seeking to move into online sales can easily and cost-effectively develop the competencies required for success. An alternate strategy in these cases is to form a co-branded partnership with an established, successful e-tailer. This approach was pioneered by Amazon.com, which leveraged its established competencies in searching, product recommendations, and fulfilment in online book retailing into a wide range of other products.

On a smaller scale, this strategy can be used by other companies with established remote selling competencies. Buywell recognises that their expertise in remote selling and service delivery has created a trusted service brand that is of value to other potential e-tailers. They have recently formed a co-branded partnership with a leading children's-wear brand:

We've integrated them into us so they don't duplicate. At one stage they had their own distribution centre, but we said, "Hey, this is complicating things. Why don't you just come into here (our distribution centre), we'll handle your distribution."

The managing director sees potential for future growth in this area:

I would like a Web site for Buywell that has on the home page icons for a whole range of products like pharmaceuticals, financial services, and whatever. I mean, Buywell is your delivery mechanism; we portray a brand. People think, "Oh look, its Buywell; I trust them because I bought clothing from them. I will buy their financial services."

This offers an alternative strategy for reducing the perceived risks of apparel e-commerce, particularly the risks originating with the vendor. Co-branding assumes that the product is already known and trusted, so the customer's perception of performance risk associated with the product will be low. However, customers may be wary about the financial, psychological, and time-loss risks associated with purchasing the product remotely from an unknown or unproven online vendor. Developing a co-branded offering with a vendor with an established reputation for online service delivery can mitigate these risks.

Conclusion

The apparel market is challenging for both buyers and sellers. For buyers, inconsistent sizing, often based on historical rather than current demographics and body shapes, means that many customers struggle to find a good product range in their size. Increasingly time-poor customers are unwilling to spend time searching for clothing and turn to the Internet for variety, convenience, and one-stop shopping. For sellers, competition is tough in a market where cost-conscious customers are reducing their spending on clothing. Heterogeneity in size, shape, and preferences are compounded by clothing moments that lead to differing requirements in different shopping events for individuals.

The increase in women on the Internet is bolstering an increase in online apparel sales to the point where apparel is now among the 10 most frequently sold items in mature e-commerce markets. The anywhere, anytime nature of the Internet offers the convenience many apparel customers are seeking, and superior search capabilities reduce the risk of time-loss and psychological stress from unsuccessful shopping expeditions. However, some risks associated with the product or vendor remain. The product fit, quality, colour, or texture may not meet expectations, and the vendor may be slow to deliver, unwilling to accept returns, or may simply not fulfil the order.

In this study, we set out to explain the changes, examine the risks for customers, and identify strategies that might mitigate customer risk. To achieve this, we investigated the strategies employed by a successful apparel multichannel retailer in New Zealand. This company had successfully transferred competencies developed in catalogue selling to online selling. They employed a range of strategies to mitigate vendor and product risks, and these are summarised in Figure 7. Together, the strategies form a strong service brand that others may call upon through co-branding.

Financial risks may arise from the vendor or the product. Perceptions of financial risk are diminished when the vendor has a strong service brand including a reputation for service delivery and easy returns. The strong service brand is built upon other essential strategies: good logistics, customer service, deep customer knowledge, and strong product management. Time-loss risk is a major factor in apparel purchasing because apparel is a seasonal fashion item and a popular choice for gift giving. Strong logistics that provide first-time fulfilment and a hassle-free return policy mitigate this risk. Customer-management systems that provide knowledge of customers and individual service in identifying products to meet their needs also reduces time loss.

Psychological risk is the outcome of other risks, particularly time-loss and financial consequences, which can lead to stress and anxiety. Mitigating

Figure 7. Risk sources that lead to risk consequences for customers, and the strategies that mitigate them

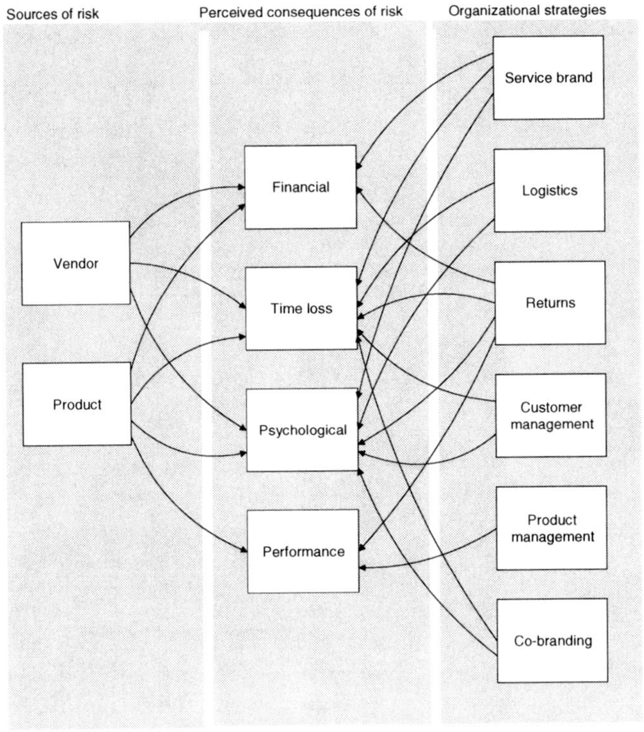

psychological risks, therefore, requires strategies that reduce time-loss and financial consequences. At a more general level, the customer can be reassured if the vendor is easy and pleasant to deal with, has efficient and easy-to-learn processes for logistics and returns, and has excellent customer management. Once again, an established reputation, either directly or from a co-branded partner, will increase customer confidence.

Performance risk is particularly high in online apparel purchasing because of the high-touch nature of apparel and the variability in the market overall. Extensive and sophisticated product-management processes are needed to manage these risks, including processes to deliver consistent products and to provide convincing virtual experiences. Expert personal advice from sales staff acting in proxy for the customer's five senses also diminishes performance risk.

There is no question that selling apparel online is demanding. Only the best will succeed. However, the lure of a share of one of the largest Internet markets makes the quest worthwhile. Those entering the market should be mindful of the six key strategies identified at Buywell, and use these to bolster success and growth in online apparel sales.

- *Manage products for quality and consistency* from manufacturing through ordering and receipt to imaging and merchandising. In apparel online selling, be sure to match product sizing to the target market and provide opportunities for virtual experiences of products.
- *Develop strong logistics management* for reliable, timely, first-time order fulfilment. In the case of seasonal or fashionable products, break the rules when required to ensure delivery by the required date.
- *Provide an easy return policy* for those times when the product does not meet the customers' requirements. Easy returns lead to repeat business.
- *Practice customer management and personalised selling* to increase customer confidence and save customers' time. For high-touch products, the availability of informed customer-focused staff to act as the sensor for the customer is crucial.
- *Build a strong service brand* based on a track record for consistency, quality, service delivery, and service recovery in every contact with the customer. This leads to repeat purchasing, loyalty, and the most valuable advertising: word-of-mouth recommendations.
- *Negotiate co-branded partnerships with a successful e-tailer* if your firm lacks the essential competencies or recognized service brand. This can jump-start your online offering and reduce both the labour and capital investment required.

It has sometimes been said, "Beauty is more than skin deep." This is true in apparel e-tailing. Successful apparel e-tailing requires more than a presented brand; it needs excellent product engineering, a quality online experience, a highly efficient distribution and fulfilment infrastructure, and personalised customer service. Establishing a service brand inclusive of both presented and delivered service brand requires a total organisational commitment that is much more than skin deep.

References

Bahn, D., & Fischer, P. (2003). Clicks and mortar: Balancing brick and mortar business strategy and operations with auxiliary electronic commerce. *Information Technology and Management, 4*(2-3), 319-334.

Barua, A., Konana, P., Whinston, A. B., & Yin, F. (2001). Driving e-business excellence. *MIT Sloan Management Review, 43*(1), 36-44.

Berry, L. (2000). Cultivating service brand equity. *Journal of the Academy of Marketing Science, 28*(1), 128-137.

Brookman, F. (1999, February 22). Inner city lacks marketing. *Discount Store News*, 38.

Brown, S., & Iorio, R. (2000). Specialty apparel: Fit, feel and brand. *Stores, 82*(1), 74.

Chen, Z., & Dubinsky, A. (2003). A conceptual model of perceived customer value in e-commerce: A preliminary investigation. *Psychology & Marketing, 20*(4), 323-347.

Chernatony, L., Drury, S., & Segal-Horn, S. (2003). Building a services brand: Stages, people and orientations. *The Services Industry Journal, 23*(3).

Corbitt, B., Thanasankit, T., & Yi, H. (2003). Trust and e-commerce: A study of consumer perceptions. *Electronic Commerce Research and Applications, 2*, 203-215.

Cuneo, A. (1999). Lands' End ads pitch "ultimate direct merchant." *Advertising Age* (Midwest region ed.), *70*(17), 85.

Danneels. (1996). Market segmentation: Normative model versus business reality: An exploratory study of apparel retailing in Belgium. *European Journal of Marketing, 30*(6), 36-51.

Dowling, G. R., & Staelin, R. (1994). A model of perceived risk and intended risk handling activity. *Journal of Consumer Research, 21*, 119-134.

Festervand, T., & Snyder. (1986). Influence of catalog versus store shopping and prior satisfaction on perceived risk. *Journal of the Academy of Marketing Science, 14*, 28-36.

Fiore, A., & Jin, H. J. (2003). Influence of image interactivity on approach responses towards an online retailer. *Internet Research: Electronic Networking Applications and Policy, 13*(1), 38-49.

Gardyn, R. (2003). The shape of things to come. *American Demographics, 25*(6), 24-30.

Ghoshal, S., & Gratton, L. (2002). Integrating the enterprise. *MIT Sloan Management Review, 44*(1), 31-47.

Goersch, D. (2002). *Multi-channel integration and its implications for retail websites*. Paper presented at the European conference on information systems, Gdansk, Poland.

Greenspan, R. (2003). *Apparel sales apparent online*. Retrieved August 1, 2003, from *http://cyberatlas.internet.com/markets/retailing/article/0,,6061_2171361,00.html*

Hammond, J., & Kohler, K. (2002). *In the virtual dressing room returns are a real problem*. Retrieved October 20, 2004, from *http://hbsworkingknowledge.hbs.edu/item.jhtml?id=2883&t=marketing*

Jarvenpaa, S. L., Tractinsky, N., & Vitale, M. (2000). Consumer trust in an Internet store. *Information Technology and Management, 1*(1-2), 45-71.

Kaufman-Scarborough, C., & Lindquist, J. D. (2002). E-Shopping in a multiple-channel environment. *Journal of Consumer Marketing, 19*(4/5), 333-350.

Lee, H. L., & Whang, S. (2001). Winning the last mile of e-commerce. *MIT Sloan Management Review, 42*(4), 54-62.

Lim, N. (2003). Consumers' perceived risk: Source versus consequences. *Electronic Commerce Research and Applications, 2*, 216-228.

McKnight, D. H., Cummings, L. L., & Chervany, N. L. (1998). Initial trust formation in new organizational relationships. *The Academy of Management Review, 23*(3), 473-490.

Miyazaki, A., & Fernandez, A. (2001). Consumer perceptions of privacy and security risks for online shopping. *The Journal of Consumer Affairs, 35*(1), 27.

Multi-channel retail report 2.0, The. (2001). *Shop.org*. Retrieved May 20, 2003, from *http://www.shop.org/research/TMCRR.html*

Nyshadham, E. (2000). Privacy policies of air travel websites: A survey and analysis. *Journal of Air Transport Management, 6*, 143-152.

Pyke, D. F., Johnson, M. E., & Desmond, P. (2001). E-Fulfilment: It's harder than it looks. *Supply Chain Management Review*, 26-32.

Retail February 2003 data overview: A gender analysis of online shopping behaviors. (2003). *Forrester*. Retrieved February 20, 2004, from *http://www.forrester.com/ER/Research/DataOverview/Summary/0,2740,16089,00.html*

Reynolds, J. (2002). Charting the multi-channel future: Retail choices and constraints. *International Journal of Retail and Distribution Management, 30*(11).

RIP: The online consumer, 1998 to 2003. (2003). *Forrester*. Retrieved August 1, 2003, from *http://www.forrester.com/ER/Research/Brief/Excerpt/0,1317,17225,00.html*

Rogers, D. (1983). America's maturing innovation: Off-price apparel stores. *Retail and Distribution Management, 11*(5), 29.

Schneider, G., & Perry, J. (2001). *Electronic commerce.* Boston: Thomson Learning.

Setlow, C. (1999, February 22). Comfort rules the roost — but looks are important. *Discount Store News*, 38.

Shopping spree: Labels launch online sales for customers. (1999). *Sporting Goods Business, 32*, 36.

Steinfield, C., Bouwman, H., & Adelaar, T. (2002). The dynamic of click-and mortar electronic commerce: Opportunities and management strategies. *International Journal of Electronic Commerce, 7*(1).

Tan, M., & Teo, T. (2000). Factors influencing the adoption of Internet banking. *Journal of the Association of Information Systems, 1*(5), 1-42.

Tate, M., Coker, B., & Hope, B. (in press-a). Moving to multi-channel e-commerce: A case study of an apparel and home-ware catalogue company. *Journal of Internet Commerce.*

Tate, M., Coker, B., & Hope, B. (2004). *Theory and practice in multi-channel e-commerce strategies: A case study of an apparel and homeware retailer.* Paper presented at the Australasian Conference in Information Systems (ACIS), Hobart, Australia.

Turban, E., & King, D. (2003). *Introduction to e-commerce.* Upper Saddle River, NJ: Prentice Hall.

Verhage, B. J., Yavas, U., & Green, G. T. (1990). Perceived risk: A cross-cultural phenomenon. *International Journal of Market Research, 7*(4), 297-303.

Ward, M. R. (2001). Will online shopping compete more with traditional retailing or catalog shopping? *Netnomics, 3*(2), 103-117.

Willcocks, L. P., & Plant, R. (2001). Pathways to e-business leadership: Getting from bricks to clicks. *MIT Sloan Management Review, 42*(3), 50-59.

Zeng, M., & Reinartz, W. (2003). Beyond online search: The road to profitability. *California Management Review, 45*(2), 107-117.

About the Authors

Mehdi Khosrow-Pour, D.B.A., is currently the executive director of the Information Resources Management Association (IRMA) and senior academic editor for Idea Group Reference. Previously, he served on the faculty of the Pennsylvania State University as an associate professor of information systems for 20 years. He has written or edited more than 20 books in information technology management, and he is also the editor-in-chief of the *Information Resources Management Journal*, *Journal of Electronic Commerce in Organizations*, *Journal of Cases on Information Technology*, and *International Journal of Cases on Electronic Commerce*.

* * *

Amit Agrahari (*agrahari.03@astra.xlri.ac.in*) is a research student at XLRI, Jamshedpur, India. He received his MBA (information systems) from Davi Ahilya University, Indore, India, and BSc (statistics) degree from Jiwaji University, Gwalior, India, and is currently finishing his doctoral dissertation on e-procurement. His research focuses on interorganizational information systems, the impact of IS on SMEs (small and medium-sized enterprises), and the economics of IS. He is a member of the Association for Information Systems.

Stuart J. Barnes is chair and professor of management at the University of East Anglia, U.K. Stuart has been teaching and researching in the information systems field for over a decade. His academic background includes a first-class degree in economics from University College London and a PhD in business administration from Manchester Business School. He has published three books and more than 70 articles including those in journals such as *Communications of the ACM*, the *International Journal of Electronic Commerce*, the *e-Service Journal*, *Electronic Markets*, and the *Journal of Electronic Commerce Research*. Two more books are in progress for 2005.

Shirley Ann Becker was a professor of management information systems and director of the National Center for Small Business Information at Florida Institute of Technology, USA. Dr. Becker has published over 80 articles in Web usability and accessibility, database technologies, telemedicine, and software engineering. She has received funding from Texas Instruments, IBM, NSF, and JPL to conduct research. Dr. Becker is an associate editor for the *Journal of Database Management, Journal of Electronic Commerce in Organizations*, and *International Journal of Cases on Electronic Commerce*. She was the recipient of Northern Arizona University's Mark Layton Award for Research Excellence.

Anthony Berkemeyer (*ahb@ti.com*) received his BS in computer engineering and his MS in software engineering from Florida Institute of Technology, Melbourne, Florida. He is currently pursuing his PhD in computer science as a Texas Instruments Scholar at Florida Institute of Technology, USA. Mr. Berkemeyer has experience in embedded-systems testing, database design, and application development, including Web-based software systems. He has coauthored several papers on data quality in database systems and Web usability with an emphasis on e-commerce user-interface designs.

Rahul Bhaskar is an associate professor at the California State University - Fullerton, USA. He earned his PhD from the University of Wisconsin - Madison. Prior to joining academia, he worked as a director and senior IT manager with various companies including Manugistics Inc., Cisco Systems Inc., and Talus Solutions Inc. in the areas of revenue management and data warehousing. He continues to use his experience to help companies with their automation projects. His research interests include knowledge based decision support systems, security technologies and marketing and sales automation systems. He has published in various academic- and industry-oriented journals.

Brent Coker is a PhD student of the School of Information Management at Victoria University of Wellington, New Zealand. He completed a bachelor's of commerce and administration in electronic commerce degree, and a bachelor's of commerce and administration degree with honors in information systems at Victoria University. Brent's PhD dissertation focuses on online buyer behavior.

Robert H. Ducoffe is a professor of marketing and acting associate dean of Zicklin School of Business, Baruch College (CUNY), USA. He received his PhD from Michigan State University, his MA from the University of Southern California, and his BA from McGill University. His administrative accomplishments at Baruch include the initiation and creation of a full-time honors MBA program, an accelerated part-time program, an English communication immersion program, and a revised core curriculum for full-time MBA students, among others. His research has appeared in publications including the *Journal of Advertising Research*, *Journal of Public Policy and Marketing*, *Journal of Current Issues and Research in Advertising*, *Journal of Promotion Management*, *Advances in Business Marketing and Purchasing*, *Journal of Direct Marketing*, *Journal of Media Economics*, *Journal of Marketing Education*, and in various texts on advertising and media economics. His research focuses on the advertising industry and on advertising theory and evaluation, and he has developed a unique approach for evaluating advertising based on its perceived value to consumers.

Janet Edwards is a lecturer in the Department of Computer Science at Loughborough University, U.K. After graduating with an engineering first degree and a master's by research in Robotic Control from Loughborough, she worked in industry as a software engineer. During her time in industry, she worked for a number of companies on projects ranging from device drivers, navigational simulators to expert systems. Since retuning to Loughborough, she lectures on the taught master's program and is responsible for undergraduate projects. She is a member of the Knowledge Management Research Group at Loughborough. Her main research interests are in the areas of knowledge management, e-commerce and CSCW.

Yuan Gao is an assistant professor of information systems at Ramapo College of New Jersey, USA. He received his MBA and PhD in business from Zicklin School of Business, Baruch College (CUNY). He also holds a master's degree in computer and information science from Brooklyn College. His research interests include human-computer interaction, user acceptance of technology, Web interface design, online consumer behavior, and current issues in electronic commerce. He is the editor of a recent book *Web Systems Design and Online Consumer Behavior*, published by Idea Group Publishing. He is published in numerous conference proceedings, scholarly books, and academic journals like

The Electronic Library and the *Journal of Electronic Commerce in Organizations*.

Peter R. Gibson is an associate professor in the Graduate School of Business and Professional Development at the University of Wollongong, Australia. He has worked extensively in the area of supply chain management and is part of the Logistic and Supply Chain Management Group at the University of Wollongong. He graduated with a PhD from Loughborough University, Department of Manufacturing Engineering (1984). He is a full member of the Institution of Electrical Engineers.

William Golden is a member of the Centre for Innovation and Structural Change and a lecturer in information systems at the National University of Ireland, Galway. He has held this position since 1991. He completed his doctorate in B2B (business-to-business) electronic commerce at the University of Warwick, England. He has presented papers at both national and international conferences. He has coauthored a book, contributed chapters to other texts, and published papers in the areas of electronic commerce and information systems, among others, which have appeared in *Omega*, the *International Journal of Management Science*, *International Journal of Electronic Commerce*, *Journal of End User Computing*, and *Journal of Decision Systems*.

Jatinder N.D. Gupta is eminent scholar of management; professor of management information systems, industrial and systems engineering, and engineering management; and chairperson of the Department of Accounting and Information Systems at The University of Alabama in Huntsville, USA. He serves on the editorial boards of several national and international journals. Recipient of the Outstanding Faculty and Outstanding Researcher awards from Ball State University, he has published numerous papers in such journals as the *Journal of Management Information Systems*, *International Journal of Information Management*, and *Mathematics of Operations Research*. His current research interests include information technology; scheduling, planning, and control; organizational learning and effectiveness; systems education; and knowledge management. Dr. Gupta's membership in academic and professional societies includes the Production and Operations Management Society, the Decision Sciences Institute, and the Information Resources Management Association.

Beverley G. Hope is a faculty member in the School of Information Management at Victoria University of Wellington, New Zealand. She completed BSc and MBA degrees at the University of Kansas and a PhD at the University of Hawaii at Manoa. Beverley's research focuses on information needs for quality initiatives, quality in online service delivery, performance measurement, electronic commerce, and information systems education. In her work she takes a holistic or system view of organizations and the issues that face them. She both publishes and referees for journals, book publishers, and regional and international conferences in the areas of information systems, decision sciences, and evaluation.

Martin Hughes is a member of the Centre for Innovation and Structural Change and a lecturer in information systems at the National University of Ireland, Galway. He is currently pursuing a PhD on interorganizational systems at the University of Bath, England. His research interests include electronic commerce, interorganizational systems and risk, and electronic government. He has been published in leading international IS conference proceedings and has published papers in the *Journal of End User Computing*, *Journal of Electronic Commerce in Organisations*, and the *Business Process Management Journal*.

Thomas James is a chartered town planner who has five years local government experience. He has experience working at Sevenoaks District Council, located on the edge of London where his role is to control the various types of developments occurring in the district and to contribute to the implementation of new technology in a local government environment.

Luiz Antonio Joia has over 20 years of experience in major technology-based companies, holding executive positions in the areas of information technology and business development, namely in PROMON Engenharia e Telecomunicações (manager of computer science and manager of IS, 1979-1995), TREND Tecnologia Educacional (director of new business, 1995-1998), and W3E://World Wide Web for education (principal, 1999-2000). He has also been an adjunct professor of the School of Engineering of Rio de Janeiro State University, Brazil since 1982. He is a guest speaker at conferences and continuing-education programs for executives. He was the academic coordinator of the MBA degrees in e-management (strategic management and information technology) and FGV management. He was also the academic coordinator of the MBA degree of EBAPE/FGV and a consultant and advisor to the World Bank in the area of educational technology applied to the training of human capital. He is a member of the advisory board of the Journal of Intellectual Capital and a coordinator of e:lab (Laboratory for Research into IT applied to Corporate and Public Management) of EBAPE/FGV.

Liz Lee-Kelley is postgraduate lecturer in e-commerce and project management at the School of Management, University of Surrey, U.K. She has extensive industry experience at senior positions in logistics and distribution, engineering and clinical research. Her research interests are in technology-enabled virtual organisations (in particular, virtual team dynamics), project leadership and project management issues, and the socio-psychology of technology and information orientations of modern businesses.

Marios Koufaris is an assistant professor of computer information systems at Baruch College (CUNY), in New York City. He received his PhD in information systems from the Stern School of Business of New York University. He has a BSc in decision sciences from the Wharton School of Business and a BA in psychology from the College of Arts and Sciences, both at the University of Pennsylvania. His research interests include consumer behavior in Web-based commerce, end-user behavior, and the social impact of IT. His work has been published in *Information Systems Research*, the *International Journal of Electronic Commerce*, *Information & Management*, *DATA BASE for Information Systems*, and *Communications of the ACM*.

Anthony Lafferty graduated from the Manchester Metropolitan University Business School (U.K.) with a first-class honors degree in business information technology in 2000. He then spent two years as a teaching company scheme (TCS) associate working on the deployment of e-commerce systems at Partwell, a small manufacturing and supply company based in Bolton. At Partwell, Anthony developed an intranet and two Web sites that have significantly enhanced the company's competitive position and operational effectiveness. Following this, he became a freelance ICT consultant working with companies throughout Europe. He worked on a range of Web-based projects for both business and academia. His latest project involves the development of a novel intranet application to create a virtual community for the tenants and residents of the borough of Rochdale, U.K. This is one of the first projects of its kind in the U.K. and has attracted interest from local and national governments.

Uwe Leimstoll is a research associate in e-business at the Institute for Business Economics (IAB), University of Applied Sciences, Basel (FHBB), Switzerland. He studied Industrial Engineering and Management at the University of Applied Sciences Offenburg and Economics at the University of Freiburg im Breisgau (Germany). After working several years as consultant and lecturer, he received his doctorate in the Faculty of Economics at the University of Freiburg im Breisgau (July 2001). He is managing different research projects in the fields of personalization, Web analysis, group support systems (GSS) and e-business in SMEs.

Scott J. Lloyd, holding a PhD in management information systems from Kent State University, is an assistant professor in the College of Business Administration at the University of Rhode Island, USA. His research is in the areas of database management, optimization of file access for database management systems, knowledge management, data mining, and system analysis and design. Dr. Lloyd has had his research published in the *Journal of Database Management, Industrial Management, Industrial Mathematics, Software Engineering in the 21st Century, Midwest Decision Sciences Proceedings, Simulators International, Modeling and Simulation*, and in conference proceedings. He serves on the editorial board of the *Journal of Database Management* and is an ad hoc reviewer of the *Journal of Electronic Commerce in Organizations*.

Robert MacGregor is senior lecturer and head of discipline in information systems at the University of Wollongong, Australia. His research expertise lies in the area of electronic commerce in small business. Rob is also the editor of the *Australasian Journal of Information Systems* and was conference chair of the Australian Conference of Information Systems in 1992. In his spare time, Rob writes music. His most recent work is the symphony "Alba."

Ashis K. Pani (akpani@xlri.ac.in) is chairman of the information systems and operations management area at XLRI, Jamshedpur, India, and the coordinator of the satellite education programs. His research and teaching focus on how businesses can effectively use information technology in general and the Internet in particular. His current areas of interest are e-business, e-SCM, e-CRM, e-security, IT outsourcing, and the application of AI (artificial intelligence) techniques. Presently, he is a member of the Indian Association of Research in Computing Sciences (IARCS) and Computer Society of India (CSI).

Vikramaditya Pant is an undergraduate student at the College of Commerce and Finance at Villanova University, PA, USA. He is dual-majoring in management information sciences and finance. His research interests are enterprise computing, data interchanges and artificial intelligence. His current research is focused on customer relationship management and strategic enterprise management. He has an extensive computing background and has provided consulting services to many businesses. He has worked as a technical editor for Prentice-Hall Publications on numerous business technology and information technology books. As a teenager, his articles were published in various newspapers and magazines including Young Expressions and Opinion Express on a variety of themes. He is very active on campus and participates in many extra-curricular activities.

Elizabeth F. Purinton, holding a PhD from the University of Rhode Island, is an assistant professor at Marist College in Poughkeepsie, New York, USA. Dr. Purinton is a fellow of the AMA-Sheth Foundation Doctoral Consortium. Dr. Purinton's research programs include Web site design, high-tech marketing and marketing orientation with emphasis on TQM techniques, marketing channel-partnership survival, and mature marketing relationships. Dr. Purinton's research is published in the *Academy of Marketing Science Review*, *Journal of Electronic Commerce in Organizations*, the *Journal of Business Research*, and in conference proceedings.

Deborah E. Rosen, holding a PhD from the University of Tennessee, Knoxville, is an associate professor in the College of Business Administration at the University of Rhode Island, USA. Dr. Rosen's research interests include Web site design, online word of mouth (mouse), interorganizational relationships, and quality management. Her research has appeared in the *Journal of Business Research*, *Journal of Electronic Commerce in Organizations*, *International Journal of Services Industry Management*, *Academy of Marketing Science Review*, and in conference proceedings.

Murray Scott is a member of the Centre for Innovation and Structural Change and a lecturer in information systems at the National University of Ireland, Galway. He is currently pursuing a PhD on electronic government at the National University of Ireland. His research interests include electronic government, stakeholder management theory, and electronic commerce. His research on electronic government has been published in leading international IS conferences, in the *Journal of Electronic Commerce in Organizations*, the *Business Process Management Journal*, and the *International Journal of Services and Standards*.

Sushil K. Sharma is currently an associate professor in the Department of Information Systems and Operations Management at Ball State University, Muncie, Indiana, USA. Coauthor of two textbooks (*Programming in C* and *Understanding Unix*) and coeditor of four edited books, Dr. Sharma has made research contributions that have appeared in many peer-reviewed national and international journals, and conference and seminar proceedings. He has contributed several book chapters in premier books that are used by many schools worldwide for their graduate and undergraduate MIS and MBA programs on subjects such as e-commerce, knowledge management, and learning organizations. Dr. Sharma's primary teaching and research interests are in e-commerce, networking environments, network security, ERP systems, database-management systems, and knowledge management. Dr. Sharma has also conducted a number of executive development programs for corporate world and government organizations on e-commerce, networking security, ERP systems, and database-related subjects.

M. Susan Stiner received her JD from the University of Nebraska and her LLM (Taxation) from Temple University in Philadelphia. She became a CPA (Delaware) in 1988, practiced public accounting in the estates and trusts area with a medium-sized Wilmington, DE, USA accounting firm and now maintains a small tax practice of her own. She joined the Department of Accountancy at Villanova University (USA) in 1988, where she teaches undergraduate and graduate tax. Her research interests are taxation and a course in Western accounting, team-taught over the Internet for over ten years with a Japanese accounting professor. Professor Stiner is a Girl Scout leader in her hometown and an active member of the DE Society of CPAs.

Petra Schubert is professor for E-Business at the University of Applied Sciences in Basel (FHBB), Switzerland. She received her doctorate in Information Systems from the University of St. Gallen. Her research interests include the study of management of e-commerce applications, specifically personalization and virtual communities. She co-edited four books containing business cases on successful e-business implementation strategies, e-fulfillment, e-procurement and e-business integration. She is a board member of Ecademy, the Swiss Competence Network for E-Business and E-Government of the Swiss Universities of Applied Sciences.

Paul Sutherland was a postgraduate student in the Department of Management Science and Information Systems, The University of Auckland, New Zealand. His research looked at combining the fields of information systems and marketing in the online environment. He is currently working as an Internet marketing consultant with New Zealand's premium search engine marketing agency and website marketing effectiveness consultancy.

Felix B. Tan is professor of Information Systems and Head, School of Computer and Information Sciences at Auckland University of Technology, New Zealand. He serves as editor-in-chief of the *Journal of Global Information Management*. Dr. Tan is internationally known for his work in the global IT field and is a frequent guest speaker at international conferences. His current research interests are in electronic commerce, global information management, business-IT alignment, and the management of IT. He is actively using cognitive mapping and narrative inquiry methods in his research. Dr. Tan has published in

MIS Quarterly, Information & Management, Journal of Information Technology as well as other journals and refereed conference proceedings. Dr. Tan has more than 20 years of experience in information systems management and consulting with large multinationals, as well as university teaching and research in Singapore, Canada and New Zealand.

Mary Tate is a faculty member in the School of Information Management at Victoria University of Wellington, New Zealand. She completed her BA (honors) at Massey University. Following that, Mary had an extensive career in information technology, with roles that include business analysis, project management, service delivery, and consultancy. Since joining Victoria University in 2001, Mary's research has focused on online service quality, electronic commerce strategy, and technology in IS education.

David Tucker is a senior learning and teaching fellow at the Manchester Metropolitan University Business School in the U.K. Following a career as an ICT consultant in the manufacturing industry, he returned to full-time study. In 1996 he received his PhD from the University of Manchester for his work on computer-integrated manufacturing methodologies. His current research interests focus on the development of models and methodologies to improve the deployment of electronic commerce in small manufacturing companies. He has published widely in this regard. He also has a particular interest in developing e-learning material for use at postgraduate and undergraduate levels, as well as for use as training material within small businesses.

Richard Vidgen is a reader in information systems in the School of Management at the University of Bath, U.K. After working in the industry in information systems development for many years, he joined the University of Salford in 1992, where he completed a PhD in systems thinking and IS quality. His current research interests include Web site quality, e-commerce transformation in the automotive industry, IS-development methodologies, and XML- (extensible markup language) and Web-Service-based information systems. He is the author of *Developing Web Information Systems* (Butterworth Heinemann, 2002) and has published many research papers in leading international journals.

Lejla Vrazalic is a lecturer in information systems at the University of Wollongong, Australia. She was awarded the University Medal in 1999. Her research interests are in human-computer interaction and e-commerce adoption in small business. As part of her PhD research, Lejla developed and validated the Distributed Usability Evaluation Method, a novel method for assessing the usability and usefulness of computer interfaces based on the cultural, historical activity theory. Lejla received the Vice Chancellor's Award for Outstanding Contribution to Teaching and Learning at the University of Wollongong in 2004.

William P. Wagner has been teaching and conducting research in Information Systems since 1988 at Villanova University, PA, USA. His research spans the areas of artificial intelligence, ERP systems and e-commerce and has appeared in internationally known journals such as *Expert Systems*, *Journal of Computer Information Systems*, and *Internet Research*. He recently co-authored the first text book on XML entitled *Introduction to Applied XML Technologies for Business* (Prentice Hall, 2002) and is currently co-authoring a CRM textbook. He has been invited to contribute to the Encyclopedia of Information Systems numerous times. He has presented numerous seminars and research papers at regional and international conferences such as Decision Science Institute, INFORMS, and AIS. At Villanova University he has developed MIS curricula for e-commerce, distance learning, CRM and ERP.

Index

D

E

F

G

H

I

K

L

M

N

O

CPSIA information can be obtained at www.ICGtesting.com
Printed in the USA
238910LV00008B/4/P